THE LOVE OF CHRIST

From the original title page of this work

BOWELS
OPENED,
OR

A DISCOVERY OF THE
Neere and deere Love, Union and
Communion betwixt Christ and the
Church, and consequently betwixt
Him and every beleeving soul.
Delivered in divers Sermons on the Fourth Fifth
and Sixt Chapters of the CANTICLES
By that Reverend and Faithfull Minister of the
Word, DOCTOR SIBS, late Preacher unto
the Honourable Societie of *Grayes Inne*, and Master
of Katharine Hall in Cambridge.
Being in part finished by his owne pen in his life
time, and the rest of them perused and corrected
by those whom he intrusted with the
publishing of his works.

CANT. 4.10.
*Thou hast ravished my heart, my Sister, my Spouse: thou hast
ravished my heart with one of thine eyes, and with one chaine of
thy necke.*

THE LOVE OF
CHRIST

*Expository Sermons on Verses from
Song of Solomon Chapters 4-6*

Richard Sibbes

THE BANNER OF TRUTH TRUST

THE BANNER OF TRUTH TRUST
3 Murrayfield Road, Edinburgh EH12 6EL, UK
P.O. Box 621, Carlisle, PA 17013, USA

*

First published as *Bowels Opened*, 1639
Reprinted from the 1862 Nichol edition of
The Complete Works of Richard Sibbes, Volume 2
This edition © The Banner of Truth Trust, 2011

ISBN: 978 1 84871 144 0

*

Typeset in 10/12 pt Minion Pro at
The Banner of Truth Trust, Edinburgh

Printed in the USA by
Versa Press, Inc.,
East Peoria, IL

CONTENTS

Editorial Note:

The Nichol Edition of Sibbes' *Works* was edited by Rev. Alexander B. Grosart of Kinross. Footnotes by him are attributed either to 'G.' or 'Ed.' as they appear in the 1862 edition. One or two notes of merely academic interest have been excluded. The present publisher has added explanations of a few words which may not be familiar today—these are attributed to 'P.' A small number of spellings has been modernised, and most Latin renderings removed, as the English meanings are usually given in the text. A few Scripture references have been found to be incorrect, and have been amended.

FOREWORD

IN his original preface, John Dod wrote that this book is 'so full of heavenly treasure, and such lively expressions of the invaluable riches of the love of Christ' that it serves 'to kindle in the heart all heavenly affections unto Jesus Christ'. Indeed it does! And that was very much what Richard Sibbes was about in all his ministry. As he himself put it, 'one main end of our calling, the ministry, is, to lay open and unfold the unsearchable riches of Christ; to dig up the mine, thereby to draw the affections of those that belong to God to Christ'.

Richard Sibbes (1577-1635) is rather less well known now than some other Puritan luminaries, but in his own day he was enormously influential. In his latter years he managed to hold three prominent posts simultaneously, as master of Katharine Hall, Cambridge, 'lecturer' at Holy Trinity Church in Cambridge, and preacher to the prestigious Gray's Inn, one of the London Inns of Court. More tellingly, though, Sibbes was widely and deeply loved. He became known as 'the heavenly Doctor', and that, not because of any remote other-worldliness, but because of his sheer loving kindness and good-natured amiability. Still today, his recorded sermons glow with sunny warmth.

The Love of Christ is a series of sermons Sibbes preached on Song of Solomon 4:16-6:3, originally published under the title *Bowels Opened* (a reference to the deep, gut desires explored or 'opened' in the book). For Sibbes, the Song of Solomon 'is nothing else but a plain demonstration and setting forth of the love of

Christ to his church, and of the love of the church to Christ', and as such it gets to the very heart of the gospel as he understood it. Christianity, he believed, was essentially a love story in which Christ the bridegroom comes to win his bride, the church.

Such imagery and use of the Song of Solomon was not only popular in Sibbes's day (and supported by the notes of the *Geneva Bible*), it also had a distinguished place in Reformation history. When, in his *The Freedom of a Christian,* Martin Luther first explained his mature understanding of justification by grace alone, it was to the Song of Solomon that he turned for illustration. For the understanding that the relationship between Christ and his people is a marital one changed everything. In medieval Roman Catholicism, Christ had been a distant figure, doling out his 'grace' from afar, approachable only through other mediators such as priests and saints. Before him one could never have confidence or know intimacy. But if Christ is the church's loving bridegroom, what place is there for mediators between him and us? And what now would the church want from him? Not some *thing* called 'grace', but the bridegroom himself, freely offered. Plus, a bride can have assurance in her love.

> Let us oft think of this nearness between Christ and us, if we have once given our names to him, and not be discouraged for any sin or unworthiness in us. Who sues a wife for debt, when she is married? . . . Therefore answer all accusations thus: 'Go to Christ.' If you have anything to say to me, go to my husband (*Works* 2.25).

Sibbes does not defend his interpretation of the Song of Solomon; in his generation he did not need to. Today, though, the majority of commentators do not agree that the Song of Solomon is a parable of the love between Christ and the church. More normally it is treated as a poem on common romance. Now, even if Sibbes is misappropriating the Song of Solomon, the wonderful truths he expounds still stand. In that case, he is preaching Christ beautifully, but simply from the wrong text. But is he misreading the Song of

Solomon? Is this fanciful allegorising (as is possible with any inter-pretation), or is he heading in the direction the text leads?

Certainly Solomon seemed to enjoy allusion. The architecture of the temple he built shows that: from the cherubim to the sea of cast metal, everything was designed to be a copy and shadow of spiritual reality (*Heb.* 8:5). One expects Solomon to be always alluding to spiritual reality. And one expects books of Scripture to be about God and his relations with his people. So we have a reasonable *expectation* as we approach the Song of Solomon.

Jonathan Edwards argued that the very title 'Song of Songs' then confirms this expectation:

> The name by which Solomon calls this song confirms me in it that it is more than an ordinary love song, and that it was designed for a divine song, and of divine authority; for we read, 1 Kings 4:32, that Solomon's 'songs were a thousand and five'. This he calls the 'song of songs' [*Canticles* 1:1], that is, the most excellent of all his songs, which it seems very probable to me to be upon that account, because it was a song of the most excellent subject, treating of the love, union, and communion between Christ and his spouse, of which marriage and conjugal love was but a shadow.

Then to the text itself. The Song of Solomon has two main characters: the lover and his beloved. The lover is a shepherd-king like David (1:4, 7); but he is the son of David (3:7). He stands at the door and knocks (5:2, 3). His carriage in chapter three looks like the tabernacle/temple; and like the Lord in the Exodus, he comes up from the wilderness like a pillar of smoke (3:6), all perfumed with the scents of the temple. The beloved is described as being like Israel, coming up from the wilderness leaning on her lover (8:5). Like Israel in Isaiah 5:1-7, she is repeatedly compared to a vineyard, and to Jerusalem (8:10-12). And while she is his bride, she is also his sister (4:9): Christ is the church's bridegroom and brother, but given the taboo on marrying one's sister in Leviticus 18:9 it seems highly unlikely that this could describe an ordinary Jewish romance.

Ordinary lovers are parted by death, but the love of these lovers is as strong as death. Not even floodwaters can wash it away (8:6, 7). It all looks as if the Song of Solomon is describing that unique story of the love between Christ and the church. And the overall similarity of the book to Psalm 45, which definitely refers to Christ and his marriage, is striking. It is no wonder, then, that the Song of Solomon, like Revelation, ends with the bride calling 'Come!'

The Song of Solomon does not simply mouth a doctrine, though. Its sensuous imagery sings its message. It is as if the love story is played on violins. The reader is thus brought, not simply to understand, but to taste and share the delights of the lovers. But this is precisely what Christ's people need, Sibbes knew: it is not enough to be *aware* of Christ's love; we must sense, grasp and *enjoy* it. Only then will we truly love the Lord our God with all our hearts.

Knowing that, Sibbes could never allow preaching to be a mere recital of bare facts: if his listeners were to delight in Christ, they would need a preacher who 'opened' to them how delightful and good he is. And in his sermons on the Song of Solomon here, Sibbes shows what a masterful preacher he was, bringing his audience actually to *feel* the love of Christ. That, in fact, is one reason why so many avoid books like this one: they want information, and they want it fast. But Sibbes intends to affect you, to hold your eyes on Jesus that you might develop a stronger appetite for him. Such work cannot be fast work, but it is profoundly transforming. I urge you, then, to give this book time; if you do, I think I can guarantee more benefit than from ten others.

MICHAEL REEVES
Oxford,
August 2011

PREFACE

THE perusal of this book being committed unto me by an ancient and a faithful friend of mine, I found it, I confess, so full of heavenly treasure, and such lively expressions of the invaluable riches of the love of Christ towards all his poor servants that sue and seek unto him, that I sent unto the godly and learned author, earnestly entreating him to publish the same, judging it altogether unmeet that so precious matter should be concealed from public use: when he excused himself, by undervaluing his own meditations; but withal signified his desire of the church's good, if by anything in his works it might never so little be promoted. I could not but declare myself in recommending this treatise as a very profitable and excellent help both to the understanding of that dark and most divine Scripture, and also to kindle in the heart all heavenly affections unto Jesus Christ.

It is well known how backward I am and ever have been to cumber the press, but yet I would not be guilty in depriving the dear children of God of the spiritual and sweet consolations which are here very plentifully offered unto them.

And the whole frame of all these sermons is carried with such wisdom, gravity, piety, judgment, and experience, that it commends itself unto all that are godly wise; and I doubt not but that they shall find their temptations answered, their fainting spirits revived, their understandings enlightened, and their graces confirmed, so as they shall have cause to praise God for the worthy author's godly and painful labours. And thus desiring the Father of all mercies and the God of all comfort to bless this work to the consolation and edification of those that seek his favour and desire to fear his holy name, I rest

Thine in Jesus Christ,

J[OHN] DOD
(1549-1645)

SERMON 1

I am come into my garden, my sister, my spouse: I have gathered
my myrrh with my spice; I have eaten my honeycomb with my
honey; I have drunk my wine with my milk: eat, O friends;
drink, yea, drink abundantly, O beloved.
SONG OF SOLOMON 5:1

OTHER books of Solomon lie more obvious and open to common understanding; but, as none entered into the holy of holies but the high priest (*Lev.* 16:2ff., *Heb.* 9:7), so none can enter into the mystery of this Song of songs, but such as have more near communion with Christ. Songs, and specially marriage songs, serve to express men's own joys, and others' praises. So this book contains *the mutual joys and mutual praises betwixt Christ and his church.*

And as Christ and his church are the greatest persons that partake of human nature, so whatsoever is excellent in the whole world is borrowed to set out the excellencies of these two great lovers.

It is called 'Solomon's Song,' who, next unto Christ, was the greatest son of wisdom that ever the church bred, whose understanding, as it was 'large as the sand of the sea' (*1 Kings* 4:29), so his affections, especially that of love, were as large, as we may see by his many wives, and by the delight he sought to take in whatsoever nature could afford. Which affection of love, in him misplaced, had been his undoing, but that he was one beloved of God, who by his Spirit raised his soul to lovely objects of a higher

1

nature. Here in this argument there is no danger for the deepest wit, or the largest affection, yea, of a Solomon, to overreach. For the knowledge of the love of Christ to his church is above all knowledge (*Eph.* 3:19). The angels themselves may admire it, though they cannot comprehend it. It may well, therefore, be called the 'Song of Solomon'; the most excellent song of a man of the highest conceit[1] and deepest apprehension, and of the highest matters, *the intercourse betwixt Christ, the highest Lord of lords, and his best beloved contracted spouse.*

There are divers things in this song that a corrupt heart, unto which all things are defiled, may take offence; but 'to the pure all things are pure' (*Titus* 1:15). Such a sinful abuse of this heavenly book is far from the intention of the Holy Ghost in it, which is by stooping low to us, to take advantage to raise us higher unto him, that by taking advantage of the sweetest passage of our life, *marriage,* and the most delightful affection, *love,* in the sweetest manner of expression, *by a song,* he might carry up the soul to things of a heavenly nature. We see in summer that one heat weakens another; and a great light being near a little one, draws away and obscures the flame of the other. So it is when the affections are taken up higher to their fit object; they die unto all earthly things, whilst that heavenly flame consumes and wastes all base affections and earthly desires. Amongst other ways of mortification, there be two remarkable—

1. *By embittering all earthly things unto us, whereby the affections are deaded[2] to them.*

2. *By showing more noble, excellent, and fit objects*, that the soul, issuing more largely and strongly into them, may be diverted, and so by degrees die unto other things. The Holy Spirit hath chosen this way in this song, by elevating and raising our affections and love, to take it off from other things, that so it might run in its right

[1] That is, imagination.—G.

[2] That is, deadened.—G.

channel. It is pity that a sweet stream should not rather run into a garden than into a puddle. What a shame is it that man, having in him such excellent affections as love, joy, delight, should cleave to dirty, base things, that are worse than himself, so becoming debased like them! Therefore the Spirit of God, out of mercy and pity to man, would raise up his affections, by taking comparison from earthly things, leading to higher matters, that only deserve love, joy, delight, and admiration. Let God's stooping to us occasion our rising up unto him. For here the greatest things, the 'mystery of mysteries', the communion betwixt Christ and his church, is set out in the familiar comparison of a marriage, that so we might the better see it in the glass of comparison, which we cannot so directly conceive of; as we may see the sun in water, whose beams we cannot so directly look upon. Only our care must be not to look so much on the colours as the picture, and not so much on the picture as on the person itself represented; that we look not so much to the resemblance as to the person resembled.[1]

Some would have Solomon, by a spirit of prophecy, to take a view here of all the time, from his age to the second coming of Christ, and in this song, as in an abridgment, to set down the several passages and periods of the church in several ages, as containing divers things which are more correspondent to one age of the church than another.[2] But howsoever this song may contain, we deny not, a story of the church in several ages, yet this hinders not, but that most passages of it agree to the spiritual estate of the church in every age, as most interpreters have thought. In this song there is,

[1] That is, represented.—G.

[2] 'Some would have Solomon, by a spirit of prophecy, to take a view here of all the time', &c. For a very full and valuable, though, in respect of the early English expositors (of whom there are many in whole or part), defective and meagre, 'Historical Sketch of the Exegesis of the Book' consult Ginsburg's *Song of Songs . . . with a Commentary, Historical and Critical* (London: Longman, 1857, 8vo) pp. 20-101. The opinions referred to by Sibbes will be found duly recorded.—G.

1. A strong desire of the church of nearer communion with Christ; and then,

2. Some declining again in affection.

3. After this we have her recovery and regaining again of love; after which,

4. The church falls again into a declining of affection; whereupon follows a further strangeness of Christ to her than before, which continues until,

5. That the church, perceiving of Christ's constant affection unto her, notwithstanding her unkind dealing, recovers, and cleaves faster to Christ than ever, chapter 3.

These passages agree to the experience of the best Christians in the state of their own lives. This observation must carry strength through this whole song, that *there is the same regard of the whole church, and of every particular member, in regard of the chiefest privileges and graces that accompany salvation.* There is the same reason of every drop of water as of the whole ocean, all is water; and of every spark of fire as of the whole element of fire, all is fire. Of those homogeneal bodies, as we call them, there is the same respect of the part and of the whole. And therefore, as the whole church is the spouse of Christ, so is every particular Christian; and as the whole church desires still nearer communion with Christ, so doth every particular member. But to come to the words, 'I am come into my garden', &c.

This chapter is not so well broken and divided from the former as it might have been, for it were better and more consequent[1] that the last verse of the former chapter were added to the beginning of this.

'Awake, O north wind; and come, thou south; blow upon my garden, that the spices thereof may flow out. Let my beloved come into his garden, and eat his pleasant fruits' (*Song of Sol.* 4:16).

And therefore, by reason of connection of this chapter with

---

[1] That is, in sequence.—G.

the former verse, we will first speak somewhat of it briefly, only to make way for that which follows. The words contain—

1. *A turning of Christ's speech to the winds to blow upon his garden, with the end why,* 'that the spices thereof may flow out'.

2. *We have an invitation of Christ, by the church, to come into his garden,* with the end, 'to eat his pleasant fruits'.

Quest. It may be a question whether this command be the words of Christ or the desire of his spouse?

Ans. The words are spoken by Christ, because he calls it '*my* garden', and the church after invites him to eat of '*his* pleasant fruits', not of hers. Yet the words may be likewise an answer to a former secret desire of the church, whereof the order is this: The church being sensible of some deadness of spirit, secretly desires some further quickening. Christ then answers those desires by commanding the winds to blow upon her. For ordinarily Christ first stirs up desires, and then answers the desires of his own Spirit by further increase, as here, 'Awake, thou north wind; and come, thou south; and blow upon my garden', &c.

I. For the first point named, we see here that Christ *sends forth his Spirit, with command to all means,* under the name of 'north and south wind', to further the fruitfulness of his church. The wind is nature's fan. What winds are to the garden, that the Spirit of Christ, in the use of means, is to the soul. From comparison fetched from Christ's commanding the winds, we may in general observe, that *all creatures stand in obedience to Christ, as ready at a word, whensoever he speaks to them.* They are all, as it were, asleep until he awakes them. He can call for the wind out of his treasures when he pleases: he holds them in his fist (*Prov.* 30:4).

Use. Which may comfort all those that are Christ's, that they are under one that hath all creatures at his beck under him to do them service, and at his check to do them no harm. This drew the disciples in admiration to say, 'What manner of man is this, that even the winds and the seas obey him?' (*Matt.* 8:27). And cannot the same power still the winds and waves of the churches and States, and cause a sudden calm, if, as the disciples, we awake him with our prayers.

Secondly, we see here that Christ speaks to *winds contrary one to another,* both in regard of the coasts from whence they blow, and in their quality; but both agree in this, that both are necessary for the garden: where we see that *the courses that Christ takes, and the means that he uses with his church, may seem contrary; but by a wise ordering, all agree in the wholesome issue.* A prosperous and an afflicted condition are contrary: a mild and a sharp course may seem to cross one another; yet sweetly they agree in this, that as the church needeth both, so Christ useth both for the church's good. The north is a nipping wind, and the south a cherishing wind; therefore the south wind is the welcomer and sweeter after the north wind hath blown. But howsoever, all things are ours: 'Paul, Apollos, Cephas, things present and to come, life, death', &c. (*1 Cor.* 3:21, 22); 'all things work together for good to us, being in Christ' (*Rom.* 8:28).

Use 1. Hence it is that the manifold wisdom of Christ *maketh use of such variety of conditions;* and hence it is that the Spirit of Christ is mild in some men's ministries, and sharp in others: nay, in the very same minister, as the state of the soul they have to deal withal requires.

Use 2. Sometimes, again, *the people of God need purging, and sometimes refreshing.* Whereupon the Spirit of God carries itself suitably to both conditions; and the Spirit in the godly themselves draws good out of every condition, sure [as] they are that all winds blow them good, and [that] were it not for their good, no winds should blow upon them. But in regard that these times of ours, by long peace and plenty, grow cold, heavy, and secure, we need therefore all kinds of winds to blow upon us, and all little enough. Time was when we were more quick and lively, but now the heat of our spirits is¹ abated. We must therefore take heed of it, and 'quicken those things that are ready to die' (*Rev.* 3:2); or else, instead of the north and south wind, God will send an east wind that shall dry up all, as it is, Hosea 13:15.

Use 3. Again, if Christ can raise or lay, bind up or let loose, all kind of winds at his pleasure, then if means be wanting or fruitless, it is he that says to the clouds, Drop not, and to the winds, Blow not. Therefore, *we must acknowledge him in want or plenty of means.* The Spirit of Christ in the use of means is a free agent, sometimes blows strongly, sometimes more mildly, sometimes not at all. No creature hath these winds in a bag at command, and therefore it is wisdom to yield to the gales of the Spirit. Though in some other things, as Solomon observes, it may hinder to observe the winds (*Eccles.* 11:4), yet here it is necessary and profitable to observe the winds of the Spirit.

Now, for the clear understanding of what we are to speak of, let us first observe—

1. Why the Spirit of God, in the use of the means, is compared to wind. And then,

2. Why the church is compared to a garden; which shall be handled in the proper place.

But first for the wind.

1. 'The wind bloweth where it listeth', as it is John 3:8. So the Spirit of God blows freely, and openeth the heart of some, and poureth grace plentifully in them.

2. The wind, especially the north wind, *hath a cleansing force.* So the Spirit of God purgeth our hearts 'from dead works to serve the living God, making us partakers of the divine nature' (2 *Pet.* 1:4).

3. The wind *disperseth and scattereth clouds, and makes a*

---

¹ It is printed 'are'. But such inaccuracy is not uncommon in Sibbes and his contemporaries. If the nearer noun be plural, it, and not the nominative proper, regulates the use of the verb. This remark is made once for all, that apparent misprints may not be placed to oversight.—G.

serenity in the air. So doth the Spirit disperse such clouds as corruption and Satan raise up in the soul, that we may clearly see the face of God in Jesus Christ.

4. The wind hath *a cooling and a tempering quality, and tempers the distemper of nature.* As in some hot countries there be yearly anniversary winds, which blow at certain times in summer, tempering the heat; so the Spirit of God allayeth the unnatural heats of the soul in fiery temptations, and bringeth it into a good temper.

5. The wind being subtle, *searcheth into every corner and cranny.* So the Spirit likewise is of a searching nature, and discerneth betwixt the joints and the marrow, betwixt the flesh and the Spirit, &c., searching those hidden corruptions, that nature could never have found out.

6. The wind hath *a cherishing and a fructifying force.* So the Spirit is a quickening and a cherishing Spirit, and maketh the heart, which is as a barren wilderness, to be fruitful.

7. The wind hath *a power of conveying sweet smells in the air, to carry them from one to another.* So the Spirit in the Word conveyeth the seeds of grace and comfort from one to another. It draws out what sweetness is in the spirits of men, and makes them fragrant and delightful to others.

8. The wind, again, *bears down all before it, beats down houses, and trees, like the cedars in Lebanon,* turns them up by the roots, and lays all flat. So the Spirit is mighty in operation. There is no standing before it. It brings down mountains, and every high thing that exalts itself, and lays them level; nay, the Roman and those other mighty empires could not stand before it.

For these respects and the like, the 'blowing of the Spirit' is compared to wind. For which end Christ here commands the wind to 'blow upon his garden'.

1. *To blow,* &c. See here the order, linking, and concatenation[1] of things one under another. To the prospering of a poor flower or

---

[1] A series of items linked together in a chain-like way.—P.

plant in a garden, not only soil is needful, but air and wind also, and the influence of heaven; and God commanding all, as here the winds to blow upon his garden. To this end, as a wonderful mercy to his people, it is said, 'And it shall come to pass in that day, I will hear, saith the Lord: I will hear the heavens, and they shall hear the earth; and the earth shall hear the corn, the wine, and the oil; and they shall hear Jezreel' (*Hos.* 2:21, 22). As the creatures are from God, so the order and dependence of creatures one from another, to teach us not only what to pray for, but also what to pray fitly for; not only to pray for the dew of heaven, but also for seasonable and cherishing winds. It is not the soil, but the season, that makes fruitful, and that from seasonable winds and influences. So in spiritual things there is a chain of causes and effects: prayer comes from faith (*Rom.* 10:14); faith from the hearing of the Word; hearing from a preacher, by whom God by his Spirit blows upon the heart; and a preacher from God's sending. If the God of nature should but hinder and take away one link of nature's chain, the whole frame would be disturbed. Well, that which Christ commands here, is for the winds to 'blow upon his garden'.

And we need blowing: our spirits will be becalmed else, and stand at a stay; and Satan will be sure by himself, and such as are his bellows, to blow up the seeds of sinful lusts in us. For there are two spirits in the church, the one always blowing against the other. Therefore, the best had need to be stirred up; otherwise, with Moses (*Exod.* 17:12) their hands will be ready to fall down, and abate in their affection. Therefore we need blowing—

1. In regard of our natural inability.

2. In regard of our dullness and heaviness, cleaving to nature occasionally.

3. In regard of contrary winds from without.

Satan hath his bellows filled with his spirit, that hinders the work of grace all they can; so that we need not only Christ's blowing, but also his stopping other contrary winds, that they blow not (*Rev.* 7:1).

4. In regard of the estate and condition of the new covenant, wherein all beginning, growth, and ending, is from grace, and nothing but grace.

5. Because old grace, without a fresh supply, will not hold against new crosses and temptations.

Use. Therefore when Christ draws, let us run after him; when he blows, let us open unto him. It may be the last blast that ever we shall have from him. And let us set upon duties with this encouragement, that Christ will blow upon us, not only to prevent us, but also to maintain his own graces in us. But O! where is this stirring up of ourselves, and one another, upon these grounds!

Quest. But, *why is the church compared to a garden?*

Ans. Christ herein takes all manner of terms to express himself and the state of the church, as it is to him, to show us that wheresoever we are, we may have occasion of heavenly thoughts, to raise up our thoughts to higher matters. His church is his 'temple', when we are in the temple; it is a 'field' when we are there; a 'garden', if we walk in a garden. It is also a 'spouse' and a 'sister', &c. But more particularly the church is resembled to a garden.

1. *Because a garden is taken out of the common waste ground, to be appropriated to a more particular use.* So the church of Christ is taken out of the wilderness of this waste world, to a particular use. It is in respect of the rest, as Goshen to Egypt (*Exod.* 9:26), wherein light was, when all else was in darkness. And indeed wherein doth the church differ from other grounds, but that Christ hath taken it in? It is the same soil as other grounds are; but, he dresseth and fits it to bear spices and herbs.

2. *In a garden nothing comes up naturally of itself, but as it is planted and set.* So nothing is good in the heart, but as it is planted and set by the heavenly husbandman (*John* 15:4 and *Matt.* 15:13). We need not sow the wilderness, for the seeds of weeds prosper naturally. The earth is a mother to weeds, but a stepmother to

herbs. So weeds and passions grow too rank naturally, but nothing grows in the church of itself, but as it is set by the hand of Christ, who is the author, dresser, and pruner of his garden.

3. Again, *in a garden nothing is planted but what is useful and delightful.* So there is no grace in the heart of a Christian, but it is useful, as occasion serves, both to God and man.

4. Further, *in a garden there are variety of flowers and spices,* especially in those hot countries. So in a Christian, there is somewhat of every grace. As some cannot hear of a curious flower, but they will have it in their garden, so a Christian cannot hear of any grace but he labours to obtain it. They labour for graces for all seasons, and occasions. They have for prosperity, temperance and sobriety; for adversity, patience and hope to sustain them. For those that are above them, they have respect and obedience; and for those under them, suitable usage in all conditions of Christianity. For the Spirit of God in them is a seminary[1] of spiritual good things. As in the corruption of nature, before the Spirit of God came to us, there was the seminary of all ill weeds in us, so when there is a new quality and new principles put in us, therewith comes the seeds of all graces.

5. Again, *of all other places, we most delight in our gardens to walk there and take our pleasure*, and take care thereof, for fencing, weeding, watering, and planting. So Christ's chief care and delight is for his church. He walks in the midst of the 'seven golden candlesticks' (*Rev.* 2:1); and if he defend and protect States, it is that they may be a harbour to his church.

6. And then again, as in gardens there had wont to have *fountains and streams which run through their gardens* (as paradise had four streams which ran through it); so the church is Christ's paradise; and his Spirit is a spring in the midst of it, to refresh the souls of his upon all their faintings, and so the soul of a Christian becomes as a watered garden.

[1] A seed-bed.—P.

11

7. So also, 'their fountains were sealed up' (*Song of Sol.* 4:12); so the joys of the church and particular Christians are, as it were, sealed up. A stranger, it is said, 'shall not meddle with this joy of the church' (*Prov.* 14:10).

8. Lastly, *a garden stands always in need of weeding and dressing.* Continual labour and cost must be bestowed upon it; sometimes planting, pruning, and weeding, &c. So in the church and hearts of Christians, Christ hath always somewhat to do. We would else soon be overgrown and turn wild. In all which, and the like respects, Christ calleth upon the winds 'to blow upon his garden'.

Use 1. If then the church be a severed portion, then *we should walk as men of a severed condition from the world*, not as men of the world, but as Christians; to make good that we are so, by feeling the graces of God's Spirit in some comfortable measure, that so Christ may have something in us, that he may delight to dwell with us, so to be subject to his pruning and dressing. For, it is so far from being an ill sign, that Christ is at cost[1] with us, in following us with afflictions, that it is rather a sure sign of his love. For, the care of this blessed husbandman is to prune us, so as to make us fruitful. Men care not for heath and wilderness, whereupon they bestow no cost. So when God prunes us by crosses and afflictions, and sows good seed in us, it is a sign he means to dwell with us, and delight in us.

Use 2. And then also, we should not strive so much for *common liberties* of the world that common people delight in, but for *peculiar graces*, that God may delight in us as his garden.

Use 3. And then, let us learn hence, *not to despise any nation or person*, seeing God can take out of the waste wilderness whom he will, and make the desert an Eden.

Use 4. Again, *let us bless God for ourselves,* that our lot hath fallen into such a pleasant place, to be planted in the church, the place of God's delight.

Use 5. And this also should move us *to be fruitful*. For men

[1] That is, expense.—G.

12

will endure a fruitless tree in the waste wilderness, but in their garden who will endure it? Dignity should mind us of duty. It is strange to be fruitless and barren in this place that we live in, being watered with the dew of heaven, under the sweet influence of the means. This fruitless estate being often watered from heaven, how fearfully is it threatened by the Holy Ghost, that 'it is near unto cursing and burning' (*Heb.* 6:8). For in this case, visible churches, if they prosper not, God will remove the hedge, and lay them waste, having a garden elsewhere. Sometimes God's plants prosper better in Babylon, than in Judea. It is to be feared God may complain of us, as he doth of his people, 'I have planted thee a noble vine; how art thou then come to be degenerated?' (*Jer.* 2:21). If in this case we regard iniquity in our heart, the Lord will not regard the best thing that comes from us, as our prayers (*Heb.* 12:17). We must then learn of himself, how and wherein to please him. Obedience from a broken heart is the best sacrifice. Mark in [the] Scriptures what he abhors, what he delights in. We used to say of our friends, Would God I knew how to please them. Christ teacheth us, that 'without faith it is impossible to please him' (*Heb.* 11:6). Let us then strive and labour to be fruitful in our places and callings. For it is the greatest honour in this world, for God to dignify us with such a condition, as to make us fruitful. 'We must not bring forth fruit to ourselves', as God complains of Ephraim [Israel] (*Hos.* 10:1). Honour, riches, and the like, are but secondary things, arbitrary at God's pleasure to cast in; but, to have an active heart fruitful from this ground, that God hath planted us for this purpose, that we may do good to mankind, this is an excellent consideration not to profane our calling. The blessed man is said to be, 'a tree planted by the water side, that brings forth fruit in due season' (*Psa.* 1:3). But it is not every fruit; not that fruit which Moses complains of (*Deut.* 32:32), the wine of dragons, and the gall of asps: but good fruit, as John speaks (*John* 15); 'Every tree that bringeth not forth good fruit, is hewn down, and cast into the fire' (*Matt.* 3:10).

Use 6. Lastly, in that the church is called Christ's garden, this may *strengthen our faith in God's care and protection.* The church may seem to lie open to all incursions, but it hath an invisible hedge about it, a wall without it, and a well within it (*Zech.* 2:5). God himself is a wall of fire about it, and his Spirit a well of living waters running through it to refresh and comfort it. As it was said of Canaan, so it may be said of the church, 'The eye of the Lord is upon it all the year long' (*Deut.* 11:12), and he waters it continually. From which especial care of God over it, this is a good plea for us to God, 'I am thine, save me'; I am a plant of thine own setting; nothing is in me but what is thine, therefore cherish what is thine. So, for the whole church the plea is good: 'The church is thine; fence it, water it, defend it, keep the wild boar out of it.' Therefore the enemies thereof shall one day know what it is to make a breach upon God's vineyard. In the meantime, let us labour to keep our hearts as a garden, that nothing that defileth may enter. In which respects the church is compared to a garden, upon which Christ commands the north and south wind, all the means of grace, to blow.

But to what end must these winds blow upon the garden?

'That the spices thereof may flow out.'

The end of this blowing is, you see, 'that the spices thereof may flow out'. Good things in us lie dead and bound up, unless the Spirit let them out. We ebb and flow, open and shut, as the Spirit blows upon us; without blowing, no flowing. There were gracious good things in the church, but they wanted blowing up and further spreading, whence we may observe, that,

Obs. 1. *We need not only grace to put life into us at the first, but likewise grace to quicken and draw forth that grace that we have.* This is the difference betwixt man's blowing and the Spirit's. Man, when he blows, if grace be not there before, spends all his labour upon a dead coal, which he cannot make take fire. But the Spirit first kindles a holy fire, and then increases the flame. Christ had in the use of means wrought on the church before, and now further promoteth his own work. We must first take in, and then send out; first be cisterns to contain, and then conduits to convey. The wind first blows, and then the spices of the church flow out. We are first sweet in ourselves, and then sweet to others.

Obs. 2. Whence we see further, that *it is not enough to be good in ourselves, but our goodness must flow out*; that is, grow more strong, useful to continue and stream forth for the good of others. We must labour to be, as was said of John, burning and shining Christians (*John* 5:35). For Christ is not like a box of ointment shut up and not opened, but like that box of ointment that Mary poured out, which perfumes all the whole house with the sweetness thereof. For the Spirit is herein like wind; it carries the sweet savour of grace to others. A Christian, so soon as he finds any rooting in God, is of a spreading disposition, and makes the places he lives in the better for him. The whole body is the better for every good member, as we see in Onesimus (*Philem.* 11). The meanest persons, when they become good, are useful and profitable; of briars, become flowers. The very naming of a good man casts a sweet savour, as presenting some grace to the heart of the hearer. For then we have what we have to purpose, when others have occasion to bless God for us, for conveying comfort to them by us. And for our furtherance herein, therefore, the winds are called upon to awake and blow upon Christ's garden, 'that the spices thereof may flow out'.

Obs. 3. Hence we see, also, that *where once God begins, he goes on, and delights to add encouragement to encouragement, to maintain new setters up in religion*, and doth not only give them a stock of grace at the beginning, but also helps them to trade. He is not only Alpha, but Omega, unto them, the beginning and the ending (*Rev.* 1:8). He doth not only plant graces, but also watereth and cherisheth them. Where the Spirit of Christ is, it is an encouraging Spirit; for not only it infuseth grace, but also stirs it up, that we may be ready prepared for every good work, otherwise we cannot do that which we are able to do. The Spirit must bring all into exercise, else the habits of grace will lie asleep. We need a present Spirit to do every good; not only the power to will, but the will itself; and not only the will, but the deed, is from the Spirit, which should stir us up to go to Christ, that he may stir up his own graces in us, that they may flow out.

Use. Let us labour, then, in ourselves to be full of goodness, that so we may be fitted to do good to all. As God is good, and does good to all, so must we strive to be as like him as may be; in which case, for others' sakes, we must pray that God would make the winds to blow out fully upon us, 'that our spices may flow out' for their good. For a Christian in his right temper thinks that he hath nothing good to purpose, but that which does good to others.

Thus far of Christ's command to the north and south wind to awake and blow upon his garden, that the spices thereof may flow out. In the next place we have—

II. Christ's invitation by the church to come into his garden, with the end thereof, 'to eat his pleasant fruits'.

Which words show *the church's further desire of Christ's presence to delight in the graces of his own Spirit in her.* She invites him to come and take delight in the graces of his own Spirit; and she calls him 'beloved', because all her love is, or should be, imparted and spent on Christ, who gave himself to a cursed death for her. Our love should run in strength no other way, therefore the church calls Christ her 'beloved'. Christ was there before, but she desires a further presence of him, whence we may observe, that

Wheresoever grace is truly begun and stirred up, there is still a further desire of Christ's presence; and approaching daily more and more near to the soul, the church thinks him never near enough to her until she be in heaven with him. The true spouse and the bride always, unless in desertion and temptation, crieth, 'Come, Lord Jesus, come quickly' (*Rev.* 22:20). Now, these degrees of Christ's approaches to the soul, until his second coming, are, that he may manifest himself more and more in defending, comforting, and enabling his church with grace. Every further manifestation of his presence is a further coming.

Quest. But why is the church thus earnest?

Reason 1. First, *because grace helps to see our need of Christ*, and so helps us to prize him the more; which high esteem breeds a hungering, earnest desire after him, and a desire of further likeness and suitableness to him.

Reason 2. Secondly, because the church well knows that when Christ comes to the soul *he comes not alone, but with his Spirit, and his Spirit with abundance of peace and comfort.* This she knows, what need she hath of his presence, that without him there is no comfortable living; for wheresoever he is, he makes the soul a kind of heaven, and all conditions of life comfortable.

Use. Hence we may see that those that do not desire the presence of Christ in his ordinances are, it is to be feared, such as the wind of the Holy Ghost never blew upon. There are some of such a disposition as they cannot endure the presence of Christ, such as antichrist and his limbs,[1] whom the presence of Christ in his ordinances blasts and consumes. Such are not only profane and worldly persons, but proud hypocrites, who glory in something of their own; and therefore their hearts rise against Christ and his ordinances, as laying open and shaming their emptiness and carnalness. The Spirit in the spouse is always saying to Christ, 'Come.' It hath never enough of him. He was now in a sort present; but the church, after it is once blown upon, is not satisfied without a further presence. It is from the Spirit that we desire more of the Spirit, and from the presence of Christ that we desire a further presence and communion with him. Now,

[1] That is, members = adherents.—G.

17

The end and reason why Christ is desired by the church to come into his garden is 'to eat his pleasant fruits;' that is, to give him contentment. And is it not fit that Christ should eat the fruit of his own vine? have comfort of his own garden? to taste of his own fruits? The only delight Christ hath in the world is in his garden, and that he might take the more delight in it, he makes it fruitful; and those fruits are precious fruits, as growing from plants set by his own hand, relishing of his own Spirit, and so fitted for his taste. Now, the church, knowing what fitted Christ's taste best, and knowing the fruits of grace in her heart, desireth that Christ would delight in his own graces in her, and kindly accept of what she presented him with. Whence we see that

A gracious heart is privy to its own grace and sincerity when it is in a right temper, and so far as it is privy is bold with Christ in a sweet and reverend[1] manner. So much sincerity, so much confidence. If our heart condemn us not of insincerity, we may in a reverend[1] manner speak boldly to Christ. It is not fit there should be strangeness betwixt Christ and his spouse; neither, indeed, will there be, when Christ hath blown upon her, and when she is on the growing hand. But mark the order.

First, Christ blows, and then the church says, 'Come.' Christ begins in love, then love draws love. Christ draws the church, and she runs after him (*Song of Sol.* 1:4). The fire of love melts more than the fire of affliction.

Again, we may see here in the church a carefulness to please Christ. As it is the duty, so it is the disposition of the church of Christ, to please her husband.

1. The reason is, first, our happiness stands in his contentment, and all cannot but be well in that house where the husband and the wife delight in, and make much of, each other.

2. And again, after that the church hath denied herself and the vanities of the world, entering into a way and course of mortifica-

[1] That is, reverent.—Ed.

tion, whom else hath she to give herself to, or receive contentment from? Our manner is to study to please men whom we hope to rise by, being careful that all we do may be well taken of them. As for Christ, we put him off with anything. If he likes it, so it is; if not, it is the best that he is like to have.

Use 1. Oh! let us take the apostle's counsel, 'To labour to walk worthy of the Lord, &c., unto all well-pleasing, increasing in knowledge, and fruitfulness in every good work' (*Col.* 1:9, 10). And this knowledge must not only be a general wisdom in knowing truths, but a special understanding of his good-will to us, and our special duties again to him.

Use 2. Again, that we may please Christ the better, labour to be cleansed from that which is offensive to him: let the spring be clean. Therefore the psalmist, desiring that the words of his mouth and the meditations of his heart might be acceptable before God, first begs 'cleansing from his secret sins' (*Psa.* 19:12).

Use 3. And still we must remember that he himself must work in us whatsoever is well-pleasing in his sight, that so we may be perfect in every good thing to do his will, having grace whereby we may serve him acceptably. And one prevailing argument with him is, that we desire to be such as he may take delight in: 'the upright are his delight'. It cannot but please him when we desire grace for this end that we may please him. If we study to please men in whom there is but little good, should we not much more study to please Christ, the fountain of goodness? Labour therefore to be spiritual; for 'to be carnally minded is death' (*Rom.* 8:8), and 'those that are in the flesh cannot please God'.

The church desires Christ to come into his garden, 'to eat his pleasant fruits,' where we see, *the church gives all to Christ.* The garden is his, the fruit his, the pleasantness and preciousness of the fruit is his. And as the fruits please him, so the humble acknowledgment that they come from him doth exceedingly please him. It is enough for us to have the comfort, let him have the glory. It came from a good spirit in David when he said, 'Of thine own, Lord, I give thee,' &c. (*1 Chron.* 29:14). God accounts the works and fruits that come from us to be ours, because the judgment and resolution of will, whereby we do them, is ours. This he doth to encourage us; but because the grace whereby we judge and will aright, comes from God, it is our duty to ascribe whatsoever is good in us, or comes from us, unto him; so God shall lose no praise, and we lose no encouragement. The imperfections in well-doing are only ours, and those Christ will pardon, as knowing how to bear with the infirmities of his spouse, being 'the weaker vessel' (*1 Pet.* 3:7).

Use. This therefore should cheer up our spirits in the wants and blemishes of our performances. They are notwithstanding precious fruits in Christ's acceptance, so that we desire to please him above all things, and to have nearer communion with him. *Fruitfulness unto pleasingness may stand with imperfections,* so that we be sensible of them, and ashamed for them. Although the fruit be little, yet it is precious, there is a blessing in it. Imperfections help us against temptations to pride, not to be matter of discouragement, which Satan aims at. And as Christ commands the north and south wind to blow for cherishing, so Satan labours to stir up an east pinching wind, to take either from endeavour, or to make us heartless in endeavour. Why should we think basely of that which Christ thinks precious? Why should we think that offensive which he counts as incense? We must not give false witness of the work of grace in our hearts, but bless God that he will work anything in such polluted hearts as ours. What though, as they come from us, they have a relish of the old man, seeing he takes them from us, 'perfumes them with his own sweet odours' (*Rev.* 8:3), and so presents them unto God. He is our High Priest which makes all acceptable, both persons, prayers, and performances, sprinkling them all with his blood (*Heb.* 9:14).

To conclude this point, let it be our study to be in such a condition wherein we may please Christ; and whereas we are daily prone to offend him, let us daily renew our covenant with him, and in him: and fetch encouragements of well-doing from this, that what we do is not only well-pleasing unto him, but rewarded of him. And to this end desire him, that he would give command to north and south, to all sort of means, to be effectual for making us more fruitful, that he may delight in us as his pleasant gardens. And then what is in the world that we need much care for or fear?

Now, upon the church's invitation for Christ to come into his garden, follows his gracious answer unto the church's desire, in the first verse of this fifth chapter:

'I am come into my garden, my sister, my spouse: I have gathered my myrrh with my spice; I have eaten my honeycomb with my honey; I have drunk my wine with my milk: eat, O friends; drink, yea, drink abundantly, O beloved' (*Song of Sol.* 5:1).

Which words contain in them *an answer to the desire of the church in the latter part of the verse formerly handled*: 'Awake, thou north wind; and come, thou south', &c.

Then, in verse 2, is set forth *the secure estate of the church at this time,* 'I sleep, but my heart waketh'; in setting down whereof the Holy Ghost here by Solomon shows likewise,

The loving intercourse betwixt Christ and the church one with another.

Now Christ, upon the secure estate and condition of the church, desires her 'to open unto him', verse 2; which desire and waiting of Christ is put off and slighted with poor and slender excuses: verse 3, 'I have put off my coat; how shall I put it on?' &c.

The success[1] of which excuses is, that Christ seems to go away from her (and indeed to her sight and sense departs): verse 6, 'I opened to my beloved; but my beloved had withdrawn himself', &c.; whereupon she lays about her, is restless, and inquires after Christ from the watchmen, who misuse, 'wound her, and take away her veil from her', verse 7.

[1] That is, the result.—G.

Another intercourse in this chapter here is, that *the church for all this gives not over searching after Christ,* but asks the daughters of Jerusalem what was become of her beloved, verse 8; and withal, in a few words, but full of large expression, she relates her case unto them, that 'she was sick of love', and so 'chargeth them to tell her beloved', 'if they find him'. Whereupon a question moved by them, touching her beloved, verse 9, 'What is thy beloved more than another beloved?' she takes occasion, being full of love, which is glad of all occasion to speak of the beloved, to burst forth into his praises, by many elegant expressions, verses 10, 11, 12, &c.

1. In general, setting him at a large distance, beyond comparison from all others, to be 'the chiefest of ten thousand', verse 10.

2. In particulars, verse 11, &c.: 'his head is as most fine gold', &c.

The issue whereof was, that the 'daughters of Jerusalem' become likewise enamoured with him, chap. 6:1; and thereupon inquire also after him, 'Whither is thy beloved gone, O thou fairest among women?' &c. Unto which demand the church makes answer, chapter 6:2; and so, verse 3 of that chapter makes a confident, triumphant close unto all these grand passages forenamed, 'I am my beloved's, and my beloved is mine', &c.; all of which will better appear in the particulars themselves.

The first thing then which offereth itself to our consideration is *Christ's answer to the church's invitation,* chapter 4:16:

'I am come into my garden, my sister, my spouse: I have gathered my myrrh with my spice; I have eaten my honeycomb with my honey; I have drunk my wine with my milk: eat, O friends; drink, yea, drink abundantly, O beloved.' In which verse we have,

I. Christ's answer to the church's petition, 'I am come into my garden.'

II. A compellation,[1] or description of the church, 'My sister, my spouse.'

---

[1] Manner or form of address, appellation. P.

III. Christ's acceptation of what he had gotten there, 'I have gathered my myrrh with my spice; I have eaten my honeycomb with my honey.' There is,

IV. An invitation of all Christ's friends to a magnifique[1] abundant feast, 'Eat, O friends; drink, yea drink abundantly, O beloved.'

I. For the first, then, in that Christ makes such a real answer unto the church's invitation, 'I am come into my garden', &c., we see, *that Christ comes into his garden.* 'Tis much that he that hath heaven to delight in, will delight to dwell among the sons of sinful men; but this he doth for us, and so takes notice of the church's petition.

'Let my beloved come into his garden, and eat his pleasant fruit.' The right speech of the church that gives all to Christ, who, when she hath made such a petition, hears it. The order is this—

First of all, God *makes his church lovely*, planteth good things therein, and then stirs up in her good desires: both fitness to pray from an inward gracious disposition, and holy desires; after which, Christ hearing the voice of his own Spirit in her, and regarding his own preparations, he answers them graciously. Whence, in the first place, we may observe, that,

God makes us good, stirs up holy desires in us, and then answers the desires of his holy Spirit in us.

A notable place for this we have, Psalm 10:17, which shows how God first prepares the heart to pray, and then hears these desires of the soul stirred up by his own Spirit, 'Lord, thou hast heard the desires of the humble.' None are fit to pray but the humble, such as discern their own wants: 'Thou wilt prepare their hearts, thou wilt make thine ear to hear.' So (*Rom.* 8:26) it is said, 'Likewise the Spirit also helpeth our infirmities; for we know not what we should pray for as we ought: but the Spirit itself maketh

[1] That is, magnificent.—G.

23

intercession for us, with groanings which cannot be uttered.' Thus the Spirit not only stirs up our heart to pray, but also prepares our hearts unto it. Especially this is necessary for us, when our thoughts are confused with trouble, grief, and passions, not knowing what to pray. In this case the Spirit dictates the words of prayer, or else, in a confusion of thoughts, sums up all in a volley of sighs and unexpressible groans. Thus it is true, that our hearts can neither be lifted up to prayer, nor rightly prepared for it, in any frame fitting, but by God's own Spirit. Nothing is accepted of God toward heaven and happiness, but that which is spiritual: all saving and sanctifying good comes from above. Therefore God must prepare the heart, stir up holy desires, dictate prayer; must do all in all, being our 'Alpha and Omega' (*Rev.* 1:8).

1. Now God hears our prayers, First, *Because the materials of these holy desires are good in themselves, and from the person from whence they come, his beloved spouse,* as it is in Song of Solomon 2:14, where Christ, desiring to hear the voice of his church, saith, 'Let me see thy countenance, and let me hear thy voice; for sweet is thy voice, and thy countenance is comely.' Thus the voice of the spouse is sweet, because it is stirred up by his own Spirit, which burns the incense, and whence all comes which is savingly good. This offering up of our prayers in the name of Christ, is that which with his sweet odours perfumes all our sacrifices and prayers; because, being in the covenant of grace, God respects whatsoever comes from us, as we do the desires of our near friends (*Rev.* 8:3).

2. And then, again, God hears our prayers, *because he looks upon us as we are in election, and choice of God the Father, who hath given us to him.* Not only as in the near bond of marriage, husband and wife, but also as he hath given us to Christ; which is his plea unto the Father (*John* 17:6), 'Thine they were, thou gavest them me', &c. The desires of the church please him, because they are stirred up by his Spirit, and proceed from her that is his; whose voice he delights to hear, and the prayers of others for his church are accepted, because they are for her that is his beloved.

To confirm this further, see Isaiah 58:9, 'Thou then shalt cry, and the Lord shall answer; thou shalt call, and presently he shall say, Here I am', &c. So as soon as Daniel had ended that excellent prayer, the angel telleth him, 'At the beginning of thy supplications the decree came forth', &c. (*Dan.* 9:23). So because he knows what to put into our hearts, he knows our desires and thoughts, and therefore accepts of our prayers and hears us, because he loves the voice of his own Spirit in us. So it is said, 'He fulfils the desires of them that fear him; and he is near to all that call upon him, to all that call upon him in truth' (*Psa.* 145:18, 19). And our Saviour, he saith, 'Ask and ye shall receive', &c. (*Matt.* 7:7). So we have it in 1 John 5:14, 'And we know if we ask anything according to his will, he heareth us.'

Use 1. Let it therefore be a singular comfort to us, that in all wants, so in that of friends, when we have none to go to, yet we have God, to whom we may freely pour out our hearts. There being no place in the world that can restrain us from his presence, or his Spirit from us, he can hear us and help us in all places. What a blessed estate is this! None can hinder us from driving this trade with Christ in heaven.

Use 2. And let us make another use of it likewise, to be a means to stir up our hearts to make use of our privileges. What a prerogative is it for a favourite to have the fare[1] of his prince! Him we account happy. Surely he is much more happy that hath God's care, him to be his father in the covenant of grace; him reconciled, upon all occasions, to pour out his heart before him, who is merciful and faithful, wise and most able to help us. 'Why are we discouraged, therefore; and why are we cast down' (*Psa.* 42:11), when we have such a powerful and such a gracious God to go to in all our extremities? He that can pray can never be much uncomfortable.

Use 3. So likewise, it should stir us up to keep our peace with God, that so we may always have access unto him, and communion with him. What a pitiful case is it to lose other comforts, and

---

[1] Qu. care or fare?—Ed.

THE LOVE OF CHRIST

therewith also to be in such a state, that we cannot go to God with any boldness! It is the greatest loss of all when we have lost the spirit of prayer; for, if we lose other things, we may recover them by prayer. But when we have lost this boldness to go to God, and are afraid to look him in the face, as malefactors the judge, this is a woeful state.

Now there are divers cases wherein the soul is not in a state fit for prayer. As that first (*Psa*. 66:18), 'If I regard iniquity in my heart, the Lord will not regard my prayer.' If a man hath a naughty heart, that purposeth to live in any sin against God, he takes him for an enemy, and therefore will not regard his prayer. Therefore we must come with a resolute purpose to break off all sinful courses, and to give up ourselves to the guidance of God's Spirit. And this will be a forcible reason to move us thereunto, because so long as we live in any known sin unrepented of, God neither regards us nor our prayers. What a fearful estate is this, that when we have such need of God's favour in all estates; in sickness, the hour of death, and in spiritual temptation, to be in such a condition as that we dare not go to God! Though our lives be civil,[1] yet if we have false hearts that feed themselves with evil imaginations, and with a purpose of sinning, though we act it not, the Lord will not regard the prayers of such a one; they are abominable. The very 'sacrifice of the wicked is abominable' (*Prov*. 15:8).   .

2. Another case is, when we will not forgive others. We know it is directly set down in the Lord's Prayer. 'Forgive us our trespasses, as we forgive them that trespass against us' (*Matt*. 6:12); and there is further added, verse 15, 'If you forgive not men their trespasses, neither will your heavenly Father forgive you.' If our hearts tell us we have no disposition to pardon, be at peace and agreement, then we do but take God's name in vain when we ask him to forgive our sins, and we continue in envy and malice. In this case God will not regard our prayers, as it is said, 'I care not for your

---

[1] That is, moral.—G.

prayers, or for any service you perform to me.' Why? 'For your hands are full of blood' (*Isa.* 1:15). You are unmerciful, of a cruel, fierce disposition, which cannot appear before God rightly, nor humble itself in prayer. If it doth, its own bloody and cruel disposition will be objected against the prayers, which are not mingled with faith and love, but with wrath and bitterness. Shall I look for mercy, that have no merciful heart myself? Can I hope to find that of God, that others cannot find from me? An unbroken disposition, which counts 'pride an ornament' (*Psa.* 73:6), that is cruel and fierce, it cannot go to God in prayer. For, whosoever would prevail with God in prayer must be humble; for our supplications must come from a loving, peaceable disposition, where there is a resolution against all sin (*Psa.* 73:1). Neither is it sufficient to avoid grudging and malice against these, but we must look that others have not cause to grudge against us, as it is commanded: 'If thou bring thy gifts to the altar, and there rememberest that thy brother hath ought against thee; leave there thy gift before the altar, and go thy way; first be reconciled to thy brother, and then come and offer thy gift' (Matt. 5:23-25). So that if we do not seek reconciliation with men unto whom we have done wrong, God will not be reconciled to us, nor accept any service from us.

If then we would have our prayers and our persons accepted or respected, let us make conscience of that which hath been said, and not lose such a blessed privilege as this is, that God may regard our prayers. But here may be asked—

Quest. How shall I know whether God regard my prayers or not?

Ans. 1. First, *When he grants the thing prayed for, or enlargeth our hearts to pray still.* It is a greater gift than the thing itself we beg, to have a spirit of prayer with a heart enlarged; for, as long as the heart is enlarged to prayer, it is a sign that God hath a special regard of us, and will grant our petition in the best and fittest time.

Ans. 2. When *he answers us in a better and higher kind*, as Paul when he prayed for the taking away of the prick of the flesh, had promises of sufficient grace (2 *Cor.* 12:7–9).

Ans. 3. When, again, *he gives us inward peace*, though he gives not the thing, as Philippians 4:6, 'In nothing be careful, but in all things let your requests be made to God with prayer and thanksgiving.'

Obj. But sometimes he doth not answer our requests.

Ans. It is true he doth not, but 'the peace of God which passeth all understanding guards our hearts and minds in the knowledge and love of God' (*Phil.* 4:7). So though he answers not our prayers in particular, yet he vouchsafes inward peace unto us, assuring us that it shall go well with us, though not in that particular we beg. And thus in not hearing their prayers, yet they have their hearts' desire when God's will is made known. Is not this sufficient for a Christian, either to have the thing, or to have inward peace, with assurance that it shall go better with them than if they had it; with a spirit enlarged to pray, till they have the thing prayed for. If any of these be, God respects our prayers.

Again, in that Christ is thus ready to come into his garden upon the church's invitation, we may further observe, that

Christ vouchsafes his gracious presence to his children upon their desire of it.

The point is clear. From the beginning of the world, the church hath had the presence of Christ always; for either he hath been present in sacrifices, or in some other things, signs of his presence, as in the 'bush' (*Exod.* 3:2), or some more glorious manifestation of his presence, the ark (*Exod.* 25:22), and in the cloud and pillar of fire (*Exod.* 13:21), and after that more gloriously in the temple. He hath ever been present with his church in some sign or evidence of his presence; he delighted to be with the children of men. Sometimes before that he assumed a body, and afterward laid it down again, until he came, indeed, to take our nature upon him, never to leave it again. But here is meant a spiritual presence most of all, which the church in some sort ever had, now desires, and he offers, as being a God 'hearing prayer' (*Psa.* 65:2). And to instance in one place for all, to see how ready Christ hath always been to show his presence to the church upon their desire. What else is the burden of the 107th Psalm but a repetition of God's readiness to show his presence in the church, upon their seeking unto him, and unfeigned desire of it, notwithstanding all their manifold provocations of him to anger? which is well summed up (*Psa.* 106:43, 44), 'Many times did he deliver them, but they provoked him with their counsel, and were brought low for their iniquity. Nevertheless, he regarded their affliction when he heard their cry.'

It doth not content the church to have a kind of spiritual presence of Christ, but it is carried from desire to desire, till the whole desire be accomplished; for as there are gradual presences of Christ, so there are suitable desires in the church which rise by degrees. Christ was present, 1, by his gracious spirit; and then, 2, more graciously present in his incarnation, the sweetest time that ever the church had from the beginning of the world until then. It being 'the desire of nations' (*Hag.* 2:7), for the description of those who lived before his coming is from 'the waiting for the consolation of Israel (*Luke* 2:25)' that is, for the first coming of Christ. And then there is a third and more glorious presence of Christ, that all of us wait for, whereby we are described to be such 'as wait for the coming of Christ' (*Mark* 15:43). For the soul of a Christian is never satisfied until it enjoy the highest desire of Christ's presence, which the church knew well enough must follow in time. Therefore, she especially desires this spiritual presence in a larger and fuller measure, which she in some measure already had. So, then, Christ is graciously present in his church by his Holy Spirit. 'I will be with you', saith he, 'unto the end of the world' (*Matt.* 28:20). It is his promise. When I am gone myself, 'I will not leave you comfortless' (*John* 14:18), but leave with you my vicar-general, the Holy Spirit, the Comforter, who shall be always with you. But—

Quest. How shall we know that Christ is present in us?

Ans. To know this, we shall not need to pull him from heaven. We may know it in the Word and sacraments, and in the communion of saints; for these are the conveyances whereby he manifests himself, together with the work of his own gracious Spirit in us; for, as we need not take the sun from heaven to know whether or not it be up, or be day, which may be known by the light, heat, and fruitfulness of the creature; and as in the spring we need not look to the heaven to see whether the sun be come near us or not, for looking on the earth we may see all green, fresh, lively, strong, and vigorous; so it is with the presence of Christ. We may know he is present by that light which is in the soul, convincing us of better courses to be taken, of a spiritual life, to know heavenly things, and the difference of them from earthly, and to set a price upon them. When there is, together with light, a heat above nature, the affections are kindled to love the best things, and to joy in them; and when, together with heat, there is strength and vigour to carry us to spiritual duties, framing us to a holy communion with God, and one with another; and likewise when there is every way cheerfulness and enlargement of spirit, as it is with the creature when the sun approacheth. For these causes the church desires Christ, that she may have more light, life, heat, vigour, strength, and that she may be more cheerful and fruitful in duties. The soul, when it is once made spiritual, doth still desire a further and further presence of Christ, to be made better and better.

What a comfort is this to Christians, that they have the presence of Christ so far forth as shall make them happy, and as the earth will afford. Nothing but heaven, or rather Christ in heaven itself, will content the child of God. In the meantime, his presence in the congregation makes their souls, as it were, heaven. If the king's presence, who carries the court with him, makes all places where he is a court, so Christ he carries a kind of heaven with him. Wheresoever he is, his presence hath with it life, light, comfort, strength, and all; for one beam of his countenance will scatter all the clouds of grief whatsoever. It is no matter where we be, so Christ be with us. If with the three children in a fiery furnace, it is no matter, if 'a fourth be there also' (*Dan.* 3:25). So if Christ be with us, the flames nor nothing shall hurt us. If in a dungeon, as Paul and Silas were (*Acts* 16:24), if Christ's presence be there, by his Spirit to enlarge our souls, all is comfortable whatsoever. It changeth the nature of all things, sweeteneth everything, besides that sweetness which it brings unto the soul, by the presence of the Spirit; as we see in the Acts, when they had received the Holy Ghost more abundantly, they cared not what they suffered, regarded not whipping; nay, were glad 'that they were accounted worthy to suffer anything for Christ' (*Acts* 5:41). Whence came this fortitude? From the presence of Christ, and the Comforter which he had formerly promised.

So let us have the Spirit of Christ that comes from him; then it is no matter what our condition be in the world. Upon this ground let us fear nothing that shall befall us in God's cause, whatsoever it is. We shall have a spirit of prayer at the worst. God never takes away the spirit of supplication from his children, but leaves them that, until at length he possess them fully of their desires. In all Christ's delays, let us look unto the cause, and to our carriage therein; renew our repentance, that we may be in a fit state to go to God, and God to come to us. Desire him to fit us for prayer and holy communion with him, that we may never doubt of his presence.

SERMON 2

I am come into my garden, my sister, my spouse: I have gathered
my myrrh with my spice; I have eaten my honeycomb with my
honey; I have drunk my wine with my milk: eat, O friends;
drink, yea, drink abundantly, O beloved.
SONG OF SOLOMON 5:1

THIS song is a mirror of Christ's love, a discovery of which
we have in part in this verse; wherein Christ accepts of the
invitation of the church, and comes into his garden; and
he entertains her with the terms of sister and spouse.

II. Herein observe *the description of the church, and the sweet*
compellation, 'my sister, my spouse'; where there is both affinity
and consanguinity, all the bonds that may tie us to Christ, and
Christ to us.

1. His sister, by blood.

2. His spouse, by marriage.

Christ is our brother, *and the church, and every particular true*
member thereof, is his sister. 'I go', saith Christ, 'to my Father and to
your Father, to my God and to your God' (*John* 20:17). 'Go', saith he,
'and tell my brethren'. This was after his resurrection. His advancement did not change his disposition. Go, tell my brethren that left
me so unkindly; go, tell Peter that was most unkind of all, and most
cast down with the sense of it. He became our brother by incarnation, for all our union is from the first union of two natures in one
person. Christ became bone of our bone and flesh of our flesh, to
make us spiritually bone of his bone and flesh of his flesh.

Therefore let us labour to be like to him, who for that purpose became like to us, Immanuel, God with us (*Isa.* 7:14); that we might be like him, and 'partake of the divine nature' (2 *Pet.* 1:4). Whom should we rather desire to be like than one so great, so gracious, so loving?

Again, 'Christ was not ashamed to call us brethren' (*Heb.* 2:11), nor 'abhorred the virgin's womb', to be shut up in those dark cells and straits; but took our base nature, when it was at the worst, and not only our nature, but our miserable condition and curse due unto us. Was he not ashamed of us? and shall we be ashamed to own him and his cause? Against this cowardice it is a thunderbolt which our Saviour Christ pronounceth, 'He that is ashamed of me before men, him will I be ashamed of before my Father, and all the holy angels' (*Mark* 8:38). It argues a base disposition, either for frown or favour to desert a good cause in evil times.

Again, *It is a point of comfort to know that we have a brother who is a favourite in heaven*; who, though he abased himself for us, is yet Lord over all. Unless he had been our brother, he could not have been our husband; for husband and wife should be of one nature. That he might marry us, therefore, he came and took our nature, so to be fitted to fulfil the work of our redemption. But now he is in heaven, set down at the right hand of God: the true Joseph, the high steward of heaven; he hath all power committed unto him; he rules all. What a comfort is this to a poor soul that hath no friends in the world, that yet he hath a friend in heaven that will own him for his brother, in and through whom he may go to the throne of grace boldly and pour out his soul (*Heb.* 4:15, 16). What a comfort was it to Joseph's brethren that their brother was the second person in the kingdom.

Again, *It should be a motive to have good Christians in high estimation, and to take heed how we wrong them*, for their brother will take their part. 'Saul, Saul, why persecutest thou me?' (*Acts* 9:4), saith the Head in heaven, when his members were trodden on upon earth. It is more to wrong a Christian than the world takes it for, for Christ takes it as done to himself. Absalom was a man wicked and unnatural, yet he could not endure the wrong that was done to his sister Tamar (*2 Sam.* 13). Jacob's sons took it as a high indignity that their sister should be so abused (*Gen.* 34). Hath Christ no affections, now he is in heaven, to her that is so near him as the church is? Howsoever he suffer men to tyrannise over her for a while, yet it will appear ere long that he will take the church's part, for he is her brother.

'My sister, my spouse.'

The church is the daughter of a King, begotten of God; the sister and spouse of a King, because she is the sister and spouse of Christ, and the mother of all that are spiritual kings. The church of Christ is every way royal. Therefore we are kings because we are Christians. Hence the Holy Ghost doth add here to sister, spouse. Indeed, taking the advantage of such relations as are most comfortable, to set out the excellent and transcendent relation that is between Christ and his church; all other are not what they are termed, so much as glasses to see better things. Riches, beauty, marriage, nobility, &c., are scarce worthy of their names. These are but titles and empty things. Though our base nature make great matters of them, yet the reality and substance of all these are in heavenly things. True riches are the heavenly graces; true nobility is to be born of God, to be the sister and spouse of Christ; true pleasures are those of the Spirit, which endure for ever, and will stand by us when all outward comforts will vanish. That mystical union and sweet communion is set down with such variety of expressions, to show *that whatsoever is scattered in the creature severally is in him entirely.* He is both a friend and a brother, a head and a husband, to us; therefore he takes the names of all. Whence we may observe further,

That *the church is the spouse of Christ.* It springs out of him; even as Eve taken out of Adam's rib, so the spouse of Christ was taken out of his side. When it was pierced, the church rose out of his blood and death; for he redeemed it, by satisfying divine justice; we being in such a condition that Christ must redeem us before he would wed us. First, he must be *incarnate in our nature* before he could be a fit husband; and then, because we were in bondage and captivity, we must be redeemed before he could marry us: 'he purchased his church with his own blood' (*Acts* 20:28). Christ hath right to us, he bought us dearly.

Again, another foundation of this marriage between Christ and us, is *consent*. He works us by his Spirit to yield to him. There must be consent on our part, which is not in us by nature, but wrought by his Spirit, &c. We yield to take him upon his own terms; that is, that we shall leave our father's house, all our former carnal acquaintance, when he hath wrought our consent. Then the marriage between him and us is struck up.

Some few resemblances will make the consideration of this the more comfortable.

1. The husband takes his wife under his own name. She, losing her own name, is called by his. So we are called Christians, of Christ.

2. The wife is taken with all her debt, and made partaker of the honours and riches of her husband. Whatsoever he hath is hers, and he stands answerable for all her debts. So it is here: we have not only the name of Christ upon us, but we partake his honours, and are kings, priests, and heirs with him (*Rev.* 1:5, 6). Whatsoever he hath, he hath taken us into the fellowship of it; so that his riches are ours, and likewise, whatsoever is ours that is ill, he hath taken it upon him, even the wrath due to us. For he came between that and us, when he was made sin and a curse for us (*2 Cor.* 5:21); so there is a blessed change between Christ and us. His honours and riches are ours. We have nothing to bestow on him, but our beggary, sins and miseries, which he took upon him.

3. Those that bring together these two different parties, are the friends of the bride; that is, the ministers, as it is in John 3:23. They are the *paranymphi*, the friends of the bride, that learn of Christ

what to report to his spouse, and so they woo for Christ, and open the riches, beauty, honour, and all that is lovely in him, which is indeed the especial duty of ministers—to lay open his unsearchable riches, that the church may know what a husband she is like to have, if she cleave to him; and what an one she leaves, if she forsake him. It was well said in the council of Basil, out of Bernard,—'None commits his wife to a vicar, for none is the husband of the church.' To be husband of the church is one of the incommunicable titles of Christ, yet usurped by the pope. Innocent the Third was the first that wronged Christ's bed by challenging the title of Sponsus, husband of the church. Bernard forbids his scholar Eugenius this title (Epist. ccxxxvii. *ad Eugenium*). It is enough for ministers to be friends of the bride. Let us yield him to be husband of the church, that hath given himself to sanctify it with washing of water and blood (*Eph.* 5:26). We are a wife of blood to him.

In this sweet conjunction we must know, that by nature we are clean otherways than spouses; for what was Solomon's wife, Pharaoh's daughter? A heathen, till she came to be Solomon's spouse. And as we read in Moses, the strange woman must have her hair cut off, and her nails pared (*Deut.* 21:12). Before she should be taken into the church, there must be an alteration; so before the church, which is not heathenish, but indeed hellish by nature, and led by the spirit of the world, be fit to be the spouse of Christ, there must be an alteration and a change of nature (*Isa.* 11:6-8, *John* 3:3). Christ must alter, renew, purge, and fit us for himself. The apostle saith (*Eph.* 5:25-27), it was the end of his death, not only to take us to heaven, but to sanctify us on earth, and prepare us that we might be fit spouses for himself.

Use 1. *Let us oft think of this nearness between Christ and us*, if we have once given our names to him, and not be discouraged for any sin or unworthiness in us. Who sues a wife for debt, when she is married? Therefore answer all accusations thus:—'Go to Christ.' If you have anything to say to me, go to my husband. God is just, but he will not have his justice twice satisfied, seeing whatsoever is due thereunto is satisfied by Christ our husband. What a comfort is this to a distressed conscience! If sin cannot dismay us, which is the ill of ills and cause of all evil, what other ill can dismay us? He that exhorts us to bear with the infirmities one of another, and hath enjoined the husband to bear with the wife, as the weaker vessel (*1 Pet.* 3:7), will not he bear with his church as the weaker vessel, performing the duty of an husband in all our infirmities?

Use 2. Again, his desire is to make her better, and not to cast her away for that which is amiss. And for outward ills, they are but to refine, and make us more conformable to Christ our husband, to fit us for heaven, the same way that he went. They have a blessing in them all, for he takes away all that is hurtful, he pities and keeps us 'as the apple of his eye' (*Zech.* 2:8). Therefore, let us often think of this, since he hath vouchsafed to take us so near to himself. Let us not lose the comfort that this meditation will yield us. We love for goodness, beauty, riches; but Christ loves us to make us so, and then loves us because we are so, in all estates whatsoever.

Use 3. And if Christ be so near us, *let us labour for chaste judgments*, that we do not defile them with errors, seeing the whole soul is espoused to Christ. Truth is the spouse of our understandings. It is left[1] to us to be wanton in opinions, to take up what conceit we will of things. So we ought to have chaste affections, not cleaving to base things. It hath been ofttimes seen, that one husband hath many wives, but never from the beginning of the world, that one wife hath had many husbands. God promiseth to betroth his church to him in righteousness and faithfulness, that is, as he will be faithful to her, so she shall by his grace be faithful to him; faithfulness shall be mutual; the church shall not be false to Christ. So there is no Christian soul must think to have many

---

[1] Qu. not left?—Ed.

husbands; for Christ in this case is a jealous husband. Take heed therefore of spiritual harlotry of heart, for our affections are for Christ, and cannot be better bestowed. In other things we lose our love, and the things loved; but here we lose not our love, but this is a perfecting love, which draws us to love that which is better than ourselves. We are, as we affect;[1] our affections are, as their objects be. If they be set upon better things than ourselves, they are bettered by it. They are never rightly bestowed, but when they are set upon Christ; and upon other things as they answer and stand with the love of Christ. For the prime love, when it is rightly bestowed, it orders and regulates all other loves whatsoever. No man knows how to use earthly things, but a Christian, that hath first pitched his love on Christ. Then seeing all things in him, and in all them, a beam of that love of his, intending happiness to him, so he knows how to use everything in order. Therefore let us keep our communion with Christ, and esteem nothing more than his love, because he esteems nothing more than ours.

Quest. But how shall we know, whether we be espoused to Christ or not?

Ans. 1. Our hearts can tell us, *whether we yield consent to him or not.* In particular, whether we have received him, as he will be received, as a right husband, that is, *whether we receive him to be ruled by him,* to make him our head. For the wife, when she yields to be married, therewith also surrenders up her own will, to be ruled by her husband. So far she hath denied her own will; she hath no will of her own. Christ hath wisdom enough for us, and himself too, whose wisdom and will must be ours. To be led by divine truths so far as they are discovered unto us, and to submit ourselves thereunto, is a sign of a gracious heart, that is married to Christ.

Ans. 2. Again, *a willingness to follow Christ in all conditions as he is discovered*[2] *in the Word.* To suffer Christ to have the

---

[1] That is, choose.—G.

[2] Revealed.—P.

sovereignty in our affections, above all other things and persons in the world; this is the right disposition of a true spouse. For as it was at the first institution, there must be a leaving of father, and mother, and all, to cleave to our husband:[1] so here, when anything and Christ cannot stand together, or else we shall never have the comfort of his sweet name. Many men will be glad to own Christ to be great by him, but as St Augustine complains in his time, Christ Jesus is not loved for Jesus his own sake. *Vix diligitur Jesus propter Jesum*, but for other things, that he brings with him, peace, plenty, &c.—as far as it stands with these contentments. If Christ and the world part once, it will be known which we followed. In times of peace this is hardly[2] discerned. If he will pay men's debts, so as they may have the credit and glory of the name to be called Christians, if he will redeem them from the danger of sin, all is well; but only such have the comfort of this communion, as love him for himself. Let us not so much trouble ourselves about signs as be careful to do our duty to Christ, and then will Christ discover his love clearly unto us.

Use 4. Now, they that are not brought so near to this happy condition by Christ, may yet have this encouragement, there is yet place of grace for them. Let them therefore consider but these three things.

1. The excellency of Christ, and of the state of the church, when it is so near him.

2. The necessity of this, to be so near him.

3. That there is hope of it.

There is in Christ whatsoever may commend a husband; birth, comeliness, riches, friends, wisdom, authority, &c.

1. The excellency of this condition to be one with Christ, is, *that all things are ours.* For he is the King, and the church the Queen of all. All things are serviceable to us. It is a wondrous

[1] See Genesis 2:24, Matthew 19:5, Mark 10:7, but it is wife, not husband.—G.

[2] That is, with difficulty.—G.

nearness, to be nearer to Christ than the angels, who are not his body, but servants that attend upon the church. The bride is nearer to him than the angels, for, 'he is the head and husband thereof, and not of the angels' (*Heb.* 2:16). What an excellent condition is this for poor flesh and blood, that creeps up and down the earth here despised!

2. But especially, if we consider *the necessity of it*. We are all indebted for more than we are worth. To divine justice we owe a debt of obedience, and in want of that we owe a debt of punishment, and we cannot answer one for a thousand. What will become of us if we have not a husband to discharge all our debts, but to be imprisoned for ever?

A person that is a stranger to Christ, though he were an Ahithophel for his brain, a Judas for his profession, a Saul for his place, yet if his sins be set before him, he will be swallowed up of despair, fearing to be shut up eternally under God's wrath. Therefore, if nothing else move, yet let necessity compel us to take Christ.

3. Consider not only how suitable and how necessary he is unto us, but *what hope there is to have him*, whenas he sueth to us by his messengers, and wooeth us, whenas we should rather seek to him; and with other messengers sendeth a privy messenger, his Holy Spirit, to incline our hearts. Let us therefore, as we love our souls, suffer ourselves to be won. But more of this in another place. The next branch is,

III. *Christ's acceptation.* 'I have gathered my myrrh with my spice', &c. So that, together with Christ's presence, here is a gracious acceptance of the provision of the church, with a delight in it, and withal, a bringing of more with him. The church had a double desire, 1, That Christ would come to accept of what she had for him of his own grace, which he had wrought in her soul; and 2, She was also verily persuaded that he would not come empty handed,

41

only to accept of what was there, but also would bring abundance of grace and comfort with him. Therefore she desires acceptation and increase; both which desires he answers. He comes to his garden, shows his acceptation, and withal he brings more. 'I have gathered my myrrh with my spice. I have eaten my honeycomb with my honey; I have drunk my wine with my milk', &c. Whence we observe,

That God accepts of the graces of his children, and delights in them.

First, Because *they are the fruits that come from his children, his spouse, his friend.* Love of the person wins acceptance of that which is presented from the person. What comes from love is lovingly taken.

Second, They are the graces of his Spirit. If we have anything that is good, all comes from the Spirit, which is first in Christ our, husband, and then in us. As the ointment was first poured on Aaron's head (*Psa.* 133:2), and then ran down upon his rich garments, so all comes from Christ to us. St Paul calls the wife 'the glory of her husband' (*1 Cor.* 11:7), because, as in a glass, she resembleth the graces of her husband, who may see his own graces in her. So it is with Christ and the church. Face answereth to face, as Solomon saith in another case (*Prov.* 27:19). Christ sees his own face, beauty, glory, in his church; she reflects his beams; he looks in love upon her, and always with his looks conveys grace and comfort; and the church doth reflect back again his grace. Therefore Christ loves but the reflection of his own graces in his children, and therefore accepts them.

Third, His kindness is such *as he takes all in good part.* Christ is love and kindness itself. Why doth he give unto her the name of spouse and sister, but that he would be kind and loving, and that we should conceive so of him? We see, then, the graces of Christ accepting of us and what we do in his strength. Both we ourselves are sacrifices, and what we offer is a sacrifice acceptable to God, through him that offered himself as a sacrifice of sweet smelling savour, from which God smells a savour of rest. God accepts of Christ first, and then of us, and what comes from us in him. We may boldly pray, as Psalm 20:3, 'Lord, remember all our offerings, and accept all our sacrifices.' The blessed Apostle St Paul doth will us 'to offer up ourselves' (*Rom.* 12:1), a holy and acceptable sacrifice to God, when we are once in Christ. In the Old Testament we have divers manifestations of this acceptation. He accepted the sacrifice of Abel, as it is thought, by fire from heaven, and so Elijah's sacrifice, and Solomon's, by fire (*1 Kings* 18:38, *2 Chron*, 7:1). So in the New Testament he showed his acceptation of the disciples meeting together, by a mighty wind, and then filling them with the Holy Ghost (*Acts* 2:4). But now the declaration of the acceptation of our persons, graces, and sacrifice that we offer to him, is most in peace of conscience and joy in the Holy Ghost, and from a holy fire of love kindled by the Spirit, whereby our sacrifices are burned. In the incense of prayer, how many sweet spices are burned together by this fire of faith working by love; as humility and patience in submitting to God's will, hope of a gracious answer, holiness, love to others, &c.

Use 1. If so be that God accepts the performances and graces, especially the prayers of his children, let it be an argument to encourage us *to be much in all holy duties.* It would dead the heart of any man to perform service where it should not be accepted, and the eye turned aside, not vouchsafing a gracious look upon it. This would be a killing of all comfortable endeavours. But when all that is good is accepted, and what is amiss is pardoned, when a broken desire, a cup of cold water shall not go unrespected, nay, unrewarded (*Matt.* 10:42), what can we desire more? It is infidelity which is dishonourable to God and uncomfortable to ourselves, that makes us so barren and cold in duties.

Use 2. Only let our care be *to approve our hearts unto Christ.* When our hearts are right, we cannot but think comfortably of

43

Christ. Those that have offended some great persons are afraid, when they hear from them, because they think they are in a state displeasing to them. So a soul that is under the guilt of any sin is so far from thinking that God accepts of it, that it looks to hear nothing from him but some message of anger and displeasure. But one that preserves acquaintance, due distance, and respect to a great person, hears from him with comfort. Before he breaks open a letter, or sees anything, he supposes it comes from a friend, one that loves him. So, as we would desire to hear nothing but good news from heaven, and acceptation of all that we do, let us be careful to preserve ourselves in a good estate, or else our souls will tremble upon any discovery of God's wrath. The guilty conscience argues, what can God show to me, being such a wretch? The heart of such an one cannot but misgive, as, where peace is made, it will speak comfort. It is said of Daniel that he was a man of God's desires (*Dan.* 9:23; 10:11, 19); and of St John, that Christ so loved him that he leaned on his breast (*John* 21:20). Everyone cannot be a Daniel, nor one that leans on Christ's bosom. There are degrees of favour and love; but there is no child of God but he is beloved and accepted of him in some degree. But something of this before in the former chapter.

'I have gathered my myrrh with my spice; I have eaten my honeycomb with my honey', &c.

That is, I have taken contentment in thy graces, together with acceptation. There is a delight, and God not only accepts, but he delights in the graces of his children. 'All my delight', saith David, 'is in those that are excellent' (*Psa.* 16:8). But this is not all, Christ comes with an enlargement of what he finds.

Christ comes, and comes not empty whensoever he comes, but with abundance of grace. If St Paul, who was but Christ's instrument, could tell the Romans, 'I hope to come to you in abundance of grace and comfort' (*Rom.* 15:29), because he was a blessed instrument to convey good from Christ to the people of God, as a conduit-pipe, how much more shall Christ himself, where he is present, come with graces and comfort! Those that have communion with Christ, therefore, have a comfortable communion, being sure to have it enlarged, for 'to him that hath shall be given' (*Matt.* 25:29). It is not only true of his last coming, when he shall come to judge the quick and the dead, 'I come, and my reward is with me' (*Rev.* 22:12); but also of all his intermediate comings that are between. When he comes to the soul, he comes not only to accept what is there, but still with his reward with him, the increase of grace, to recompense all that is good with the increase thereof. This made his presence so desired in the gospel with those that had gracious hearts. They knew all was the better for Christ, the company the better, for he never left any house or table where he was, but there was an increase of comfort, and of grace. And as it was in his personal, so it is in his spiritual presence. He never comes, but he increases grace and comfort.

Therefore, let us be stirred up to have communion with Christ, by this motive, that thus we shall have an increase of a further measure of grace. Let us labour to be such as Christ may delight in, for our graces are honey and spices to him, and where he tastes sweetness he will bring more with him. To him that overcometh he promiseth 'the hidden manna' (*Rev.* 2:17). They had manna before, but he means they shall have more abundant communion with me, who am 'the hidden manna'. There is abundance in him to be had, as the soul is capable of abundance. Therefore we may most fruitfully and comfortably be conversant in holy exercises and communion with Christ, because our souls are fit to be enlarged more and more, till they have their fulness in heaven; and still there is more grace and comfort to be had in Christ, the more we have to deal with him.

But to come to show what is meant by honey and wine, &c. Not to take uncertain grounds from these words, but that which may be a foundation for us to build comfort and instruction on, we will not show in particular what is meant by wine and honey (for that is not intended by the Holy Ghost), but show in general how acceptable the graces of the Spirit of Christ are to him, that they feed him and delight him, as wine and honey do us, because in the covenant of grace he filleth us by his Spirit of grace, to have comfort in us as we have in him. For, except there be a mutual joy in one another, there is not communion. Therefore Christ furnisheth his church with so much grace as is necessary for a state of absence here, that may fit her for communion with him for ever in heaven. As Isaac sent Rebecca, before the marriage, jewels and ornaments to wear (*Gen.* 24:22), that she might be more lovely when they met, so our blessed Saviour, he sends to his spouse from heaven jewels and ornaments, that is, graces, wherewith adorned, he may delight in her more and more till the marriage be fulfilled. Therefore in this book the church is brought in, delighting in Christ, and he in the church. 'Thy love', saith the church to him, 'is sweeter than wine' (*Song of Sol.* 1:2). Christ saith to the church again, 'Thy love is sweeter than wine.' Whatsoever Christ saith to the church, the church saith back again to Christ, and he back again to the church. So there is a mutual contentment and joy one in another. 'Eat, O friends, drink', &c.

IV. Here is an invitation. When he comes stored with more grace and comfort, he stirs them up; both the church, others, and all that bear good-will to his people, that they would delight in the graces and comforts of his church. Whence observe, that

Obs. We ought to rejoice in the comforts and graces of others, and of ourselves.

He stirreth up the church here, as well as others; for he speaks to all, both to the church and the friends of it. He had need to stir her up to enjoy the comfort of her own grace; for they are two distinct benefits, to have grace, and to know that we have it, though one Spirit work both (*1 Cor.* 2:12). The Spirit works grace, and shows us the things that God hath given us, yet sometimes it doth the one, and not the other. In the time of desertion and of temptation, we have grace, but we know it not; right to comfort, but we feel it not. There is no comfort of a secret, unknown treasure; but so it is with the church, she doth not always take notice of her own graces, and the right she hath to comfort.

We have need to have Christ's Spirit to help us to know what good is in us. And indeed a Christian should not only examine his heart for the evil that is in him, to be humbled; but what good there is, that he may joy and be thankful. And since Christ accepts the very first fruits, the earnest, and delights in them, we should know what he delights in, that we may go boldly to him; considering that it is not of ourselves, but of Christ, whatsoever is graciously good. Therefore we ought to know our own graces; for Christ, when he will have us comfortable indeed, will discover to us what cause we have to rejoice, and show us what is the work of his own Spirit, and our right to all comfort.

And so, for others, we should not only joy in ourselves, and in our own condition and lot; but also in the happy condition of every good Christian. There is joy in heaven at the conversion of one sinner (*Luke* 15:10). God the Father joys to have a new son; God the Son to see the fruit of his own redemption, that one is pulled out of the state of damnation; and God the Holy Ghost, that he hath a new temple to dwell in; the angels, that they have a new charge to look to, that they had not before, to join with them to praise God. So there is joy in heaven; the Father, Son, and Holy Ghost, with the angels, joy at it; and all true-hearted Christians joy in the graces one of another.

Reasons. For, 1, God, Christ, and the Holy Ghost have glory by it; and 2, the church hath comfort by the increase of a saint. 3, the prayer of a Christian adds new strength to the church. What a happy condition is it when God's glory, the church's comfort and strength, and our own joy, meet together. So that we should all take notice of the grace of God in others.

We ought to take notice of the works of God in creation and providence, when we see plants, stars, and such like, or else we dishonour God. What then should we do for his gifts and graces in his children, that are above these in dignity? should we not take notice of what is graciously good, and praise God for it? Thus they did for Paul's conversion, 'they glorified God'. For when they saw that Paul of a wolf was become not only a sheep, but a shepherd and leader of God's flock, they glorified God (*Gal.* 1:24).

So the believing Jews, when the Gentiles were converted, 'they glorified God, that he had taken the Gentiles to be his garden and people' (*Acts* 11:18). When Paul and others had planted the gospel, and God gave the increase, the godly Jews rejoiced at that good. So, we that are Gentiles, should rejoice to hear of the conversion of the Jews, and pray for it; for then there will be a general joy when that is. Want of joy shows want of grace.

There is not a surer character of a Satanical and Cainish disposition, than to look on the graces of God's children with a malignant eye: as Cain, who hated his brother, because his works were better than his (*1 John* 3:12). Those that deprave[1] the graces of God in others, and cloud them with disgraces, that they may not shine, and will not have the sweet ointment of their good names to spread, but cast dead flies into it, show that they are of his disposition that is the accuser of the brethren. It is a sign of the child of the devil. All that have grace in them, are of Christ's and of the angels' disposition. They joy at the conversion and growth of any Christians. Here, such as they, are styled friends and beloved; and indeed none but friends and beloved can love as Christ loves, and delight as Christ delights.

---

[1] That is, speak evil of.—G.

SERMON 3

I am come into my garden, my sister, my spouse: I have gathered
my myrrh with my spice; I have eaten my honeycomb with my
honey; I have drunk my wine with my milk: eat, O friends;
drink, yea, drink abundantly, O beloved.
I sleep, but my heart waketh, &c.

SONG OF SOLOMON 5:1, 2

IT hath been showed how Christ and the church were feasting together. She entreated his company 'to come into his garden and eat his pleasant fruits'. He, according to her desire, was come; and not only feasted on the church's provision, but also brought more with him. Christ taking walks in his garden, that is, his church, and every particular soul, which is as a sweet paradise for him to delight in, is much refreshed; and in witness of acceptance brings increase. What greater encouragement can we wish, than that we, being by nature as the earth, since the fall, accursed, should be the soil of Christ's delight, planted and watered by him; and that what we yield should be so well taken of him. We are under so gracious a covenant that all our services are accepted; not only our honey, but honeycomb; not only our wine, but our milk; our weak services as well as our strong; because the Spirit which we have from him sweeteneth all. As in nature there is one common influence from heaven, but yet variety of flowers, violets, roses, gilliflowers, spices, all sweet in their several kind, with a different kind of sweetness: so all graces have their beginning from the common influence of Christ's Spirit, though they differ

49

one from another; and are all accepted of the 'Father of lights', from whence they come (*James* 1:17). Christ wonders at his own grace, 'O woman, great is thy faith' (*Matt.* 15:28); and 'Who is this that cometh out of the wilderness like pillars of smoke, perfumed with myrrh and frankincense, with all powders of the merchant?' (*Song of Sol.* 3:6).

Let not the weakest of all others be discouraged. Christ looks not to what he brings, so much as out of what store; that which is least in quantity may be most in proportion, as the widow's mite was more in acceptance than richer offerings (*Luke* 21:3). 'A pair of turtle doves' (*Lev.* 5:7), was accepted in the law, and those that brought but goats' hair to the building of the tabernacle (*Exod.* 35:6).

The particulars here specified that Christ took delight in, and inviteth others to a further degree of delight in, are

Myrrh and spice, honey and honeycomb, milk.

Which show, 1. The sweetness of grace and spiritual comfort. 2. The variety. 3. The use.

Myrrh and spices, 1, refresh the spirits, and 2, preserve from putrefaction; which are therefore used in embalming. If the soul be not embalmed with grace, it is a noisome, carrion soul; and as it is in itself, so whatsoever cometh from it is abominable.

Milk and honey nourish and strengthen; and *wine* increaseth spirits; and thereupon encourageth and allayeth sorrow and cares. 'Give wine to him that is ready to die' (*Prov.* 31:6). The sense of the love of Christ is sweeter than wine; it banisheth fears, and sorrow, and care.

From this mutual delight between Christ and his spouse we observe next, that

There is a mutual feasting betwixt Christ and his church. The church bringeth what she hath of his Spirit; and Christ comes with more plenty.

For there being so near a covenant between him and us, we are by his grace to perform all offices on our part. We invite him, and he inviteth us. There is not the meanest Christian in whom there is not somewhat to welcome Christ withal; but Christ sends his provision before, and comes, as we say, to his own cost. He sends a spirit of faith, a spirit of love, a spirit of obedience. 1. Some are content to invite others, but are loath to go to others, as if it were against state. They would have wherewith to entertain Christ, but are unwilling to be beholden to Christ. 2. Some are content to have benefit by Christ, as his righteousness to cover them, &c., but they desire not grace to entertain Christ; but a heart truly gracious desireth both to delight in Christ, and that Christ may delight in it. It desireth grace together with mercy, holiness with happiness. Christ could not delight in his love to us, if we by his grace had not a love planted in our hearts to him. But to come to speak of this feast.

We see it pleaseth Christ to veil heavenly matters with comparisons fetched from earthly things, that so he may enter into our souls the better by our senses.

1. Christ maketh us *a feast, a marriage feast, a marriage feast with the King's Son*, of all feasts the most magnificent. A feast, first, in regard of the choice rarities we have in Christ. We have the best, and the best of the best. 'Fat things, and the marrow of fatness; wine, and wine on the lees' (*Isa.* 25:6), refined, that preserveth the strength. The comforts we have from Christ, are the best comforts; the peace, the best peace; the privileges, the highest privileges. 'His flesh', crucified for us, to satisfy divine justice, 'is meat indeed; his blood, shed for us, is drink indeed' (*John* 6:55); that is, the only meat and drink to refresh our souls; because these feed our souls, and that to eternal life. The love of God the Father in giving Christ to death; and Christ's love in giving himself, together with full contentment to divine justice; this gift it is that the soul especially feeds on. What could Christ give, better than himself to feed on? He thought nothing else worthy for the soul to feed on; and this it daily feeds on, as daily guilt riseth from the breakings out of the remainder of corruption. Other dainties are

from this; from hence we have the Spirit, and graces of the Spirit. If he giveth himself, will he not give all things with himself?

2. As Christ maketh a feast of choice things for his elect and choice spouse, *so there is variety*, as in a feast. 'Christ is made to us of God, wisdom, righteousness, sanctification, and redemption' (*1 Cor.* 1:30), that we should not be too much cast down with thought of our own folly, guilt, unholiness, and misery. There is that in Christ which answereth to all our wants, and an all-sufficiency for all degrees of happiness. Therefore, he hath terms from whatsoever is glorious and comfortable in heaven and earth. Christ is all marrow, all sweetness. All the several graces and comforts we have, and the several promises whereby they are made over and conveyed unto us, are but Christ dished out in several manner, as the need of every Christian shall require. Christ himself is the ocean, issuing into several streams, to refresh the city of God. We can be in no condition, but we have a promise to feed on, and 'all promises are yea and amen' (*2 Cor.* 1:20), made to us 'in Christ', and performed to us 'for Christ'.

3. Therefore, as we have in Christ a feast for variety, so for *sufficiency of all good*. No man goeth hungry from a feast. It was never heard for any to famish at a feast. In Christ there is not only abundance, but redundance, a diffusive and a spreading goodness; as in breasts to give milk, in clouds to drop down showers, in the sun to send forth beams. As Christ is full of grace and truth, so he fully dischargeth all his offices. There is an overflowing of all that is good for our good. He that could multiply bread for the body, he can multiply grace for our soul. If he giveth life, he giveth it in abundance (*John* 10:10). If he giveth water of life, he giveth rivers, not small streams (*John* 7:38). If he giveth peace and joy, he giveth it in abundance; his scope is to fill up our joy to the full. As he is able, so 'is he willing to do for us far more abundantly than we are able to think or speak' (*Eph.* 3:20). Where Christ is present, he bringeth plenty with him. If wine be wanting at the first, he will rather turn water into wine, than there should be a fail.

4. In a feast there is variety of *friendly company*; so here friends are stirred up to refresh themselves with us. We have the blessed Trinity, the angels, and all our fellow-members in Christ to come with us.

There is no envy in spiritual things, wherein whatsoever the one hath, the other hath not the less.

5. In a feast, because it is intended for rejoicing, *there is music*; and what music like to the sweet harmony between God, reconciled in Christ, and the soul, and between the soul and itself, in inward peace and joy of the Holy Ghost, shedding the love of Christ in the soul. We do not only joy, but glory, under hope of glory, and in afflictions, and in God now as ours, in whom now by Christ we have an interest (*Rom.* 6:2-10). When we come sorrowful to this feast, we depart cheerful. This, as David's harp, stills all passions and distempers of spirit.

The founder and master of the feast is Christ himself; and withal is both guest, and banquet, and all. All graces and comforts are the fruits of his Spirit; and he alone that infused the soul, can satisfy the soul. He that is above the conscience can only quiet the conscience. He is that wisdom that 'sends forth maids' (*Prov.* 9:3), his ministers, to invite to his feast. It is he that cheereth up his guests, as here. Those that invited others, brought ointment, and poured it out upon them, to show their welcome, and to cheer them up, as may appear by our Saviour's speech to the Pharisee that invited him (*Luke* 7:44). So we have from Christ both the oil of grace and oil of gladness. 'He creates the fruits of the lips to be peace' (*Isa.* 57:19), speaking that peace and joy to the heart that others do to the ear. 'He raiseth pastors according to his own heart, to feed his sheep' (*Jer.* 3:15).

The vessels wherein Christ conveyeth his dainties are the ministry of the Word and sacraments. By the Word and sacraments we come to enjoy Christ and his comforts and graces; and by this feast of grace we come at length to the feast of feasts, that feast of glory, when we shall be satisfied with the image of God, and enjoy fulness of pleasures for evermore; and, which adds to the fulness, we shall fully know that it shall be a never-interrupted joy.

We see, then, that we cannot please Christ better than in showing ourselves welcome, by cheerful taking part of his rich provision. It is an honour to his bounty to fall to; and it is the temper of spirit that a Christian aims at, to 'rejoice always in the Lord' (*Phil.* 4:4), and that from enjoying our privileges in him. We are not bidden to mourn always, but to 'rejoice always', and that upon good advisement; 'Rejoice', and 'I say again', saith St Paul, 'rejoice'. Indeed, we have causes of mourning, but it is that the seed of joy should be sown in mourning; and we can never be in so forlorn a condition, wherein, if we understand Christ and ourselves, we have not cause of joy. 'In me', saith Christ, 'ye shall have peace' (*John* 16:33). The world will feed us with 'bread of affliction' (*Hos.* 9:4). If the world can help it, we shall have sorrow enough; and Christ knows that well enough, and stirs us up to a cheerful feeding on that he hath procured for us. He hath both will, and skill, and power, and authority to feed us to everlasting life, for the Father sent him forth, and sealed him to that purpose. All the springs of our joy are from him (*Psa.* 87:7).

Our duty is to accept of Christ's inviting of us. What will we do for him, if we will not feast with him? We will not suffer with him, if we will not feast with him; we will not suffer with him, if we will not joy with him, and in him. Happy are they that come, though compelled by crosses and other sharp ways. If we rudely and churlishly refuse his feast here, we are like never to taste of his feast hereafter. Nothing provokes so deeply as kindness despised. It was the cause of the Jews' rejection. 'How shall we escape', not if we persecute, but 'if we do but neglect so great salvation?' (*Heb.* 2:8).

That which we should labour to bring with us is a taste of these dainties, and an appetite to them. The soul hath a taste of its own, and as all creatures that have life have a taste to relish and distinguish of that which is good for them, from that which is offensive, so wheresoever spiritual life is, there is likewise a taste suitable to the sweet relish that is in spiritual things. God should lose the glory of many excellent creatures if there were not several senses to discern of several goodness in them. So if there were not a taste in the soul, we could never delight in God, and his rich goodness in Christ.

Taste is the most necessary sense for the preservation of the creature, because there is nearest application in taste; and that we should not be deceived in taste, we hear, see, and smell before, and if these senses give a good report of the object, then we taste of it and digest it, and turn it into fit nourishment. So the spirit of man, after judgment of the fitness of what is presented, tastes of it, delights in it, and is nourished by it. There is an attractive, drawing power in the soul, whereby every member sucks that out of the food that is convenient for it. So the soul draws out what is well digested by judgment, and makes it its own for several uses.

The chief thing that Christ requireth is a good stomach to these dainties.

1. The means to procure an appetite. We are first *to be sensible of spiritual wants and misery.* The passover lamb was eaten with sour herbs; so Christ crucified, relisheth best to a soul affected with bitterness of sin. Whilst men are rich in their conceit, they go empty away. The duties and performances they trust to, are but husks, windy, empty chaff. Swelling is not kind nourishment.

2. *That which hinders the sharpness of the stomach are, cold defluxions,*[1] *that dull and flat the edge of it.* So upon plodding upon the world, cold distillations drop upon the soul, and take away the savour and desire of heavenly things. These things fill not. There is both a vanity of emptiness, and a vanity of short continuance in them. 'Why should we lay out our money' (*Isa.* 55:2), spend our time, our wits, our endeavour so much about them? This makes so many starvelings in religion.

[1] A discharge of fluid in the body.—P.

THE LOVE OF CHRIST

Besides, there be other noisome affections to be purged, as 1 Peter 2:1 ['Wherefore laying aside all malice, and all guile, and hypocrisies, and envies, and all evil speakings', which breed a distaste and disaffection to spiritual things]; as malice and guile, &c. How can Christ be sweet to that soul unto which revenge is sweet!

3. *Exercise quickens appetite.* Those that exercise themselves unto godliness, see a need of spiritual strength to maintain duty. A dull formalist keeps his round, and is many years after where he was before; sees no need of further growth or strength. A Christian life, managed as it should be indeed, as it hath much going out, so it must have much coming in. It will not else be kept up. Those that have a journey to go, will refresh themselves for afterward, lest they faint by the way.

4. *Company likewise* of such as 'labour for that blessed food that endureth to life eternal' (*John* 6:27), provoketh to fall too as the rest do, especially if they be equal or go beyond us in parts. For we will reason with ourselves, Have not I as much need as they? If these things be good for them, then they are good for me.

Thus St Paul foretelleth, that the example of the Gentiles should provoke the Jews to come in, and taste of the banquet Christ hath provided for both (*Rom.* 11:25, 26). Especially this should stir us up earnestly to take our part in that Christ hath provided, because we know not how soon the table may be taken away. When men see the dishes in removing, though before they have discoursed away much time of their supper, yet then they will fall fresh to it. We know not how long wisdom will be inviting of us. It will be our wisdom to take our time, lest we put off so long, as wisdom herself laughs at our destruction; and a famine be sent, of all famines the most miserable, a famine of the Word, and then we may pine away eternally without comfort. Christ will not always stand inviting of us. If we will none of his cheer, others will, and shall, when we shall starve.

Let this draw us on, that we see here Christ's hearty and free welcome, the gracious look that we are like to have from him. He counts it an honour, since he hath made such rich provision, for us to take part, and for our part, show our unwillingness, that such free kindness should be refused. We cannot honour his bounty more than to feed liberally of that he liberally sets before us. We are glad to perceive our friends upon invitation to think themselves welcome. Let us open our mouth wide, since Christ is so ready to fill it. We are not straitened in his love, but in our own hearts. The widow's oil failed not till her vessels failed (2 *Kings* 4:6). We are bidden to delight in the Lord, and in whom should we delight, but where all fulness is to be had to delight in? Our spirits are not so large as those blessed comforts are which we are called to the enjoyment of. If the capacity of our souls were a thousand times larger, yet there is so large a sea of comfort in Christ, as they are not able to comprehend it. A taste of these good things breeds 'joy unspeakable', and 'peace that passeth all understanding' (*Phil.* 4:7). What will the fulness do? This taste we feel in the ordinances will bring us to that fulness hereafter. Oh, let us keep our appetites for these things which are so delightful, so suitable to the soul. How great is that goodness which he both lays up for hereafter, and lays out for his, even here in this life!

In some ages of the church, the feasts that Christ hath made have been more solemn and sumptuous than in other thereafter, as Christ hath been more or less clearly and generally manifested. At Christ's first coming there was a greater feast than before; because the riches of God's love in Christ were then laid open, and the pale of the church was enlarged by the coming in of the Gentiles. So will there be a royal feast, when the Jews shall be converted. 'Blessed then shall those be that shall be called to the supper of the Lamb' (*Rev.* 19:9). Suppers are in the end of the day, and this supper shall be furnished towards the end of the world.

But then will be the true magnificent supper, when all that belong to God's election shall meet together, and feed upon that heavenly manna for ever. Then there will be nothing but marrow itself, and wine without all dregs. In all our contentments here, there is some mixture of the contrary; then nothing but pure quintessence. In the meantime, he lets fall some manna in this our wilderness, he lets us relish that now. It will not putrefy as the other manna did, but endure, and make us endure for ever. It's the true 'bread of life'.

Mark how Christ draws his spouse on to drink, and drink abundantly. There is no danger of taking too much. Where the spring is infinite, we can never draw these wells dry, never suck these breasts of consolation too much; and the more strong and cheerful we are, the better service we shall perform, and the more accepted. Delight is as sugar, sweet in itself, and it sweetens all things else. The joy of the Lord is our strength. Duties come off more gracefully, and religion is made more lovely in the eyes of all, when it comes forth in strength and cheerfulness. Christ's housekeeping is credited hereby. In our Father's house is plenty enough (*Luke* 15:17). When the martyrs had drunk largely of this wine, it made them forget friends, riches, honours, life itself. The joy stirred up by it, carried them through all torments.

If any be hindered by conceit[1] of unworthiness, if affected deeply with it, let them consider what kind of men were compelled to the banquet, the blind, the lame (*Luke* 14:21). See a lively picture of God's mercy in the example of the prodigal. He fears sharp chiding, and the father provides a rich banquet. He *goeth* to his father, but the father *runs* to meet him (*Luke* 15:20). Did Christ ever turn back any that came unto him, if they came out of a true sense of their wants?

'Eat, O friends.' Christ, out of the largeness of his affections, multiplieth new titles and compellations—'beloved' and 'friends'.

---

[1] Conception or idea.—P.

Christ provides a banquet, and invites his friends, not his enemies. Those good things that neither 'eye hath seen, nor ear hath
heard, that are above our conceit to apprehend' (*1 Cor.* 2:9); these
are provided for 'those that love him', not that hate him. He min-
gles another cup for them, 'a cup of wrath', and they are to 'drink
up the very dregs of it' (*Psa.* 75:8). Friendship is the sweetness,
intimateness, and strength of love. In our friends our love dwells
and rests itself. Conjugal friendship is the sweetest friendship. All
the kinds and degrees of friendship meet in Christ towards his
spouse. It is the friendship of a husband, of a brother; and if there
be any relation in the world wherein friendship is, all is too little
to express the love of Christ.

In friendship there is mutual consent, an union of judgment
and affections. There is a mutual sympathy in the good and ill one
of another, as if there were one soul in two bodies.[1] There be mutual friends and mutual enemies. 'Do I not hate them', saith David,
'that hate thee?' (*Psa.* 139:21). There is mutual love of one another
for their own sakes. In flattery, men love themselves most; in sem-
blance, love others, but all is in reflection to themselves.

There is liberty which is the life of friendship; there is a free
intercourse between friends, a free opening of secrets. So here
Christ openeth his secrets to us, and we to him. We acquaint him
with the most hidden thoughts of our hearts, and we lay open all
our cares and desires before him. Thus Abraham was called God's
friend (*2 Chron.* 20:7), and the disciples Christ's friends (*John*
15:15). It is the office of the Spirit to reveal the secrets of Christ's
heart to us, concerning our own salvation. He doth not reveal
himself to the world.

In friendship, there is mutual solace and comfort one in another. Christ delighteth himself in his love to his church, and his

---

[1] This definition of friendship, which is again and again introduced by Sibbes and
his contemporaries, is ascribed to Aristotle by Diogenes Laertius (v. § 20), cf.
Aristotle, *Eth. Nic.*, ix. 8, § 2, Ovid. *Trist.*, iv. 4, 72. Probably Sibbes derived it from
Augustine (a favourite with him), who applies it to his friend Nebridius.—G.

church delighteth herself in her love to Christ. Christ's delight was to be with the sons of men, and ours is to be with him.

In friendship there is a mutual honour and respect one of another; but here is some difference in this friendship. For though Christ calls us friends, and therein in some sort brings himself down to us, yet we must remember that this is a friendship of unequals. Christ's honouring of us is his putting honour upon us. Our honouring of him is the giving him the 'honour due to his name' (1 Chron. 16:29). This friendship must be maintained by due respect on our parts. As he is our friend, so he is our king, and knows how to correct us if we forget our distance. If he here seem to use us hardly, it is that he may use us the more kindly after. He suffers much for us, therefore we may well allow him the liberty of seasonable correcting of us.

He that inspireth friendship into others will undoubtedly keep the laws of friendship himself, will count our enemies his enemies. The enemies of the church shall one day know that the church is not friendless.

And as his friendship is sweet, so constant in all conditions. He useth not his friends as we do flowers, regard them only when they are fresh; but he breeds that in us that may make us such as he may still delight in us. If other friends fail, as friends may fail, yet this friend will never fail us. If we be not ashamed of him, he will never be ashamed of us. How comfortable would our life be if we could draw out the comfort that this title of *friend* affordeth! It is a comfortable, a fruitful, an eternal friendship.

'I sleep, but my heart waketh.' Here the church expresseth a changeable passage of her spiritual condition, after she had recovered herself out of a former desertion, expressed in the beginning of the third chapter; and enjoyed a comfortable intercourse with Christ. Now she falleth into a deeper desertion and temptation, from the remainder of corruption getting strength. The church now falleth asleep, then was awake in the night, and sought her beloved. Here is no present awaking, no seeking; there no misusage by the watchmen, as here. There she findeth him more speedily; here she falls sick with love before Christ discovereth himself.

Before we come to the words, observe in general,

Obs. 1. *That the state of the church and every Christian is subject to spiritual alterations.* The church is always 'beloved', a 'spouse', a 'friend'; but in this one state there falleth out variety of changes. No creature [is] subject to so many changes as man. From a state of innocency he fell into a state of corruption. From that he, by grace, is restored to a state of grace, and from grace to glory, where his condition shall be as Christ's now is, and as heaven the place is, altogether unchangeable. And in that state of grace, how many intercourses be there! the foundation of God's love to us, and grace in us always remaining the same. Once beloved, for ever beloved.

We see here, after a feast, the church falleth asleep. See it in Abraham, sometimes 'strong in faith', sometimes fearful. David sometimes standing, sometimes falling, sometimes recovering himself and standing faster, sometimes triumphing, 'The Lord is the light of my countenance, whom shall I fear?' (*Psa.* 27:1); sometimes, again, 'I shall one day fall by the hands of Saul' (*1 Sam.* 27:1). In the very same psalm he begins with 'Rebuke me not in thy wrath', and ends with 'Away, ye wicked' (*Psa.* 6:1, 10). Elijah, though zealous, yet after flies for his life (*1 Kings* 19). So Job, Peter, sometimes resolute and valiant, other while sinks for fear (*Job* 6, *Matt.* 14:30).

The reason. The ground is, by reason of variety of outward occurrences working upon the diversity of principles in us, nature and grace. Both nature and grace are always active in us in some degree. When corruption gets strength, then we find a sick state creeping upon us, and lose our former frame. It is with the soul as with the body. In a certain period of time it gathereth ill humours, which break out into aguish distempers at length; so the relics of a spiritual disease not carried away, will ripen and gather to a head. This should teach us, when we are well, to study to keep an even course, and to watch over the first stirrings, and likewise, if we see some unevenness in our ways, not to censure ourselves or others over harshly. Exact evenness is to be striven after here, but to be enjoyed in another world.

Obs. 2. We see, by comparing the state of the church here with the state of it in the third chapter, that *where corruption is not thoroughly purged, and a careful watch kept over the soul, there-after[1] a recovery, will follow a more dangerous distemper.* Corruption will not only strive for life, but for rule. If there had been a thorough reformation in the church after her former trouble, and a thorough closing with Christ, she would not thus have fallen into a more dangerous condition. We see David, in his later times, falls to 'numbering of the people' (2 *Sam.* 24:1ff.); and Samson, after he had done great services for the church, at length shamefully betrays his strength; and he that had ruled others submits to be ruled by a base strumpet (*Judg.* 16). Jonah, for not thorough repenting for his running from his calling, falls after to quarrel with God himself (*Jon.* 4:9). It is the best, therefore, to deal thoroughly with our hearts, else flesh unsubdued will owe us a greater shame, and we shall dishonour our own beginnings. Yet this is the comfort, that this will occasion deeper humility and hatred of sin in those that are God's, and a faster cleaving to God than ever before, as we see in the church here. Afterwards grace will have the better at last.

Obs. 3. *We may observe the ingenuity[2] of the church in laying open her own state.* It is the disposition of God's people to be ingenuous in opening their state to God, as in David, Nehemiah, Ezra, &c.

The reason is thus :—

(1.) By a free and full confession *we give God the honour of his*

---

[1] Qu. there, after.—Ed.

[2] That is, ingenuousness [frankness, free from deception.—P.].—G.

wisdom in knowing of our own condition, secret and open. We give him the honour of mercy that will not take advantage against us, the honour of power and authority over us, if he should show his strength against us. We yield unto him the glory of all his chief prerogatives; whereupon Joshua moveth Achan to a free confession, 'My son, give glory to God' (*Josh.* 7:19).

(2.) *We shame Satan,* who first takes away shame of sinning, and then takes away shame for sin. He tempts us not to be ashamed to do that we are ashamed to confess, so we, by silence, keep Satan's counsel against our own souls. If we accuse ourselves, we put him out of office who is the 'accuser of the brethren' (*Rev.* 12:10).

(3.) *We prevent, likewise, malicious imputations from the world.* Augustine answered roundly and well when he was upbraided with the sins of his former age: 'What thou', saith he, 'findest fault with, I have condemned in myself before.'

(4.) This ingenuous dealing *easeth the soul,* giving vent to the grief of it. Whiles the arrow's head sticks in the wound, it will not heal. Sin unconfessed is like a broken piece of rusty iron in the body. It must be gotten out, else it will, by rankling and festering, cause more danger. It is like poison in the stomach, if it be not presently cast up it will infect the whole body. Is it not better to take shame to ourselves now, than to be shamed hereafter before angels, devils, and men? How careful is God of us, by this private way to prevent future shame!

(5.) This faithful dealing with ourselves is oft a means of *present delivery out of any trouble.* David, in Psalm 32:4, was in a great distemper both of body and spirit; his moisture was turned into the drought of summer. It is thought he made this psalm between the time of his sin and his pardon. What course taketh he? 'I said', saith he, that is, 'I resolved to confess my sin, and thou forgavest the iniquity of my sin,' verse 5. Upon a free and full, a faithful and ingenuous confession, without all guile of spirit, he found ease presently, both in soul and body. The cause of God's severe dealing with us is, that we should deal severely with ourselves. The best trial of religion in us is by those actions whereby we reflect on ourselves by judging and condemning of ourselves, for this argueth a spirit without guile. Sin and shifting[1] came into the world together. The subtlety of proud nature, especially in eminency, is such that sins may pass for virtues, because sin and Satan are alike in this, they cannot endure to appear in their own colour and habit, and so those that oppose it shall be accounted opposers of good. This guile of spirit hath no blessedness belonging to it. Take heed of it.

Obs. 4. Mark, further, one sign of a gracious soul, *to be abased for lesser defects, sleepiness, and indisposition to good.* One would think drowsiness were no such great matter. O, but the church had such sweet acquaintance with Christ, that every little indisposition that hindered any degree of communion was grievous to her! You shall have a Judas, a Saul, an enormous offender confess great falls that gripe his conscience. All shall be cast up, that the conscience, being disburdened, may feel a little ease; but how few have you humbled for dullness of spirit, want of love, of zeal, and cheerfulness in duty? This, accompanied with strife against it, argues a good spirit indeed.

A carnal man is not more humbled for gross sins than a gracious Christian for wants in good actions, when it is not with him as it hath been, and as he would. The reason is, where there is a clear and heavenly light, there lesser motes are discernible; and spiritual life is sensible of any obstruction and hindrance. This goeth in the world for unnecessary nicety.[2] The world straineth

---

[1] That is, evasions, expedients.—G.

[2] This reminds us of an anecdote of the saintly Richard Rogers, who was remarkable for seriousness and gravity in all kinds of company. Being once engaged in conversation with one of the 'wits', who said to him, 'Mr Rogers, I like you and your company very well, only you are *too precise*'; he replied, 'Oh, sir, I serve a *precise* God.'—Firmin's *Real Christian*, p. 67, ed. 1670.—G.

not at these gnats. But those upon whose hearts the sun of right-eousness hath shined have both a clear sight and a tender heart.

To come to the words, 'I sleep'. The church fetcheth a comparison from the body to express the state of the soul. It is one use of our body to help us in spiritual expressions. Whilst the soul dwelleth in the body, it dependeth much in the conceiving of things upon the imagaination, and the imagination upon the senses. We come to conceive of spiritual sleep by sleep of the body, which we are all well enough acquainted with.

The church, as she consists of a double principle, flesh and spirit mingled together in all parts, as darkness and light in the twilight and dawning of the day; so here she expresseth her condition in regard of either part. So far as she was carnal, she slept; so far as she was spiritual, she was awake.

In this mixed condition the flesh for the present prevailed, yet so as the spirit had its working; 'she slept, but her heart waked'.

The words contain a confession, 'I sleep'; and a correction, 'but my heart waketh'. She hath a double aspect, one to the ill, 'her sleeping'; the other to the good, 'the heart in some degree awaked'. The Spirit of God is a discerning Spirit, it discovereth what is flesh and what is spirit.

So that we must not conceive this sleep to be that dead sleep all men are in by nature, nor to be that judicial sleep, that spirit of slumber, which is a further degree of that natural sleep to which God giveth up some, as a seal of their desperate condition; but here is meant that sleep that ariseth out of the remainder of corruption unsubdued, and now, is here in the church, prevailing over the better part. Flesh and spirit have both their intercourse in us, as Moses and Amalek had. Unless we stand upon our guard, the flesh will get the upper ground, as we see here. The best are no further safe than they are watchful.

For the clear understanding of this, observe some correspondency in the resemblance; wherein too much curiosity is loathsome,[1] and postill-like;[2] and calleth the mind too much from the kernel to the shell.

Bodily and spiritual sleep resemble each other in the causes, in the effects, and in the dangerous issue.

[First, to the causes of bodily and spiritual sleep.]

1. The sleep of the body cometh from the *obstruction and binding up of the senses by vapours which arise out of the stomach*. So there be spiritual fumes of worldly cares and desires that obstruct the senses of the soul. Therefore our blessed Saviour counts it a spiritual surfeiting,[3] when the soul is oppressed with care about the world (*Luke* 21:34). Lusts bring the soul a-bed. Prosperity is a strong vapour. If it overcome not the brain, yet it weakeneth it, as strong waters do. See it in Solomon himself.

2. The disciples fell asleep in the garden when they were *oppressed with heaviness and sorrow* (*Luke* 22:45), which passions will have the like effect upon the soul.

3. Sleep ariseth oft from *weariness and want of spirits*. So there is a spiritual weariness arising from discouragements and too much expense[4] of the strength of the soul upon other matters; upon impertinencies that concern not the best state of the soul.

4. Some are brought asleep by *music*. So many, by flattering enticements and insinuations of others, joining with their own flattering, deceitful heart, are cast into a spiritual sleep.

5. Sleep ariseth from *want of exercise*. When there is a cessation from spiritual exercise, about the proper object of it, there followeth a spiritual sleep. Exercise keeps waking.

6. Sleep ariseth oft from *cold diseases, as lethargies*; from cold,

---

[1] That is, offensive.—G.

[2] The allusion, no doubt, is to the over-subtle distinctions and uselessly curious speculations of the *scholastic* expositions of Scripture, which are called 'Postilla'. Various had been translated in the time of Sibbes, under the title of 'Postils'.—G.

[3] Indulging to excess.—P.

[4] That is, expenditure.—G.

gross humours. Cold, earthly, gross affections about the things here below, benumb the soul, and bring it into a heavy, drowsy, sleepy temper.

7. Sometimes sleep is caused by *some kind of poison*, especially the poison of asps, which kills in sleeping. And do not sinful delights do the like to the soul? Insensible evils are the most dangerous evils.

8. Otherwhile *slothful, yawning company* dispose to sleep. There is no more ordinary cause of spiritual sleep, than conversing with spiritual sluggards, that count it a high point of wisdom not to be forward in religion. These formal, proud persons, as they are cold themselves, so they labour to cast water upon the heat of others. Nay, those that are otherwise good, if declining in their first love, will incline others to a fellowship in the same secure temper, lest they should be upbraided by the vigilancy of others.

They are like *in the effects.*

1. Men disposed to be asleep *desire to be alone.* Those likewise that are disposed to take a spiritual nap, will avoid company, especially of such as would awake them. They will hardly endure rousing means.

2. Men will *draw the curtains and shut out light*, when they mean to compose themselves to rest. So when men favour themselves in some ways not allowable, they are afraid to be disquieted by the light. Light both discovereth, awaketh, and stirs up to working. And men when they are loath to do what they know, are loath to know what they should do. 'They that sleep, sleep in the night' (*1 Thess.* 5:7). Asa, otherwise a good king, shut up the prophet in prison for doing his duty (*2 Chron.* 16:10). Much of the anger that men bear against the Word laid open to them, is because it will not suffer them to sleep quietly in their sins. Such as will suffer them to live quietly in their sins,—they are quiet and honest men. There cannot be a worse sign than when men will

not endure wholesome words. It is a sign they are in an ill league with that they should above all wage war against.

3. In sleep, *imagination ruleth, and dreams in imagination.* Men in sleep dream of false good, and forget true danger.

Many cherish golden dreams; dream of meat, and when they awake, their soul is empty (*Isa.* 29:8). Vain hopes are the dreams of waking men, as vain dreams are all the waking of sleeping and carnal men, whose life is but a dream.

In sleep, there is no exercise of senses or motion. As then, men are not sensible of good or ill, they move neither to good or ill. Motion followeth sensibleness. What good we are not sensible of, we move not unto. Hence sleep is of kin to death, for the time, depriving us of the use of all senses; and a secure professor in appearance differs little from a dead professor. Both of them are unactive in good; and what they do, they do it without delight, in an uncomely and unacceptable manner, unbeseeming the state of a Christian. It is all one to have no senses, and not to use them. We may say of men in this sleepy temper, as the Scripture speaks of idols, 'they have eyes and see not, ears and hear not', &c. (*Psa.* 115:5).

So likewise they are alike in danger. In sleep, the preciousest thing men carry about them is taken away without resistance; and they are ready to let loose what they held fast before, were it never so rich a jewel. And it is so in spiritual sleepiness. Men suffer the profession of the truth to be wrung from them, without much withstanding; and with letting fall their watch, let fall likewise, if not their grace, yet the exercise of their graces, and are in danger to be robbed of all.

There is no danger but a man in sleep is fair for, and exposed unto. Sisera was slain asleep (*Judg.* 5:26), and Ishbosheth at noonday (2 *Sam.* 4:7); and there is no temptation, no sin, no judgment, but a secure, drowsy Christian is open for; which is the ground of so oft enforcing watchfulness by the Spirit of God in the Scriptures. As spiritual deadness of spirit is a cause of other sin, so likewise it is a punishment of them. God poureth a spirit of 'dead sleep upon men, and closeth up their eyes' (*Isa.* 29:10), till some heavy judgment falleth upon them; and how many carnal men never awake in this world, till they awake in hell! No wonder therefore that Satan labours to cast men into a dead sleep all that he can; and deludes them, with dreams of a false good, that their estate is good, and like so to continue; that tomorrow shall be as today; that no danger is near, though God's wrath hangeth over their head, ready to be revealed from heaven.

Thus we see how the resemblance holds. Some apply this to Constantine's time, about three hundred years after Christ, when the church upon peace and plenty grew secure, and suffered ecclesiastical abuses to creep in. Religion begat plenty, and the daughter devoured the mother. This made the writers of the ecclesiastical stories, to question whether the church hath more hurt by open persecution or peace, when one Christian undermineth and rageth against another.[1] Human inventions were so multiplied, that not long after, in Augustine's time, he complained that the condition of the Jews was more tolerable than theirs;[2] for though the Jews were under burdens, yet they were such as were imposed by God himself, and not human presumptions. But Gerson many hundred years after increaseth his complaint. If, O Augustine, thou saidst thus in thy time, what wouldst thou have said if thou hadst lived now, when men, as a toy[3] taketh them in the head, will multiply burdens? And he was not afraid to say, that the number of human constitutions[4] was such, that if they were observed in rigour, the greatest part of the church would be damned. Thus, whilst the husbandmen slept, the envious man Satan slept

[1] Theodoret, lib 5.—G.

[2] Augustine, *Epist. ad Januar.* cxix. —G.

[3] That is, trifle.—G.

[4] Laws, regulations, customs.—P.

not, but sew[1] his tares. Thus popery grew up by degrees, till it overspread the church, whilst the watchmen that should have kept others awake, fell asleep themselves. And thus we answer the papists, when they quarrel with us about the beginning of their errors. They ask of us, when such and such an heresy began? We answer, that those that should have observed them, were asleep. Popery is a mystery that crept into the church by degrees, under glorious pretences.[2] Their errors had modest beginnings. Worshipping of images arose from reserving the pictures of friends, and after that [they] were brought into the church. Invocation of saints arose from some of the fathers' figurative turning of their speech to some that were dead. Transubstantiation had rise from some transcendent, unwary phrases of the fathers. The papacy itself, from some titles of the Romish Church and bishop. Nothing in popery so gross, but had some small beginnings, which being neglected by those that should have watched over the church, grew at length unsufferable. No wonder if the papists be cast into a dead sleep; they have drunk too deep of the whore's cup. They that worship images are, as the Scripture saith, 'like unto them, they have eyes and see not', &c. (*Psa.* 115:5). They cannot discern of their errors, though they be never so ridiculous and senseless, as prayer in an unknown tongue, and such like.

And upon this state of the church let us add this caution.

A Caution. If the best men be so prone to sleep, then we cannot safely at all times build upon their judgment. The fathers of the church were not always awake. There be few of them, but in some things we may appeal from themselves sleeping, to themselves waking. The best, having some darkness left in their understandings, and some lusts unsubdued in their affections, may write and speak sometimes out of the worst part and principle that is in them, as well as out of the best, when they keep not close to the rule.

[1] That is, sowed.—G.

[2] See the Memoir of Sibbes in Volume 1 of the *Works*, p. lxv.

When our adversaries press us with the authority of fathers, we appeal to them, where they speak advisedly and of purpose. When they were not awaked by heretics, they speak sometimes unworthily, and give advantages to heretics that followed. It is the manner of our adversaries to make the unwarrantable practice of the ancienter time a rule of their practice, and the doubtful opinions of the ancients their own grand tenets; wherein in both they deal unsafely for themselves, and injuriously towards us, when we upon grounds in some things dissent; which liberty (oft when they should not) they will take to themselves.

But howsoever this sleepy condition agreeth to the former times of the church, yet I wish there were not cause to apply it to ourselves, in this latter age of the church, wherein many of the ancient heresies are revived; and besides, the evils that accompany long peace take hold of us, and will prevail too far, if we do not rouse up ourselves. The church is in the commonwealth, and usually they flourish and fall together. When there is a sleep of the church, for the most part there is a sleep of the State. A civil sleep is, when in grounds of danger there is no apprehension of danger; and this sleep is a punishment of spiritual sleep, when with Ephraim a State hath 'grey hairs, and knoweth it not' (*Hos.* 7:9); when judgments abroad will not awake men. When noise and pinching will not awake, the sleep must needs be deep. The whole world almost is in combustion round about us; and many countries thought themselves as safe, a little before their troubles, as we now think ourselves. If fear of outward dangers will not awake, then spiritual dangers will not, as being more secret, and not obvious to sense. No wonder, then, if few will believe our report of the fearful condition of wicked men in the world to come. A man may be startled and awaked with outward dangers that is spiritually sottish,[1] but he that is careless of outward danger, will be regardless of what we say in spiritual dangers. The fear of danger

---

[1] Foolish, stupid or numbed by alchoholic drink.—P.

may be the greater, when, as it was amongst the Jews, those that should be watchful themselves, and awake others, instead of awaking, rock the cradle, and cry 'Peace, peace, the temple of the Lord, the temple of the Lord' (*Jer.* 7:4). Yet we must never forget to be mindful, with thankfulness, for peace and the gospel of peace, which yet by God's blessing we enjoy, always suspecting the readiness of nature to grow secure under the abundance of favours, and so to bless ourselves in that condition.

Signs of a sleepy state. 1. Now we know that sleep is creeping upon us, by *comparing our present condition with our former,* when we were in a more wakeful frame, when the graces of God's Spirit were in exercise in us. If we differ from that we were, then all is not well.

2. Compare ourselves again with that *state and frame that a Christian should be in*; for sometimes a Christian goes under an uncomfortable condition all the days of his life, so that he is not fit to make himself his pattern. The true rule is, that description that is in the Word, of a waking and living Christian. What should a man be, take him at the best, the varying from that is a sleepy estate. As, for instance, a Christian should walk 'in the comfort of the Holy Ghost' (*Acts* 9:31), live and walk by faith; he should depend upon God, and resist temptations. Faith should work by love, and love to ourselves should move us to honour ourselves as members of Christ, to disdain to defile ourselves by sin. Our hope, if it be waking, will purge us, and make us suitable to the condition we hope for in heaven, and the company we hope to have fellowship with there.

3. Again, *look to the examples of others that are more gracious.* I have as many encouragements to be thankful to God, and fruitful. They enjoy no more means than I; and yet they abound in assurance, are comfortable in all conditions. I am down in a little trouble, subject to passion, to barrenness, and distrust, as if there were no promises of God made to sowing in righteousness. Thus

a man may discern he is asleep, by comparing himself with others that are better than himself.

4. Again, it is evident that we are growing on to a sleepy condition by this, when we find *a backwardness to spiritual duties*, as to prayer, thanksgiving, and spiritual conference. It should be the joy of a Christian, as it is his prerogative, to come into the presence of Christ, and to be enabled to do that, that is above himself. When what is spiritual in a duty will not down with us, it is a sign our souls are in a sleepy temper. There is not a proportion between the soul and the business in heavenly duties. Whom do we speak to but God? whom do we hear speak in the Word but God? what should be the temper of those that speak to God, and hear him speak to them? It should be regardful, reverent, observant. Those that are watchful to the eye of a prince, what observance they show, when they are to receive anything from him or to put up any request to him. 'Offer this to thy king', saith the Lord by Malachi (*Mal.* 1:8). When a man comes drowsily to God, to sacrifice, to hear, to pray, &c., offer this carriage to man; will he take it at thy hands? Oh the mercy of our patient God, that will endure such services as we most frequently perform! By this indisposedness to duty more or less, may we discover our sleepiness.

5. When the soul begins to *admire outward excellencies*; when it awakes much to profits, pleasures, and honours; when men admire great men, rich men, great places. The strength and fat of the soul are consumed by feeding on these things; so that when it comes to spiritual things it must needs be faint and drowsy. By these and the like signs, let us labour to search the state of our souls.

Motives against sleepiness. 1. And to stir us up the more, *consider the danger of a secure, sleepy estate*. There is no sin but a man is exposed unto in a secure estate. Therefore the devil labours all he can to cast men into this temper; which he must do before

73

he can make him fall into any gross sin. When he is asleep, he is in a fit frame for any ill action; he is in a temper fit for the devil to work upon; to bring into any dream or error; to inflame the fancies and conceits with outward excellencies. The devil hath a faculty this way, to make outward things great that are nothing worth, and to make such sins little as, if we were awake, would affright us. He works strongest upon the fancy, when the soul is sleepy or a little drowsy.

There is no man that comes to gross sin suddenly. But he falls by little and little; first to slumber, and from slumber to sleep, and from sleep to security; and so from one degree to another. It is the inlet to all sins, and the beginning of all danger. Therefore the Lord takes a contrary course with his. When he would preserve a State or person, he plants in them first a spirit of faith, to believe that there is such a danger, or such a good to be apprehended, upon watching and going on in a course befitting that condition; and then faith, if it be a matter of threatening, stirs up fear, which waketh up care and diligence. This is God's method, when he intends the preservation of any.

2. A man in his sleep *is fit to lose all.* A sleepy hand lets anything go with ease. A man hath grace and comfort; he lets it go in his spiritual sleepiness,—grace in a great measure, and the sense and comfort of it altogether. A Christian hath always the divine nature in him, that works in some degree; yet notwithstanding in regard of his present temper and feeling, he may be in such a case, that he shall differ nothing from a reprobate, nay, he may come to feel more than any ordinary wicked man feels whiles he lives in the world, as divers good Christians do. And all this, through their carelessness,—that they suffer themselves to be robbed of first beginnings, by yielding to delights, company, and contentments. Feeding their conceits with carnal excellencies, so favouring corruptions, and flattering that that is naught in them, they lose the comfort of all that is good. Who would do this for the

gaining of a little broken sleep; I say broken sleep, for the better a man is, the more unquietly shall he sleep in such a state. He shall feel startlings and frights in the midst of his carnal delights if he belong to God.

3. Besides, *God meets them with some crosses in this world,* that they shall gain nothing by it. There is none of God's children that ever gained by yielding to any corruption, or drowsiness, though God saved their souls. It is always true, a secure state is a sure forerunner of some great cross, or of some great sin. God cannot endure such a temper of soul; lifeless and unfeeling performances and sacrifices, to him that hath given us such encouragements. It must needs be distasteful to God, when we go drowsily and heavily about his work. 'Cursed is he that doth the work of the Lord negligently' (*Jer.* 48:10). If it were to sheath his sword in the bowels of his enemy, to which man is exceedingly prone, yet if it be not done with diligence and an eye to God, a man is cursed in it.

4. And it is an *odious temper to God.* For doth not he deserve cheerful service at our hands? hath he been a 'wilderness' to us? doth he not deserve the marrow of our souls? doth not his greatness require it at our hands, that our senses be all waking? and doth not his mercy deserve, that our love should take all care, to serve him that is so gracious and good to us? Is it not the fruit of our redemption to serve him without fear, in holiness and righteousness all the days of our lives? (*Luke* 1:14).

5. It is a state not only odious to God, but *irksome to our own spirits.* The conscience is never fully at peace in a drowsy state or in drowsy performances.

Likewise it is not graceful to others. It breeds not love in them to good things, but dislike. Carnal men, let them see a Christian not carry himself waking, as he should, though they be a thousand times worse themselves, yet notwithstanding they think it should not be so. Such a course doth not suit with so much knowledge and so much grace.

Let a man consider, wherefore God hath given the powers of the soul and the graces of the Spirit. Are they not given for exercise, and to be employed about their proper objects? A man is not a man, a Christian is not a Christian, when he is not waking. He so far degenerates from himself, as he yields unto any unbeseeming carriage. Wherefore hath God given us understanding, but to conceive the best things? Wherefore have we judgment, but to judge aright between the things of heaven and earth? Wherefore have we love planted in us, but to set it on lovely objects? Wherefore faith, but to trust God over all? Wherefore hatred, but to fly ill? Wherefore have we affections, but for spiritual things? When therefore our affections are dull, and lose their edge to these things, being quick only to earthly things, what a temper is this! How doth a man answer his creation, the state of a new creature! Wherefore are all graces planted in the soul, as faith and love, and hope and patience, but to be in exercise, and waking? To have these, and to let them sleep and lie unexercised, so far a Christian forgets himself, and is not himself. A Christian as a Christian, that is, in his right temper, should be in the act and exercise of what is good in him, upon all occasions; as we say of God, he is a pure act, because he is always in working. The Spirit of God is a pure act, in whom is no suffering but all action, about that that is fit for so glorious a nature. So it is with the spirit of a man, that hath the Spirit of God. He is in act, in exercise, in operation, as the Spirit is more or less in him. So he is more or less in operation, more or less fruitful. What a world of good might Christians do, if they were in a right temper! What a deal of ill might they escape and avoid that they lie in, if they would rouse up their souls to be as Christians should be, and as their soul and conscience tells them they ought and might be, did they rightly improve the means they have!

SERMON 4

I sleep, but my heart waketh, &c.
Song of Solomon 5:2

THE words, as it hath been showed, contain a confession, 'I sleep', and a correction, 'my heart waketh'. The confession hath been handled, now something of the correction or exception.

'My heart waketh.' The word heart, you know, includes the whole soul, for the understanding is the heart, 'an understanding heart' (*Job* 38:36). To 'lay things up in our hearts' (*Luke* 2:51), there it is memory; and to cleave in heart is to cleave in will (*Acts* 11:28). To 'rejoice in heart' (*Isa.* 30:29), that is in the affection. So that all the powers of the soul, the inward man, as Paul calleth it (2 *Cor.* 4:16), is the heart.

'I sleep, but my heart waketh.' Indeed the church might have said, My heart sleepeth, but my heart waketh. For it is the same faculty, the same power of the soul, both in the state of corruption, and of grace, in which the soul is; as in the twilight we cannot say, this is light and that is darkness, because there is such a mixture. In all the powers of the soul there is something good and something ill, something flesh and something spirit. The heart was asleep, and likewise was awake. 'I sleep, but my heart waketh.'

Obs. 1. You see here, then, first of all, in this correction, that *a Christian hath two principles in him*, that which is good, and that which is evil, whence issueth the weakness of his actions and affections. They are all mixed, as are the principles from which they come forth.

Obs. 2. We may observe, further, that *a Christian man may know how it is with himself.* Though he be mixed of flesh and spirit, he hath a distinguishing knowledge and judgment whereby he knows both the good and evil in himself. In a dungeon where is nothing but darkness, both on the eye that should see and on that which should be seen, he can see nothing; but where there is a supernatural principle, where there is this mixture, there the light of the Spirit searcheth the dark corners of the heart. A man that hath the Spirit knoweth both; he knoweth himself and his own heart. The Spirit hath a light of its own, even as reason hath. How doth reason know what it doth? By a reflect act inbred in the soul. Shall a man that is natural reflect upon his state, and know what he knows, what he thinks, what he doth, and may not the soul that is raised to an higher estate know as much? Undoubtedly it may. Besides, we have the Spirit of God, which is light, and self-evidencing. It shows unto us where it is, and what it is. The work of the Spirit may sometimes be hindered, as in times of temptation. Then I confess a man may look wholly upon corruption, and so mistake himself in judging by that which he sees present in himself, and not by the other principle which is concealed for a time from him. But a Christian, when he is not in such a temptation, he knows his own estate, and can distinguish between the principles in him of the flesh and spirit, grace and nature.

Again, we see here in that the church saith, 'but my heart waketh', that she doth acknowledge there is good as well as evil. As the church is ingenious[1] to confess that which is amiss, 'I sleep', so she is as true in confessing that which is good in herself, 'but my heart waketh', which yields us another observation.

Obs. 3. *We should as well acknowledge that which is good as that which is evil in our hearts.*

---

[1] That is, ingenuous.—G.

Because we must not bear false witness, as not against others, much less against ourselves. Many help Satan, the accuser, and plead his cause against the Spirit, their comforter, in refusing to see what God seeth in them. We must make conscience of this, to know the good as well as the evil, though it be never so little.

To come in particular, what is that good the church here confesseth, when she saith that 'her heart waketh'?

1. She in her sleepy estate, *first*, hath her *judgment sound in that which is truth, of persons, things, and courses.* Christians are not so benighted when they sleep, or given up to such a reprobate judgment, as that they discern not differences. They can discern that such are in a good way, and such are not; that such means are good, and such are not. A Christian ofttimes is forced to do work out of judgment, in case his affections are asleep or distracted; and such works are approved of God, as they come from a right judgment and conviction, though the evil of them be chastised.

2. But all is not in the judgment. The child of God asleep hath a *working in the will.* Choosing the better part, which he will cleave to, he hath a general purpose 'to please God in all things', and no settled purpose in particular for to sleep. Thus answerable to his judgment, therefore, he chooseth the better part and side; he owns God and his cause, even in evil times, cleaving in resolution of heart to the best ways, though with weakness.

Take David in his sleepy time between his repentance and his foul sin. If one should have asked him what he thought of the ways of God and of the contrary, he would have given you an answer out of sound judgment thus and thus. If you should have asked him what course he would have followed in his choice, resolution, and purpose, he would have answered savourly.

3. Again, there remaineth *affection answerable to their judgment*, which, though they find, and feel it not for a time, it being perhaps scattered, yet there is a secret love to Christ, and to his cause and side, joined with joy in the welfare of the church and

people of God; rejoicing in the prosperity of the righteous, with a secret grief for the contrary. The pulses will beat this way, and good affections will discover themselves. Take him in his sleepy estate, the judgment is sound in the main, the will, the affections, the joy, the delight, the sorrow. This is an evidence his heart is awake.

4. *The conscience likewise is awake.* The heart is taken ofttimes for the conscience in Scripture. A good conscience, called a merry heart, is 'a continual feast' (*Prov.* 15:15). Now, the conscience of God's children is never so sleepy but it awaketh in some comfortable measure. Though perhaps it may be deaded[1] in a particular act, yet notwithstanding there is so much life in it, as upon speech or conference, &c., there will be an opening of it, and a yielding at the length to the strength of spiritual reason. His conscience is not seared. David was but a little roused by Nathan, yet you see how he presently confessed ingeniously[2] that he had sinned (2 *Sam.* 12:13). So, when he had numbered the people, his conscience presently smote him (2 *Sam.* 24:10); and when he resolved to kill Nabal and all his family, which was a wicked and carnal passion, in which there was nothing but flesh; yet when he was stopped by the advice and discreet counsel of Abigail, we see how presently he yielded (1 *Sam.* 25:32ff.). There is a kind of perpetual tenderness of conscience in God's people. All the difference is of more or less.

5. And answerable to these inward powers is the *outward obedience of God's children*. In their sleepy estate they go on in a course of obedience. Though deadly and coldly, and not with that glory that may give others good example or yield themselves comfort, yet there is a course of good duties. His ordinary way is good, howsoever he may step aside. His fits may be sleepy when his estate is waking. We must distinguish between a state and a fit. A man may have an aguish fit in a sound body. The state of a

---

[1] That is, deadened.—G.

[2] That is, ingenuously.—G.

Christian is a waking state in the inward man. The bye-courses he falleth into are but fits, out of which he recovers himself.

Use 1. Whence, for use, let us magnify the goodness of God, that will remain by his Spirit, and let it stay to preserve life in such hearts as ours are, so prone to security and sleepiness. Let it put us in mind of other like merciful and gracious doings of our God for us, that he gave his Spirit to us when we had nothing good in us, when it met with nothing but enmity, rebellion, and indisposedness. Nay, consider how he debased himself and became man, in being united to our frail flesh, after an admirable¹ nearness, and all out of mercy to save us.

Use 2. If so be that Satan shall tempt us in such occasions, let us enter into our own souls, and search the truth of grace, our judgment, our wills, our constant course of obedience, and the inward principle whence it comes, that we may be able to stand in the time of temptation. What upheld the church but this reflect act, by the help of the Spirit, that she was able to judge of the good as well as of the ill? Thus David, 'The desires of our souls are towards thee' (*Psa*. 38:9); and though all this have befallen us, yet have we not forgotten thy name (*Psa*. 44:20). This will enable us to appeal to God, as Peter, 'Lord, thou knowest I love thee' (*John* 21:15). It is an evidence of a good estate.

Obs. 1. 'My heart waketh.' *God's children never totally fall from grace*. Though they sleep, yet their heart is awake. The prophet Isaiah, speaking of the church and children of God (*Isa*. 6:13), saith, 'It shall be as a tree, as an oak whose substance is in them, when they cast their leaves.' Though you see neither fruit nor leaves, yet there is life in the root, 'the seed remains in them'. There is always a seed remaining. It is an immortal seed that we are begotten by. Peter, when he denied his Master, was like an oak that was weather-beaten; yet there was life still in the root (*1 Pet*. 1:3, *Matt*. 26:32ff.). For, questionless, Peter loved Christ from his

¹ That is, wonderful.—G.

heart. Sometimes a Christian may be in such a poor case, as the spiritual life runneth all to the heart, and the outward man is left destitute; as in wars, when the enemy hath conquered the field, the people run into the city, and if they be beaten out of the city, they run into the castle. The grace of God sometimes fails in the outward action, in the field, when yet it retireth to the heart, in which fort it is impregnable. 'My heart waketh.'

When the outward man sleeps, and there are weak, dull performances, and perhaps actions amiss, too, yet notwithstanding 'the heart waketh'. As we see in a swoon or great scars, the blood, spirits, and life, though they leave the face and hands, &c., yet they are in the heart. It is said in the Scripture of Eutychus, 'His life is in him still', though he seemed to be dead (*Acts* 20:9). As Christ said of Lazarus (*John* 11:4), so a man may say of a Christian in his worst state, 'His life is in him still; he is not dead, but sleeps; 'his heart waketh.'

Obs. 2. *This is a sound doctrine and comfortable, agreeable to Scripture and the experience of God's people.* We must not lose it, therefore, but make use of it against the time of temptation. There are some pulses that discover life in the sickest man, so are there some breathings and spiritual motions of heart that will comfort in such times. These two never fail on God's part, his love, which is unchangeable, and his grace, a fruit of his love; and two on our part, the impression of that love, and the gracious work of the new creature. 'Christ never dies', saith the apostle (*Heb.* 7:25). As he never dies in himself, after his resurrection, so he never dies in his children. There is always spiritual life.

Use for comfort. 'The heart waketh.' This is a secret of God's sanctuary, only belonging to God's people. Others have nothing to do with it. They shall ever love God, and God will ever love them. The apostle (*1 Cor.* 13:8), saith, 'Love never fails.' Gifts, you know, shall be abolished, because the manner of knowing we now use shall cease. 'We see through a glass', &c., 'but love abideth'

(*1 Cor.* 13:12). Doth our love to God abide for ever, and doth not his love to us, whence it cometh? Ours is but a reflection of God's love. Let us comfort ourselves, therefore, in this for the time to come, that in all the uncertainty of things in this life we have today and lose tomorrow, as we see in Job, there is somewhat a saint may build on that is constant and unmoveable. 'I am the Lord, I change not; therefore you sons of Jacob are not consumed' (*Mal.* 3:6). God should deny himself, as it were, which he cannot do, and his own constant nature, if he should vary this way.

Obs. 3. *A Christian is what his heart and inward man is.* It is a true speech of divines, God and nature begin there. Art begins with the face and outward lineaments, as hypocrisy, outward painting and expressions; but grace at the centre, and from thence goes to the circumference. And therefore the church values herself here by the disposition and temper of her heart. Thus I am for my outward carriage, &c. 'I sleep, but my heart, that waketh.'

Therefore, let us enter into our consciences and souls, for the trial of our estates, how it is with our judgments. Do we allow of the ways of God and of the law of the inward man? How is it with our affections and bent to good things? how with our hatred, our zeal? Is it not more for outward things than for inward? We know what Jehu said to Jonadab, when he would have him into his chariot, 'Is thine heart as mine? Then come to me' (*2 Kings* 10:15). So saith Christ, Is thine heart as mine? then give me thy hand. But first God must have our hearts, and then our hands. A man otherwise is but a ghost in religion, which goes up and down, without a spirit of its own; but a picture that hath an outside, and is nothing within. Therefore, especially, let us look to our hearts. 'Oh, that there were such an heart in this people', saith God to Moses, 'to fear me always, for their good' (*Deut.* 5:29). This is it that God's children desire, that their hearts may be aright set. 'Wash thy heart, O Jerusalem', saith the prophet, 'from thy wickedness', &c. (*Jer.* 4:14). Indeed, all the outward man depends upon this. Therefore, Satan, if he can get this fort, he is safe, and so Satan's vicar (*Prov.* 4:23). It was a watchword that was in Gregory XIII, his time, in Queen Elizabeth's days, 'My son, give me thy heart. Dissemble, go to church, and do what you will; but, *da mihi cor*, be in heart a papist, and go where you will.'[1] God is not content with the heart alone. The devil knows if he have the heart he hath all; but God, as he made all, both soul and body, he will have all. But yet in times of temptation the chief trial is in the heart.

And from hence we may have a main difference between one Christian and another. A sound Christian doth what he doth from the heart; he begins the work there. What good he doth he loves in his heart first, judgeth it to be good, and then he doeth it.

An hypocrite doth what he doth outwardly, and allows not inwardly of that good he doth. He would do ill, and not good, if it were in his choice. The good that he doth is for by-ends, for correspondence, or dependence upon others, or conformity with the times, to cover his designs under formality of religion, that he may not be known outwardly, as he is inwardly, an atheist and an hypocrite. So he hath false aims; his heart is not directed to a right mark. But it is otherwise with God's child. Whatsoever good he doth, it is in his heart first; whatsoever ill he abstains from, he doth it from his heart, judging it to be naught; therefore he hates it, and will not do it. Here is a main difference of the church from all others. It wakes in the heart, though the outward man sleeps. But other men's hearts sleep when they wake, as you know some men will walk and do many things in their sleep. An hypocrite is such a kind of man. He walks and goes up and down, but his heart is asleep. He knows not what he doth, nor doth he the thing out of judgment or love, but as one asleep, as it were. He hath no inward affection unto the things he doth. A Christian is the contrary; his heart is awake when he is asleep.

---

[1] Jesuitism, even in its present working, proceeds on this maxim, of which there have been many startling evidences.—G.

Another difference from the words you may have thus. A Christian, by the power of God's Spirit in him, is sensible of the contrarieties in him, complains, and is ashamed for the same. But an hypocrite is not so; he is not sensible of his sleepiness. 'I sleep', saith the church. So much as the church saith she slept, so much she did not sleep; for a man that is asleep cannot say he is asleep, nor a dead man that he is dead. So far as he saith he is asleep, he is awake. Now, the church confesseth that she was asleep by that part that was awake in her. Other men do not complain, are not sensible of their sleepiness and slumbering, but compose themselves to slumber, and seek darkness, which is a friend of sleep. They would willingly be ignorant, to keep their conscience dull and dumb as much as they can, that it may not upbraid them. This is the disposition of a carnal man; he is not sensible of his estate as here the church is.

Obs. 4. *A waking state is a blessed state.* The church you see supports and comforts herself that she was waking in her inward man, that she was happy in that respect.

Quest. How shall we do to keep and preserve our souls in this waking condition, especially in these drowsy times?

Ans. 1. *Propound unto them waking considerations.* What causeth our sleeps but want of matters of more serious observation? None will sleep when a thing is presented of excellency more than ordinary. To see, and know, and think of what a state we are now advanced unto in Christ; what we shall be ere long, yet the fearful estate we should be in, if God leave us to ourselves! a state of astonishment, miserable and wretched, beyond speech, nay, beyond conceit![1] Thus did the blessed souls in former times exercise their thoughts, raise, and stir them up by meditation, that so they might hold their souls in a high esteem of the best things, and not suffer them to sleep. We never fall to sleep in earthly and carnal delights, till the soul let its hold go of the best things, and ceaseth to think of, and to wonder at them. What made Moses to fall from

---

[1] That is, conception.—G.

the delights of Egypt? He saw the basest things in religion were greater than the greatest things in the court, yea, in the world. 'He esteemed the reproach of Christ better than the greatest treasures of Egypt' (*Heb.* 11:26).

2. *Make the heart think of the shortness and vanity of this life,* with the uncertainty of the time of our death; and of what wondrous consequent[1] it is to be in the state of grace before we die. The uncertainty of the gales of grace, that there may be a good hour which, if we pass, we may never have the like again (*Luke* 19:42, *Matt.* 23:37); as the angel descended at a certain hour into the pool of Bethesda (*John* 5:4), when those that entered not immediately after, went away sick as they came. So there are certain good hours which let us not neglect. This will help to keep us waking.

3. *The necessity of grace,* and then the free dispensing of it in God's good time, and withal the terror of the Lord's-day, 'Remembering', saith St Paul, 'the terror of the Lord, I labour to stir up all men', &c. (*2 Cor.* 5:11). Indeed it should make us stir up our hearts when we consider the terror of the Lord; to think that ere long we shall be all drawn to an exact account, before a strict, precise judge. And shall our eyes then be sleeping and careless? These and such like considerations out of spiritual wisdom we should propound to ourselves, that so we might have waking souls, and preserve them in a right temper.

Ans. 2. *To keep faith waking.* The soul is as the object is that is presented to it, and as the certainty of the apprehension is of that object. It conduceth much therefore to the awakening of the soul to keep faith awake. It is not the greatness alone, but the presence of great things that stirs us. Now it is the nature of faith to make things powerfully present to the soul; for it sets things before us in the word of Jehovah, that made all things of nothing, and is Lord of his Word, to give a being to whatsoever he hath spoken (*Heb.*

[1] That is, consequence.—G.

11:1). Faith is an awakening grace. Keep that awake, and it will keep all other graces waking.

When a man believes, that all these things shall be on fire ere long; that heaven and earth shall fall in pieces; that we shall be called to give an account, [and that] before that time we may be taken away—is it not a wonder we stand so long, when cities' stone walls fall, and kingdoms come to sudden periods? When faith apprehends, and sets this to the eye of the soul, it affects the same marvellously. Therefore let faith set before the soul some present thoughts according to its temper. Sometimes terrible things to awaken it out of its dullness; sometimes glorious things, promises and mercies, to waken it out of its sadness, &c. When we are in a prosperous estate let faith make present all the sins and temptations that usually accompany such an estate, as pride, security, self-applause, and the like. If in adversity, think also of what sins may beset us there. This will awaken up such graces in us, as are suitable to such an estate, for the preventing of such sins and temptations, and so keep our hearts in 'exercise to godliness' (*1 Tim.* 4:7); than which, nothing will more prevent sleeping.

Ans. 3. And withal, *labour for abundance of the Spirit of God.* For what makes men sleepy, and drowsy? The want of spirits. We are dull, and overloaden with gross humours, whereby the strength sinks and fails. Christians should know, that there is a necessity, if they will keep themselves waking, to keep themselves spiritual. Pray for the Spirit above all things. It is the life of our life, the soul of our soul. What is the body without the soul, or the soul without the Spirit of God? Even a dead lump. And let us keep ourselves in such good ways, as we may expect the presence of the Spirit to be about us, which will keep us awake.

Ans. 4. *We must keep ourselves in as much light as may be.* For all sleepiness comes with darkness. Let us keep our souls in a perpetual light. When any doubt or dark thought ariseth, upon yielding thereunto comes a sleepy temper. Sleepiness in the affections ariseth from darkness of judgment. The more we labour to increase our knowledge, and the more the spiritual light and beams of it shine in at our windows, the better it will be for us, and the more shall we be able to keep awake. What makes men in their corruptions to avoid the ministry of the Word, or anything that may awake their consciences? It is the desire they have to sleep. They know, the more they know, the more they must practise, or else they must have a galled[1] conscience. They see religion will not stand with their ends. Rich they must be, and great they will be; but if they suffer the light to grow upon them, that will tell them they must not rise, and be great, by these and such courses. A gracious heart will be desirous of spiritual knowledge especially, and not care how near the Word comes; because they ingeniously[2] and freely desire to be spiritually better. They make all things in the world yield to the inward man. They desire to know their own corruptions and evils more and more. And therefore love the light 'as children of the light, and of the day' (1 Thess. 5:5). Sleep is a work of darkness. Men therefore of dark and drowsy hearts desire darkness, for that very end that their consciences may sleep.

Ans. 5. Labour to preserve the soul in the fear of God: because fear is a waking affection, yea, one of the wakefullest. For, naturally we are more moved with dangers, than stirred with hopes. Therefore, that affection, that is most conversant about danger, is the most rousing and waking affection. Preserve therefore the fear of God by all means. It is one character of a Christian, who, when he hath lost almost all grace, to his feeling, yet the fear of God is always left with him. He fears sin, and the reward of it, and therefore God makes that awe the bond of the new covenant. 'I will put my fear into their hearts, that they shall never depart from me' (*Jer.* 32:39). One Christian is better than another, by how much more he wakes, and fears more than another. Of all Christians,

---

[1] Irritated or aggravated.—P.

[2] That is, ingenuously.—G.

mark those [that] are most gracious, spiritual, and heavenly, that are the most awful and careful of their speeches, courses, and demeanours; tender even of offending God in little things. You shall not have light and common oaths come from them, nor unsavoury speeches. Sometimes a good Christian may in a state of sleepiness be faulty some way. But he grows in the knowledge of the greatness of God, and the experience of his own infirmities, as he grows in the sense of the love of God. He is afraid to lose that sweet communion any way, or to grieve the Spirit of God. Therefore, always as a man grows in grace, he grows in awfulness, and in jealousy of his own corruptions. Therefore let us preserve by all means this awful affection, the fear of God. Let us then often search the state of our own souls; our going backward or forward; how it is between God and our souls; how fit we are to die, and to suffer; how fit for the times that may befall us. Let us examine the state of our own souls, which will preserve us in a waking estate; especially examine ourselves in regard of the sins of the place, and the times where we live; of the sins of our own inclination, how we stand affected and biassed in all those respects, and see how jealous we are of dangers in this kind. Those that will keep waking souls, must consider the danger of the place where they live, and the times; what sins reign, what sins such a company as they converse with are subject unto, and their own weakness to be led away with such temptations. This jealousy is a branch of that fear that we spake of before, arising from the searching of our own hearts, and dispositions. It is a notable means to keep us awake, when we keep our hearts in fear of such sins as either by calling, custom, company, or the time we live in, or by our own disposition, we are most prone to.

There is no Christian, but he hath some special sin, to which he is more prone than to another, one way or other, either by course of life, or complexion. Here now is the care and watchfulness of a Christian spirit, that knowing by examination, and trial of his own heart, his weakness, he doth especially fence against that, which he is most inclined to; and is able to speak most against that sin of all others, and to bring the strongest arguments to dishearten others from practice of it.

Ans. 6. In the last place it is a thing of no small consequence, that *we keep company with waking and faithful Christians,* such as neither sleep themselves or do willingly suffer any to sleep that are near them.

It is a report, and a true one, of the sweating sickness, that they that were kept awake by those that were with them, escaped; but the sickness was deadly if they were suffered to sleep. It is one of the best fruits of the communion of saints, and of our spiritual good acquaintance, to keep one another awake. It is an unpleasing work on both sides. But we shall one day cry out against all them that have pleased themselves and us, in rocking us asleep, and thank those that have pulled us 'with fear' (*Jude* 23) out of the fire, though against our wills.

Let us labour upon our own hearts in the conscionable[1] use of all these means, in their several times and seasons, that we may keep our hearts waking; and the more earnest ought we to be, from consideration of the present age and season in which we live.

Certainly a drowsy temper is the most ordinary temper in the world. For would men suffer idle words, yea, filthy and rotten talk to come from their mouths if they were awake? Would a waking man run into a pit? or upon a sword's point? A man that is asleep may do anything. What do men mean when they fear not to lie, dissemble, and rush upon the pikes of God's displeasure? When they say one thing and do another, are they not dead? or take them at the best, are they not asleep? Were they awake, would they ever do thus? Will not a fowl that hath wings, avoid the snare? or will a beast run into a pit when it sees it? There is a

---

[1] That is, conscientious.—G.

snare laid in your playhouses, gaming houses, common houses, that gentlemen frequent that generally profess religion, and take the communion. If the eye of their souls were awake, would they run into these snares, that their own conscience tells them are so? If there be any goodness in their souls, it is wondrous sleepy. There is no man, even the best, but may complain something, that they are overtaken in the contagion of these infectious times. They catch drowsy tempers, as our Saviour saith, of those latter times. 'For the abundance of iniquity, the love of many shall wax cold' (*Matt.* 24:12). A chill temper grows ever from the coldness of the times that we live in, wherein the best may complain of coldness; but there is a great difference. The life of many, we see, is a continual sleep.

Let us especially watch over ourselves, in the use of liberty and such things as are in themselves lawful. It is a blessed state, when a Christian carries himself so in his liberty, that his heart condemns him not for the abuse of that which it alloweth, and justly in a moderate use. Recreations are lawful; who denies it? To refresh a man's self, is not only lawful, but necessary. God knew it well enough, therefore hath allotted time for sleep, and the like. But we must not turn recreation into a calling, to spend too much time in it.

Where there is least fear, there is most danger always. Now because in lawful things there is least fear, we are there in most danger. It is true for the most part, *licitis perimus ommes,* more men perish in the church of God by the abuse of lawful things, than by unlawful; more by meat, than by poison. Because every man takes heed of poison, being[1] he knows the venom of it, but how many men surfeit, and die by meat! So, many men die by lawful things. They eternally perish in the abuse of their liberties, more than in gross sins. Therefore let us keep awake, that we may carry ourselves so in our liberties, that we condemn not ourselves in

[1] That is, seeing it is.—G.

the use of them. We will conclude this point with the meditation of the excellency of a waking Christian. When he is in his right temper, he is an excellent person, fit for all essays.[1] He is then impregnable. Satan hath nothing to do with him, for he, as it is said, is then a wise man, and 'hath his eyes in his head' (*Eccles.* 3:4). He knows himself, his state, his enemies, and adversaries, the snares of prosperity and adversity, and of all conditions, &c. Therefore, he being awake, is not overcome of the evil of any condition, and is ready for the good of any estate. He, that hath a waking soul, he sees all the advantages of good, and all the snares that might draw him to ill (*Mark* 13:37). What a blessed estate is this! In all things therefore watch; in all estates, in all times, and in all actions. There is a danger in everything without watchfulness. There is a scorpion under every stone, as the proverb is, a snare under every blessing of God, and in every condition, which Satan useth as a weapon to hurt us; adversity to discourage us, prosperity to puff us up: when, if a Christian hath not a waking soul, Satan hath him in his snare, in prosperity to be proud and secure; in adversity to murmur, repine,[2] be dejected, and call God's providence into question. When a Christian hath a heart and grace to awake, then his love, his patience, his faith is awake, as it should be. He is fit for all conditions, to do good in them, and to take good by them.

Let us therefore labour to preserve watchful and waking hearts continually, that so we may be fit to live, to die, and to appear before the judgment seat of God; to do what we should do, and suffer what we should suffer, being squared for all estates whatsoever.

[1] That is, attempts. Sibbes' spelling is assaies,—Qu. assaults?—G.

[2] Complain or grumble.—P.

SERMON 5

It is the voice of my beloved that knocketh, saying, Open to me, my sister, my love, my dove, my undefiled; for my head is filled with dew, and my locks with the drops of the night.
SONG OF SOLOMON 5:2

HITHERTO, by God's assistance, we have heard largely both of the church's sleeping and heart-waking; what this sleeping and heart-waking is; how it comes; the trials of these opposite dispositions; of the danger of sleeping, and excellency of heart-waking; and of the helps and means, both to shun the one and preserve the other. Now, the church, having so freely and ingeniously[1] confessed what she could against herself, proceeds yet further to acquaint us with the particulars in her heart-waking disposition, which were twofold. She heard and discerned 'the voice of her beloved', who, for all her sleep, was her beloved still; and more than that, she remembers all his sweet words and allurements, whereby he pressed her to open unto him, saying, 'Open to me, my love, my dove, my undefiled;' which is set out and amplified with a further moving argument of those inconveniences Christ had suffered in his waiting for entertainment in her heart, 'For my head is filled with dew, and my locks with the drops of the night', all which aggravates her offence; and his rare goodness and patience towards miserable sinners, so to wait from time to time for admission into our wretched souls, that he may rule and govern them by his Holy Spirit. Therefore, we had great

[1] That is, ingenuously.—G.

93

reason to shun this sleepy distemper of soul, which for the present so locks up 'the everlasting gates of our soul, that the King of glory cannot enter in' (*Psa.* 24:7), and to strive for this blessed heart-waking disposition, which may help us at all times to see our dangers, and, by God's blessing, recover us out of them, as here the church doth at length, though first smarting and well beaten by the watchmen, in a world of perplexities ere she can recover the sense of her former union and communion with Christ.

And surely we find by experience what a woeful thing it is for the soul which hath once tasted how gracious the Lord is, to be long without a sense of God's love; for when it looks upon sin as the cause of this separation, this is for the time as so many deaths unto it. Therefore, the church's experience must be our warning-piece to take heed how we grieve the Spirit, and so fall into this spiritual sleep. Wherein yet this is a good sign, that yet we are not in a desperate dead sleep when we can with her say,

'It is the voice of my beloved that knocks, saying, Open unto me', &c.

In which words you have,

1. The church's acknowledgment of Christ's voice.

2. Of his carriage towards her.

1. Her acknowledgment is set down here, 'It is the voice of my beloved.'

2. His carriage, 'He knocks', &c. Wherein,

(1.) His patience in suffering things unworthy and utterly unbeseeming for him. He doth not only 'knock', but he continues knocking, till 'his head was filled with dew, and his locks with the drops of the night'.

(2.) His friendly compellation, 'Open to me, my love, my dove, my undefiled.' Lo, here are sweet actions, sweet words, and all to melt the heart of the spouse!

First, *the church's acknowledgment* is to be considered, confessing, 'It is the voice of her beloved.' The first thing to be observed in this acknowledgment is, that the church, however sleepy and drowsy she was, yet notwithstanding, her heart was so far awake as to know the voice of her husband. The point is this,

Obs. That *a Christian soul doth know and may discern the voice of Christ, yea, and that even in a lazy, sleepy estate, but much more when in a good and lively frame.* God's believers are Christ's sheep (*John* 10:3). Now, 'My sheep', saith Christ, 'hear my voice' (verse 4). It is the ear-mark, as it were, of a Christian, one of the characters of the new man, 'to taste words by the ear' as Job saith (*Job* 12:11). He hath a spiritual taste, a discerning relish in his ear, because he hath the Spirit of God, and therefore relisheth what is connatural,[1] and suitable to the Spirit. Now, the voice of Christ without in the ministry, and the Spirit of Christ within in the heart, are connatural, and suitable each to other.

And surely so it is, that *this is one way to discern a true Christian from another, even by a taste in hearing.* For those that have a spiritual relish, they can hear with some delight things that are most spiritual. As the heathen man said of a meadow, that some creatures come to eat one sort of herbs, others another, all that which is fit for them; men to walk therein for delight; all for ends suitable to their nature; so, in coming to hear the Word of God, some come to observe the elegancy of words and phrases, some to catch advantage perhaps against the speaker, men of a devilish temper; and some to conform themselves to the customs of the places they live in, or to satisfy the clamours of a troubled conscience, that will have some divine duty performed, else it goes on with much vexation. But every true Christian comes and relisheth what is spiritual; and when outward things can convey in similitudes spiritual things aptly to the mind, he relisheth this, not as elegant and pleasing his fancy so much, as for conveying the voice of Christ unto his soul, so that a man may much be helped to know his state in grace and what he is, by his ear.

---

[1] Of the same or similar nature.—P.

'Itching ears' (2 *Tim.* 4:3) usually are such as are 'led with lust', as the apostle saith, and they must be clawed.[1] They are sick, and nothing will down with them. They quarrel with everything that is wholesome, as they did with manna. No sermons will please them, no bread is fine and white enough; whereas, indeed, it is their own distemper that is in fault. As those that go in a ship upon the sea, it is not the tossing but the stomach that causeth a sickness, the choler[2] within, and not the waves without, so the disquiet of these men, that nothing will down with them, is from their own distemper. If Christ himself were here a-preaching, they would be sure to cavil at[3] something, as then men did when he preached in his own person, because they labour of lusts, which they resolve to feed and cherish.

And again, observe it against our adversaries. What say they? How shall we know that the word is the Word of God? For this heretic saith thus, and this interprets it thus. This is the common objection of the great rabbis amongst them in their writings, how we can know the word to be God's, considering there are such heresies in the churches, and such contrariety of opinions concerning the Scriptures read in the churches.

Even thus to object and ask is an argument and testimony that these men have not the Spirit of Christ, for 'his sheep know his voice' (*John* 10:3), who, howsoever they cannot interpret all places of Scripture, yet they can discern in the Scripture what is suitable food for them, or in the unfolding of the Scriptures in preaching they can discern agreeable food for them, having a faculty to reject that which is not fit for nourishment, to let it go. As there is in nature passages fit for concoction and digestion and for rejection, so there is in the soul to work out of the Word, even out of that which is hard, yet wholesome, what is fit for the

---

[1] Cut or lanced—P.

[2] Bile, biliousness; anger, irritability. —P.

[3] Find fault with or criticise.—P.

soul and spirit. If it be cast down, it feeds upon the promises for direction and consolation; and what is not fit for nourishment, that it rejects, that is, if it be of a contrary nature, heterogeneal. Therefore, we answer them thus, that 'God's sheep hear his voice' (*John* 10:4); that his Word left in the church, when it is unfolded, his Spirit goes together with it, breeding a relish of the Word in the hearts of people, whereby they are able to taste and relish it, and it hath a supernatural power and majesty in it which carries its own evidence with it. How shall we know light to be light? It carries evidence in itself that it is light. How know we that the fire is hot? Because it carries evidence in itself that it is so. So if you ask how we know the Word of God to be the Word of God; it carries in itself inbred arguments and characters, that the soul can say none but this word can be the Word of God; it hath such a majesty and power to cast down, and raise up, and to comfort, and to direct with such power and majesty, that it carries with it its own evidence, and it is argument enough for it (*1 Cor.* 14:24, 25; *2 Cor.* 10:4, 5). And thus we answer them, which they can answer no way but by cavils.[1] 'God's sheep hear the voice of Christ.' He speaks, and the church understands him, 'and a stranger's voice they will not hear' (*John* 10:5).

And indeed, this is the only sure way of understanding the word to be of God, from an inbred principle of the majesty in the Word, and a powerful work thereof on the soul itself; and an assent so grounded is that which makes a sound Christian. If we should ask, what is the reason there be so many that apostatize, fall away, grow profane, and are so unfruitful under the gospel, notwithstanding they hear so much as they do? The answer is, their souls were never founded and bottomed upon this, that it is the Word of God, and divine truth, so as to be able to say, I have felt it by experience, that it is the voice of Christ. Therefore they so soon apostatize, let Jesuits, or seducers set upon them. They were

---

[1] Objections or criticisms.—P.

never persuaded from inbred arguments, that the voice of Christ is the Word of God. Others from strictness grow profane, because they were never convinced by the power and majesty of the truth in itself; and then in the end they despair, notwithstanding all the promises, because they were never convinced of the truth of them. They cannot say Amen to all the promises. But the church can say confidently, upon sound experience, 'It is the voice of my beloved', &c.

Again, whereas the church saith here, It is the voice of my beloved, &c., and knows this voice of her beloved, we may note—

Obs. That the church of God, and every Christian, takes notice of the means that God useth for their salvation.

A Christian is sensible of all the blessed helps he hath to salvation. To a dead heart, it is all one whether they have means or no means; but a Christian soul takes notice of all the means. 'It is the voice of my beloved that knocketh.' It seeth Christ in all.

And mark what the church saith, moreover, 'It is the voice of my beloved.' She acknowledgeth Christ to be beloved of her, though she were asleep. So then here is a distinction between the sleep of a Christian and the dead sleep of another natural man. The one when he sleeps, his heart doth not only wake, but it is awake to discern the voice of Christ. It can relish in reading what is spiritual and good, what is savoury, and what not. And likewise take a Christian at the worst: when he is asleep, he loves Christ, he will do nothing against him. 'I can do nothing', saith Paul, 'against the truth, but for the truth' (2 *Cor.* 13:8). He will do nothing against the cause of religion. There is a new nature in him, that he cannot do otherwise. He cannot but love; he cannot sin with a full purpose, nor speak against a good cause, because he hath a new nature, that leads him another way. Christ is her beloved still though she sleep.

Obs. Take a Christian at the lowest, his heart yearns after Christ.
Acknowledging him to be his beloved, there is a conjugal

chastity in the soul of a Christian. Holding firm to the covenant and marriage between Christ and it, he keeps that unviolable. Though he may be untoward, sleepy, and drowsy, yet there is always a conjugal, spouse-like affection. 'It is the voice of my beloved', &c.

Now, leaving the church's notice of the voice of Christ, we come to Christ's carriage towards her.

1. 'He knocketh'; and then we have—

2. His patience in that carriage. 'My head is filled with dew, and my locks with the drops of the night', &c. Here is patience and mercy, to endure this indignity at the church's hand, to stand at her courtesy to come in; besides,

3. The compellation, afterwards to be spoken of. The general observation from Christ's carriage is this—

Obs. That *Christ still desires a further and further communion with his church.*

Even as the true soul that is touched with the Spirit, desires nearer and nearer communion with Christ; so he seeks nearer and nearer communion with his spouse, by all sanctified means. Christ hath never enough of the soul. He would have them more and more open to him. Our hearts are for Christ, who hath the heaven of heavens, and the soul of a believing Christian for himself to dwell in. He contents not himself to be in heaven alone, but he will have our hearts. He knocks here, waits, speaks friendly and lovingly, with such sweet words, 'My love, my dove', &c. We had a blessed communion in the state of innocency, and shall have a glorious communion in heaven, when the marriage shall be consummated; but now the time of this life is but as the time of the contract, during which there are yet many mutual passages of love between him and his spouse, a desire of mutual communion of either side. Christ desires further entertainment in his church's heart and affection, that he might lodge and dwell there. And likewise there is the like desire in the church, when she is in a right temper; so that if any strangeness be between Christ and any man's soul, that hath tasted how good the Lord is, let him not blame Christ for it, for he delights not in strangeness. He that knocks and stands knocking, while his locks are bedewed with the drops of the night, doth he delight in strangeness, that makes all this love to a Christian's soul? Certainly no.

Therefore look for the cause of his strangeness at any time in thine own self. As, *whether we cast ourselves imprudently into company, that are not fit to be consulted withal*, in whom the Spirit is not, and who cannot do us any good, or they cast themselves to us. Evil company is a great damping, whereby a Christian loseth his comfort much, especially that intimate communion with God; whence we may fall into security.

Again, *discontinuing of religious exercises doth wonderfully cause Christ to withdraw himself.* He makes no more love to our souls, when we neglect the means, and discontinue holy exercises, and religious company, when we stir not up the graces of God's Spirit. Being this way negligent, it is no wonder that Christ makes no more love to our souls, when we prize and value not the communion that should be between the soul and Christ, as we should. 'Whom have I in heaven but thee?' (*Psa.* 73:25). 'Thy lovingkindness is better than life', saith the psalmist (*Psa.* 63:3). When we prize not this, it is just with Christ to make himself strange. Where love is not valued and esteemed, it is estranged, and for a while hides itself. So that these, with other courses and failings, we may find to be the ground and reason of the strangeness between Christ and the soul, for certainly the cause is not in him. For we see here, he useth all means to be entertained by a Christian soul: 'he knocks'.

You know what he says to the church of Laodicea—'Behold, I stand at the door, and knock' (*Rev.* 3:20); so here—'It is the voice of my beloved that knocketh'. Therefore, in such a case, search your own hearts, where, if there be deadness and desertion of spirit, lay the blame upon yourselves, and enter into a search of your own ways, and see what may be the cause.

Now, to come more particularly to Christ's carriage here, knocking at the heart of the sleepy church, we see that *Christ takes not the advantage and forfeiture of the sins of his church, to leave them altogether, but makes further and further love to them.* Though the church be sleepy, Christ continues knocking. The church of Laodicea was a lukewarm, proud, hypocritical church; yet 'Behold', saith Christ, 'I stand at the door, and knock' (*Rev.* 3:20); and it was such a church as was vainglorious and conceited. 'I am rich, and want nothing, when she was poor, blind, and naked' (*Rev.* 3:17). And here he doth not only stand knocking, but he withal suffereth indignities—'the dew' to fall upon him, which we shall speak more of hereafter. Christ, therefore, refuseth not weak sinners. He that commands, 'that we should receive him that is weak in the faith' (*Rom.* 14:1), and not cast him off from our fellowship and company, will he reject him that is weak and sleepy? No. What father will pass by or neglect his child, for some failings and weaknesses? Nature will move him to respect him as his child.

Now, Christ is merciful both by his office and by his nature. Our nature he took upon him, that he might be a merciful Redeemer (*Heb.* 2:17). And then as God also, he is love, 'God is love' (*1 John* 4:16): that is, whatsoever God shows himself to his church, he doth it in love. If he be angry in correcting, it is out of love; if merciful, it is out of love; if he be powerful in defending his church, and revenging himself on her enemies, all is love. 'God is love', saith John (*1 John* 4:8): that is, he shows himself only in ways, expressions, and characters of love to his church. So Christ, as God, is all love to the church. And we see the Scriptures also to set out God as love, both in his essence and in his relations.

1. In relations of love to his church, he is a father: 'As a father pitieth his child, so the Lord pities them that fear him' (*Psa.* 103:13). And,

2. Also in those sweet attributes of love, which are his essence, as we see in Exodus 34:6. When God describes himself to Moses, after his desire to know him, in the former chapter, 'Thou canst not see me and live;' yet he would make him know him, as was fit for him to be known—'Jehovah, Jehovah, strong, merciful, gracious, long-suffering', &c. (*Exod.* 34:6). Thus God will be known in these attributes of consolation. So Christ, as God, is all love and mercy. Likewise Christ, as man, he was man for this end, to be all love and mercy. Take him in his office as Jesus, to be a Saviour; he carrieth salvation in his wings (*Mal.* 4:2), both by office and by nature.

And here how excellently is the expression of Christ's mercy, love, and patience set out! He knocks, 'my beloved knocks', &c., saying, 'Open.' He knocks for further entrance, as was showed before. Some he had already, but he would have further. As you know we have divers rooms and places in our houses. There is the court, the hall, the parlour, and closet: the hall for common persons, the parlour for those of better fashion, the closet for a man's self, and those that are intimate friends. So a Christian hath room in his heart for worldly thoughts, but his closet, his inmost affections, are kept for his inmost friend Christ, who is not content with the hall, but will come into the very closet. He knocks, that we should open, and let him come into our hearts, into our more intimate affections and love. Nothing will content him but intimateness, for he deserves it. As we shall see, he knocks for this end. But how doth he knock?

Every kind of way. 1. It is taken from the fashion of men in this kind, God condescending to speak to us in our own language. Sometimes, you know, there is a knocking or calling for entrance by voice, when a voice may serve, and then there needs no further knocking.

Sometimes both by voice and knocking. If voice will not serve, knocking comes after. So it is here. Christ doth knock and speak, useth a voice of his Word, and knocks by his works, and both together sometimes, whether by works of mercy or of judgment. He labours to enter into the soul, to raise the sleepy soul that way. He begins with mercy usually.

(1.) By *mercies*. All the creatures and blessings of God carry in them, as it were, a voice of God to the soul, that it would entertain his love. There goes a voice of love with every blessing. And the love, the mercy, and the goodness of God in the creature, is better than the creature itself. As we say of gifts, the love of the giver is better than the gift itself. So the love of God in all his sweet benefits is better than the thing itself. And so in that we have. There is a voice, as it were, entreating us to entertain God and Christ in all his mercies, yea, every creature, as one saith, and benefit, speaks, as it were, thus to us: We serve thee, that thou mayest serve him that made thee and us. There is a speech, as it were, in every favour. Which mercies, if they cannot prevail, then,

(2.) Come *corrections*, which are the voice of God also. 'Hear the rod, and him that smiteth' (*Mic.* 6:9).

2. But hath the rod a voice? Yes, for what do corrections speak, but amendment of the fault we are corrected for? So we must hear the rod. All corrections tend to this purpose. They are as knockings, that we should open to God and Christ. And because corrections of themselves will not amend us, God to this kind of knocking adds a voice. He teacheth and corrects together, 'Happy is that man that thou correctest, and teachest out of thy law', saith the psalmist (*Psa.* 94:12). Correction without teaching is to little purpose. Therefore God adds instruction to correction. He opens the conscience, so that it tells us it is for this that you are corrected; and together with conscience, gives his Spirit to tell us it is for this or that you are corrected; you are to blame in this, this you have done that you should not have done. So that corrections are knockings, but then especially when they have instruction thus with them. They are messengers from God, both blessings and

corrections (*Lev.* 26:24ff.). They will not away, especially corrections, till they have an answer, for they are sent of God, who will add seven times more; and if the first be not answered, then he sends after them. He will be sure to have an answer, either in our conversion or confusion, when he begins once.

3. Many other ways he useth to knock at our hearts. *The examples of those we live among that are good, they call upon us* (*Luke* 13:2, 3, *1 Cor.* 10:33). The patterns of their holy life, the examples of God's justice upon others, are speeches to us. God knocks at our door then. He intends our correction when he visits another, when, if we amend by that, he needs not take us in hand.

4. But besides all this, there is a more near knocking that Christ useth to the church, *his ministerial knocking*. When he was here in the days of his flesh, he was a preacher and prophet himself, and now he is ascended into heaven, he hath given gifts to men, and men to the church (*Eph.* 4:11ff.), whom he speaks by, to the end of the world. They are Christ's mouth, as we said of the penmen of holy Scripture. They were but the hand to write; Christ was the head to indite.[1] So in preaching and unfolding the Word they are but Christ's mouth and his voice, as it is said of John (*Matt.* 3:3). Now he is in heaven, he speaks by them, 'He that heareth you heareth me, he that despiseth you despiseth me' (*Luke* 10:16). Christ is either received or rejected in his ministers, as it is said of Noah's time, 'The Spirit of Christ preached in the days of Noah to the souls now in prison', &c. (*1 Pet.* 3:19). Christ as God did preach, before he was incarnate, by Noah to the old world, which is now in prison, in hell, because they refused to hear Christ speak to them by Noah. Much more now, after the days of his flesh, that he is in heaven, he speaks and preacheth to us, which, if we regard not, we are like to be in prison, as those souls are now in prison for neglecting the preaching of Noah. So the ministers are Christ's mouth. When they speak, he speaks by them, and they are as

---

[1] To compose or to write.—P.

ambassadors of Christ, whom they should imitate in mildness. 'We therefore, as ambassadors, beseech and entreat you, as if Christ by us should speak to you; so we entreat you to be reconciled unto God' (*2 Cor.* 5:20). And you know what heart-breaking words the apostle useth in all his epistles, especially when he writes to Christians in a good state, as to the Philippians, 'If there be any bowels of mercy, if there be any consolation in Christ', then regard what I say, 'be of one mind' (*Phil.* 2:1). And among the Thessalonians he was as a nurse to them (*1 Thess.* 2:7). So Christ speaks by them, and puts his own affections into them, that as he is tender and full of bowels[1] himself, so he hath put the same bowels into those that are his true ministers.

He speaks by them, and they use all kind of means that Christ may be entertained into their hearts. They move all stones, as it were, sometimes threatenings, sometimes entreaties, sometimes they come as 'sons of thunder' (*Mark* 3:17); sometimes with the still voice of sweet promises. And because one man is not so fit as another for all varieties of conditions and spirits, therefore God gives variety of gifts to his ministers, that they may knock at the heart of every man by their several gifts. For some have more rousing, some more insinuating gifts; some more legal, some more evangelical spirits, yet all for the church's good. John Baptist, by a more thundering way of preaching, to make way for Christ to come, threateneth judgment. But Christ, then he comes with a 'Blessed are the poor in spirit', 'blessed are they that hunger and thirst for righteousness', &c. (*Matt.* 5:3, 6). All kind of means have been used in the ministry from the beginning of the world.

5. And because of itself this ministry it is a dead letter; therefore he joins that with the Word, which knocks at the heart together with the Word, not severed from it, but is the life of it. *Oh! the Spirit is the life, and soul of the Word*; and when the inward

---

[1] Compassion, sympathy, mercy or affection, the bowels being regarded as the seat of the affections.—P.

word, or voice of the Spirit, and the outward word or ministry go together, then Christ doth more effectually knock and stir up the heart.

Now this Spirit with sweet inspirations knocks, moves the heart, lightens the understanding, quickens the dull affections, and stirs them up to duty: 'And thine ears shall hear a voice behind thee saying, This is the way, walk ye in it' (*Isa.* 30:21). The Spirit moves us sweetly, agreeable to our own nature. It offers not violence to us; but so as in Hosea 11:4, 'I drew them by the cords of a man.' That is, by reasons and motives befitting the nature of man, motives of love. So the Spirit, together with the word, works upon us, as we are men by rational motives, setting good before us, if we will let Christ in to govern and rule us; and by the danger on the contrary, so moving and stirring up our affections. These be 'the cords of a man.'

6. And besides his Spirit, God hath planted in us a *conscience* to call upon us, to be his vicar; a little god in us to do his office, to call upon us, direct us, check and condemn us, which in great mercy he hath placed in us.

Thus we see what means Christ useth here—his voice, works, and Word; works of mercy and of correction; his Word, together with his Spirit; and the conscience, that he hath planted, to be, as it were, a god in us, which together with his Spirit may move us to duty. This Augustine speaks of when he says, 'God spake in me oft, and I knew it not.'[1] He means it of conscience, together with the Spirit, stirring up motives to leave his sinful courses. God knocked in me, and I considered it not. I put off God, now I will, and now I will, but I had no moderation, I knew no limits. And whilst Christ thus knocketh, all the three persons may be said to do it. For as it is said elsewhere, that 'God was and is in Christ reconciling the world', &c. (2 *Cor.* 5:19). For whatsoever Christ did, he did it as anointed, and by office. And therefore God doth

---

[1] This is the touching burden of the early chapters of Augustine's *Confessions.*—G.

it in Christ, and by Christ, and so in some sort God died in his human nature, when Christ died. So here the Father beseecheth when Christ beseecheth, because he beseecheth, that is sent from him, and anointed of the Father. And God the Father stoops to us when Christ stoops, because he is sent of the Father, and doth all by his Father's command and commission (*John* 5:27). So besides his own bowels, there is the Father and the Spirit with Christ, who doth all by his Spirit, and from his Father, from whom he hath commission. Therefore God the Father, Son, and Holy Ghost knock at the heart. 'Open to me, my love, my dove, my undefiled;' but Christ especially by his Spirit, because it is his office.

Obj. But some may object, Christ can open to himself, why doth he not take the key and open, and make way for himself? Who will knock, when he hath the key himself? and who will knock, when there is none within to open? Christ can open to himself, and we have no free will, nor power to open.

Bellarmine makes this objection, and speaks very rudely, that he is an unwise man to knock, where there is no man within to open; and that if Christ knock, and we cannot open, it is a delusion to exhort to open, and that therefore there must needs be free will in us to open.

The answer is, *first*, Christ speaks to the spouse here, and so, many such exhortations are given to them that have the Spirit of God already, who could by the help thereof open. For good and gracious men are moved first by the Spirit, and then they move; they are acted first by the Spirit, and then they do act by it, not of themselves; as the inferior orbs move not, but as they are moved by the superior. The question is not of them in the state of grace, but at their first conversion, when especially we say that Christ speaks to them that he means to convert. He knocks at their hearts, and opens together with his speech. Then there goes a power that they shall open; for his words are operative words. As it was in the creation, 'Let there be light', it was an operative word, 'and there was light' (*Gen.* 1:3). Let there be such a creature, it was an operative working word, and there was such a creature presently. So he opens together with that word. With that invitation and command there goes an almighty power to enable the soul to open. Were it not a wise reason to say, when Christ called to Lazarus to 'come forth' (*John* 11:43), that we should reason he had life to yield to Christ, when he bade him come forth? No, he was rotten, in his grave, almost; but with Christ's speaking to Lazarus, there went an almighty power, that gave life to him, by which life he heard what Christ said, 'Arise, Lazarus.' So Christ by his Spirit clothes his word in the ministry, when he speaks to people with a mighty power. As the minister speaks to the ear, Christ speaks, opens, and unlocks the heart at the same time; and gives it power to open, not from itself, but from Christ. Paul speaks to Lydia's ear, Christ to her heart, and opened it, as the text says (*Acts* 16:13), whereby she believes;[1] so Christ opens the heart.

Quest. But why doth he thus work?

Ans. Because he will preserve nature, and the principles thereof; and so he deals with us, working accordingly. The manner of working of the reasonable creature, is to work freely by a sweet inclination, not by violence. Therefore when he works the work of conversion, he doth it in a sweet manner, though it be mighty for the efficaciousness of it. He admonisheth us with entreaty and persuasion, as if we did it ourselves. But though the manner be thus sweet, yet with this manner there goeth an almighty power. Therefore he doth it strongly as coming from himself, and sweetly, as the speaking is to us, preserving our nature. So the action is from him, which hath an almighty power with it. As holy Bernard saith, 'Thou dealest sweetly with my soul in regard of myself;' that is, thou workest upon me, as a man with the words of love, yet strongly in regard of thyself. For except he add strength

---

[1] *Lydia's Heart Opened* is the title of one of Sibbes' most delightful minor books.—G.

with sweetness, the work will not follow; but when there are both, an almighty work is wrought in the soul of a Christian; and so wrought, as the manner of man's working is preserved in a sweet and free manner, whilst he is changed from contrary to contrary. And it is also with the greatest reason that can be, in that now he sees more reason to be good, than in the days of darkness he did to be naught, God works so sweetly. God speaks to us after the manner of men, but he works in us as the great God. He speaks to us as a man in our own language, sweetly; but he works in us almightily, after a powerful manner, as God. So we must understand such phrases as these, 'I knock; open to me, my love, my dove', &c. We may take further notice,

Obs. That *the heart of a Christian is the house and temple of Christ.*

He hath but two houses to dwell in; the heavens, and the heart of an humble brokenhearted sinner (*Isa.* 57:15).

Quest. How can Christ come into the soul?

Ans. He comes into the heart by his Spirit. It is a special entertainment that he looks for. Open thine ears that thou mayest hear my word; thy love, that thou mayest love me more; thy joy, that thou mayest delight in me more; open thy whole soul that I may dwell in it. A Christian should be God's house, and a true Christian is the true temple of God. He left the other two temples therefore; but his own body, and his church he never leaves. For a house is for a man to solace himself in, and to rest in, and to lay up whatsoever is precious to him. So with Christ. A man will repair his house, so Christ will repair our souls, and make them better, and make them more holy, and spiritual, and every way fit for such a guest as he is.

Quest. How shall we know whether Christ dwells in our hearts or not?

Ans. We may know by the servants what master dwells in an house. If Christ be in the soul, there comes out of the house good speeches. And we watch the senses, so as there comes nothing in to defile the soul, and disturb Christ, and nothing goes out to offend God. When we hear men full of gracious sweet speeches, it is a sign Christ dwells there. If we hear the contrary, it shows Christ dwells not there. For Christ would move the whole man to do that which might edify and comfort.

Again, where Christ comes, *assistance comes there.* When Christ was born, all Jerusalem was in an uproar; so, when Christ is born in the soul, there is an uproar. Corruption arms itself against grace. There is a combat betwixt flesh and spirit. But Christ subdues the flesh by little and little. God's image is stamped upon the soul where Christ is; and if we have opened unto the Lord of glory, he will make us glorious.

Christ hath never enough of us, nor we have never enough of him till we be in heaven; and, therefore, we pray, 'Thy kingdom come.' And till Christ comes in his kingdom, he desires his kingdom should come to us. Open, saith he. It is a stupendous condescendence, when he that hath heaven to hold him, angels to attend him, those glorious creatures; he that hath the command of every creature, that do yield presently homage when he commands, the frogs, and lice, and all the host of heaven are ready to do his will! for him to condescend and to entreat us to be good to our own souls, and to beseech us to be reconciled to him, as if he had offended us, who have done the wrong and not he, or as if that we had power and riches to do him good; here greatness beseecheth meanness, riches poverty, all-sufficiency want, and life itself comes to dead, drowsy souls. What a wondrous condescending is this! Yet, notwithstanding, Christ vouchsafes to make the heart of a sinful, sleepy man to be his house, his temple. He knocks, and knocks here, saying, 'Open to me', &c.

Use 1. This is useful many ways, as *first, cherish all the good conceits*[1] *we can of Christ.* Time will come that the devil will set

---

[1] That is, conceptions.—G.

upon us with sharp temptations, fiery darts, temptations to despair, and present Christ amiss, as if Christ were not willing to receive us. Whenas you see he knocks at our hearts to open to him, useth mercies and judgments, the ministry of his Spirit and conscience, and all. Will not he then entertain us, when we come to him, that seeks this entertainment at our hands? Certainly he will. Therefore, let us labour to cherish good conceits of Christ. This is the finisher and beginning of the conversion of a poor sinful soul, even to consider the infinite love and condescendence of Christ Jesus for the good of our souls. We need not wonder at this his willingness to receive us, when we first know that God became man, happiness became misery, and life itself came to die, and to be 'a curse for us' (*Gal.* 3:13). He hath done the greater, and will he not do the less? Therefore, think [it] not strange that he useth all these means, considering how low he descended into the womb of the virgin for us (*Eph.* 4:9).

Now such considerations as these, being mixed with the Spirit and set on by him, are effectual for the conversion of poor souls. Is there such love in God to become man, and to be a suitor to woo me for my love? Surely, thinks the soul then, he desires my salvation and conversion. And to what kind of persons doth he come? None can object unworthiness. I am poor: 'He comes to the poor' (*Isa.* 14:32; 29:19). I am laden and wretched: 'Come unto me, all ye that are weary and laden' (*Matt.* 11:28). I have nothing: 'Come and buy honey, milk, and wine, though you have nothing' (*Isa.* 55:1). He takes away all objections. But I am stung with the sense of my sins: 'Blessed are they that hunger and thirst', &c. (*Matt.* 5:6). But I am empty of all: 'Blessed are the poor in spirit' (*Matt.* 5:3). You can object nothing, but it is taken away by the Holy Ghost, wisely preventing[1] all the objections of a sinful soul. This is the beginning of conversion, these very conceits. And when we are converted, these thoughts, entertained with admiration of Christ's

---

[1] That is, anticipating.—G.

condescending, are effectual to give Christ further entrance into the soul, whereby a more happy communion is wrought still more and more between Christ and the soul of a Christian.

Use 2. *Oh, but take heed that these make not any secure.* For, if we give not entrance to Christ, all this will be a further aggravation of our damnation. How will this justify the sentence upon us hereafter, when Christ shall set us on the left hand, and say, 'Depart from me' (*Matt.* 25:41), for I invited you to come to me, I knocked at the door of your hearts, and you would give me no entrance. Depart from us, said you; therefore, now, Depart you from me. What do profane persons in the church but bid Christ depart from them, especially in the motions of his Spirit? They entertain him in the outward room, the brain; they know a little of Christ, but, in the heart, the secret room, he must not come there to rule. Is it not equal that he should bid us, 'Depart, ye cursed, I know you not' (*Matt.* 25:12, 41)?; you would not give entrance to me, I will not now to you, as to the foolish virgins he speaks (*Matt.* 25:12, *Prov.* 1:28). Wisdom knocks, and hath no entrance; therefore, in times of danger, they call upon her, but she rejoiceth at their destruction. Where God magnifies his mercy in this kind, in sweet allurements, and inviting by judgments, mercies, ministry, and Spirit, he will magnify his judgment after. Those that have neglected heaven with the prerogatives and advantages in this kind, they shall be cast into hell. 'Woe to thee, Chorazin', &c. (*Matt.* 11:21), as you know in the gospel. This is one thing that may humble us of this place and nation, that Christ hath no further entrance, nor better entertainment after so long knocking! for the entertaining of his Word is the welcoming of himself. 'Let the word of God dwell plentifully in you' (*Col.* 3:16). And, 'Let Christ dwell in your hearts by faith' (*Eph.* 3:17). Compare those places; let the Word dwell plenteously in you by wisdom, and let Christ dwell in your hearts by faith. For then doth Christ dwell in the heart, when the truth dwells in us. Therefore, what entertainment we give to his truth, we give to himself. Now what means of knocking hath he not used among us a long time? For works of all sorts, he hath drawn us by the cords of a man, by all kind of favours. For mercies, how many deliverances have we had (no nation the like; we are a miracle of the Christian world) from foreign invasion, and domestical conspiracies at home? How many mercies do we enjoy! Abundance, together with long peace and plenty. Besides, if this would not do, God hath added corrections with all these, in every element, in every manner. Infection in the air, judgments in inundations. We have had rumours of wars, &c. Threatenings, shakings of the rod only, but such as might have awaked us. And then he hath knocked at our hearts by the example of other nations. By what he hath done to them, he hath showed us what he might justly have done to us. We are no better than they.

As for his ministerial knocking: above threescore years we have lived under the ministry of the gospel. This land hath been Goshen, a land of light, when many other places are in darkness. Especially we that live in this Goshen, this place, and such like, where the light shines in a more abundant measure. Ministers have been sent, and variety of gifts. There hath been piping and mourning, as Christ complains in his time, that they were like froward children, that neither sweet piping nor doleful mourning would move to be tractable to their fellows. 'They had John, who came mourning' (*Matt.* 11:18), and Christ comforting with blessing in his mouth. All kind of means have been used.

And for the motions of his Spirit, who are there at this time, who thus live in the church under the ministry, who cannot say that God thereby hath smote their hearts, those hard rocks, again and again, and awaked their consciences, partly with corrections public and personal, and partly with benefits? Yet notwithstanding, what little way is given to Christ! Many are indifferent, and lukewarm either way, but rather incline to the worst.

Let us then consider of it. The greater means, the greater judgments afterwards, if we be not won by them. Therefore let us labour to hold Christ, to entertain him. Let him have the best room in our souls, to dwell in our hearts. Let us give up the keys to him, and desire him to rule our understandings, to know nothing but him, and what may stand with his truth, not to yield to any error or corruption. Let us desire that he would rule in our wills and affections; sway all, give all to him. For that is his meaning, when he says, 'Open to me', so that I may rule, as in mine own house, as the husband rules in his family, and a king in his kingdom. He will have all yielded up to him. And he comes to beat down all, whatsoever is exalted against him; and that is the reason men are so loath to open unto him. They know if they open to the Spirit of God, he will turn them out of their fool's paradise, and make them resolve upon other courses of life, which, because they will not turn unto, they repel the sweet motions of the Spirit of Christ, and pull away his graces, building bulwarks against Christ, as lusts, strange imaginations, and resolutions (2 *Cor.* 10:3-5). Let the ministers say what they will, and the Spirit move as he will, thus they live, and thus they will live. Let us take notice, therefore, of all the means that God useth to the State, and to us in particular, and everyone labour to amend one. Every soul is the temple, the house, Christ should dwell in. Let every soul, therefore, among us, consider what means Christ useth to come into his soul to dwell with him, and to rule there.

And what shall we lose by it? Do we entertain Christ to our loss? Doth he come empty? No; he comes with all grace. His goodness is a communicative, diffusive goodness. He comes to spread his treasures, to enrich the heart with all grace and strength, to bear all afflictions, to encounter all dangers, to bring peace of conscience, and joy in the Holy Ghost. He comes, indeed, to make our hearts, as it were, a heaven. Do but consider this. He comes not for his own ends; but to empty his goodness into our hearts. As a breast that desires to empty itself when it is full; so this fountain hath the fulness of a fountain, which strives to empty his goodness into our souls. He comes out of love to us. Let these considerations melt our hearts for our unkindness, that we suffer him to stand so long at the door knocking, as it is said here.

If we find not our suits answered so soon as we would, remember, we have made him also wait for us. Perhaps to humble us, and after that to encourage us, he will make us wait; for we have made him wait. Let us not give over, for certainly he that desires us to open, that he may pour out his grace upon us, he will not reject us when we come to him (*Matt.* 7:7, *Hab.* 2:3). If he answers us not at first, yet he will at last. Let us go on and wait, seeing there is no one duty pressed more in Scripture than this. And we see it is equity, 'He waits for us' (*Isa.* 30:18). It is good reason we should wait for him. If we have not comfort presently when we desire it, let us attend upon Christ, as he hath attended upon us, for when he comes, he comes with advantage (*Isa.* 60:16). So that when we wait, we lose nothing thereby, but are gainers by it, increasing our patience (*Isa.* 64:4, *James* 1:4). The longer we wait, he comes with the more abundant grace and comfort in the end, and shows himself rich, and bountiful to them that wait upon him (*Isa.* 40:1ff.).

SERMON 6

*It is the voice of my beloved that knocketh, saying, Open
to me, my sister, my love, my dove, my undefiled; &c.*
SONG OF SOLOMON 5:2

IN the first part of this verse hath been handled the church's
own condition, which she was in, after some blessed feelings
that she had of the love of Christ.

Now, in the next words, the church sets down an acknowledgment of the carriage of Christ to her in this her sleepy condition.
'It is the voice of my beloved that knocks, saying, Open to me, my
sister, my love, my dove', &c. She acknowledgeth Christ's voice in
her sleepy estate, and sets down his carriage thus, 'how he knocks',
and then also speaks, 'Open to me', and then sets down what he
suffered for her, 'My head is filled with dew, and my locks with the
drops of the night.' And that nothing might be wanting that might
move her heart to respect this his carriage towards her, he useth
sweet titles, a loving compellation, 'Open to me', saith he, 'my sister, my love, my dove, my undefiled', as so many cords of love to
draw her. So here wants neither loving carriage, sweet words, nor
patience. 'It is the voice of my beloved that knocketh.'

The church, as she takes notice of the voice of Christ, so she
doth also of the means he useth, and seeth his love in them all. 'It
is the voice of my beloved that knocketh, saying, Open to me', &c.
Here is also another distinguishing note of a sound Christian from
an unsound. A sanctified spirit sees Christ in the means. This is,
says the heart, the word of Christ, and this the mercy of Christ, to

take such pains with my soul, to send his ministers, to provide his ordinances, to give gifts to men, and men to the church (*Eph.* 4:11, 12). 'It is the voice of my beloved that knocketh.'

But we must especially understand it of the ministerial voice, whereby Christ doth chiefly make way for himself into the heart, and that by all kind of ways dispensed therein: as gifts of all sorts, some rougher, some milder, all kind of methods and ways in the ministry to make way for himself. First of all by the threatenings of the law, and by terrors. As John was sent before Christ, and as the storm went before the still and calm voice, wherein God came to Elijah (*1 Kings* 19:12), so he useth all kinds of courses in the ministry. And ministers, by the direction of the Spirit, turn themselves, as it were, into all shapes and fashions, both of speech and spirit, to win people to God, in so much, that God appeals to them, 'What could I have done more for my church, that I have not done?' (*Isa.* 5:4).

Use. Therefore let us take notice of this voice of Christ in the word, and not think as good Samuel thought, that Eli spake, when God spake (*1 Sam.* 3:5). Let us think that God speaks to us in the ministry, that Christ comes to woo us, and win us thereby.

And we ministers are the friends of the Bridegroom, who are to hear what Christ saith and would have said to the church; and we must pray to him, that he would teach us what to teach others. We are to procure the contract, and to perfect it till the marriage be in heaven. That is our work.

And you that are hearers, if you do not regard Christ's sweet voice in the ministry, which God hath appointed for the government of the world, know that there is a voice that you cannot shake off. That peremptory voice at the day of judgment, when he will say, 'Go, ye cursed, into hell fire', &c. (*Matt.* 25:30). And that God who delights to be styled 'a God hearing prayer' (*Psa.* 65:2), will not hear thee, but saith, 'Such a one as turns his ear away from hearing the law, his prayer is abominable' (*Prov.* 28:9). It is a doleful thing, that he that made us, and allureth us in the ministry, that follows us with all evidences of his love, and adds, together with the ministry, many sweet motions of his Spirit, that he should delight in the destruction of his creatures, and not endure the sight of them, 'Depart away from me, ye cursed, into hell fire', &c. There are scarce any in the church, but Christ hath allured at one time or other to come in, and in many he opens their understandings in a great measure and knocks upon their hearts, that they, as it were, half open unto Christ, like Agrippa, that said to Paul, 'Thou almost persuadest me to be a Christian' (*Acts* 26:28). So Herod 'did many things, and he heard gladly' (*Mark* 6:20). They are half open, seem to open, but are not effectually converted. But at last they see, that further yielding will not stand with that which they resolve not to part with, their lusts, their present condition, that they make their God, and their heaven. Whereupon they shut the door again. When they have opened it a little to the motions of God's Spirit, they dare give no further way, because they cannot learn the first lesson in Christ's school, to deny themselves and take up their cross.

This is an undoubted conclusion. Our blessed Saviour giveth such means and motions of his Spirit to the vilest persons in the church, that their own hearts tell them, they have more means and sweeter motions than they yield to, and that the sentence of condemnation is not pronounced upon them for merely not knowing of Christ, but upon some grounds of rebellion, in that they go not so far as they are provoked,[1] and put on[2] by the Spirit of God. They resist the Holy Spirit. There can be no resistance where there is not a going beyond the desire and will of him whom he resisteth (*Acts* 7:51). A man doth not resist, when he gives way as far as he is moved. There is no wicked man in the church, that gives so much way as he is moved and stirred to by the Spirit and Word of God.

[1] That is, stirred up.—G.

[2] That is, incited.—G.

Away then with these impudent, ungracious objections about God's decree for matter of election. Let us make it sure. And for any ill conceits that may rise in our hearts about that other of reprobation, let this damp them all, that in the church of God, he offers unto the vilest wretch so much means, with the motions of his Spirit, as he resisting, proves inexcusable; his own rebellion therefore being the cause of his rejection. Let men cease from cavilling;[1] God hath that in their own breast, in the heart of every carnal man, which will speak for God against him, and stop his mouth that he shall be silent and speechless at the day of judgment (*Matt.* 22:12).

Thus we see that Christ doth condescend so low as to account it almost a part of his happiness to have our souls for a temple to dwell in, to rule there. Therefore he makes all this earnest suit, with strong expressions what he suffereth.

And since Christ bears this great and large affection to his poor church, it may encourage us to pray heartily for the same, and to spread before God the state thereof. Why, Lord? it is that part of the world that is thy sister, thy love, thy dove, thy undefiled; the communion with whom thou lovest above all the world besides. It is a strong argument to prevail with God. Therefore let us commend the state of the church at this time, or at any time, with this confidence. Lord, it is the church that thou lovest. They thought they prevailed much with Christ when they laboured to bring him to Lazarus, saying, 'Lord, he whom thou lovest is sick' (*John* 11:3). So say we, the church whom thou lovest, that is, thy only love, in whom thy love is concenterate,[2] as it were, and gathered to a head, as though thou hadst no other love in the world but thy church, this thy love is in this state and condition. It is good to think of prevailing arguments; not to move God so much as our own hearts; to strengthen our faith to prevail with

[1] Raising empty, trifling objections.—P.

[2] That is, concentrated.—G.

God, which is much fortified with the consideration of Christ's wondrous loving expression to his poor church. Then come to Christ, offer thyself, and he will meet thee. Are not two loving well-wishers well met? When thou offerest thyself to him, and he seeks thy love, will he reject thee when thou comest to him that seeks thy love, and seeketh it in this passionate, affectionate manner, as he doth? Therefore, be of good comfort. He is more willing to entertain us than we are to come to him.

And for those that have relapsed any kind of way, let them not be discouraged to return again to Christ. The church here was in a drowsy, sleepy estate, and used him unkindly; yet he is so patient, that he waits her leisure, as it were, and saith, 'Open to me, my sister, my love', &c. Thomas was so untoward, that he would not believe, 'unless he did see the print of the nails', &c., in Christ's body. Yet Christ was so gracious as he condescendeth to poor Thomas (*John* 20:27). So to Peter after he was fallen (*Mark* 16:7), and to the church after backsliding.

'Open to me, my sister', &c. Hence observe further,

That Christ hath never enough of his church till he hath it in heaven, where are indeed the kisses of the spouse, and of Christ. In the meanwhile 'Open, open', still. Christ had the heart of the spouse in some measure already; but yet there were some corners of the heart that were not so filled with Christ as they should be. He was not so much in her understanding, will, joy, delight, and love, as he would be. Therefore, open thy understanding more and more to embrace me, and divine truths that are offered thee. Open thy love to solace me more and more. For God in Christ, having condescended to the terms of friendship, nay, to intimate terms of friendship in marriage with us; therefore[1] the church in her right temper, hath never enough of Christ, but desires further union, and communion still. It being the description of the people of God, that 'they love the appearance of Christ' (*2 Tim.* 4:8, *Rev.* 22:20),

[1] As, deleted here.—G.

as they loved his first appearance, and waited for 'the consolation of Israel' (*Luke* 2:25); so they love his second appearing, and are never quiet, till he comes again in the flesh, to consummate the marriage begun here. So Christ also he is as desirous of them, yea, they are his desires that breed their desires. 'Open to me, my sister, my love, my dove', &c. Again his love and pity moves him to desire further to come into us. Christ knows what is in our hearts. If he be not there, there is that that should not be there. What is in the brain where Christ is not? A deal of worldly projects, nothing worth. What is in our joy if Christ be not there? Worldly joy, which cleaves to things worse than itself. If a man were anatomised, and seen into, he would be ashamed of himself, if he did see himself. Christ therefore, out of pity to our souls, would not have the devil there. Christ knows it is good for our souls to give way to him, therefore he useth all sweet allurements, 'Open to me, my sister, my love', &c. Christ hath never his fill, till he close with the soul perfectly; so that nothing be in the soul above him, nothing equal to him. Therefore 'Open, open', still.

Again, he sets down, to move the church the more to open to him, the inconveniences that he endured, 'My head is filled with dew', &c. Wherein he shows what he suffered, which sufferings are of two sorts: in himself; in his ministers. In himself, and in his own blessed person, what did he endure! What patience had he in enduring the refractory[1] spirits of men, when he was here! How many indignities did he digest[2] in his disciples after their conversion! Towards his latter end, his head was not only filled with the drops, but his body filled with drops of blood. Drops of blood came from him, because of the anguish of his spirit, and the sense of God's wrath for our sins. Upon the cross, what did he endure there! That sense of God's anger there, was only for our sins. 'My God, my God, why hast thou forsaken me?' (*Matt.* 27:46). What

[1] Obstinate.—P.

[2] That is, bear.—G.

should we speak of his going up and down doing good, preaching in his own person, setting whole nights apart for prayer! And then for what he suffers in his ministers. There he knocks, and saith, 'Open', in them. And how was he used in the apostles that were after him, and in the ministers of the church ever since! What have they endured! for he put a spirit of patience upon them. And what indignities endured they in the primitive church, that were the publishers of the gospel! Those sweet publishers thereof, drawing men to open to Christ, were killed for preaching. So cruel is the heart, that it offereth violence to them that love them most, that love their souls. And what greater love than the love of the soul! Yet this is the Satanical temper and disposition of men's hearts. They hate those men most, that deal this way most truly and lovingly with them. It is not that the gospel is such an hard message. It is the word of reconciliation, and the word of life; but the heart hates it, because it would draw men from their present condition; and 'therefore condemnation is come into the world, in that men hate the light, because their works are evil' (*John* 3:19). Is there anything truly and cordially hated but grace? and are any persons heartily and cordially hated in the world so much as the promulgers and publishers of grace, and the professors of it? because it upbraids most of all, and meddles with the corruptions of men, that are dearer to them than their own souls.

Now, what patience is there in Christ to suffer himself in his messengers, and his children to be thus used! Nor it is not strange to say that Christ stands thus in his ministers; for it is said, 'That Christ by his Spirit preached in the days of Noah, to the souls now in prison' (*1 Pet.* 3:19). Christ preached in Noah's time, before he was incarnate, much more doth he preach now. And as he was patient then to endure the old world, unto whom Noah preached a hundred and twenty years; so he is patient now in his ministers to preach still by the same Spirit, even to us still, and yet the entertainment[1] in many places is, as Paul complains, 'Though the more I love you, yet the less I am beloved of you' (*2 Cor.* 12:15).

Use 1. *Let these things move us to be patient towards God and Christ, if we be corrected in any kind,* considering that Christ is so patient towards us, and to wait upon him with patience. How long hath he waited for our conversion! How long doth he still wait for the thorough giving up of our souls to him! Shall we think much, then, to wait a little while for him?

Use 2. *And let this Spirit of Christ strengthen us likewise in our dealing with others,* as to bear with evil men, and as it is, 'to wait, if God will at any time give them repentance' (*2 Tim.* 2:25, 26). Neither may we be so short-spirited, that if we have not an answer, presently to give over. We should imitate Christ here. Never give over as long as God continues life with any advantage and opportunity to do good to any soul. Wait, if God at any time will give them grace. 'Open to me, my sister, my love', &c.

Use 3. *Let this again work upon us, that our Saviour Christ here would thus set forth his love, and his patience in his love,* in bearing with us thus, under the resemblance of a silly suitor that comes afar off, and stands at the door, and knocks. That Christ should stoop thus in seeking the good of our souls, let this win and quicken our hearts with all readiness and thankfulness to receive him when he comes to work in our souls. Considering that Christ hath such a care of us by himself, his ministers, and the motions of his Spirit, who joins with his ministry, let not us therefore be careless of our own souls, but let it move our hearts to melt to him. The motives may be seen more in the particular compellations. 'Open to me, my sister, my love', &c.

'My sister'. This was spoken of before in the former verse. The church of God is Christ's sister and spouse. We are knit to him both by consanguinity and by affinity. The nearest affinity is marriage, and the nearest consanguinity is sister. So that there are all bonds to knit us to Christ. Whatsoever is strong in any bond, he

---

[1] That is, the reception, treatment.—P.

knits us to him by it. Is there any love in an husband, a brother, a mother, a friend, in an head to the members? in anything in the world? Is there any love scattered in any relation, gather it all into one, and all that love, and a thousand times more than that, is in Christ in a more eminent manner. Therefore he styles himself in all these sweet relations, to show that he hath the love of all. Will a sister shut out a brother, when the brother comes to visit her, and do her all good? Is this unkindness even in nature, to look strangely upon a man that is near akin, that comes and saith, 'Open to me, my sister'? If the sister should shut out the brother, were it not most unnatural? And is it not monstrous in grace, when our brother comes for our good, and in pity to our souls, to let him stand without doors? Remember that Christ hath the same affections, to account us brothers and sisters, now in heaven, as he had when he was upon the earth. For after his resurrection, saith he to his disciples, 'I go to my God, and to your God, to my Father, and to your Father' (*John* 20:17). He calls himself our brother, having one common Father in heaven, and one Spirit, and one inheritance, &c. This is a sweet relation. Christ being our brother, his heart cannot but melt towards us in any affliction. Joseph dissembled a while, out of politic wisdom (*Gen.* 42:7ff.), but because he had a brother's heart to Benjamin, therefore at last he could not hold, but melted into tears, though he made his countenance as though he had not regarded. So our Joseph, now in heaven, may seem to withdraw all tokens and signs of brotherly love from us, and not to own us; but it is only in show, he is our brother still. His heart, first or last, will melt towards his brethren, to their wonderful comfort. 'My sister', &c.

'My love'. That word we had not yet. It is worthy also a little standing on, for all these four words be, as it were, the attractive cords to draw the spouse, not only by showing what he had suffered, but by sweet titles, 'My love, My dove'.

What, had Christ no love but his spouse? Did his love go out of his own heart to her, as it were? It is strange, yet true. Christ's love is so great to his church and children, and so continual[1] to it, that his church and people and every Christian soul is the seat of his love. That love in his own breast being in them, they are his love, because he himself is there, and one with them (*John* 17:26).

He loves all his creatures. They have all some beams of his goodness, which he must needs love. Therefore he loves them as creatures, and as they be more or less capable of a higher degree of goodness; but for his church and children, they are his love indeed.

Quest. But what is the ground of such love?

Ans. 1. *He loves them as he beholds them in his father's choice,* as they are elected of God, and given unto himself in election. 'Thine they are, thou gavest them me' (*John* 17:6). Christ, looking on us in God's election and choice, loves us.

Ans. 2. Again, *he loves us because he sees his own graces in us.* He loves what is his in us. Before we be actually his, he loves us with a love of good will, to wish all good to us. But when we have anything of his Spirit, that our natures are altered and changed, he loves us with a love of the intimatest friendship, with the love of an head, husband, friend, and what we can imagine. He loves his own image. Paul saith that 'the wife is the glory of her husband' (*1 Cor.* 11:7), because whatsoever is in a good husband, the wife expresseth it by reflection. So the church is the glory of Christ; she reflects his excellencies, though in a weak measure. They show forth his virtues or praises, as Peter speaks (*1 Pet.* 2:9). Thus he sees his own image in her, and the Holy Ghost in his church. He loves her, and these in her, so as whether we regard the Father or himself or his Spirit, the church is his love.

Ans. 3. *If we consider also what he hath done and suffered for her,* we may well say the church is his love. Besides the former favours, not to speak of election, he chose us before we were. In time he did choose us by actual election, by which he called

---

[1] That is, abiding.—G.

us. We had an existence, but we resisted. He called us when we resisted. And then also he justified us, and clothed us with his own righteousness, and after feeds us with his own body. As the soul is the most excellent thing in the world, so he hath provided for it the most excellent ornaments. It hath food and ornaments proportionable. What love is this, that he should feed our souls with his own body, and clothe us with his own righteousness! 'He loved me', saith Paul (*Gal.* 2:20). What was the effect of his love? 'He gave himself for me.' He gave himself, both that we might have a righteousness to clothe us with in the sight of God, and he gave himself that he might be the bread of life, 'My flesh is meat indeed, and my blood is drink indeed' (*John* 6:55). The guilty, the self-accusing soul feeds upon Christ dying for its sins. Again (*Rev.* 1:5), you have his love set forth, 'He loved us;' and how doth he witness it? 'He hath washed us with his own blood, and hath made us kings, and priests', &c. The like you have, 'He loved us, and gave himself a sweet sacrifice to God for us' (*Eph.* 5:2). When this world is at an end, we shall see what his love is. He is not satisfied till we be all in one place. What doth he pray for to his Father? 'Father, I will that those whom thou hast given me be with me where I am', &c. (*John* 17:24). Run through all the whole course of salvation, election, vocation, justification, glorification, you shall see his love in all of them. But it were an infinite argument to follow to show the love of Christ, which is beyond all knowledge (*Eph.* 3:19); and it is too large for us to know all the dimensions of it, to see the height, breadth, depth, and length of it, which we should ever think, speak, and meditate of, because the soul is then in the most fit temper to serve, love, and glorify God, when it is most apprehensive of his great love.

This phrase imports divers things.

1. *That there is no saving love to any out of the church*, which is his *love*. It is, as it were, confined in the church, as if all the beams of his love met in that centre, as we see when the beams of the sun

meet in a glass, they burn, because many are there united. So in the church all his love doth meet.

2. Then the church is his love also, *because whatsoever she hath or hopes for is from his love, and is nothing but his love.* The church, as it is a church, is nothing but the love of Christ. That there is a church so endowed, so graced, so full of the hope of glory, it is out of his love.

And for the properties of it.

1. It is *a free love, a preventing love*. He loved us before ever we could love him. He loved us when we resisted him, and were his enemies.

2. It is *a most tender love,* as you have it in Isaiah 49:15, 'Can a mother forget her sucking child? If she should, yet will not I forget thee. Thou art written on the palms of my hands', &c. He hath us in his heart, in his eye, in his hand, in a mother's heart, and beyond it. He hath a tender eye and a powerful hand to maintain his church (*Deut.* 33:3).

3. It is *a most transcendent and careful love.* All comparisons are under it.

4. And it is *a most intimate invincible love*, that nothing could quench it.

As we see here the church droopeth, and had many infirmities, yet she is Christ's love. So that the love of Christ is a kind of love that is unconquerable; no water will ever quench it; no sin of ours; no infirmity. So as it is very comfortable that the church considered under infirmities is yet the love of Christ. 'I sleep, but my heart waketh', yet Christ comes with, 'My love, my dove', &c.

Quest. But what, cannot Christ see matter of weakness, sinfulness, hatred, and dislike in the church?

Ans. Oh yes, to pity, help, and heal it, but not at all to diminish his love, but to manifest it so much the more. His love is a tender love, sensible of all things wherewith we displease him, yet it is so invincible and unconquerable, that it overcomes all. Again, he sees ill indeed in us, but he sees in us some good of his own also, which moves him more to love, than that that is ill in us, moves him to hate. For what he sees of ours, he sees with a purpose to vanquish, mortify, and eat it out. The Spirit is as fire to consume it. He is as water to wash it. But what he sees of his own, he sees with a purpose to increase it more and more, and to perfect it. Therefore he says, 'my love', notwithstanding that the church was asleep.

Use. This therefore serves greatly for our comfort, to search what good Christ by his Spirit hath wrought in our hearts; what faith, what love, what sanctified judgment, what fire of holy affections to him, and to the best things. O let us value ourselves by that that is good, that Christ hath in us. We are Christ's love notwithstanding we are sleepy. If we be displeased with this our state; that as Christ dislikes it, so if we by the Spirit dislike it, the matter is not what sin we have in us, but how we are affected to it. Have we that ill in us, which is truly the grief of our hearts and souls, which as Christ dislikes, so we abhor it, and would be purged, and rid of it; and it is the grief of our hearts and souls, that we cannot be better, and more lovely in Christ's eye! then let us not be discouraged. For Christ esteems of his church highly, even as his very love, even at that time when she was sleepy; and may teach us in time of temptation not to hearken to Satan, who then moves us to look altogether upon that which is naught in us, thereby to abate our love to Christ, and our apprehension of his to us. For he knows if we be sensible of the love of Christ to us, we shall love him again. For love is a kind of fire, an active quality, which will set us about glorifying God, and pulling down Satan's kingdom. As we say in nature, fire doth all; (what work almost can a man work without fire, by which all instruments are made and heated? &c.). So grace doth all with love. God first doth manifest to our souls his love to us in Christ, and quicken us by his Spirit, witnessing his love to us, wherewith he warms our hearts, kindles and inflames them so with love, that we love him again; which love hath a constraining, sweet violence to put us upon all duties, to suffer, to do, to resist anything. If a man be in

THE LOVE OF CHRIST

love with Christ, what will be harsh to him in the world? The devil knows this well enough; therefore one of his main engines and temptations is to weaken our hearts in the sense of God's love and of Christ's. Therefore let us be as wise for our souls as he is subtle, and politic against them; as watchful for our own comfort, as he is to discomfort us, and make us despair. Let us be wise to gather all the arguments of Christ's love that we can.

Quest. But how shall we know that Christ loves us in this peculiar manner?

Ans. 1. *First*, search what course he takes and hath taken to *draw thee nearer unto him.* 'He chastiseth everyone that he loveth' (*Heb.* 12:6). Seasonable corrections sanctified, is a sign of Christ's love; when he will not suffer us to thrive in sin; when we cannot speak nor do amiss; but either he lasheth us in our conscience for it, and by his Spirit checks us, or else stirs up others, one thing or other to make us out of love with sin.

Ans. 2. Again, we may gather Christ's love by this, *if we have any love to divine things, and can set a great price upon the best things;* upon the Word, because it is Christ's Word; upon grace, prizing the image of Christ, and the new creature. When we can set an high value upon communion with Christ, the sense of his love in our hearts, and all spiritual prerogatives and excellencies above all things, this is an excellent argument of Christ's love to us. Our love is but a reflection of his; and therefore if we have love to anything that is good, we have it from him first. If a wall that is cold become hot, we say, the sun of necessity must shine on it first, because it is nothing but cold stone of itself. So if our hearts, that are naturally cold, be heated with the love of divine things, certainly we may say, Christ hath shined here first; for naturally our hearts are of a cold temper. There is no such thing as spiritual love growing in our natures and hearts.

You have many poor souls helped with this, who cannot tell whether Christ love them or no; but this helps them a little, they can find undoubted arguments of their love to Christ, his image, and servants, and of relishing the Word, though they find much corruption: and this their love to divine things tells them by demonstrations from the effects, *that Christ loves them*, because there is no love to divine and supernatural things without the love of Christ first. And the graces in our hearts, they are love tokens given to the spouse. Common favours he gives, as Abraham [gave] gifts to his servants and others, but special gifts to his spouse. If therefore there be any grace, a tender and soft heart, a prizing of heavenly things, love to God's people and truth, then we may comfortably conclude Christ loves us; not only because they are reflections of God's love, but because they are jewels and ornaments that Christ only bestows upon his spouse; and not upon reprobates, such precious jewels as these (*John* 15:15).

3. *By discovering his secrets to us* (*Psa.* 25:14), for that is an argument of love. Doth Christ by his Spirit discover the secret love he hath borne to us before all worlds? Doth he discover the breast of his Father, and his own heart to us? This discovery of secret affections, of entire love, showeth our happy state. For that is one prerogative of friendship, and the chiefest discovery of secrets, when he gives us a particular right to truths, as our own, that we can go challenge them, these are mine, these belong to me, these promises are mine. This discovery of the secret love of God, and of the interests we have in the promises, is a sign that Christ loves us, and that in a peculiar manner we are his love.

Use 1. Let us be like our blessed Saviour, that where we see any saving goodness in any, let us love them; for should not our love meet with our Saviour's love? Shall the church of God be the love of Christ, and shall it be our hatred? Shall a good Christian be Christ's love, and shall he be the object of my hatred and scorn? Can we imitate a better pattern? O let us never think our estate to be good, except every child of God be our love as he is Christ's love. Can I love Christ, and cannot I love[1] him in whom I see

---

[1] That is, can I not love.—Ed.

Christ? It is a sign that I hate himself, when I hate his image. It is to be wondered at that the devil hath prevailed with any so much, as to think they should be in a good estate, when they have hearts rising against the best people, and who, as they grow in grace, so they grow in their dislike of them. Is here the Spirit of Christ?

Use 2. And let them likewise be here reproved that are glad to see any Christian halt, slip, and go awry. The best Christians in the world have that in part, which is wholly in another man; he hath flesh in him. Shall we utterly distaste a Christian for that? The church was now in a sleepy condition, and yet, notwithstanding, Christ takes not the advantage of the weakness of the church to cashier,[1] and to hate her, but he pities her the more, and takes a course to bring her again into a good state and condition. Let us not therefore be glad at the infirmities and failings of any, that discover any true goodness in them. It may be our own case ere long. It casts them not out of Christ's love, but they dwell in his love still; why should we then cast them out of our love and affections? Let them be our loves till, as they are the love of Christ, notwithstanding their infirmities.

[1] That is, dismiss.—G.

SERMON 7

*My love, my dove, my undefiled: for my head is filled with dew,
and my locks with the drops of the night. I have put off
my coat; how shall I put it on? I have washed
my feet; how shall I defile them?*
SONG OF SOLOMON 5:2, 3

THAT the life of a Christian is a perpetual conflicting, appears evidently in this book, the passages whereof, joined with our own experiences, sufficiently declare what combats, trials, and temptations the saints are subject unto, after their new birth and change of life; now up, now down, now full of good resolutions, now again sluggish and slow, not to be waked, nor brought forward by the voice of Christ, as it was with the church here. She will not out of her sleep to open unto Christ, though he call, and knock, and stand waiting for entrance. She is now desirous to pity herself, and needs no Peter to stir her up unto it.[1] The flesh of itself is prone enough to draw back, and make excuses, to hinder the power of grace from its due operation in us. She is laid along, as it were, to rest her; yet is not she so asleep, but she discerns the voice of Christ. But up and rise she will not.

Thus we may see the truth of that speech of our Saviour verified, 'That which is born of the flesh is flesh, and that which is born of the Spirit is spirit' (*John* 3:6). The flesh pulls her back: the

---

[1] The allusion is to Matthew 16:22. In our translation it is rendered, 'Be it far from thee, Lord', which obscures the pathos of the devoted apostle's mistaken, but most loving appeal. It should be 'Pity thyself.' Hence Sibbes' reference.—G.

Spirit would raise her up to open to Christ. He in the meanwhile makes her inexcusable, and prepares her by his knocking, waiting, and departing; as for a state of further humiliation, so for an estate of further exaltation. But how lovingly doth he speak to her!

1. 'Open unto me, my love.' He calls her my love, especially for two respects; partly because *his love was settled upon her.* It was in his own breast, but it rested not there, but seated itself upon, and in the heart of his spouse, so that she became Christ's love. We know the heart of a lover is more where it loves than where it lives, as we use to speak; and indeed, there is a kind of a going out, as it were, to the thing beloved, with a heedlessness of all other things. Where the affection is in any excess, it carries the whole soul with it.

2. But, besides this, when Christ saith my love, he shows, that as his love goes, and plants, and seats itself in the church, *so it is united to that, and is not scattered to other objects.* There are beams of God's general love scattered in the whole world; but this love, this exceeding love, is only fastened upon the church. And, indeed, there is no love comparable to this love of Christ, which is above the love of women, of father, or mother, if we consider what course he takes to show it. For there could be nothing in the world so great to discover his love, as this gift, and gift of himself. And therefore he gave himself, the best thing in heaven or in earth withal, to show his love. The Father gave him, when he was God equal with his Father. He loved his church, and gave himself for it. How could he discover his love better, than to take our nature to show how he loved us? How could he come nearer to us, than by being incarnate, so to be bone of our bone, and flesh of our flesh; and took our nature to show how he loved it (*Eph.* 5:30). Love draws things nearer wheresoever it is. It drew him out of heaven to the womb of the virgin, there to be incarnate; and, after that, when he was born not only to be a man, but a miserable man, because we could not be his spouse unless he purchased us by his death. We must be his spouse by a satisfaction made to

divine justice. God would not give us to him, but with salving[1] his justice. What sweet love is it to heal us not by searing, or lancing, but by making a plaster of his own blood, which he shed for those that shed his, in malice and hatred. What a wondrous love is it, that he should pour forth tears for those that shed his blood! 'O Jerusalem, Jerusalem', &c. (*Matt.* 23:37); that he prayed for those that persecuted him (*Luke* 23:34); and what wondrous love is it now that he sympathiseth with us in heaven, accounting the harm that is done to the least member he hath, as done to himself! 'Saul, Saul, why persecutest thou me?' (*Acts* 9:4), and that he should take us into one body with himself, to make one Christ (*1 Cor.* 12:27). And he doth not content himself with anything he can do for us here, but his desire is, that we may be one with him more and more, and be for ever with him in the heavens, as you have it in that excellent prayer in John 17:24.

Use 1. Now this should stir us up *to be fully persuaded of his love, that loves us so much.* Christ's love in us, is as the loadstone to the iron. Our hearts are heavy and downwards of themselves. We may especially know his love by this, that it draws us upwards, and makes us heavenly minded. It makes us desire further and further communion with him. Still there is a magnetical attractive force in Christ's love. Wheresoever it is, it draws the heart and affections after it.

Use 2. And we may know from hence one argument to prove *the stability of the saints, and the immortality of the soul,* because Christ calls the church his love. The want of love again, where it is entire, and in any great measure, is a misery. Christ therefore should suffer, if those he hath planted his love upon, whom he loves truly, either should fall away for ever, or should not be immortal for ever. Christ will not lose his love. And as it is an argument of persevering in grace, so is it of an everlasting being, that this soul of ours hath; because it is capable of the love of Christ,

[1] That is, preserving.—G.

seeing there is a sweet union and communion between Christ and the soul. It should make Christ miserable, as it were, in heaven, the place of happiness, if there should not be a meeting of him and his spouse. There must therefore be a meeting; which marriage is for ever, that both may be for ever happy one in another (*Hos.* 2:20).

Use 3. Let us often *warm our hearts with the consideration hereof, because all our love is from this love of his.* Oh the wonderful love of God, that both such transcendent majesty, and such an infinite love should dwell together. We say majesty and love never dwell together, because love is an abasing of the soul to all services. But herein it is false, for here majesty and love dwell together in the heart of one Christ, which majesty hath stooped as low as his almighty power could give leave. Nay, it was an almighty power that he could stoop so low and yet be God, keeping his majesty still. For God, to become man, to hide his majesty for a while, not to be known to be God, and to hide so far in this nature as to die for us: what an almighty power was this, that could go so low and yet preserve himself God still! Yet this we see in this our blessed Saviour, the greatest majesty met with the greatest abasement that ever was, and all out of love to our poor souls. There was no stooping, no abasement that was ever so low as Christ was abased unto us, to want for a time even the comfort of the presence of his Father. There was an union of grace; but the union of solace and comfort that he had from him was suspended for a time, out of love to us. For he had a right in his own person to be in heaven presently. Now for him to live so long out of heaven, and ofttimes, especially towards his suffering, to be without that solace (that he might be a sacrifice for our sins), to have it suspended for a time, what a condescending was this? It is said (*Psa.* 113:6), that God stoops 'to behold the things done here below'. It is indeed a wondrous condescending, that God will look upon things below; but that he would become man, and out of love to save us, suffer as he did here, this is wondrous humility to astonishment! We think humility is not a proper grace becoming the majesty of God. So it is not indeed, but there is some resemblance of that grace in God, especially in Christ, that he should, to reveal himself, veil himself with flesh, and all out of love to us. The consideration of these things are wondrous effectual, as to strengthen faith, so to kindle love. Let these be for a taste to direct our meditations herein. It follows,

'My dove'. We know when Christ was baptized, the Holy Ghost appeared in the shape of a dove (*Matt.* 3:16), as a symbol of his presence, to discover thus much:

1. *That Christ should have the property and disposition of a dove.* 'And be meek and gentle.' For indeed he became man for that end, to be 'a merciful Saviour'. 'Learn of me, for I am meek and lowly' (*Matt.* 11:28, 29). 'And I will not quench the smoking flax, nor break the bruised reed', &c. (*Matt.* 12:20), said he; and therefore the Spirit appeared upon him in the shape of a dove. As likewise,

2. *To show what his office should be.* For even as the dove in Noah's ark was sent out, and came home again to the ark with an olive branch, to show that the waters were abated; so Christ was to preach deliverance from the deluge of God's anger, and to come with an olive leaf of peace in his mouth, and reconciliation, to show that God's wrath was appeased. When he was born, the angels sung, 'Glory to God on high, on earth peace, and goodwill towards men' (*Luke* 2:14). Now, as Christ had the Spirit in the likeness of a dove; so all that are Christ's, the spouse of Christ, have the disposition of Christ. That Spirit that framed him to be like a dove, frames the church to be a dove; as the ointment that was poured on Aaron's head: it ran down upon the lowest skirts of his garments (*Psa.* 133:2).

Now, the church is compared to a dove, partly *for the disposition that is and should be in the church resembling that creature;* and partly, also, *for that the church is in a mournful suffering condition.*

I. *For the like disposition as is found in a dove.* There is some good in all creatures. There is no creature but it hath a beam of God's majesty, of some attribute; but some more than others. There is an image of virtue even in the inferior creatures. Wherefore the Scripture sends us to them for many virtues, as the sluggard to the ant (*Prov.* 6:6). And indeed we may see the true perfection of the first creation, the state of it, more in the creatures than in ourselves; for there is no such degeneration in any creature as there is in man.

Now, that which in a dove the Scripture aims at,

1. We should resemble a dove in is, his *meekness* especially. The church is meek both to God and man, not given to murmurings and revengement. Meek: that is, 'I held my tongue without murmuring', as it is in the psalm; 'I was dumb', &c. (*Psa.* 39:2): which is a grace that God's Spirit frames in the heart of the church, and every particular Christian, even to be meek towards God by an holy silence; and likewise towards men, to put on the 'bowels of meekness', as we are exhorted, 'As the elect of God, put on the bowels of meekness and compassion', &c. (*Col.* 3:12). Hereby we shall show ourselves to be Christ's, and to have the Spirit of Christ. And this grace disposeth us to a nearer communion with God than other graces. It is a grace that God most delights in, and would have his spouse to be adorned with, as is showed in 1 Peter 3:4, where the apostle tells women, it is the best jewel and ornament that they can wear, and is with God of great price. Moses, we read, was a mighty man in prayer, and a special means to help and fit him thereunto, was because he was the meekest man on earth (*Num.* 12:3); and therefore, 'seek the Lord, seek meekness' (*Zeph.* 2:3); and it fits a man for communion with God, 'for God resisteth the proud, and giveth grace to the meek and humble' (*1 Pet.* 5:5). It is a grace that empties the soul of self-conceit, to think a man's self unworthy of anything, and so makes it capacious, low, and fit for God to fill with a larger measure of his Spirit. It takes away the roughness and swelling of the soul, that keeps out God

and grace. Therefore in that grace we must especially be like this meek creature, which is no vindictive creature, that hath no way to revenge itself.

Again,

2. *It is a simple creature, without guile.* It hath no way to defend itself, but only by flight. There is a simplicity that is sinful, when there is no mixture of wisdom in it. There is a simplicity that is a pure simplicity; and so God is simple, which simplicity of God is the ground of many other attributes. For thereupon he is eternal, because there is nothing contrary in him; there is no mixture in him of anything opposite. So that is a good simplicity in us, when there is no mixture of fraud, no duplicity in the soul. 'A double-hearted man is inconstant and unstable in all his ways' (*James* 1:8). Now simplicity, as it is a virtue, so we must imitate the dove in it; for there is a sinful, dove-like silliness. For in Hosea 7:11, Ephraim is said there to be 'like a silly dove without heart; they call to Egypt, they go to Assyria'. There is a fatal simplicity, usually going before destruction, when we hate those that defend us, and account them enemies, and rely more upon them that are enemies indeed than upon friends. So it was with Ephraim before his destruction: 'He was a silly dove without heart; he called to Egypt, and went to Assyria', false friends, that were enemies to the church of God; yet they trusted them more than God or the prophets. Men have a world of tricks to undermine their friends, to ruin them, and to deserve ill of those that would with all their hearts deserve well of them, when yet in the meantime they can gratify the enemy, please them, and hold correspondence with them, as here Ephraim did. 'Ephraim is a silly dove', &c. This, therefore, is not that which we must aim at, but to be simple and children concerning evil, but not in ignorance and simplicity that way.

3. Again, *this creature is a faithful creature.* That is mainly here aimed at. It is faithful to the mate. So the Christian soul, by the Spirit of God, it is made faithful to Christ, it keeps the judgment chaste, is not tainted with errors and sins. He keeps his affections

chaste likewise, sets nothing in his heart above Christ. 'Whom hath he in heaven but him, and what is there in earth he desires beside him?' (*Psa.* 73:25). You know in the Revelation, the spouse of Christ is brought in like a virgin contracted, but the Romish Church like a whore. Therefore the church of God must take heed of the Roman Church, for that is not a dove. We must be virgins, who must keep chaste souls to Christ, as you have it—'Those that follow the Lamb wheresoever he goeth, they have not defiled themselves with women' (*Rev.* 14:4). The meaning is spiritual, namely, that they have not defiled themselves with idolatry and spiritual fornication; they have chaste hearts to Christ. So in this respect they resemble the dove. These, therefore, that draw away from the love of religion to mixture, to be meretrices[1] and harlots in religion, they are not Christ's doves. As far as they yield to this, it is an argument that they have false hearts. Christ's church is a dove. She keeps close and inviolate to him.

4. Again, *this creature is of a neat[2] disposition*. It will not lodge where it shall be troubled with stench, and annoyed that way; and likewise feeds neatly on pure grain; not upon carrion, as you see in the ark, when the raven was sent out it lights upon carrion, of which there was then plenty, and therefore never came into the ark again (*Gen.* 8:7). But the dove, when she went out, would not light upon carrion or dead things; and so finding no fit food, came back again to the ark. So the Christian soul in this respect is like a dove, that will not feed upon worldly carrion, or sinful pleasures, but upon Christ and spiritual things. The soul of a carnal and a natural man useth to feed upon dust, earth and earthly things. When the soul of a true Christian, that hath the taste of grace, feeds neatly, it will not feed on that which is base and earthly, but upon heavenly and spiritual things.

5. It is *a bird that loves communion and fellowship*, as the prophet speaks, 'Who are those that flock to the windows as doves' (*Isa.*

---

[1] That is, courtesans [court mistresses, whores.—P]—G.

[2] That is, cleanly.—G

60:8); for so they use to flock to their houses by companies. So the children of God love the communion and fellowship one of another, and keep severed from the world as soon as ever they are separated from it, delighting in all those of the same nature. Doves will consort with doves, Christians with Christians, and none else. They can relish no other company. These and such like properties may profitably be considered of the dove. The much standing upon these were to wrong the intendment[1] of the Spirit of God; to neglect them altogether were as much. Therefore we have touched upon some properties only.

II. Now, *for the sufferings of the church* it is like a dove in this. *The dove is molested by all the birds of prey*, it being the common prey of all other ravenous birds. So the poor church of God is persecuted and molested. 'Oh that I had wings like a dove', &c., saith holy David (*Psa.* 55:6). It is an old speech, and is for ever true, that crows and such, escape better than doves. The punishment that should light on ravens, ofttimes it lights on doves. Thus God's dove, God's church, is used.

But what defence hath God's poor church? Why, no defence. But,

First, *flight*, even as the dove hath nothing but flight. It hath no talons to wound, but it hath flight. So we are to fly to God as to our mountain; fly to the ark, that God may take us in. The church of *God hath no other refuge but to be housed in God and Christ (Prov.* 18:10). He is our ark.

Secondly, and to *mourn*; as Hezekiah saith of himself, 'He mourned as a dove, and chattered like a crane' (*Isa.* 38:14). The state of the church of God is like the turtle's,[2] to mourn in all afflictions, desertions, and molestations of wicked men; to mourn to God, who hears the bemoanings of his own Spirit in them. And woe to all other birds, the birds of prey, when the turtles do

[1] That is, design.—G.

[2] That is, turtle-doves.—P.

THE LOVE OF CHRIST

mourn because of their cruelty. It is a presage of ruin to them, when they force the turtle to sorrow and mourning.

And then, thirdly, they have another refuge besides flight and mourning, which is *to build high from vermin* that would otherwise molest them. Instinct teacheth them thus to escape their enemies by building high, and so to secure themselves. So there is in God's children a gracious instinct put, an antipathy to the enemies of it; which tends to their safety, in that they mingle not themselves with them. And likewise God breeds in them a familiarity with himself, and stirs them to build in him as on a rock, to be safe in him.

Obj. But you will object, If the church of God be his dove, why is it so with it as it is, that God should suffer his love, and his dove, and his turtle thus as it were to be preyed upon? 'Give not the soul of the turtle to the beasts', saith the psalmist (*Psa.* 74:19). If the church were God's dove, he would esteem more of it than he doth, and not suffer it to be persecuted thus?

Ans. God never forsakes his dove, but is an ark for it to fly to, a rock for it to build on. The dove hath always a refuge in God and in Christ in the worst times. You have a notable place for this, 'Though you have lain among the pots', that is, smeared and sullied, 'yet they shall be as the wings of a dove covered with silver, and her feathers with yellow gold. When the Almighty scattered kings in it, it was white as the snow in Salmon' (*Psa.* 68:13, 14). So though the church of God lies among the pots awhile, all smeared, and soiled, and sullied with the ill-usage of the world, yet as long as it keeps itself a dove, unspotted of the filth of the world and sin (though it be smeared with the ill-usage thereof), we see what God promiseth here, 'yet shall they be as the wings of a dove covered with silver, and her feathers with yellow gold'. So God will bring forth his dove with glory out of all these abasements at length. So much for the title of dove. It follows,

'My undefiled'. Undefiled is a high word to be applied to the church of God here; for the church, groaning under infirmities, to be counted perfect and undefiled. But Christ, who judgeth aright of his church, and knows best what she is, he yet thus judgeth of her. But, how is that? The church is undefiled, especially *in that it is the spouse of Christ, and clothed with the robes of his right-eousness.* For there is an exchange so soon as ever we are united to Christ. Our sins are upon him, and his righteousness is made ours; and therefore in Christ the church is undefiled. Christ himself the second person is the first lovely thing next the Father; and in Christ all things as they have relation to him are loved, as they are in him. Christ's human nature is next loved to the second person. It is united, and is first pure, holy, and beloved. Then, because the church is Christ mystical, it is near to him; and, in a manner, as near as that sacred body of his, both making up one Christ mystical. And so is amiable and beloved even of God himself, who hath pure eyes; yet in this respect looks upon the church as undefiled.

Christ and his church are not to be considered as two when we speak of this undefiledness, but as one. And the church having Christ, with all that is Christ's, they have the field, and the pearl[1] in the field together. And Christ giving himself to the church, he gives his righteousness, his perfection, and holiness; all is the church's.

Quest. But how can it be the church's, when it is not in the church, but in Christ?

Ans. It is safe for the church that it is in Christ, who is perfect and undefiled for us; to make us appear so. And so it is in Christ, the second Adam, for our good. It is not in him as another person, but it is in him as the church's Head, that make both one Christ. The hand and the foot see not; but both hand and foot have benefit by the eye, that sees for them. There is no member of the body [that] understands, but the head does all for them. Put the case we have not absolute righteousness and undefiledness in our own natures and persons inhering in us. Yet we have it in

[1] That is, treasure. See *Matt.* 13:44.—G.

143

Christ, that is one with us, who hath it for our good. It is ours, for all the comfort and good that we may have by it; and thereupon the church in Christ is undefiled; yea, even then when it feels its own defilements. And here ariseth that wondrous contradiction that is found in a believer's apprehension. The nature of faith is to apprehend righteousness in the sense of sin, happiness in the sense of misery, and favour in the sense of displeasure.

And the ground of it is, because that at the same time the soul may be in some measure defiled in itself, and yet notwithstanding be undefiled in her head and husband Christ. Hence the guilty soul, when it feels corruption and sin, yet notwithstanding doth see itself holy and clean in Christ the head. And so at once there is a conscience of sin, and no more conscience of sin, as the apostle saith (*Heb.* 10:2), when we believe in Christ, and are purged with his blood, that is, there is no more guilt of sin binding over to eternal damnation, yet notwithstanding always there is a conscience of sin, for we are guilty of infirmities, 'And if we say we have no sin, we lie, and deceive ourselves' (*1 John* 1:8).

Obj. But, how can this be, that there should be conscience of sin, and no conscience of sin, a sinner, and yet a perfect saint and undefiled?

Ans. 1. *The conscience knows its own imperfection, so it is defiled, and accuseth of sin. And as it looks to Christ, so it sees itself pure, and purged from all sin.* Here is the conquest, fight, and the victory of faith in the deepest sense of sin, pollution, and defilement in ourselves, at the same time to see an absolute and perfect righteousness in Jesus Christ. Herein is even the triumph of faith, whereby it answers God. And Christ, who sees our imperfections, but it is to purge and cleanse them away, not to damn us for them, at the same time he sees us in his own love clothed with his righteousness, as one with himself, endowed with whatsoever he hath; his satisfaction and obedience being ours as verily as anything in the world is. Thus he looks on us, and thus faith looks upon him too, and together with the sight and sense of sin, at the same time it apprehends righteousness, perfect righteousness, and so is undefiled. This is the main point in religion, and the comfort of Christians, to see their perfection in Christ Jesus, and to be lost in themselves, as it were, and to be only 'found in him, not having their own righteousness, but the righteousness of God in him' (*Phil.* 3:9). This is a mystery which none knows but a believing soul. None see corruption more, none see themselves freed more. They have an inward sight to see corruption, and an inward faith to see God takes not advantage at it. And surely there can be no greater honour to Christ than this. In the sense of sin, of wants, imperfections, stains, and blemishes, yet to wrap ourselves in the righteousness of Christ, God-man; and by faith, being thus covered with that absolute righteousness of Christ, with boldness to go, clothed in the garments of this our elder brother, to the throne of grace. This is an honour to Christ, to attribute so much to his righteousness, that being clothed therewith, we can boldly break through the fire of God's justice, and all those terrible attributes, when we see them all, as it were, satisfied fully in Christ. For Christ, with his righteousness, could go through the justice of God, having satisfied it to the full for us. And we being clothed with this his righteousness and satisfaction, may go through too.

Ans. 2. But besides that, there is another undefiledness in the church, in respect to which she is called undefiled, that is, *in purity of disposition, tending to perfection*. And God respects her according to her better part, and according to what he will bring her in due time. For we are chosen unto perfection, and to be holy in his sight; and perfectly holy, undefiled, and pure. We are not chosen to weak beginnings.

In choosing us, what did God aim at? Did he aim at these imperfect beginnings, to rest there? No; we were elected and chosen to perfection. For, as it is in this natural life, God purposed that we should not only have all the limbs of men, but grow from infancy to activeness and perfection. As God at first intended so much for our bodies, no question he intends as much also for the soul, that we should not only have the lineaments[1] of Christianity, a sanctified judgment, with affections in part renewed, but he hath chosen us to perfection by degrees. As the seed first lies rotting in the ground, then grows to a stalk, and then to an ear, so God's wisdom shines here, by bringing things by degrees to perfection and undefiledness. His wisdom will have it thus (or else his power might have it otherwise), because he will have us to live by faith, to trust his mercy in Christ, and not to the undefiledness that is begun in us, but to admire that which we have in Christ himself.

And, indeed, it is the character of a judicious believing Christian soul, that he can set a price and value the righteousness of Christ, out of himself, labouring, living, and dying to appear in that; and yet to comfort and sustain himself during this conflict and fight between the flesh and the Spirit, that in time this inherent grace shall be brought to perfection.

And Christ, he looks upon us as he means to perfect the work of grace in us by little and little, as he means to purge and cleanse us (*Eph.* 5:26, 27). The end of redemption is, that he might purge his church, and so never leave it till he have made it 'a glorious spouse in heaven'. He looks upon us as we shall be ere long, and therefore we are said 'to be dead to sin', while we are but dying to it. And, saith he, 'you have crucified the flesh with the affections, and lusts thereof' (*Gal.* 5:24), when we are but crucifying it. But it is said so because it is as sure to be done as if it were done already. As a man, when he is condemned, and going to his execution, he is a dead man, so there is a sentence passed upon sin and corruption. It shall be abolished and die. Therefore it is dead in sentence, and is dying in execution. It is done; 'They that are in Christ have

---

[1] Features, distinguishing marks.—P.

crucified the flesh, with the lusts thereof' (*Gal.* 5:24). It is as sure to faith as if it were done already. So we are said 'to sit in heavenly places with Christ' (*Eph.* 2:6). We are with him already. For Christ having taken us so near in affection to himself, he will never leave us till he have made us such as he may have full contentment in, which is in heaven, when the contract between him and us shall be fulfilled in consummation of the marriage. Thus faith looks, and Christ looks thus upon us. Which should comfort us in weakness, that God regards us not in our present imperfections, but as he means to make us ere long. In the mean time, that he may look upon us in love, he looks upon us in the obedience of his Son, in whom whatsoever is good shall be perfected at the last.

Use 1. What should we do then, if Christ doth make his church thus, 'his love', 'his dove', 'his undefiled', by making his love to meet in it as the centre thereof, whereunto he doth confine all his love, as it were? *We should confine our love to him again; and have no love out of Christ*, since he hath no love out of us. There should be an everlasting mutual shining and reflection between him and the soul. We should lay open our souls to his love, as indeed he desires especially the communion of our affections. We should reflect love to him again. This perpetual everlasting intercourse between Christ and his spouse, is her main happiness here, and her eternal happiness in heaven. In looking on him who hath done so much for us, he shines on us, and we look back again upon him. Doth Christ love us so intimately, and so invincibly, that no indignities nor sin could overcome his love, which made, that he endured that which he hates most,[1] 'to become sin for us' (*2 Cor.* 5:21), nay, the want of that, which was more to him than all the world, the want of the sense of the favour of God for a time. 'My God, my God, why hast thou forsaken me?' Hath Christ thus infinitely loved us, and shall not we back again make him our love? In their degree the saints of God have all done so. It was a

[1] That is, which made him to endure .—P.

THE LOVE OF CHRIST

good speech of Ignatius the martyr, 'My love Christ was cruci-fied!'[1] So a Christian should say, 'My love was crucified', 'My love died', 'My love is in heaven.' And for the things on earth, I love them as they have a beam of him in them; as they lead me to him. But he is my love, there my love is pitched, even upon him. This is the ground of these Scripture phrases, 'But our conversa-tion is in heaven, from whence we look for the Saviour, the Lord Jesus Christ', &c. (*Phil.* 3:20); and 'set your affections on the things that are above' (*Col.* 3:1). Why? Christ our love is there. The soul is more where it loves, than where its residence is. It dies, as it were, to other things, and lives in the thing it loves. Therefore our thoughts and affections, our joy and delight should be drawn up to Christ; for indeed his love hath such a magnetical attractive force, that where it is, it will draw up the heavy iron, the gross soul; and make it heavenly. For there is a binding, a drawing force in this excellent affection of love.

Use 2. 'My love, my dove', &c. *There are all words of sweetness.* He labours to express all the affection he can. For the conscience is subject to upbraid, and to clamour much. So that there must be a great deal of persuasion to still the accusing conscience of a sinner, to set it down, make it quiet, and persuade it of God's love. Therefore he useth all heavenly rhetoric to persuade and move the affections.

Use 3. In this that the church is undefiled in Christ, let us learn when afflicted in conscience, *not so much to judge of ourselves by what we feel in ourselves, as by what faith suggests.* In Christ there-fore let us judge of ourselves by what we are as in him. We are poor in ourselves, but have riches in him. We die in ourselves in regard of this life, but we have a life in him, an eternal life; and we are sinners in ourselves, but we have a righteousness in him

---

[1] There are various sayings resembling this in the epistles of Ignatius, e.g., *to the Ephesians,* c. xviii., *to the Trallians,* c. ix.-xi., *to the Romans,* c. ii.-iv., and vi. Probably Sibbes refers to the ancient narrative of the 'martyrdom of Ignatius'. Cf. § 2. *Patrum Apostolicorum Opera,* ed, Hefele. 8vo. 1847.—G.

whereby we are righteous in his sight (*2 Cor.* 5:21). We are foolish, unskilful, and ignorant in ourselves, but he is our wisdom in all whatsoever is amiss in us. Let us labour to see a full supply of our wants made up in Christ. This is to glorify God as much as if we could fulfil the law perfectly. If we were as undefiled as Adam was, we could not glorify God more, than when we find ourselves and our conscience guilty of sins, yet thus by the Spirit of God to go out of ourselves, and to see ourselves in Christ, and thus to cast ourselves on him, embrace him, and take that gift of God given us, Christ offered to us, because God so commands (*John* 4:10). We honour God more than if we had the obedience that Adam had at first before his fall. For now in the covenant of grace, he will be glorified in his mercy, in his forgiving, forbearing, rich, transcendent mercy, and in going beyond all our unworthiness and sins, by showing that there is a righteousness provided for us, the righteousness of God-man; whose obedience and satisfaction is more than our disobedience, because it is the disobedience of man only, but his obedience and righteousness is the obedience and righteousness of God-man. So it satisfieth divine justice, and therefore ought to satisfy conscience to the full. Our faith must answer Christ's carriage to us. We must therefore account ourselves in him 'undefiled', because he accounts us so. Not in ourselves, but as we have a being in him, we are undefiled.

Use 4. Again, see here, Christ accounts us, even in regard of habitual grace, *undefiled, though we have for the present many corruptions.* Let us therefore learn a lesson of moderation of so excellent a teacher; let us not be ashamed to learn of our Saviour. What spirit shall we think they have, that will unchurch churches, because they have some defilement and unbrotherly brethren, accounting them no churches, no brethren, because they have some imperfections? Why hath not Christ a quarrel to the church then? is he blind? doth his love make him blind? No; he seeth corruption, but he seeth better things; somewhat of his own, that makes him overlook those imperfections, because they are such as he means to mortify, subdue, wear away, and to fire out by the power of his Spirit, which as fire shall waste all those corruptions in time. So it is with the church. Put the case, she hath some corruptions; that it be not with her as it should be, yet she is a church notwithstanding. The church of Corinth, we see, Paul styles them saints and brethren, with all those sweet names (*1 Cor.* 1:1, 2), notwithstanding they had many corruptions among them.

Use 5. We have a company of malignant spirits, worse than these a great deal, atheistical persons, that have no religion at all, who, out of malice and envy, *watch for the halting of good Christians*; who can see nothing but defilement in those that have any good in them, nothing but hypocrisy, moppishness,[1] all that is naught; who, if they can devise any blemish, put it upon them. Whereas Christ sees a great deal of ill in the church, but he sees it to pardon, subdue, and to pity the church for it, extolling and magnifying its goodness. What spirits are those of that watch to see imperfections in others, that their hearts tell them are better than they, that they may only disgrace them by it; for goodness they will see none.

Use 6. And likewise, it should teach us *not to wrong ourselves with false judgment.* We should have a double eye: one eye to see that which is amiss in us, our own imperfections, thereby to carry ourselves in a perpetual humility; but another eye of faith, to see what we have in Christ, our perfection in him, so to account of ourselves, and glory in this our best being, that in him we have a glorious being,—such an one whereby God esteems us perfect, and undefiled in him only. The one of which sights should enforce us to the other, which is one end, why God in this world leaves corruption in his children. Oh, since I am thus undefiled, shall I rest in myself? Is there any harbour for me to rest in mine own righteousness? Oh, no; it drives a man out of all harbour. Nay, I

---

[1] A negative emotional state, such as melancholia, mainly used of the uneducated classes.—P.

will rest in that righteousness which God hath wrought by Christ, who is God-man. That will endure the sight of God, being clothed with which, I can endure the presence of God. So, this sight of our own unworthiness and wants should not be a ground of discouragement, but a ground to drive us perfectly out of ourselves, that by faith we might renew our title to that righteousness, wherein is our especial glory. Why should we not judge of ourselves as Christ doth? Can we see more in ourselves than he doth? Yet, notwithstanding all he sees, he accounts us as undefiled.

Use 7. Again, since he accounts us undefiled, because he means to make us so, and now looks on us as we shall be, in all our foils[1] and infirmities, let us comfort ourselves, *it shall not thus be always with us.* Oh, this flesh of mine shall fall and fall still, and shall decay as Saul's house [2 *Sam.* 3:1], and the Spirit at the last shall conquer in all this! I am not chosen to this beginning, to this conflicting course of life. I am chosen to triumph, to perfection of grace: this is my comfort. Thus we should comfort ourselves, and set upon our enemies and conflict in this hope of victory: 'I shall get the better of myself at the last.' Imperfection should not discourage, but comfort us in this world. We are chosen to perfection. Let us still rejoice, in that 'we are chosen to sanctification', which is a little begun, being an earnest[2] of other blessings. Let us not rest in the pledge or in the earnest, but labour for a further pledge of more strength and grace. For those that have the Spirit of Christ, will strive to be as much unspotted and as heavenly as they can, to fit themselves for that heavenly condition as much as may be. When, because they cannot be in heaven, yet they will converse there as much as they can; and because they cannot be with such company altogether, they will be as much as they may be; labouring as they are able to be that which they shall be hereafter. Imperfection contents them not, and therefore they pray still in

---

[1] That is, falls.—G.

[2] A first instalment or downpayment that guarantees all that is yet to come.—P.

THE LOVE OF CHRIST

the Lord's Prayer, 'Thy kingdom come' (*Matt.* 6:10). While there is any imperfection, their hearts are enlarged more and more; nothing contents them but perfection. And indeed God accounts us thus unspotted for this end, because he would encourage us. Where he sees the will and endeavour, he gives the title of the thing desired.

I have put off my coat; how shall I put it on? I have washed my feet; how shall I defile them? (verse 3).

Here is an ingenious[1] confession made by the church of her own untowardness. Notwithstanding all Christ's heavenly rhetoric and persuasion that he did use, yet she draws back, and seems to have reason so to do. 'I have put off my coat; how shall I put it on again' to let thee in? 'I have washed my feet', &c. It is a phrase taken from the custom of those hot countries, wherein they used to wash their feet. 'I have washed my feet; how shall I defile them' to rise and open the door to thee? There is a spiritual meaning herein, as if she had said, I have some ease by this sleepy profession, some freedom from evil tongues, and some exemption and immunity from some troubles I was in before. I was then, perhaps, too indiscreet. Now wilt thou call me again to those troubles, that I have wisely avoided? No; 'I have put off my coat; how shall I put it on? I have washed my feet, how shall I defile them?' I affect[2] this estate very well; I am content to be as I am, without troubling of myself. Thus the church puts off Christ. This I take to be the meaning of the words. That which is observable is this: that *it is not an easy matter to bring the soul and Christ together into near fellowship*. We see here how the church draws back; for the flesh moves either not to yield at all to duty, or to be cold, uncertain, and unsettled therein. The flesh knows that a near communion with Christ cannot stand with favouring any corruption, and therefore the flesh will do something, but not enough. It will yield

[1] That is, ingenuous.—G.

[2] That is, like.—G.

to something, but not to that that it should do, to that communion and fellowship that we ought to have with Christ. To instance in some particulars, as a rule and measure to somewhat of which we should be.

Obs. 1. *A Christian life should be nothing but a communion and intercourse with Christ,* a walking in the Spirit; and to be spiritual, and to favour the things of the Spirit altogether, he should study to adorn his profession by a lively and cheerful performance of duty (*Matt.* 5:16), and be exemplary to others; and should be in such a frame as he should 'walk continually in the comforts of the Holy Ghost' undismayed and undaunted, 'and abound in the fruits of the Spirit' (*Acts* 9:31), and do all the good he can wheresoever he comes. He should 'keep himself unspotted of the world' (*James* 1:27), go against the stream, and be continually in such a temper, as it should be the joy of his heart to be dissolved, and to be with Christ (2 *Tim.* 4:6). One might go on thus in a world of particulars, which would be too long. If we could attain to this excellency, it were an happy life, a heaven upon earth. This we should aim at. Will the flesh endure this, think you? No, it will not; which you shall see more particularly in this next observation, which is,

Obs. 2. That *one way, whereby the unregenerate part in us hinders this communion with Christ,* and the shining of a believer in a Christian course, *is by false pretences, reasons, and excuses.* 'I have washed my feet; I have put off my coat', &c.

The flesh never wants[1] excuses and pretences (there was never any yet came to hell, but they had some seeming pretence for their coming thither) to shift and shuffle off duties. There was never yet any careless, sinful course but it had the flesh to justify it with one reason or other; and therefore it is good to understand the sophistical shifts[2] of the flesh, and pretences and shows which it

---

[1] That is, lacks.—P.

[2] That is, expedients—G.

hath. And as it is good to know the truth of God, and of Christ revealed in his Word, so is it to know the falseness and deceitfulness of our own hearts. They are both mysteries almost alike, hard to be known. Labour we then more and more to know the falsehood of our own disposition, and to know the truth of God. To give instance in a few particulars. You see in the church the difficulty of her communion with Christ comes from the idle pretences and excuses she hath. Every one hath his several pretexts, as his state and condition is. We think we should be losers if we give ourselves to that degree of goodness which others do; whereas God doth curse those blessings which men get with neglect of duty to him. If we seek 'first the kingdom of heaven, all other things that are good for us shall be cast upon us' (*Matt.* 6:33).

Obj. Thou shalt lose the favour of such a one?

Ans. Never care for that favour thou canst not keep with God's favour. The favour of man is a snare. Take heed of that favour that snares thee. Thou losest their favour and company, but thou gainest the favour of Christ, and company of angels.

Obj. But they will rail on thee, and reproach thee with thy old sins?

Ans. Care not, 'God will do thee good for that', as David said when Shimei cursed him (2 *Sam.* 16:12).

Obj. But I shall lose my pleasure?

Ans. O! but such pleasures end in death. They are but pleasures of sin for a season, and thou shalt not lose by the change. 'The ways of wisdom are pleasant ways' (*Prov.* 3:17). One day religiously spent in keeping of a good conscience, what a sweet farewell hath it! Joy is in the habitation of the righteous. It becomes the righteous to be joyful. However outwardly it seems, yet there is a paradise within. Many such objections the flesh makes. Some take scandal at the prosperity of the wicked, and affliction of the saints, and from hence take occasion to rot in their dregs of sin. But what saith Christ? 'Happy is the man who is not offended in me' (*Matt.* 11:6). As for the prosperity of the wicked, envy them not. They stand in slippery places, and flourish like a green bay tree, but presently they vanish. Take no offence at them, nor at the cross. Look not at this, but at the ensuing comfort. 'Blessed are they that suffer for righteousness sake' (*1 Pet.* 3:14). Bind such words to your head as your crown. God reserves the best comforts to the worst times; his people never find it otherwise.

Obj. Ay, but if I be thus precise, the times are so bad, I shall be alone.

Ans. Complain not of the times, when thou makest them worse. Thou shouldst make the times better. The worse the times are, the better be thou; for this is thy glory, to be good in an evil generation. This was Lot's glory (*2 Pet.* 2:7). Paul tells what ill times they were; but, saith he, 'our conversation is in heaven, from whence we look for a Saviour' (*Phil.* 3:20). What brings destruction on God's people, but their joining with the wicked? When they joined with the children of men, then came the flood. These and the like pretences keep men altogether from goodness, or else from such a measure as may bring honour to God and comfort to themselves.

Or if men be great, why, this is not honourable to do thus, as you know what Michal said to David, 'How glorious was the king of Israel this day! like a fool', &c. (*2 Sam.* 6:20). To attend upon the Word of God with reverence, to make conscience of religion, Oh! it stands not with greatness, &c. But the Spirit of God answereth this in him, 'I will yet be more vile for God' (verse 22). It is a man's honour here to stand for God and for good things; and it is our honour that God will honour us so much.

Those likewise that are worldly have excuses also. 'Alas! I must tend my calling.' And they have Scripture for it too. 'He that provides not for his family is worse than an infidel' (*1 Tim.* 5:8), as if God had set up any callings to hinder the calling of Christianity; as if that were not the greatest calling, and the best part that will abide with us for ever; as if it were not the part of a Christian to redeem time from his calling to the duties of Christianity. I have no time, saith the worldling; what will you have me to do? Why, what time had David, when he meditated on the law of God day and night? (*Psa.* 1:2). He was a king. The king is bound to study the Scriptures (*Deut.* 17:18, 19). And yet whose employment is greater than the employment of the chief magistrate?

And thus every one, as their state and condition is, they have several pretences and excuses. Those that are young, their excuse is, we have time enough for these things hereafter. Others, as those that were negligent to build the second temple, 'the time is not yet, say they' (*Hag.* 1:2); whenas the uncertainty of this life of ours, the weightiness of the business, the danger of the custom of sin, the engaging of our hearts deeper and deeper into the world, makes it a more difficult thing to be a Christian. It more and more darkens our understanding, the more we sin; and the more it estrangeth our affections from good things, the more we have run out in an evil course. Time is a special mercy; but then thou hast not time only, but the means, good company, and good motions. Thou mayest never have such a gale again; thy heart may be hardened through the deceitfulness of sin. Again, who would want the comforts of religion for the present? As Augustine saith, 'I have wanted thy sweetness too long.'[1] What folly is it to want the sweetness and comfort of religion, so long as we may have it.

Some others pretend, the uncomfortableness of religion, I shall want my comforts; whenas indeed there is no sound comfort without having our hearts in a perfect communion with Christ, walking with God, and breaking off from our evil courses. What is the reason of discomforts, unresolvedness, and unsettledness? when we know not where we are, whither we go, or what our condition is. Unsettledness breeds discomfort; and indeed there is no pleasure so much as the pleasure that the serving of God

---

[1] *Confessions*, Book X. [xxvii.], 38. 'Too late loved I thee, O thou beauty of ancient days, yet ever new! too late I loved thee.'—G.

hath with it. As the fire hath light and heat always in it, so there is no holy action that we perform throughly, but as it hath an increase of strength, so there is an increase of comfort and joy annexed to it. There is a present reward annexed to all things that are spiritually good. They carry with them present peace and joy. The conscience hath that present comfort which consumes all discouragements whatsoever, as is always found in the experience of that soul that hath won so much of itself, as to break through discouragements to the practice of holy duties. Believers have a joy and comfort 'that others know not of' (*Rev.* 2:17); an hidden kind of manna and contentment.

These and a thousand such like discouragements men frame to themselves: 'My health will not serve', 'I shall endanger my life.' 'There is a lion in the way', saith the sluggard (*Prov.* 26:13), who, with his excuses, 'thinks himself wiser than the wisest in the city' (verse 16). There is none so wise as the sluggard, for belly-policy teacheth him a great many excuses, which he thinks will go for wisdom, because by them he thinks to sleep in a whole skin. He is but a sluggard for all that; and though he plead 'yet a little while', poverty, not only outward, but spiritual poverty and barrenness of soul, 'will come upon him as an armed man' (*Prov.* 6:11), and leave him destitute of grace and comfort, when he shall see at last what an evil course of life he hath led, that he hath yielded so much to his lazy flesh to be drawn away by discouragements from duties that he was convinced were agreeable to the Word. Now, what may be the grounds and causes of these false pretences and excuses which hinder us from holy duties? There be many causes.

1. First of all, one cause of this in us is this: Naturally, so far as we are not guided by a better spirit than our own, *we are inclined too much to the earthly present things of this life*, because they are present and pleasant, and we are nuzled up¹ in them, and whatsoever pulls us from them is unwelcome to us. This is one ground.

¹ That is, nestled.—G

157

2. Again, join with this, that naturally, since the fall, the soul of man having lost wisdom to guide it to that which is truly good, hath wit enough left *to devise untoward shifts,*[1] *to excuse that which is evil.* In this fallen estate the former abilities to devise things throughly good is turned to a matter of untoward wit, joined with shifting.[2] 'God made man right, but he hath sought out many inventions' (*Eccles.* 7:29). Carnal wit serves carnal will very well; and carnal lusts never want an advocate to plead for them, namely, carnal reason. From the bent, therefore, of the soul to ill things, pleasure, ease, and honour, such a condition as pleaseth the outward man since the fall, the bent and weight of the soul goeth this way, together with wit. Having lost the image of God in holy wisdom, there is shifting. This is a ground also why delays are joined with shifts.

3. Again, there is another ground, that *corrupt nature,* in this like the devil and sin, which never appear in their own colours, *sets a man on this way.* Who would not hate the devil if he should appear in his own likeness? or sin, if it should appear in its own colours? And therefore wit stretcheth itself to find out shifts. For, says the heart, unless there be some shifts and pretences to cover my shame, I shall be known to be what I am indeed, which I would be loath were done. I would have the sweet but not the shame of sin, the credit of religion, but not put myself to the cost which cometh with true religion, to deny myself. Corrupt courses never appear in their own colours. They are like the devil for this.

4. And then, again, naturally there is a great deal of *hypocrisy in us.* We may do duties to satisfy conscience, for somewhat must be done, to hear now and then, read and come to prayer betwixt sleeping and waking, yawning prayers, when we can do nothing else. Somewhat must be done. Conscience else will cry out of us that we are atheists, and shall be damned. Some slubbering[3] service

[1] That is, expedients.—G.

[2] That is, expediency.—G.

[3] That is, hurried and careless.—P.

158

must be done therefore. Yet notwithstanding, herein is our hypocrisy, that we cannot bring our hearts to do it, as it should be done, to purpose; for though it be true that there is much imperfection in the best actions, the best performances, yet this is hypocrisy when men do not do it as God may accept it, and as it may yield themselves comfort. The heart draws back. Duties it will and must do, but yet will not do them as it shall have comfort by them. This is inbred in the heart naturally. Conscience forceth to do something, though the flesh and corruption pulls back. This is the disposition of all men, till they have got the victory of their own atheistical hearts.

5. And then, again, another ground may be this, *a false conceit of God and of Christ,* that they will take anything at our hands. Because we love ourselves, and think that we do very well, we think that God is such a one as we are, as it is, 'Thou thoughtest that I was like unto thee', &c. (*Psa.* 50:21), that God will be put off with anything, and any excuse will serve the turn. You have not a swearer, a filthy, careless person, but he thinks God is merciful, and Christ died for sinners; and I was provoked to it, &c. Still he thinks to have some excuse for it, and that they will stand good with God. This atheism is in us naturally, and when we are palpably to blame in the judgment of others and ourselves in our sober wits, yet we put more ignorance and carelessness on God than on ourselves. 'Tush,[1] God regards it not.' It is the times. I would be better. It is company whom I must yield unto, &c. They think God will accept these things from them.

6. But one main ground thereof is, *the scandals that we meet withal in the world*, which, indeed, is a ground, because our own false hearts are willing to catch at anything. You see, say they, these men that make profession of religion, what they are; and then the devil will thrust some hypocrisy[2] into the profession of religion, and they judge all by one or two, and will be sure to do it.

[1] Expression of contempt, disapproval, disgust.—P.

[2] Qu, hypocrite?—G.

Therein stands their ingenuity; and if they can see any infirmity in them that are incomparably better than themselves, Oh, they are safe. Here is warrant enough to dislike religion and all good courses, because some do and so,[1] as if the course of religion were the worse for that. Thus they wrap themselves in those excuses, as men do their hands to defend them from pricks. This is the vile poison of our hearts, that will be naught, and yet, notwithstanding, will have reason to be so. The speech is, wickedness never wanted pretexts, which, as it is true of great wickedness, much more is it of that which goes in the world for drowsy lukewarm profession, under which many sink to hell before they are aware. They never want reason and pretexts to cover their sin. There is a mint and forge of them in the soul. It can coin them suddenly. Thus we see our wits do serve us excellently well to lay blocks in our own way to hinder us from heaven. We are dunces, and dull to do anything that is spiritually good, whereof we are incapable. But if it be to lay blocks in our own way to heaven, to quarrel with God and his ordinances, with the doctrine of salvation, with the instruments, teachers, and those that lead us a better way, that our wit will serve for. But to take a course to do us good another day, to lay up comforts in which we might end and close up our days, there we are backward, and have shift upon shift. This is added for the further explication of it, because of the necessity of the point; for except our hearts be discovered to us, we shall never know what religion means, save to know so much as may, through the winding, turning, shifting, and falsehood of our own nature, bring us to hell. Wherein we are worse enemies to ourselves than the devil is, who could not hurt us unless we did betray ourselves. But he hath factors[2] in us to deal for him. Our own carnal wit and affection, they hold correspondency with him; whence all the mischief that he doth us is by that intercourse that our

[1] Qu. so and so?—Ed.

[2] That is, agents.—P.

nature hath with Satan. That is the Delilah which betrayeth all the Samsons, sound worthy Christians in the world, to their spiritual enemies. Therefore, we can never be sufficiently instructed what a vile nature we have, so opposite to religion, as far as it is saving. Corrupt nature doth not oppose it so far as it is slubbered over, but so far as may bring us to that state we should be in. We have no worse enemies than our own hearts. Therefore, let us watch ourselves continually, and use all blessed means appointed of God whereby we may escape out of this dangerous, sleepy disposition of soul, which cost the church so dear, as we shall hear, God willing, hereafter.

SERMON 8

*I have put off my coat; how shall I put it on? I have washed
my feet; how shall I defile them?*
SONG OF SOLOMON 5:3

WE are now, by God's assistance, to speak of *the remedies against the lazy distempers we are prone unto in
spiritual things*; where we left off the last day.

Quest. What course should we take, then, to come forth from
this distempered laziness? That we may attain a spiritual taste and
relish of heavenly things, so as not to loathe religious exercises; or
delay and put them off with excuses?

Ans. 1. First of all, *resolve not to consult with flesh and blood in
anything.* For it always counsels us for ease, as Peter counselled
Christ, 'Master, pity thyself' (*Matt.* 16:22). So we have a nature
in us like unto Peter, Spare, favour, pity thyself. Like Eve, and
Job's wife, we have a corrupt nature that is always soliciting from[1]
God, and drawing us unto vanity (*Gen.* 3:6, *Job* 2:10). Take heed
of counselling with flesh and blood; for if men were in a city envi-
roned round about with enemies, would they consult with them
what they should do for defence of the city? Were it not a mad
part? And is it not a greater madness when Christians will consult
with flesh and blood what they should do in duties of obedience,
which will always put us upon terms of ease, the favour of men,
content, and the like, which, if a man yield to, he shall never enter
into heaven? Take heed therefore of consulting with our enemy,

---

[1] That is, away from.—G.

THE LOVE OF CHRIST

seeing Satan hath all the correspondency he hath by that enemy which we harbour in our bosom. In which case the hurt he doth us by his sophistry comes by ourselves. We betray ourselves by our carnal reason, whereby Satan mingleth himself with our imaginations and conceits. Let us therefore beware we listen not to the counsel of flesh and blood, especially when the matter comes to suffering once, for there of all other things flesh and blood doth draw back. Every one hath a Peter in himself that saith, 'Spare thyself.' Thou art indiscreet to venture thyself upon this and that hazard. But where the judgment is convinced of the goodness of the cause, whether it be religion or justice (for the first or for the second table,[1] that matters not), if the judgment be convinced of the thing, then consult not with flesh and blood, whatsoever the suffering be. It is not necessary that we should live in riches, honours, pleasures, and estimation with the world. But it is necessary we should live honest men and good Christians. Therefore, when flesh and blood objecteth in this kind, consult not with it. First, because it is an enemy, and therefore is to be suspected and neglected; secondly, because it is said, 'flesh and blood shall not inherit the kingdom of heaven' (*1 Cor.* 15:50).

Ans. 2. And therefore we should practise that first lesson in religion, *heavenly wisdom*. To aid us wherein, Christ, knowing what an enemy we are to ourselves in the ways of God, saith, 'Let a man deny himself, and take up his cross, and follow me' (*Matt.* 16:24). There is no following of Christ, considering that our flesh is so full of cavils and excuses, unless we practise that heavenly lesson of Christ, 'to deny ourselves', our whole self, our wit and reason, in the matters of God: our will and affections. Say nay to all the sluggishness of the flesh; silence all presently, as soon as ever they discourage thee from holy ways. Consider whence they come, which is enough; from God's and our enemy, and the worst

---

[1] That is of the Ten Commandments, 1-4 dealing with our duties to God and 5-10 our duty to our neighbour.—P.

enemy we have, that lieth in our own bosom. And to enable us the better, mark what Paul saith, 'We are no more debtors to the flesh', &c. (*Rom.* 8:12). We owe nothing to it. I owe not such obedience, such subjection, to the flesh and carnal reason; I have renounced it long since. What! am I obnoxious to a man unto whom I owe no service? We owe the flesh no service or obedience. What! shall we yield to that which we have long since renounced?

Ans. 3. And withal, *in spiritual courses, let us arm ourselves with resolution.* First, conclude is it so or not so. Let our judgments be convinced. For resolution is a disposition arising from the will immediately; but it is of the will, by sound judgment, convinced of the goodness of the thing, after which the will resolves. Get resolution from soundness of conviction that such things are good, and that they are best for us, and best for us at this time, the sooner the better; that there is an absolute necessity to have them, and that they are everlastingly good. Oh! these considerations will put us on amain[1] to obtain the same. It is our duty, and we shall sin against God, against our conscience, against the Spirit of God, and against others that take like liberty by our examples, if we yield to our base lusts and suggestions in this kind.

And to help resolution the more, let us have before our eyes the examples of God's worthies, who (like unto David's worthies, who brake through the host of the Philistines for water, 2 *Sam.* 23:16) have in all ages broken through all discouragements, and made a conscience more to please God, to hold communion and fellowship with Christ, than to hold any correspondency with the world. Look to blessed Paul, 'What do ye vexing of me and breaking my heart? I am ready not only to go to Jerusalem, but to die for Christ's sake' (*Acts* 21:13). And look to Christ how he shakes off Peter, 'Get thee behind me, Satan', &c. (*Matt.* 16:23). Look to Moses, how he shook off all the solicitations of a court, 'Because he had an eye to the recompence of the reward' (*Heb.* 11:26). Look

---

[1] Exceedingly or forcefully.—P.

to Joshua, 'I and mine house will serve the Lord' (*Josh*. 24:15). Let others of the world do what they will; if others will go to the devil, let them; for myself, I and my house, those that I have charge of, will serve the Lord. This was a noble resolution which was in good Nehemiah, 'Shall such a man as I flee?' (*Neh*. 6:11). What! shall I flee? shall I do this, yield to this base discouragement? shall I discourage others, like those spies of Canaan, by mine example? Hence it is that Hebrews 11th, in that notable chapter, that little 'book of martyrs', after the catalogue of those worthies set down there, that which we are exhorted and pointed to in the beginning of the next chapter, is unto the practice of the like virtues, in imitation, having before us 'such a cloud of witnesses', wherewith being compassed, the exhortation is, 'Let us therefore shake off everything that presseth down, and the sin that hangeth so fast on', &c. (*Heb*. 12:1).[1] As the cloud was a guide to them to Canaan out of Egypt, so the cloud of good examples is as it were a light to go before us to the heavenly Canaan.

In this case above all, let us look to Christ, 'who is the author and finisher of our faith' (*Heb*. 12:2). This will make us break through discouragements and resolve indeed. What could hinder him? His love is so fiery, that nothing could hinder him to come from heaven to the womb of the virgin; from thence to the cross, and so to the grave, to be abased lower than ever any creature was. His love to us so carried him through all discouragements and disgraces. 'Consider him, who endured such speaking against of sinners' (*Heb*. 12:3). The consideration of Christ's love and example will carry us through all discouragements whatsoever.

Ans. 4. And further, *let us be able by sound reasons to justify the ways of God, and to answer cavils; to give account of what we do to ourselves and others*, with reasons why we sanctify the Sabbath, have such communion with God in prayer, neglect the fashions

---

[1] Cf. Sibbes' translation, with Alford, Webster and Wilkinson, and Dr Sampson, *in loc*. He repeats this and other renderings in his various books.—G.

of the world, &c. To have reasons ready from Scripture is an excellent thing; when we are able to justify whatsoever we do by the Word, against all the quarrels of our own hearts and others. When we are led to do things only by the example of others, or by respects, then we are ofttimes put to it on the sudden by temptations, being not able to justify what we do. Let us labour therefore to do things upon good grounds, and be able to justify all the ways of religion, as they are easily justified. For nothing in this world stands with so much reason, as exactness in the ways of God. There is so much reason for nothing in the world, as to be not only Christians, but exact Christians as Paul saith to Agrippa, 'Would to God you were not almost, but altogether as I am, saving these bonds' (*Acts* 26:29), to make conscience of all ways and courses. It stands with the most reason of the world, so to justify religion by reasons unanswerable, that may set down corrupt nature, and stop the mouth of the devil himself. And herein let us propound sound and strong questions to ourselves often. Are those things that I am moved to do good, or are they not? If they be good, why do I not do them? If they be bad, why do I do them at all? If they be good, why do I stick at them? How do I prove them to be good? Have always ready some Scripture, or reason from thence, which is as good. The reasons of the Word are most divinely strong, let them be ready against all objections whatsoever, as against slight oaths, think of that of Christ, that we must give an account for all idle words (*Matt.* 12:36). How much more for atheistical oaths! So against grosser sins learn reason, a civil man, an heathen, would not do thus.

So also when the flesh moveth us to any backwardness in religious courses, let us have some Scripture ready, or reasons deducted from it. As, 1, *From the dignity of our profession, from the great hopes we have to be glorious another day.* And reason the matter, How doth this that I am moved to, suit with my hopes and expectation to come? How furthers it my journey homewards?

And consider this likewise, 2, *That no excuse will serve the turn at the day of judgment, but such an one as ariseth from an invincible infirmity, or an unremovable impediment.* Such an excuse, taken from an invincible infirmity, may then serve the turn. As, when we cannot possibly do a thing, from impediments that all the means in the world cannot remove, as, a poor man cannot be liberal, &c. Excuses also, fetched from impossible impediments, as from invincible weakness, may avail. If a man have an infirm body, then he cannot do that which another man can. These excuses, with a gracious God, will serve the turn: which are not so much excuses, as a just plea. But otherwise, our untoward excuses will not serve the turn. What hindered them in the gospel who were invited to the supper? (*Luke* 14). Excuses from oxen, wives, &c. Was it not lawful to buy oxen? and was it not lawful for the married to take content in a wife? 'Another had married a wife.' Were not all these things lawful? Very lawful. The farm hurts not, if it hinder not, nor the wife, oxen, nor anything. But in this case, when we regard these things more than the invitation to come to the feast of holy things, here is the malice of the devil, which brings that doleful message, 'They shall never taste of my feast' (*Luke* 14:24). There is such an infinite disproportion between the good of religion, peace of conscience, joy in the Holy Ghost here, and heaven and happiness hereafter, and between anything in this world, that to allege any hindrance whereby we cannot keep a good conscience, and preserve assurance of salvation, is most extreme folly and atheism. I believe not a better life, the disproportion being so great between the state of this life and a better, if I fetch excuses from the things of this life, to keep me from religion, the fear of God, and working out my salvation with fear and trembling. These excuses will not serve the turn. Not only with God at the day of judgment, but also our own consciences will tell us, that we are hypocrites to make such or such a plea. Therefore, when men become false, thereby to provide for wife or children, and take corrupt courses to keep them from religion, with pretext of their callings, lest they should lose one day in seven, this employment cannot prosper, which slights over duties under false pretences. Oh, they can toil for the pelf[1] of the world! But for matters of their souls, they turn off all shamefully, as if there were not a God to judge them, a heaven to reward them, or a hell to punish them. Will such excuses serve the turn? Oh, no; they cannot with conscience, much less with God the Judge, who is greater than our conscience. This is another way to cut off these idle cavils, to consider that these excuses cannot serve the turn, neither to comfort conscience in this world, nor to uphold us in our plea at the day of judgment. Remember that.

Ans. 5. And then again, *Let us inure[2] ourselves to bear the yoke of religion from our youth*, which will make it easy afterwards. It were an excellent thing if those who are young, in the prime of their years, would inure themselves to the exercise of religion. This would make it easy unto them, to read the Word of God, to open their spirits unto him in prayer. It may please God hereby (though they be negligent herein), yet they may be called to religion. But for an old man there is much work to do to read, to get anything into his brain, when his memory is pestered with other things, and corrupt nature in him is armed with a world of excuses, that might have been prevented by a timely and seasonable training up in a course of religion. Profane young persons know not what they do when they put off religion. Have they excuses now? They will have many more hereafter, when Satan and corruption will be much stronger. O! let them bear the yoke of religion, that is, inure themselves to duties that become Christians, which may facilitate and make it easy and pliable, that it may not be harsh to our nature. If a man do not hear, pray, and read, he can never have faith, grace, knowledge, mortification of corruption, wherein religion

[1] Riches, wealth, used in a disparaging sense—P.

[2] That is, get used, accustomed.—P.

stands. But because these lead to duties that are hard to nature, and harsh, it is wisdom to inure young ones thereto betimes, that, having used themselves to these preparing duties, they may be the more fitted for the essential ones; that, having things in the brain by reading and hearing, grace may be wrought in the heart, it being a more easy passage from the brain to the heart. When a man is converted, it is an easy matter to bring it from the brain unto the heart; whereas a man that hath been negligent in his youth must then be instructed in the principles of religion. Therefore, it is a miserable case (though men be never so politic in the world) to have been negligent herein till age. It breeds a great deal of difficulty to them, ere they can come to be in such a state as a Christian should be in. Remember this, therefore, to do as Paul adviseth Timothy, a young man, 'to exercise himself in godliness' (*1 Tim*. 4:7). It is a good thing for all that are young to exercise themselves to all duties of religion, or else pretences will grow up with age, whereby they will be indisposed every day more than other. Experience shows it generally. We may believe it. If we will not, we shall find it hereafter too true by woeful experience.

Ans. 6. And then again, by little and little, not only to be inured to the yoke of religion, but likewise *to endure difficulties, opposition, and hardship*; as the apostle stands upon it to Timothy, 'to endure hardship and afflictions from the beginning' (*2 Tim*. 2:3). If the thing be good and warrantable, neglect the speeches of the world. What are the speeches of a company of men in the state of nature, in their miserable condition, to regard them, so as not to endure hardship in such things, of the goodness whereof we are convinced? But in these days men take up a delicate profession of religion. Men will be religious, but they will suffer nothing, not a taunt or a scoff. They will part with nothing; be at no loss; suffer no cross; be at no pains with religion further than may stand with all earthly content of this world. This delicate profession, if anything among us, threateneth the removing of the gospel and blessed truths we enjoy, because we will not part with any pleasure now. How will they suffer afflictions for the gospel, if such times come, that will not part with a vain oath, a corrupt fashion of life, a superfluity,[1] that will not part with a rotten unsavoury discourse, which discovereth a rotten spirit, and infecteth others? Here is a profession of religion, indeed, that cannot have so much mastery of the corrupt heart as to deny and overcome itself in things that are grossly ill! How will a man part with his blood and life, that will not part with things that he should part withal? not only with something to the poor and to good uses, but to part with some sinful course of life, and wicked and ungodly lusts that fight against the soul; who will not endure so much as a check; who, rather than they will go under that censure wherewith the world is pleased to disgrace religion, they will live and die like atheists. This extreme tenderness in the matters of God and of salvation is the cause why many eternally perish.

Ans. 7. Again, to cut off all vain excuses, *let us oft have in thought of our heart what we should be, and what we should all aim at, and how far we come all short of it.* A Christian that hopes of good of his religion should live by faith, and depend upon God in the use of lawful means. If he be as he should be, he ought to walk with God, keep his watch with him, and do nothing unbeseeming the eye of God. When his corruption draws him to be careless, then he is not as he should be; for in a right temper, he ought to be fitted to every good work, ready for all opportunities of doing anything that is good, because the time of this life is the seedtime, the time of doing good. The time of reaping is in the world to come. When, therefore, the heart is shut, when any opportunity is offered of doing good, he may conclude certainly, I am cold and dull; pretend what I will, I am not as I should be. A Christian ought to 'abound in the work of the Lord' (*1 Cor.* 15:58), especially having such abundance of encouragements as we have.

[1] Excess.—P.

THE LOVE OF CHRIST

What a world of encouragements hath a Christian! There are none to[1] those of religion, from the inward content that it brings here, at the hour of death, and in glory hereafter. When we are drawn to be scanty, niggardly, and base to things that are good, surely this is not as it should be. Pretend what we will to the contrary, this is a fault. A Christian should at all times be fit to yield and to render up his soul unto God, because our life is uncertain. When, therefore, we are moved by corruption to live in a state that we cannot abide to die in, because we are under the guilt of some sin, then certainly, pretend what we will, our state is so far naught, as far as there is unfitness and unwillingness to die. Let us have in the eye of our soul, therefore, what a Christian should be, aim at it, and think that when we stop at a lower measure and pitch, that, pretend what we will, all is but from carnal wit and policy, the greatest enemy that religion hath.

We pray in the Lord's Prayer, 'Thy kingdom come; thy will be done in earth, as it is done in heaven:' great desires, and which should be the desires of all our hearts. But herein we play the hypocrites. Whilst we pray thus, that the kingdom of God may come, that Christ may rule in our hearts over lusts and desires; yet notwithstanding, we pretend this and that excuse, whereby we may be led with this and that lust. We cross our own prayers. Yet it showeth what pitch we should aspire to, 'To sanctify the Lord in our hearts', to delight in him, and trust in him above all. When we do not this, we fall short of our own prayers. And when we cannot bring our hearts to suffer, and to do what God would have us to do, but are led away with our own wills, we are not as we should be. Our wills should be conformable to Christ's in all things. It is our prayer, and therefore we should aim at it. Now, when flesh and blood sets up a pitch of religion, I am well enough; and yet prays, 'Hallowed be thy name; thy kingdom come; thy will be done', &c.,—such a man is an hypocrite. For his

[1] That is, there are no encouragements compared with.—Ed.

prayer leads him further and further still, till he come to heaven, where is all perfection; until when, our life is a life of endeavour and progress. Though we be never so perfect, yet Christ may more rule and set up his kingdom yet more in the heart, and further bring our will to his in all things. When flesh and blood sets up cavils against this, we play the hypocrites with God, and cross ourselves. Therefore, let us justify a measure of religion beyond our present pitch, whatsoever it is; justify it more and more still. Think, we are never as we should be till we be in heaven; and never bless ourselves, but think that we should always be on the growing hand; and whatsoever excuse comes to hinder us from zealousness and earnestness, though it carry a show of reason in the profession of religion, account it to come from our corrupt hearts.

Ans. 8. Again, *remember to do all things to God and not to man, in our callings both of religion and in our particular callings*; and then whatsoever discouragement there is from men, we should not be discouraged. We shall hear men continually complain of others, that they are unthankful persons; and why should we do anything for them? Why! do it to God. If it fall within our callings, let us do justice and show mercy. God will accept, though men do not. It cuts off many discouragements in duties. It is best to have God's reward. In this world it is good to meet with naughty unthankful persons, because else we should meet with all our reward here. It is good to do somewhat for God's sake, and for religion, let people be as unthankful as they will; to say, I did it not to you, but to God. If a man regard the discouragement of the world, he shall never do that which is good, people in the world are so unthankful and regardless to those that wish them best, and that do best to them. But if a man do a thing to God, and do it out of duty and conscience, he may hold on; have he never so many discouragements in the world, he shall lose nothing. All shall be rewarded, and is regarded.

Ans. 9. Likewise, be sure to carry this in mind, *that sin is the greatest evil, and grace and goodness the best thing in the world.* Therefore, there is no excuse for sin, from anything in the world, for it is the worst thing in the world, which stains the soul, and hinders it from comfort. And for grace and goodness in the inward man, it is the best thing in the world. Therefore, purchase this, though with disadvantage. It is best to avoid sin, though with enduring evil; yea, to avoid the least sin, by enduring the greatest evil. It is wisdom to do good with disadvantage, when the disadvantage is bounded only in this life, the thing that I do being a thing which furthers my reckoning at the day of account. Therefore, have this always in consideration, whatsoever I suffer in this world, I will not sin. This will cut off a world of excuses.

Therefore, let us labour to cut off all cavils, and to 'arm ourselves'. It is the Apostle Peter's exhortation (*1 Pet.* 4:1). As David's worthies brake through the pikes to fetch him water from the well of Bethlehem (*2 Sam.* 23:16), so all Christian worthies that look to be crowned, let them be armed inwardly with resolution for good things, take up resolutions that they will do it. As Paul tells his scholar Timothy of his purpose, 'Thou knowest my purpose, and manner of living' (*2 Tim.* 3:10). This is the manner of a Christian life: that this, I will not break for all the world. So, there is a purpose of living honestly a manner of life, not by starts, now and then to speak a word, and to do a good deed; but there is a purpose and a manner of life for it. He resolves always for the best things.

And to this end beg of God his Spirit, which is above all impediments. The more Spirit, the more strength and courage against impediments. The more we attend upon holy means, the more spiritual and heavenly light and life is set up in the soul. The more spiritual we are, the more we shall tread under foot all those things that stand between us and heaven. Let us therefore labour more and more for the Spirit, and then we shall offer an holy violence unto good things; as it was said of John Baptist's time, 'The kingdom of God suffered violence' (*Matt.* 11:12). Men were so eager of it, as that they surprised it as a castle, by violence. There is no way to take heaven but by offering violence to discouragement, corruption, and whatsoever stands in the way. The violent only takes heaven by force.[1] Now when we are spiritual, we shall not pretend, that 'there is a lion in the way', that there are difficulties, as the sluggard doth, that thinks himself wiser than many men who can render a reason. But we shall go boldly and courageously on; and know that there are more encouragements for good, and stronger, than the world hath allurements to be naught, which are but for the present life; but we have inward ones, which will hold out in the hour of death and after. Therefore, go on boldly and resolutely in good things, always remembering to beg the Spirit of God, that may arm our spirits with invincible courage.

Now the Spirit of God brings faith with it, which is a conquering, victorious grace over the world, and 'sees him that is invisible' (*Heb.* 11:27); which brings love also, 'which is strong as death' (*Song of Sol.* 8:6): wherewith the soul being warmed, it constraineth us to do duties in spite of all impediments. The Spirit of God will strengthen our hope also of heaven, which strengthens us against all discouragements which stand in our way. For this hope is on greater and better grounds than discouragements are; and he that giveth us this hope, will enable us to possess it.

Therefore labour first, *to have a clear understanding of the things of God, and of the excellency of them*; for light will cause heat. Why did the kingdom of heaven in John Baptist's time, 'suffer violence'? Why were men then so violent to cleave unto Christ? Because from that time the gospel was more clearly manifested. And heavenly truths, the more they are discovered and laid open

---

[1] This recalls the little book of Thomas Watson's, called *Heaven taken by Storm*, memorable as having been the occasion of the conversion of the celebrated Colonel Gardiner, whose life by Doddridge is one of our Christian classics.—G.

THE LOVE OF CHRIST

(there is such an excellency in them), the more they work upon the heart and affections. Therefore, 'the kingdom of heaven suffered violence'. And where are people more earnest after good things, than in these places where the evangelical truths of God are laid open most? There they break through all discouragements whatsoever.

And so, *labour for faith to believe those truths*: which is the most victorious and conquering grace, that will carry us through all discouragements whatsoever; because it will set greater things before us, than the discouragements are. Are we afraid of men? Faith, it sets hell before us. Are we allured by the world? It sets heaven before us. It conquers the world, with all the discouraging temptations thereof. Are the discouragements from impossibilities? O, it is hard, I cannot do it. Aye, but, saith Paul, 'I am able to do all things through Christ that strengthens me' (*Phil.* 4:13). There is a kind of omnipotency in faith, 'O woman, be it unto thee as thou wilt' (*Matt.* 15:28). We have abundance of strength in Christ. Faith is but an empty hand, that goes to Christ to draw from him what it hath need of; 'In Christ I can do all things.'

So, *to have our hearts warmed with love to him*. This grace of the Spirit will make us pass through all discouragements, for it hath a constraining power. 'The love of Christ constrains us', saith the apostle (*2 Cor.* 5:14). If our hearts once be warmed with the love of Christ, this will make us to think nothing too dear for Christ, and will cut off all excuses and pretences whatsoever, which come from coldness of affection. 'Love is strong as death', as we have it in this book, 'much water cannot quench it' (*Song of Sol.* 8:6). All oppositions and discouragements whatsoever, all the water which the devil and the world hath or useth, cannot quench the heavenly fire of love, when it is kindled in any measure. What carried the blessed saints and martyrs of God in all times through the pikes of all discouragements? The Spirit of God, by the spirit of love, from a spirit of faith, and heavenly conviction of the excellency and truth of the things. They saw such a light, which wrought upon their affections, and carried them amain against the stream (contrary to the stream of the times wherein they lived), that the worse the times were, the better they were.

Ans. 10. And let us consider again, *that Christ will not be always thus alluring us*; that we shall not always have these encouragements, such truths and motions of God's Spirit, as perhaps we feel now. Therefore, when we feel any good motion stirred up toward Christ, entertain it presently. Happily we shall never hear of it again. The longer we defer and put it off, the worse. As a man that is rowing in a boat, let him neglect his stroke, the neglecting of one may make him tug at it five or six times after to overtake those that are before him. So nothing is gotten by sloth and negligence. We do but cast ourselves back the more.

Ans. 11. And let us help ourselves *with setting the glory to come before our eyes*, with Moses to have a patriarch's eye to him 'that is invisible', to see 'a country afar off' (*Heb.* 11:27). Now, 'we are nearer salvation than when we believed'. Let us help our backward souls this way: that so, having still glory in our eyes, it may help us to go through all discouragements, whatsoever they be. We know Zaccheus, when he was afraid that he should not see Christ, went before the multitude; and getting up upon the top of a tree, thus helps himself. So doth grace help itself by glory. And so far is grace from objecting and pretending lets,[1] as it makes supplies in God's service; as David, who in this case was pleased to be accounted vile (*2 Sam.* 6:22). Let us look unto the recompence of the reward; not to the present discouragements, but to the prize at the end of the race. What makes a soldier to fight hard for the victory in the end? The sweetness of the triumph. What makes a husbandman go through all discouragements? He hopes to receive a crop in the end. Consider the issue which followeth after a conscionable, careful, and Christian life, after

---

[1] That is, hindrances.—G.

a more near and perfect walking with God, maintaining communion with him. Let there be what discouragements there will be in the world, 'the end thereof is peace'. 'The end of that man is peace' (*Psa.* 37:37). Upon this ground, the apostle exhorts us, 'to be fruitful and abundant in the work of the Lord; knowing that your labour is not in vain in the Lord' (*1 Cor.* 15:58).

SERMON 9

I rose to open to my beloved;
but my beloved had withdrawn himself.
SONG OF SOLOMON 5:6

NATURALLY we are prone to delays in heavenly things, and then to cover all with excuses. A man is a sophister[1] to himself, whom he first deceives, before the devil or the world deceive him; which is the reason why so oft in Scripture you have this mentioned: 'Be not deceived, God is not mocked' (*Gal.* 6:7). 'Be not deceived, neither adulterer, nor covetous person, nor such and such, shall ever enter into the kingdom of heaven' (*1 Cor.* 6:9). 'Be not deceived', which is an intimation that naturally we are very prone to be deceived in points of the greatest consequence in the world, to flatter ourselves, as the church doth here, with false excuses. 'I have put off my coat', &c. But we shall now see in this next verse what becomes of all those excuses and backwardness of the church whereby she puts off Christ.

'My beloved put in his hand by the hole of the door, and my bowels were moved for him.

'I rose to open to my beloved; and my hands dropped with myrrh, and my fingers with sweet-smelling myrrh, upon the handles of the lock.

'I rose to open to my beloved; but my beloved had withdrawn himself', &c., verses 4–6.

This comes of her sluggishness and drowsiness, that Christ

---

[1] One who reasons in a self-deceptive or fallacious manner.—P.

179

THE LOVE OF CHRIST

absented and withdrew himself. There are three things here set down in these verses now read.

1. *Christ's withdrawing of himself.*

2. *His gracious dealing, having withdrawn himself.*

He doth not altogether leave his church, but 'puts his finger into the hole of the door', and then leaves some sweetness behind him before he goes. After which is set down,

3. *The success of Christ's departure and withdrawing of himself from her.*

(1.) *Her bowels were moved in her*, which were *hard* before.

(2.) *She rose up out of her bed*, wherein formerly she had framed and composed herself to rest.

(3.) *She seeks and calls after him.*

But the doctrinal points which are to be observed out of these verses are these,

Obs. 1. *That Christ doth sometimes use to leave his children, as he did the church here.*

Obs. 2. *That the cause is from the church herself*, as we see how unkindly she had used Christ, to let him attend her leisure so long. Therefore he, taking a holy state upon him, leaves the church. The cause of his forsaking us is in ourselves. We may thank ourselves for it.

Obs. 3. That though Christ deal thus with us, yet notwithstanding *he never leaves us wholly, without some footsteps of his saving grace and everlasting love; some remainders and prints he leaves upon the soul*, so as it lingers after him, and never rests till it find him. He always leaves something. There is never a total desertion; as we see here in Christ's dealing, 'he puts his finger into the hole of the door'. He stands at the door, and leaves myrrh behind him, something in the heart that causeth a lingering and restless affection in her towards Christ.

Obs. 4. *That the church, by reason of this gracious dealing of Christ, (leaving somewhat behind him) is sensible of her former unkindness, is restless, and stirs up herself to endeavour more and*

more, till she have recovered her former communion and sweet fellowship with Christ which she had before. She never gives over till Christ and she meet again in peace, as we shall see in the prosecution.[1] These be the chief points considerable.

Obs. 1. First, *Christ doth use sometimes to leave his church,* as here he doth, 'My beloved had withdrawn himself', &c.

But what kind of leaving is it?

We must distinguish of Christ's leavings and withdrawings of himself. They are either in regard of outward or inward comforts and helps.

1. *Outward,* as Christ leaves his church sometimes *by taking away the means of salvation,* the ministry, or *by taking away outward comforts,* which is a withdrawing of his; especially if he accompany the taking of them away with some signs of his displeasure or sense of his anger, as usually it falls out. This doth embitter all crosses and losses, namely, when they come from Christ as a testimony of his anger for our former unkindness.

2. Sometimes his forsaking is *more inward,* and that is double, either in regard of *peace and joy,* sweet inward comfort that the soul had wont to feel in the holy ordinances by the Spirit of Christ; or in regard of *strength and assistance.* There is a desertion in regard of comfort and in regard of strength. Sometimes he leaves them to themselves, in regard of strength and supportation, to fall into some sin, to cure some greater sin perhaps.

Now that Christ thus leaves his church, it is true of all, both of the body and of each particular member of the church.

(1.) It is true of *the whole body of the church,* for you have the church complaining (*Isa.* 49:14, 15), 'God hath forgotten me', 'Can a mother forget her child?' saith God again. So Psalm 44:9; and in other places the church complains of forsakings. The Scripture is full of complaints in this kind.

(2.) It is true of *the several members,* and especially of the most eminent members, as we see holy Job complains, as if God had

---

[1] The process of carrying something out.—P.

'set him', as it were, 'a butt to shoot at' (*Job* 6:4), and had opposed himself against him. So David complains (*Psa.* 88:11; 77:9; and 60:1, and in other Psalms) of God's anger. 'Correct me not in thine anger' (*Psa.* 6:1). The Psalms are full of this, so as it would be time unprofitably spent to be large in a point so clear, that every one knoweth well enough who reads and understands the Psalms. So Jonah likewise felt a kind of forsaking when he was in the midst of the sea, when the waves were without and terrors within, when he was in the midst of hell, as it were (*Jon.* 2:2). Thus, you see, the instances clear the point.

The ends that God hath in it are many. (1.) *To endear his presence the more to us*, which we slighted too much before. It is our corruption, the not valuing of things till they be gone. We set not the true price upon them when we enjoy them. When we enjoy good things, we look at the grievances which are mingled with the good, and forget the good; which, when it is gone, then we remember the good. The Israelites could remember their onions and garlic, and forget their slavery (*Num.* 11:5). So, because manna was present, they despised manna, and that upon one inconvenience it had, 'it was ordinary with them' (*Num.* 21:5). Thus the corrupt heart of man is prone in the enjoying of favours. If it have any grievance, it murmurs at that; and it troubles and makes them forget all the goodness and sweetness of what they enjoy. But, on the contrary, when God withdraws those good things from us, then we forget those former inconveniences, and begin to think what good we had by them. This is the poison and corruption of our nature.

(2.) Again, Christ seems to forsake us, *to try the truth of the graces and affections in us*, whether they be true or not; and to cause us to make after him, when he seems to forsake us, as undoubtedly we shall, where there is truth of grace planted in the heart in any measure.

(3.) And in regard of others, he doth it *to teach us heavenly wisdom, how to deal with those in affliction* (2 *Cor.* 1:4). It makes us wise, tender, and successful in dealing with others, when we have felt the like particular grievance ourselves, as Galatians 6:1, 'Brethren, if a man be overtaken in a fault, you that are spiritual restore such a one in the spirit of meekness, considering thyself, lest thou also be tempted.' Experience of spiritual grief in this kind, will make us fit, able, and wise every way to deal with others.

(4.) This serves likewise *to wean us from the world, in the plenty and abundance of all earthly things.* For take a Christian that hath no cross in the world, let him find some estrangement of Christ from his spirit, that he finds not the comforts of the Holy Ghost, and that enlargement which in former times he enjoyed, and all the wealth he hath, the earthly contentments he enjoys, please him not, nor can content that soul, which hath ever felt sweet communion with Christ. Again, how should we pray with earnestness of affection, 'Thy kingdom come', in the time of prosperity, except there were somewhat in this kind to raise up the soul to desire to be gone? Now, it is our subjection to these alterations and changes, ebbings and flowings, sometimes to have the sense of God's love in Christ, and sometimes to want it; sometimes to feel his love, and sometimes again the fruits of his anger and displeasure, which serves exceedingly to stir up men's desires of heaven.

(5.) In this place here, the especial end was *to correct the security, and ill carriage of the church.*

And, likewise

(6.) *To prepare the church, by this desertion and seeming forsaking, for nearer communion.* For, indeed, Christ did not forsake her, but to her feeling, to bring her, in the sequel, to have nearer communion and union with himself than ever she had before. God forsakes, that he may not forsake. He seems strange, that he may be the more friendly. This is Christ's usage. He personates an adversary, when he intends to show the greatest effects of his love, as we may see afterwards in the passages following.

And also,

(7.) *To make us to know thoroughly the bitterness of sin*, that we may grow up to a further hatred of that which deprives us of so sweet a communion. We think sin a trifle, and never know it enough till the time of temptation; that conscience be awakened and opened; that it appears in its right colours.

And then, again,

(8.) *That we may know what Christ suffered and underwent for us, in the sense of God's wrath, in the absence of his favour for a time.* This the human nature could never have suffered, if his divinity had withdrawn itself. Now, all of us must sip of that cup, whereof Christ drank the dregs, having a taste what it is to have God to forsake us. For the most part, those believers who live any time (especially those of great parts), God deals thus with. Weaker Christians he is more indulgent unto. At such times we know of what use a Mediator is, and how miserable our condition were without such an one, both to have borne and overcome the wrath of God for us, which burden he could never have undergone, but had sunk under it, but for the hypostatical union.[1]

Use 1. Let us not, therefore, *censure any Christian, when we find that their course hath been good and gracious, yet notwithstanding they seem to want comfort.* Let us not wonder at them, as if God had utterly forsaken them. Indeed, sometimes they think themselves forsaken, and the world thinks them so too, 'that God regards them not' (*Psa.* 66:18). They are people of no respect either to God or to others, as you have the church in the Psalms complaining, as if God had forsaken them (*Psa.* 44:9); so they think themselves forsaken, and the world thinks them so too, and neglects them. Therefore, in so doing, we shall censure the generation of the righteous. It was thus with the Head of the church, with the whole church, and with every particular member. Neither is it fit we should always enjoy the sense of God's love. Christ by heavenly

---

[1] The union of the human and divine natures of Christ in one person.—P.

wisdom dispenseth of his sweetness, comforts, and peace, as may stand with our souls' best good, and we should as much take heed of censuring ourselves in that condition, as if we were rejected and cast away of God. We must judge ourselves at such times by faith, and not by feeling; looking to the promises and Word of God, and not to our present sense and apprehension.

Use 2. Again, if this be so, learn *to prepare and look for it beforehand, and to get some grounds of comfort, some promises out of the Word, and to keep a good conscience.* O it is a heavy thing, when God shall seem to be angry with us, and our conscience at the same time shall accuse us; when the devil shall lay sins hard to our charge, and some affliction at the same time lie heavy upon the sore and guilty soul. If we have not somewhat laid up beforehand, what will become of the poor soul, when heaven, and earth, and hell, and all shall seem to be against it. There are few that come to heaven, but they know what these things mean. It is good, therefore, to look for them, and to prepare some comforts beforehand.

But what here should be the inward moving cause? It is in the church herself; for mark the coherence. She had turned off Christ with excuses, pretences, and dilatory answers; and now presently upon it Christ forsakes her in regard of her feeling, and of the sweet comfort she formerly enjoyed. The point is,

Obs. 2. *That the cause rests in ourselves why Christ withdraws comfort from our souls.*

If we search our own hearts we shall find it so, and usually the causes in ourselves are these, as it was in the church here:

1. *When we are unkind to Christ*, and repel the sweet motions of the Spirit.

2. *When we improve not the precious means of salvation that we enjoy.*

3. *When we are careless of our conversation and company.*

4. *When we linger after carnal liberties and ease.*

5. *When we yield to carnal policy* and shifts to keep us off from the power of religion, to go on in a lukewarm course.

6. *When we linger after earthly things and comforts*, and wrap ourselves up in fleshly policy for ease.

7. *When we tremble not at God's judgments and threatenings, and at the signs of them*; with many such things. Where these dispositions are, we need not wonder if we find not the comforts of Christ and of the Holy Ghost in us, with the gracious presence of his Spirit. The cause is in ourselves. But security hath been at large spoken of before, where the church's sleep was handled.[1] Therefore, the point shall not be here enlarged, but only some use made of it, as may serve for the present purpose.

Use 1. If Christ should take away the comforts that we enjoy, and remove himself and his dwelling from us, for he is now yet among us and knocks at our doors, *do we not give him just cause to depart?* What a spirit of slumber possesseth us, which will be awaked with nothing to seek after Christ! How few lay hold upon God, press upon him, wrestle with him by prayer, to hide themselves before the evil day come, as they should do! Therefore, if Christ have absented himself a long time from the church in general, and withdrawn the comfort and presence of his ordinances; and, in particular, withheld the sweet comforts of our spirits and our peace, so that we see him in the contrary signs of his displeasure and anger, as if he did not regard and respect us, we have given him just cause so to do. We see here how the church used Christ; and so do we, with the like security, and a spirit of slumber, with unkindness. Notwithstanding all the provocations that Christ useth to win us, he leaves us not, until he be left first, for he desires to have nearer acquaintance, communion, and fellowship with the soul, as we have seen in the former verse, 'My love, my dove, my undefiled, open to me', &c. Therefore, if we do not enjoy more acquaintance with Christ than we do, and walk more in the

[1] See Sermons 3 and 4.—P.

comforts of the Holy Ghost, it is merely from our own indisposition and security (*Acts* 9:31). Therefore, let us censure ourselves in this kind, and not call Christ an enemy, as if he had forgotten, and God had forsaken. Take heed of such a spirit of murmuring. If such a state befall us, let us labour to lay our hand upon our mouth and to justify Christ. It is just with thee thus to leave me, to give me over to this terror, to deal thus with me, that have dealt so unkindly with thee. So to justify God, and accuse ourselves, is the best way to recover spiritual comfort.

Obs. 3. Well, for the third point. *That howsoever Christ be provoked by the church's ingratitude, drowsiness, and careless carriage, to leave her in regard of her feeling, and of inward comfort; yet notwithstanding he is so gracious, as to leave something behind him, that shows indeed, that he had not left the church altogether, but only in some regard.* For howsoever Christ, in regard of some order of his providence, leave it, yet in regard of another order of his providence, care and mercy, he doth not leave it, so as one way which he takes must sometimes give place to another way of his working in ordering things. Sometimes he is present in a way of comfort, that is one order of his dispensation; and when he sees that that is neglected, then he withdraws his comforts and hides his gracious countenance. Yet he is then present still in another order and way, though we discern it not, that is, in a way of humbling the soul, letting it see its sin. So here, howsoever Christ had withdrawn himself in regard of this manner of his dealing, in respect of comfort, that the church did not now see his grace and favour; yet he left behind him a spirit of grace, to affect her heart with grief, sorrow, and shame, and to stir up her endeavours to seek after him, as it is said here: 'I rose to open to my beloved; and my hands dropped myrrh, and my fingers sweet smelling myrrh, upon the handles of the locks.'

Here observe these three things, which shall be briefly named, because they shall be touched elsewhere.

Obs. 1. *Christ's grace is the cause of our grace.* He first leaves myrrh, and then her fingers drop myrrh. Our oil is from his oil. The head being anointed, 'the oil ran down to the skirts of Aaron's garments' (*Psa.* 133:2; 36:9); 'Out of his fulness we receive grace for grace' (*John* 1:16), that is, our grace is answerable to the grace of Christ. We have all from him, favour for his favour. Because he is beloved, we are beloved. We have the grace of sanctification from him. He was sanctified with the Spirit, therefore we are sanctified. We have grace of privilege for his grace. He is the Son of God, therefore we are sons. He is the heir of heaven, therefore we are heirs. So that of his grace it is we receive all. Whether we take grace for favour, or for the grace of sanctification, or the grace of privilege and prerogative, all our graces are from his, 'our myrrh from his myrrh'.

Use. This should teach us, *the necessity of dependence upon Christ,* for whatsoever we have or would have; which dependence upon Christ is the life of our life, the soul of our souls.

Again, observe from hence, that the church's fingers dropped myrrh when she opened the door, and stirred up herself to endeavour. When first her bowels were moved, then she makes to the door, and then her hands dropped myrrh, so that,

Obs. 2. *We find experience of the grace of Christ, especially when we stir up ourselves to endeavour.* 'Arise and be doing, and the Lord shall be with thee' (*1 Chron.* 28:20), saith David to Solomon. So let us rouse up ourselves to endeavour, and we shall find a gracious presence of Christ, and a blessed assistance of the Spirit of Christ, who will show himself in the midst of endeavours. 'To him that hath shall be given:' what is that? To him that hath, if he exercise and stir up the grace of God in him, shall be given (*Matt.* 25:29). Therefore, let us stir up the graces of God in us; let us fall upon actions of obedience, second them with prayer. Whatsoever we pray for and desire, set upon the practice thereof. We mock God else, except we endeavour for that we desire. There was myrrh left on the door, but she feels it not till she arose, opened the door, and laid her hand upon the lock.

I speak to any Christian's experience, if in the midst of obedience they do not find that comfort they looked for, and that it is meat and drink to do God's will. Therefore keep not off and say, I am dead and drowsy, therefore I shall be still so. You are deceived; fall upon obedience and practising of holy duties, and in the midst thereof thou shalt find the presence and assistance of God's Spirit. That will comfort thee.

Obs. 3. The third thing observable from hence is this, *that God's graces are sweet.* Pleasant and sweet, compared here to myrrh, which was an ingredient in the holy oil. Grace makes us sweet. Prayers are sweet (*Rev.* 8:4). Christ mingleth them with his own sweet odours, and so takes and offers them to God. Holy obedience is sweet and delightful to God and to the conscience. It brings peace and delight to others. Therefore they are called fruits. Fruit doth not only imply and show the issuing of good things from the root, but there is also a pleasantness in it. So there is a delightfulness in good works, as there is in fruit to the taste. Therefore if we would be sweet and delightful to God, let us labour to have grace. If we would think of ourselves with contentment, and have inward sweetness, let us labour for the graces of God's Spirit. These are like myrrh. 'The wicked are an abomination unto the Lord', who abhors them, and whatsoever is in them. But 'the righteous and sincere man is his delight' (*Prov.* 15:8). Therefore, if we would approve ourselves to God, and feel that he hath delight in us, labour to be such as he may delight in.

Use. Wherefore let the discouraged soul make this use of it, *not to be afraid to do that which is good, upon fear we should sin.* Indeed, sin will cleave to that we do, but Christ will pardon the sin, and accept that which is sweet of his own Spirit. Let us not esteem basely of that which Christ esteems highly of, nor let that be vile in our eyes that is precious in his. Let us labour to bring

THE LOVE OF CHRIST

our hearts to comfortable obedience, for it is a sweet sacrifice to God.

Now, whence came all this? From this that is mentioned, 'My beloved put in his hand by the hole of the door, and my bowels were moved for him', verse 4. First, for that expression, he put his finger in by the hole of the door. It implies here that Christ, before he departed, left by his Spirit an impression on the church's heart, which deeply affected her to seek after him.

The fingers spoken of are nothing but 'the power of his Spirit'. As the usual Scripture phrase is, 'This is God's finger', 'God's mighty hand' (*Exod.* 8:19), without which all ordinances are ineffectual. 'Paul may plant, and Apollos may water' (*1 Cor.* 3:6, 7), but all is nothing without the working of the Spirit, the motions whereof are most strong, being God's finger, whereby he wrought all that affection in the church which is here expressed. Christ, before he leaveth the church, 'puts his finger into the hole of the door', that is, he works somewhat in the soul by his Spirit, which stirred up a constant endeavour to seek after him. For why else follows it, 'her bowels were moved after him'? which implies a work of the Spirit upon her bowels, expressed in her grief for his absence, and shame for her refusing his entrance, and whereby her heart was moved and turned in her to seek after him. From whence, thus explained, observe,

Obs. 1. *That outward means will do no good, unless the finger of Christ come to do all that is good.*

The finger of Christ is the Spirit of Christ—that is, a kind of divine power goes from him in hearing and speaking the Word of God, and in prayer. There is more than a man's power in all this. If these work any effect, Christ 'must put his finger in'. When duties are unfolded to us in the ministry of the Word, all is to no purpose, but the sounding of a voice, unless the finger of Christ open the heart, and work in the soul.

Use 1. Let us make this use of it, therefore, *not to rest in any means whatsoever*, but desire the presence of Christ's finger to move and to work upon our hearts and souls. Many careless Christians go about the ordinances of God, and never regard this power of Christ, this mighty power, 'the finger of Christ'. Thereupon they find nothing at all that is divine and spiritual wrought in them. For, as it required a God to redeem us, to take our nature, wherein he might restore us, so likewise it requires the power of God to alter our natures. We could not be brought into the state of grace without divine satisfaction, and we cannot be altered to a frame of grace without a divine finger, the finger of God working upon our hearts and souls. This should move us, in all the ordinances of God that we attend upon, to lift up our hearts in the midst of them, 'Lord, let me feel the finger of thy Spirit writing thy Word upon my heart.' 'Turn us, O Lord, and we shall be turned' (*Jer.* 31:18). Pray for this quickening and enlivening, for this strengthening Spirit. All comes by it.

From this that it is said here, 'that Christ puts his finger into the hole of the door before he removed it', and withdrew himself, observe,

Obs. 2. How graciously Christ doth deal with us, *that he doth always leave some grace before he doth offer to depart.* Let us therefore, for the time to come, lay and store this up as a ground of comfort, that howsoever Christ may leave us, yet, notwithstanding, he will never leave us wholly; but as he gave us his Holy Spirit at first, so he will continue him in us by some gracious work or other, either by way of comfort, or of strength to uphold us. Perhaps we may need more sorrow, more humility, than of any other grace. For winter is as good for the growing of things as the spring, because were it not for this, where would be the killing of weeds and worms, and preparing of the ground and land for the spring? So it is as needful for Christians to find the presence of Christ in the way of humiliation and abasement, causing us to afflict our own souls, as to feel his presence in peace, joy, and comfort. In this life we cannot be without this gracious dispensation. We may therefore comfort ourselves, that howsoever Christ leaves us, yet he will always leave somewhat behind him, as here he left some myrrh after him upon the handle of the door. Some myrrh is left always behind him upon the soul, which keeps it in a state and frame of grace, and sweetens it. Myrrh was one of the ingredients in the holy oil (*Exod.* 30:23-25); and so this leaving of myrrh behind him signifies the oil of grace left upon the soul, that enabled the church to do all these things, which are after spoken of.

Obj. But you will say, How doth this appear, when in some desertion a Christian finds no grace, strength, or comfort at all, that nothing is left?

Ans. It is answered, *they always do.* Take those who at any time have had experience of the love of God, and of Christ formerly, take them at the worst, you shall find from them some sparkles of grace, broken speeches of tried secret comfort, some inward strength and struggling against corruptions; their spirits endeavouring to recover themselves from sinking too low, and with something withstanding both despair and corruption. Take a Christian at the worst, there will be a discovery of the Spirit of Christ left in him, notwithstanding all desertion. This is universally in all in some measure, though perhaps it is not discerned to a Christian himself, but to those that are able to judge. Sometimes others can read our evidences better than ourselves. A Christian that is in temptation cannot judge of his own estate, but others can. And so, at the very worst, he hath always somewhat left in him, whereby he may be comforted. Christ never leaves his church and children that are his wholly. Those that are wholly left, they never had saving grace, as Ahithophel, Cain, Saul, and Judas were left to themselves. But for the children of God, if ever they found the power of sanctifying grace, 'Christ whom he loves, he loves to the end' (*John* 13:1), from whom he departs not, unless he leaves somewhat behind him, that sets an edge upon the desires to seek after him.

Use 2. Make this second use of it, *to magnify the gracious love and mercy of Christ*, that when we deserve the contrary, to be left altogether, yet notwithstanding so graciously he deals with us. Behold, in this his dealing, the mercy of Christ. He will not suffer the church to be in a state of security, but will rather, to cure her, bring her to another opposite state of grief and sorrow, as we shall see in the next point, how that which Christ left in the heart of the church so afflicted her 'that her bowels were turned in her'. Whereupon she riseth, seeks, and inquires after Christ by the watchmen and others. So she saith of herself,

'My bowels were moved in me', &c. What was that? My heart was affected full of sorrow and grief for my unkind dealing with Christ. Hereby those affections were stirred up, that were afore sleepy and secure, to godly grief, sorrow, and shame. For God hath planted affections in us, and joined them with conscience, as the executioners with the judge. So that, whenas conscience accuseth of any sin, either of omission or commission, affections are ready to be the executioners within us. Thus to prevent eternal damnation, God hath set up a throne in our own hearts, to take revenge and correction by our own affections, godly sorrow and mourning, as here the church saith, 'My bowels were turned in me.' It was a shame and grief, springing out of love to Christ, that had been so kind, patient, and full of forbearance to her. 'My bowels were turned in me;' that is, sorrow and grief were upon me for my unkind dealing.

The observation from hence is,

That security and a cold, dull state produceth a contrary temper. That is, those that are cold, dull, secure, and put off Christ, he suffers them to fall into sharp sorrows and griefs.

We usually say, Cold diseases must have hot and sharp remedies. It is most true spiritually. Security, which is a kind of lethargy, a cold disease, forgetting of God and our duty to him, must have a hot and sharp cure. And the lethargy is best cured by a burning ague.[1] So Christ deals here. He puts his finger in at the

---

[1] Burning fever.—P.

hole of the door, and leaves grace behind to work upon the bowels of the church, to make her grieve and be ashamed for her unkind dealing. Thus he cures security by sorrow. This is the best conclusion of sin.

And we may observe withal, *that even sins of omission, they bring grief, shame, and sorrow.* And in the issue, through Christ's sanctifying them, these which they breed consume the parent. That is, sin brings forth sorrow, shame, and grief, which are a means to cure sin. Security breeds this moving of the bowels, which moving helps security. Would we therefore prevent sorrow, shame, and grief? Take heed then of security, the cause that leads to them; yea, of sins of omission, wherein there is more danger than in sins of commission. The sins of carnal, wicked men are usually sins of commission; most which break out outrageously, and thereby taint themselves with open sins. But the sins of God's people, who are nearer to him, are for the most part sins of omission; that is, negligence, coldness, carelessness in duty, want of zeal, and of care they should have in stirring up the graces of God in them; as the church here, which did not give way to Christ, nor shook off security.

Use. Let us esteem as slightly as we will of sins of omission and carelessness, *they are enough to bring men to hell if God be not the more merciful.* It is not required only that we do no harm, and keep ourselves from outward evils; but we must do good in a good manner, and have a care to be fruitful and watchful, which if we do not, this temper will bring grief, shame, and sorrow afterwards. As here, even for sins of omission, deadness, and dullness, we see the church is left by Christ, 'and her bowels are turned in her'. For careless neglect and omission of duty to God is a presage and forerunner of some downfall and dejection. And commonly it is true, when a man is in a secure and careless state, a man may read his destiny (though he have been never so good); nay, the rather if he be good. Such a one is in danger to fall into some sharp punishment, or into some sin; for of all states and tempers, God will not suffer a Christian to be in a secure, lazy, dead state, when he cannot perform things comfortably to God, or himself, or to others. A dead, secure estate is so hateful to him (decay in our first love, this lukewarm temper) that he will not endure it. It either goes before some great sin, cross, affliction, or judgment.

'My bowels were moved in me.' And good reason. It was a suitable correction to the sin wherein she offended. For Christ, his bowels were turned towards her in love and pity, 'My love, my dove, my undefiled', in which case, she neglecting him, it was fit she should find 'moving of bowels' in another sense, out of love too, but in shame and mourning. Christ here leaves her to seek after him, that had waited and attended her leisure before, as we shall see after.

The next thing we may hence observe in that, 'that her bowels were turned in her', from something left in the hole of the door by the Spirit of Christ, is,

That Christ hath our affections in his government.

He hath our bowels in his rule and government, more than we ourselves have. We cannot of ourselves rule our grief, shame, sorrow, or such affections as these. The wisest man in the world cannot award[1] grief and sorrow when God will turn it upon his bowels, and make a man ashamed and confounded in himself. All the wit and policy in the world cannot suppress those affections. For Christ rules our hearts, 'The hearts of kings are in his hand, as the rivers of water' (*Prov.* 21:1), as well as the hearts of ordinary persons.

If he set anything upon the soul to afflict it and cast it down, it shall afflict it, if it be but a conceit. If he will take away the reins from the soul, and leave it to its own passion, removing away its guard; for he by his Spirit guards our souls with peace, by commanding of tranquillity; so as let him but leave it to itself, and it

[1] That is, ward off.—Ed.

will tear itself in sunder, as Ahithophel, who being left to himself, did tear himself in pieces (2 *Sam.* 17:23). Cain also being thus left, was disquieted, tormented, and wracked[1] himself (*Gen.* 4:13). So Judas in this case, being divided in himself, you see what became of him (*Matt.* 27:5). Let Christ but leave us to our own passion of sorrow, what will become of us but misery? He hath more rule therefore of our passions than we ourselves have, because we cannot rule them graciously, nor can we stay them when we would.

Use. Therefore this should *strike an awe in us of God, with a care to please him.* For there is not the wisest man in the world, but if he remove his guard from his soul, and leave him to himself; if there were no devil in hell, yet he would make him his own tormentor and executioner. Therefore the apostle makes this sweet promise. He bids them pray to God; 'and the peace of God which passeth all understanding should guard their souls', &c. (*Phil.* 4:7). So the word is in the original.[2] It is a great matter for the keeping of God's people, to have their souls guarded.

'Her bowels were turned in her.'

Here again, as the conclusion of all this, we seeing this estate of the church, *may wonder at Christ's carriage towards her in this world.* Christ is wonderful in his saints, and in his goodness towards them (2 *Thess.* 1:10); sometimes alluring them, as we see Christ [and] the church here; wondrous in patience, notwithstanding their provocation of him; wondrous in his desertions; wondrous in leaving something behind him in desertions. Those that are his he will not leave them without grace, whereby they shall seek him again. Nay, the falling out of lovers shall be the renewing of fresh and new love, more constant than ever the former was. Thus our blessed Saviour goes beyond us in our deserts, taking

---

[1] Qu. racked?—G.

[2] Sibbes very frequently quotes this text; and invariably returns upon his rendering of 'guarded' instead of 'kept'. Demarest, who adopts it, may be profitably consulted (*Translation and Exposition of 1 Peter*. New York, 1851).—G.

advantage even of our security; for our greater good, making all work to good in the issue (*Rom.* 8:28); which shall end in a more near and close communion between Christ and his church than ever before. Carnal men feel not these changes, ebbings and flowings. They are not acquainted with God's forsakings. Indeed their whole life is nothing but a forsaking of God, and God's forsaking of them, who gives them outward comforts, peace and friends in the world, wherein they solace themselves. But for inward communion with him, any strength to holy duties, or against sin, for to be instruments for God's honour, and service, to do any good, they are careless. For they live here to serve their own turns, leaving their state and inheritance behind them. The Scripture saith, 'They have no changes, therefore they fear not God' (*Psa.* 55:19); and so they go down to hell quietly and securely. Oh! but it is otherwise with God's children. They are tossed up and down. God will not suffer them to prosper, or live long in a secure, drowsy, sinful state, the continuance wherein is a fearful evidence that such an one as yet hath no saving grace, nor that he yet belongs to God, seeing Christ hates such an estate, and will not suffer his to be long therein, but will shift and remove them from vessel to vessel, from condition to condition, till he have wrought in them that disposition of soul that they shall regard and love him more and more, and have nearer and nearer communion with him.

SERMON 10

*I opened to my beloved; but my beloved had withdrawn himself
and was gone: my soul failed when he spake; I sought him, but
could not find him; I called him, but he gave no answer.*
Song of Solomon 5:6

THUS we see that the life of a Christian is trouble upon
trouble, as wave upon wave. God will not suffer us to rest
in security, but one way or other he will fire us out of our
starting-holes, and make us to run after him. How much better
were it for us, then, to do our works cheerfully and joyfully, 'so to
run as we may obtain' (*1 Cor.* 9:24), than to be thus hurried up and
down, and through our own default, coming into desertions, and
there receiving rebukes and blows and delays ere we have peace
again, as it fell out with the church in the sequel; for this text is but
the beginning of her seeming misery. The watchmen, after this,
'found her, and wounded her', &c. (verse 7). But heaven is more
worth than all, now that her affections are set on fire. From thence
she bestirs herself, is resolute to find out her beloved, whom she
highly values above all this world. How her affections were stirred
by Christ's putting in his finger at the hole of the door, we have
heard. Now follows her action thereupon; for here is rising, opening, seeking, calling, and inquiring after Christ.

Action follows affection. After her bowels are moved, she ariseth and openeth; from whence we may further observe—

*Obs. 1. That where truth of affection is, it will discover itself in
the outward man, one way or other.* If there be any affection of love

199

and piety to God, there will be eyes lift up, knees bended down, and hands stretched forth to heaven. If there be any grief for sin, there will be the face dejected, the eyes looking down, some expression or other. If there be a desire, there will be a making forth to the thing desired; for the outward man is commanded by the inward, which hath a kind of sovereign commanding power over it, and says, Do this, and it doth it; Speak this, and it speaks it. Therefore, those whose courses of life are not gracious, their affections and their hearts are not good; for where the affections are good, the actions will be suitable. 'Her bowels were moved in her', and presently she shows the truth of her affection, in that she maketh after him.

1. *Her soul failed when he spake.*
2. *She makes after him.*

'My soul failed when he spake: I sought him, but I could not find him.'—Of Christ's withdrawing himself, we spake in general before, wherefore we will leave that and proceed.

'My soul failed when he spake.' That is, her soul failed when she remembered what he had spoke when he stood at the door and said, 'Open to me, my sister, my love, my dove, my undefiled: for my head is wet with the dew', &c. Now, when God's Spirit had wrought upon her, then she remembered what Christ had said. All those sweet allurements were effectual now unto her, especially when she saw that after those sweet allurements Christ had withdrawn himself; for that is the meaning of these words, 'My soul failed when he spake unto me.' He did not speak now; but her soul failed after he spake; for so it should be read, that is, after she remembered his speech to her; for now, when she opened, he was not there. Therefore, he could not speak to her.

Obs. 2. *The word of Christ, howsoever for the present it be not effectual, yet afterwards it will be in the remembrance of it.* To those that are gracious, it will be effectual when the Holy Ghost comes to seal it further upon their hearts. Christ spake many things to his disciples which they forgot; but when afterwards the Holy

Ghost the Comforter was come, his office was, 'to bring all things to their remembrance that they had forgotten before' (*John* 14:26). The Holy Ghost taught them not new things, but brought former things to their remembrance; for God will make the word effectual at one time or other. Perhaps the word we hear is not effectual for the present; it may afterwards, many years after, when God awakes our consciences.

And as this is true of God's children, the seed now sown in them will not grow up till many years after, so it is true also of those that are not God's children. They think they shall never hear again of those things they hear. Perhaps they will take order by sensuality, hardening of their hearts, and through God's judgments withal concurring, that conscience shall not awake in this world. But it shall awake one day; for it is put into the heart to take God's part, and to witness against us for our sins. It shall have and perform its office hereafter, use it as you will now; and it will preach over those things again that you now hear. You shall hear again of them, but it shall be a barren hearing. Now we may hear fruitfully to do us good, but afterwards we shall call to mind what we have heard, and it shall cut us to the heart. Dives, we know, had Moses and the prophets to instruct him, but he never heeded them in his life, until afterwards to his torment (*Luke* 16:29). So men never heed what they hear and read; they put off all, and lay their consciences asleep; but God will bring them afterwards to remembrance. But because it is a point especially of comfort to the church;—

Labour we all of us to make this use of it, to be diligent and careful to hear and attend upon the ordinances of God; for howsoever that we hear is not effectual for the present, but seems as dead seed cast into the heart, yet God will give it a body after, as the apostle speaks, at one time or other (*1 Cor.* 15:38). And that which we hear now, the Holy Ghost will bring it to our remembrance when we stand in most need of it.

'My soul failed when he spake.' She was in a spiritual swoon and deliquium[1] upon his withdrawing, whence the point considerable is,

That Christ doth leave his church sometimes, and bring it very low in their own apprehensions, that their hearts fail them for want of his presence. So it was with David (*Psa.* 38:2, 3); so with Jonah (*Jon.* 2:2); so with the church (*Lam.* 3:1ff.). We see it at large.

Reason. The necessity of our souls and of our estates requires this. As sometimes a body may be so corrupt, that it must be brought as low as possible may be, before there will be a spring of new and good blood and spirits, so we may fall into such a state of security, that nothing will bring us to a right temper but extreme purging. And usually God deals thus with strong wits and parts, if they be holy. David and Solomon were men excellently qualified; yet when they tasted of the pleasures and contentments of the world too deep, answerably they had; and so usually others shall have such desertions as will make them smart for their sweetness, as was showed before.

But upon what occasions doth a Christian think especially that God doth leave, forsake, and fail him?

First. This failing and fainting of the soul is sometimes upon an apprehension, *as if God and Christ were become enemies*, as Job saith (*Job* 7:20), and as having set us as a butt to shoot at. But this is not all that a gracious and pure heart sinks for.

But also *secondly. For the absence of Christ's love, though it feel no anger.* Even as to a loving wife, her husband not looking lovingly upon her as he used to do, is enough to cast her down, and cause her spirits to fail; so for God to look upon the soul, put the case, not with an angry, yet with a countenance withdrawn, it is sufficient to cast it down. For anyone that hath dependence upon another, to see their countenance withdrawn, and not to show their face as before, if there be but a sweet disposition in them, it is enough to daunt and dismay them.

[1] That is, fainting, sinking.—G.

Nay, *thirdly.* Moreover, *when they find not that former assistance in holy duties;* when they find that their hearts are shut up and they cannot pray as formerly when they had the Spirit of God more fully; and when they find that they cannot bear afflictions with wonted patience—certainly Christ hath withdrawn himself, say they. This is first done when we hear the Word of God, not with that delight and profit as we were wont. When they find how they come near to God in holy communion, and yet feel not that sweet taste and relish in the ordinances of God as they were wont to do, they conclude, certainly God hath hid his face. Whereupon they are cast down, their spirits fail. And do not wonder that it should be so, for it is so in nature. When the sun hides itself many days from the world, it is an uncomfortable time; the spirits of the creatures lower and wither. We see it so in the body, that the animal spirits in the brain, which are the cause of motion and sense, if they be obstructed, there follows an apoplexy and deadness. So it is between Christ and the soul. He is the 'Sun of righteousness' (*Mal.* 4:2), by whose beams we are all comforted and cheered, which when they are withheld, then our spirits decay and are discouraged. Summer and winter arise from the presence and absence of the sun. What causeth the spring to be so clothed with all those rich ornaments? The presence of the sun which comes nearer then. So what makes the summer and winter in the soul, but the absence or presence of Christ! What makes some so vigorous beyond others, but the presence of the Spirit! As it is in nature, so it is here. The presence of Christ is the cause of all spiritual life and vigour; who when he withdraws his presence a little the soul fails.

'My soul failed when he spake to me: I sought him, but I could not find him; I called, but he gave me no answer.'

Obs. 1. The church redoubleth her complaint to show her passion. *A large heart hath large expressions.* She took it to heart that Christ did not show himself in mercy. Therefore she never hath done. I sought him but I could not find him, I called but he gave me no answer. Affection makes eloquent and large expressions.

Obs. 2. But mainly observe from this failing of the church, *the difference between the true children of God and others.* The child of God is cast down when he finds not the presence of God as he was wont; his spirits fail. A carnal man, that never knew what this presence meant, regards it not, can abide the want of it. He finds, indeed, a presence of God in the creature which he thinks not of. There is a sweetness in meat, drink, rest, and a contentment in honour, preferment, and riches; and thus God is present always with him, but other presence he cares not for. Nay, he shuns all other presence of God, labouring to avoid his spiritual presence. For what is the reason that a carnal man shuns the applying of the Word and the thinking of it, but because it brings God near to his heart, and makes him present? What is the reason he shuns his own conscience; that he is loath to hear the just and unanswerable accusations that it would charge upon him, but because he cannot abide the presence of God in his conscience? What is the reason he shuns the sight of holier and better men than himself? (*1 Kings* 17:18). They present God to him, being his image, and call his sins to memory, and upbraid his wicked life. Hence comes that Satanical hatred more than human in carnal, vile men, to those that are better than themselves; because they hate all presence of God, both in the Word, ministry, and all God's holy servants. All such presence of God they hate; whereof one main reason is, because they are malefactors, wicked rebels, and intend to be so. And as a malefactor cannot endure so much as the thought of the judge, so they cannot think of God otherwise, in that course they are in, than of a judge; whereupon they tremble and quake at the very thought of him, and avoid his presence.

You know that great man, Felix, Paul spake to in the Acts (*Acts* 24:25), when he spake of the judgment to come, and those virtues, as temperance and righteousness, which he was void of, and guilty of the contrary vices; he quaked, and could not endure to hear him speak any longer. Wicked men love not to be arraigned, tormented, accused, and condemned before their time (*Mark* 5:7). Therefore, whatsoever presents to them their future terrible estate, they cannot abide it. It is an evidence of a man in a cursed condition, thus not to endure the presence of God. But what shall God and Christ say to them at the day of judgment? It was the desire of such men not to have to do with the presence of God here, and it is just with Christ to answer them there as they answer him now; 'Depart, depart, we will have none of thy ways', say they (*Job* 22:17). 'Depart, ye cursed', saith he. He doth but answer in their own language, 'Depart, ye cursed, with the devil and his angels' (*Matt.* 25:41).

But you see the child of God is clean of another temper. He cannot be content to be without the presence of God and of his Spirit, enlightening, quickening, strengthening, and blessing of him in spiritual respects. When he finds not his presence helping him, when he finds Christ his life is absent from him, he is presently discouraged. For 'Christ is our life' (*Col.* 3:4). Now, when a man's life fails all fails. When, therefore, a man finds his spiritual taste and comfort not as it was before, then Oh, 'the life of my life' hath withdrawn himself, and so is never quiet till he have recovered his life again, for 'Christ is his life' (*Col.* 3:4).

And because there is a presence of God and of Christ in the Word and sacraments—a sweet presence, the godly soul, he droops and fails if he be kept from these. He will not excommunicate himself, as many do, that perhaps are asleep when they should be at the ordinances of God. But if he be excommunicated and banished, O how takes he it to heart! 'As the hart panteth after the water brooks, so longeth my soul after thee, O God' (*Psa.* 42:1). The whole 84th Psalm is to that purpose, 'O how amiable are thy tabernacles, O Lord of hosts.' He finds a presence of God in his Word and sacraments, and when he doth not taste a sweet presence of God therein, he droops and sinks.

A carnal man never heeds these things, because he finds no sweetness in them; but the godly, finding Christ in them, they droop in the want of them, and cannot live without them. 'Whither shall we go?' saith Peter to Christ, 'thou hast the words of eternal life' (*John* 6:68). I find my soul quickened with thy speaking. So a soul that feels the quickening power of the ordinances, he will never be kept from the means of salvation, but he droops and is never well till he have recovered himself again.

Again, another difference may be observed. Carnal men, when they find the sense of God's anger, they seek not God's favour, but think of worse and worse still, and so run from God till they be in hell. But those that are God's children, when they fail and find the sense of God's displeasure, they are sensible of it, and give not over seeking to God. They run not further and further from him.

The church here, though she found not Christ present with her, yet she seeks him still and never gives over. Whence again we may observe,

Obs. 3. *That although the church be said to fail and not to find Christ, yet he is present then with her.* For who enabled her to seek him? To explain this, there is a double presence of Christ.

1. Felt.
2. Not felt.

1. *The presence felt*, is, when Christ is graciously present and is withal pleased to let us know so much, which is a heaven upon earth. The soul is in paradise then, when she feels 'the love of God shed abroad in the heart', and the favourable countenance of God shining upon her. Then she despiseth the world, the devil, and all, and walks as if she were half in heaven already. For she finds a presence and a manifestation of it, a more glorious state than the world can afford.

2. But, there is a presence of Christ *that is secret*, when he seems to draw us one way, and to drive us another, that we are both driven and drawn at once: when he seems to put us away, and yet, notwithstanding, draws us. When we find our souls go to

Christ, there is a drawing power and presence; but when we find him absent, here is a driving away. As we see here in the church and in the 'woman of Canaan' (*Matt.* 15:22ff.). We see what an answer she had from Christ, at first none, and then an uncomfortable, and lastly a most unkind answer. 'We must not give the children's bread to dogs' (*Matt.* 15:27). Christ seemed to drive her away, but, at the same time, he by his Spirit draws her to him, and was thereby secretly present in her heart to increase her faith. When Christ wrestled with Jacob, though he contended with him, yet the same time he gave Jacob power to overcome him, to be Israel, a prevailer over him (*Gen.* 32:28). So, at the same time, the church seems to fail and faint, yet, notwithstanding, there is a secret, drawing power pulling her to Christ, whereby she never gives over, but seeks and calls still after him.

It is good to observe this kind of Christ's dealing, because it will keep us that we be not discouraged when we find him absent. If still there be any grace left moving us to that which is good, if we find the Spirit of God moving us to love the Word and ordinances, to call upon him by prayer, and to be more instant, certainly we may gather there is a hidden, secret presence here that draws us to these things. Nay more, that the end of this seeming forsaking and strangeness is to draw us nearer and nearer, and at length to draw us into heaven to himself. God's people are gainers by all their losses, stronger by all their weaknesses, and the better for all their crosses, whatsoever they are. And you shall find that the Spirit of God is more forceable in them after a strangeness, to stir them up more eagerly after Christ than before, as here the church doth: for her eagerness, constancy, and instantness, it groweth as Christ's withdrawing of himself groweth.

Use 1. Let us therefore learn hence *how to judge of ourselves*, if we be in a dead, lifeless state, both in regard of comfort and of holy performances, whether we be content to be so. If we be not contented, but make towards Christ more and more, it is a good sign that he hath not forsaken us, that he will come again more gloriously than ever before, as here we shall see after, it was with the church. He seems strange, but it is to draw the church to discover her affection, and to make her ashamed of her former unkindness, and to sit surer and hold faster than she did before. All ends in a most sweet communion.

Use 2. We should labour, therefore, *to answer Christ's dealings in suitable apprehensions of soul*, when he is thus present secretly, though he seem, in regard of some comforts and former experience of his love, to withdraw himself. It should teach us to depend upon him, and to believe, though we feel not comfort, yea, against comfort, when we feel signs of displeasure. If he can love and support me, and strengthen my soul, and show it a presence of that which is fit for me, certainly I should answer thus with my faith, I will depend upon him, though he kill me, as Job did (*Job* 13:15). Our souls should never give over seeking of Christ, praying and endeavouring, for there is true love where he seems to forsake and leave. Therefore I ought in these desertions to cleave to him in life and in death.

SERMON 11

*I opened to my beloved; but my beloved had withdrawn himself
and was gone: my soul failed when he spake; I sought him, but
could not find him; I called him, but he gave no answer. The
watchmen that went about the city found me, they smote
me, they wounded me: the keepers of the
walls took away my veil from me.*
SONG OF SOLOMON 5:6, 7

THE pride and security of the spouse provokes the Lord,
her husband, oft to bring her very low, they being incompatible with Christ's residence.

Pride is an affection contrary to his prerogative; for it sets up
somewhat in the soul higher than God, the highest.

Security is a dull temper, or rather distemper, that makes the
soul neglect her watch, and rely upon some outward privilege.
Where this ill couple is entertained, there Christ useth to withdraw himself, even to the failing and fainting of the soul.

The spouse is here in her fainting fit, yet she seeks after Christ.
Still she gives not over. So Jonah, 'I am cast out of thy presence', says
he, 'yet notwithstanding I will look toward thy holy temple' (*Jon.*
2:4). And David, 'I said in my haste, I am cast out of thy sight; yet
notwithstanding thou heardest the voice of my prayer' (*Psa.* 31:22).
He said it, but he said it in his haste. God's children are surprised
on the sudden to think they are cast away; but it is in haste, and
so soon as may be, they recover themselves. 'I said it is my infirmity', said David (*Psa.* 77:10). It is but in a passion. Here then is the

difference between the children of God and others in desertions; they arise, these lie still and despair. There is 'life in the substance of the oak' (*Isa.* 6:13), that makes it lift up its head above ground, though it be cut down to the stumps. Nay, we see further here, the church is not taken off for any discouragements, but her faith grows stronger, as the woman's of Canaan did (*Matt.* 15:22ff.).

The reason whereof is—1, faith looks to the promise, and to the nature of God, not to his present dealing.

And then, 2, God, by a secret work of his Spirit, though he seem to be an enemy, yet notwithstanding draws his children nearer and nearer to him by such his dealing. All this strangeness is but to mortify some former lust, or consume some former dregs of security.

'I sought him, but I could not find him.' Here one of the greatest discouragements of all other is, when prayer, which is left to the church as a salve for all sores, hath no answer. This is the complaint, but indeed an error, of the church; for Christ did hear the church, though he seemed to turn his back.

But how shall we know that God hears our prayers?

First. Amongst many other things this is one. When he gives us inward peace, then he hears our prayers, for so is the connection (*Phil.* 4:6, 7).

Or *secondly.* If we find a spirit to pray still, a spirit to wait and to hold out, it is an argument that God either hath or will hear those prayers.

And as it is an argument that God hears our prayers, so is it of the presence of Christ. For how could we pray but from his inward presence? Christ was now present, and more present with the church when he seemed not to be found of her, than he was when she was secure; for whence else comes this eagerness of desire, this spirit of prayer, this earnestness of seeking? 'I called, but he gave no answer', &c.

Directions how to carry ourselves in such an estate. How shall we carry ourselves when it falls out that our hearts fail of that we seek for, when we pray without success, and find not a present answer, or are in any such-like state of desertion.

1. *We must believe against belief,* as it were, 'hope against hope, and trust in God' (*Rom.* 4:18), howsoever he shows himself to us as an opposite.[1] It is no matter what his present dealing with his church and children here is; the nature of faith is to break through all opposition, to see the sun behind a cloud, nay, to see one contrary in another, life in death, a calm in a storm, &c. (*2 Cor.* 6:8, 9ff.).

2. *Labour for an absolute dependence upon Christ, with a poverty of spirit in ourselves.* This is the end of Christ's withdrawing himself, to purge us of self-confidence and pride.

3. *Stir up your graces.* For as nature joining with physic[2] helps it to work and carry away the malignant humours, so by the remainder of the Spirit that is in us, let us set all our graces on work until we have carried away that that offends and clogs the soul, and not sink under the burden. For this is a special time for the exercising of faith, hope, love, diligence, care, watchfulness, and such-like graces.

And let us know for our comfort, that even this conflicting condition is a good estate. In a sick body it is a sign of life and health approaching when the humours are stirred, so as that a man complains that the physic works. So when we take to heart our present condition, though we fail and find not what we would, yet this will work to the subduing of corruption at length. It is a sign of future victory when we are discontent with our present ill estate. Grace will get the upper hand, as nature doth when the humours are disturbed.

4. Again, when we are in such a seeming forlorn estate, *let us have recourse to former experience.* What is the reason that God vouchsafes his children for the most part in the beginning of their

---

[1] That is, opponent.—G.

[2] Medicine; probably a laxative or purgative is meant.—P.

conversion, in their first love, experience of his love to ravishment? It is, that afterwards they may have recourse to that love of God then felt, to support themselves, and withal to stir up endeavours, and hope; that finding it not so well with them now as formerly it hath been, by comparing state with state, desires may be stirred up to be as they were, or rather better (*Hos.* 2:7).

And as the remembrance of former experiences serve to excite endeavour, so to stir up hope, I hope it shall be as it was, because God is immutable; I change, but Christ alters not. The inferior elementary world changes. Here is fair weather and foul, but the sun keeps his perpetual course. And as in the gloomiest day that ever was, there was light enough to make it day and to distinguish it from night, though the sun did not shine, so in the most disconsolate state of a Christian soul, there is light enough in the soul to show that the Sun of righteousness is there, and that Christ hath shined upon the soul, that it is day with the soul, and not night (*Psa.* 112:4).

5. And learn when we are in this condition *to wait God's leisure*, for he hath waited ours. It is for our good, to prepare us for further blessings, to mortify and subdue our corruptions, to enlarge the capacity of the soul, that the Lord absents himself. Therefore Bernard saith well, 'Christ comes and goes away for our good.' When he withdraws the sense of his love, the soul thereupon is stretched with desire, that it may be as it was in former time, in the days of old. Thus much for that. 'I sought, but could not find him: I called, but he gave me no answer.'

Obj. Here we must answer one objection before we leave the words. This seems to contradict other Scriptures, which promise that those that seek shall find (*Matt.* 7:7).

Ans. It is true they that seek shall find, but not presently. God's times are the best and fittest. They that seek shall find, if they seek constantly with their whole heart in all the means. Some do not find, because they seek in one means and not in another. They seek Christ in reading and not in the ordinance of hearing, in private meditation, but not in the communion of saints. We must go through all means to seek Christ, not one must be left. Thus if we will seek him, undoubtedly he will make good his promise. Nay, in some sort, 'he is found before he is sought', for he is in our souls to stir up desire of seeking him. He prevents us with desires, and answers us in some sort before we pray (*Isa.* 65:24). When he gives us a spirit of prayer, it is a pledge to us, that he means to answer us. Therefore it is a spiritual deceit when we think Christ is not in us, and we are neglected of him, because we have not all that we would have. Among many other deceits that Christians deceive themselves with in this kind, these be two.

1. That they judge grace *by the quantity and not by the value and price of it*; whereas the least measure of grace and comfort is to be esteemed, because it is an immortal seed cast into the soul by an immortal God, the Father of eternity[1] (*Isa.* 9:6).

2. Another deceit is, that we judge of ourselves *by sense and feeling, and not by faith.*

'The watchman that went about the city found me, and smote me, and took away my veil from me.' Here the poor church, after the setting down of her own exercise in her desertion, now sets out some outward ill dealing she met with, and that from those that should have been her greatest comforters. 'The watchmen that went about the city found me, they wounded me: the keepers of the walls took away my veil from me.'

Thus we see how trouble follows trouble. 'One depth calls upon another.' Inward desertion and outward affliction go many times together. The troubles of the church many times are like Job's messengers. They come fast one upon another, because God means to perfect the work of grace in their hearts. All this is for their good. The sharper the winter the better the spring. Learn hence first of all therefore in general,

---

[1] That is, the Everlasting Father of authorised translation.—G.

THE LOVE OF CHRIST

That it is no easy thing to be a sound Christian. We see here, when the church had betrothed herself to Christ and entertained him into her garden, thereafter she falls into a state of security and sleep, whence Christ labours to rouse her up. Then she useth him unkindly. After which he withdraws himself, even so far that her heart fails her. Then, as if this were not enough, the watchmen that should have looked to her, 'they smite her, wound her, and take away her veil'. See here the variety of the usage of the church and changes of a Christian; not long in one state, he is ebbing and flowing.

Therefore let none distaste the way of godliness for this, that it is such a state as is subject to change and variety, whereas carnal men are upon their lees[1] and find no changes.

Obj. But you will say, All Christians are not thus tossed up and down, so deserted of God and persecuted of others.

Ans. I answer, indeed there is difference. Whence comes this difference? From God's liberty. It is a mystery of the sanctuary, which no man in the world can give a reason of, why of Christians both equally beloved of God, some should have a fairer passage to heaven, others rougher and more rugged. It is a mystery hid in God's breast. It is sufficient for us, if God will bring us any way to heaven, as the blessed apostle saith, 'if by any means I might attain to the resurrection of the dead' (*Phil.* 3:11); either through thick or thin, if God will bring me to heaven it is no matter. 'If I by any means.'

'The watchmen that went about the city smote me', &c. By the watchmen here are meant especially governors of State and church.

Why are they called watchmen?

It is a borrowed speech, taken from the custom of cities that are beleaguered. For policy's sake they have watchmen to descry the danger they are liable unto. So magistrates be watchmen of

---

[1] Dregs or sediment of wine (normally separated or refined by pouring from bottle to bottle). cf. *Isa.* 26:6, *Jer.* 48:11, *Zeph.* 1:12.—P.

the State. Ministers are the watchmen for souls, 'watching over our souls for good' (*Heb.* 13:17).

Quest. Why doth God use watchmen?

Ans. 1. Not for any defect of power in him, but for demonstration of his goodness. For he is the great watchman, who watcheth over our commonwealths, churches, and persons. He hath an eye that never sleeps. 'He that watcheth Israel neither slumbers nor sleeps' (*Psa.* 121:4). Yet notwithstanding he hath subordinate watchmen, not for defect of power, but for demonstration of goodness. He manifests his goodness in that he will use variety of subordinate watchers.

And likewise to show his power in using many instruments, and his care for us when he keeps us together with his own subordinate means.

And in this that God hath set over us watchers, ministers especially, it implies that *our souls are in danger*. And indeed there is nothing in the world so beset as the soul of a poor Christian. Who hath so many and so bad enemies as a Christian? and amongst them all, the worst and greatest enemy he hath is nearest to him, and converseth daily with him, even himself. Therefore there must needs be watchmen to discover the deceits of Satan and his instruments, and of our own hearts; to discover the dangers of Jerusalem, and the errors and sins of the times wherein we live. The church is in danger, for God hath set watchmen. Now God and nature doth nothing in vain or needlessly.

Again, in that God takes such care for the soul, it shows the *wondrous worth of it*. Many arguments there be to show that the soul is a precious thing. It was breathed by God at first. Christ gave his life to redeem it. But this is an especial one, that God hath ordained and established a ministry and watchmen over it. And as God hath set some watchmen over others, so hath he appointed every man to be a watchman to himself. He hath given every man a city to watch over, that is, his own estate and soul.

Therefore let us not depend altogether on the watching of others. God hath planted a conscience in every [one] of us, and useth as others to our good, so our own care, wisdom, and foresight, these he elevateth and sanctifieth.

'The watchmen that went about the city found me, they smote me, they wounded me', &c.

Come we now to the carriage of these watchmen. Those that should have been defensive prove most offensive.

They smote the church and wounded her many ways, though it be not discovered here in particular. As 1, with their ill and scandalous life; and 2, sometimes with corrupt doctrine, and otherwhiles with bitter words; and 3, their unjust censures, as we see in the story of the church, especially the Romish Church. They have excommunicated churches and princes. But not to speak of those synagogues of Satan, come we nearer home and we may see amongst ourselves sometimes those that are watchmen, and should be for encouragement, they smite and wound the church, and take away her veil (3 *John* 10).

What is it to take away the veil?

You know, in the times of the Old Testament, a veil was that which covered women for modesty, to show their subjection; and it was likewise an honourable ornament. 'They took away the veil', that is, that wherewith the church was covered. They took away that that made the church comely, and laid her open, and as it were naked.

Now both these ways the church's veil is taken away by false and naughty watchmen.

1. As the veil is a token of subjection, when by their false doctrines they labour *to draw people from Christ, and their subjection to him.*

The church is Christ's spouse. The veil was a token of subjection. Now they that draw the people to themselves, as in popish churches, that desire to sit high in the consciences of people, and so make the church undutiful, 'they take away the veil of subjection', and so force Christ to punish the church, as we see in former ages.

2. As the veil is for honour and comeliness, so 'they take away the veil' of the church, when they *take away the credit and esteem of the church*; when they lay open the infirmities and weaknesses of the church. This is strange that the watchmen should do this; yet notwithstanding oftentimes it falls out so that those that by place are watchmen, are the bitterest enemies of the church. Who were bitterer enemies of the poor church in Christ's time than the scribes, Pharisees, and priests?

And so in the time of the prophets. Who were the greatest enemies the church had, but false priests and prophets?

Quest. What is the ground of this, that those men that by their standing should be encouragers, are rather dampers of the church's zeal in pursuit of it?

Ans. There are many grounds of it.

Sometimes it falls out from a spirit of envy in them at the graces of God's people, which are wanting in themselves. They would not have others better than themselves.

Sometimes from idleness, which makes them hate all such as provoke them to pains. They raise up the dignity of outward things too much, as we see in popery. They make everything to confer grace, as if they had a special virtue in them. But they neglect that wherewith God hath joined an efficacy, his own ordinances.

Use 1. This should teach us, *to be in love with Christ's government*, and to see the vanity of all things here below, though they be never so excellent in their ordinance. Such is the poison of man's heart, and the malice of Satan, that they turn the edge of the best things against the good of the church.

What is more excellent than magistracy? yet many times the point of [the] sword is directed the wrong way. 'I have said ye are gods' (*Psa.* 82:6). They should govern, as God himself would govern, and ask with themselves, Would God now, if he were a watchman of the state, do thus and thus? But I wish woeful experience did not witness the contrary.

So ministers are Christ's ambassadors (*2 Cor.* 5:20), and should carry themselves even as Christ would do. They should strengthen the feeble knees and bind up the brokenhearted, nor[1] discourage; and not sew pillows under the armholes of wicked and carnal men (*Ezek.* 13:18). But, alas! we see the edge of the ordinance is oftentimes turned another way by the corrupt, proud, unbroken hearts of men and the malice of Satan.

Use 2. Again, it should teach us *not to think the worse of any for the disgraces of the times*. The watchmen here take away the veil of the church, and her forwardness is disgraced by them. Take heed, therefore, we entertain not rash conceits of others upon the entertainment they find abroad in the world, or among those that have a standing in the church, for so we shall condemn Christ himself. How was he judged of the priests, scribes, and Pharisees in his times? And this hath been the lot of the church in all ages. The true members thereof were called heretics and schismatics. The veil was taken off. It is the poisonful pride of man's heart that, when it cannot raise itself by its own worth, it will endeavour to raise itself by the ruin of others' credit through lying slanders. The devil was first a slanderer and liar, and then a murderer (*John* 8:44). He cannot murder without he slander first. The credit of the church must first be taken away, and then she is wounded. Otherwise, as it is a usual proverb, Those that kill a dog make the world believe that he was mad first; so they always first traduced the church to the world, and then persecuted her. Truth hath always a scratched face. Falsehood many times goes under better habits than its own, which God suffers, to exercise our skill and wisdom, that we might not depend upon the rash judgment of others, but might consider what grounds they have; not what men do, or whom they oppose, but from what cause, whether from a

[1] Qu. not?—G.

spirit of envy, idleness, jealousy, and pride, or from good grounds. Else, if Christ himself were on earth again, we should condemn him, as now men do the generation of the just, whom they smite and wound, and take away their veil from them.

SERMON 12

The watchmen that went about the city found me, they smote
me, they wounded me: the keepers of the walls took away
my veil from me. I charge you, O daughters of Jerusalem,
if ye find my beloved, that ye tell him I am sick of love.
SONG OF SOLOMON 5:7, 8

THE watchmen, those that by their place and standing
should be so, they smote the church. As Bernard complains, almost five hundred years ago, 'Alas, alas!' saith he,
'those that do seek privileges in the church are the first in per-
secuting it;' and as his fashion is to speak in a kind of rhetoric,
'they were not pastors, but impostors '. There be two ordinances
without which the world cannot stand.

1. Magistracy.

2. Ministry.

Magistrates are nursing fathers and nursing mothers to the
church.

Ministers are watchmen by their place and standing.

Now, for shepherds to become wolves, for watchmen to become smiters, what a pitiful thing is it! But thus it is. The church
hath been always persecuted with these men under pretence of
religion, which is the sharpest persecution of all in the church. It
is a grievous thing to suffer of an enemy, but worse of a country-
man, worse then that of a friend, and worst of all, of the church.
Notwithstanding, by the way, we must know that the persecuted
cause is not always the best, as Augustine was forced to speak

in his time against the Donatists[1]. Sarah was a type of the true, and Hagar of the false, church. Now, Sarah, she corrected Hagar. Therefore, it follows not that the suffering cause is always the better. Therefore, we must judge of things in these kind of passages by the cause, and not by the outward carriage of things.

'They took away my veil.'

Quest. What shall we do in such cases, if we suffer any indignity, if the veil be taken off? That is, if our shame, infirmities, and weaknesses be laid open by false imputations.

Ans. In this case it is the 'innocency of the dove' that is to be laboured for, and withal the wisdom of the serpent (*Matt.* 10:16). If innocency will not serve, labour for wisdom, as indeed it will not alone. The wicked would then labour for subtlety to disgrace righteous persons.

Obj. But what if that will not serve either? Christ was wisdom itself, yet he suffered most.

Ans. When innocency and wisdom will not do it (because we must be conformable to our head), then we must labour for patience, knowing that one hair of our heads shall not fall to the ground without the providence of the Almighty.

Commend our case, as Christ did, by faith and prayer to God that judgeth.

'I charge you, O daughters of Jerusalem, if you see my beloved, that you tell him that I am sick of love ', &c.

Here the church, after her ill usage of the watchmen, is forced to the society of other Christians not so well acquainted with Christ as herself. 'I charge you, O daughters of Jerusalem, if you find my beloved ', &c., 'tell him ', &c. What shall they tell him?

'Tell him I am sick of love.'

The church is restless in her desire and pursuit after Christ till she find him. No opposition, you see, can take off her endeavour.

---

[1] For a very masterly account of this and other of the great fathers' controversies, consult Wigger's *Historical Presentation of Augustinism and Pelagianism from the Original Sources,* (ed. by Emerson. Andover, 1840. 8vo).—G.

1. Christ seems to leave her inwardly.

2. Then she goeth to the watchmen. They 'smite and wound' her.

3. Then she hath recourse to the daughters of Jerusalem for help.

Generally, before we come to the particulars, from the connection we may observe this,

That love is a fire kindled from heaven.

Nothing in the world will quench this grace (*Song of Sol.* 8:7); no opposition; nay, opposition rather whets and kindles endeavour.

The church was nothing discouraged by the ill usage of the watchmen, only she complains; she is not insensible. A Christian may without sin be sensible of indignities; only it must be the 'mourning of doves' (*Isa.* 38:14), and not the roaring of bears. It must not be murmuring and impatiency, but a humble complaining to God that he may take our case to heart, as the church doth here. But as sensible as she was, she was not a whit discouraged, but seeks after Christ still in other means. If she find him not in one, she will try in another. We see here the nature of love. If it be in any measure perfect, it casteth out all fear of discouragements.

And, indeed, *it is the nature of true grace to grow up with difficulties.* As the ark rose higher with the waters, so likewise the soul grows higher and higher, it mounts up as discouragements and oppositions grow. Nay, the soul takes vigour and strength from discouragements, as the wind increaseth the flame. So the grace of God, the more winds and waves of affliction oppose it, with so much the more violence it breaks through all oppositions, until it attain the desired hope.

To apply it: those therefore that are soon discouraged, that pull in their horns presently, it is a sign they are very cold, and have but little grace. For where there is any strength of holy affection, they will not be discouraged, nor their zeal be quenched and damped. Therefore they subordinate religion to their own ends, as your temporary believers. Where is any love to Christ, the love of Christ is of a violent nature. It sways in the heart, as the apostle speaks, 'The love of Christ constraineth us' (2 *Cor.* 5:14).

If we find this unconquerable resolution in ourselves, notwithstanding all discouragements to go on in a good cause, let us acknowledge that fire to be from heaven; let us not lose such an argument of the state of grace, as suffering of afflictions with joy. The more we suffer, the more we should rejoice, if the cause be good, as the apostles rejoiced 'that they were accounted worthy to suffer any thing' (*Acts* 5:41).

'I charge you, O daughters of Jerusalem, if you find my beloved, that ye tell him I am sick of love.'

She goes to the 'daughters of Jerusalem' for help. Whence we may learn,

That, *if we find not comfort in one means, we must have recourse to another.*

If we find not Christ present in one, seek him in another; and perhaps we shall find him where we least thought of him. Sometimes there is more comfort in the society of poor Christians, than of the watchmen themselves.

'I charge you, O daughters of Jerusalem', &c.

Where we have, 1. A charge given. 'I charge', &c.

2. The parties charged, 'the daughters of Jerusalem'.

3. The particular thing they are charged with, that is, if they find Christ, to 'tell him she is sick of love'.

The parties charged are 'the daughters of Jerusalem', the daughters of the church, which is called Jerusalem, from some resemblances between Jerusalem and the church. Some few shall be touched; to give light to the point.

1. Jerusalem was a city compact in itself, as the Psalmist saith (*Psa.* 122:3), so is the church, the body of Christ.

2. Jerusalem was chosen from all places of the world, to be the

seat of God; so the church is the seat of Christ. He dwells there in the hearts of his children.

3. It is said of Jerusalem, they went up to Jerusalem, and down to Egypt, and other places: so the church is from above (*Gal.* 4:26). 'The way of wisdom is on high' (*Prov.* 15:24). Religion is upward. Grace, glory, and comfort come from above; and draw our minds up to have our conversation and our desires above.

4. Jerusalem was 'the joy of the whole earth;' so the church of God, what were the world without it, but a company of incarnate devils?

5. In Jerusalem, records were kept of the names of all the citizens there; so all the true citizens of the church, their names are written in the book of life in heaven (*Heb.* 12:23).

The daughters of Jerusalem therefore are the true members of the church that are both bred and fed in the church (*1 Pet.* 1:20; 2:2). Let us take a trial of ourselves, whether we be daughters of Jerusalem or no. That we may make this trial of ourselves.

1. *If we find freedom in our conscience from terrors and fears.* If we find spiritual liberty and freedom to serve God, it is a sign that we are daughters of Jerusalem, because Jerusalem was free (*Gal.* 4:26).

2. Or *if we mind things above, and things of the church.* If we take to heart the cause of the truth, it is a sign we are true 'daughters of Jerusalem'. We know what the Psalmist saith, 'Let my right hand forget her cunning if I forget thee, O Jerusalem, if I do not prefer Jerusalem before my chief joy' (*Psa.* 138:5, 6). If the cause of the church go to our hearts; if we can joy in the church's joy, and mourn in the church's abasement and suffering, it is a sign we are true daughters of Jerusalem, and lively[1] members of the body of Christ. Otherwise, when we hear that the church goes down, and that the adverse part prevails, and we joy, it is a sign we are daughters of Babylon and not of Jerusalem.

[1] That is, living.—G.

THE LOVE OF CHRIST

Therefore let us ask our affections what we are, as Augustine writes excellently in his book *De Civitate Dei*.[1] 'Ask thy heart of what city thou art.'

But what saith the church to the daughters of Jerusalem? In the first place, 'I charge you.'

It is a kind of admiration supplied thus: 'I charge you, as you love me your sister, as you love Christ, as you tender my case that am thus used, as you will make it good that you are daughters of Jerusalem and not of Babylon, 'tell my beloved, that I am sick of love'. It is a strong charge, a defective speech, which yields us this observation,

That true affections are serious in the things of God and of religion.

She lays a weight upon them, 'I charge you, O daughters of Jerusalem.' True impressions have strong expressions. Therefore are we cold in matters of religion in our discourses; it is because we want these inward impressions. The church here was full, she could not contain herself, in regard of the largeness of her affections. 'I charge you, O daughters of Jerusalem ', &c.

We may find the truth of grace in the heart, by the discoveries and expressions in the conversation in general.

'I charge you, O daughters of Jerusalem, if you find my beloved, that ye tell him I am sick of love.'

The church here speaks to others meaner than herself. She would have the church tell Christ, by prayer, the surest intelligencer, how she was used, how she languished, and was sick for him, and cannot be without him.

Quest. Why did not the church tell Christ herself?

Ans. So she did as well as she could, but she desired the help of the church this way also. Sometimes it is so with the children of God that they cannot pray so well as they should, and as they would do; because the waters of the soul are so troubled, that they

[1] *The City of God.*—P.

226

can do nothing but utter groans and sighs, especially in a state of desertion, as Hezekiah could but chatter (*Isa.* 38:14); and Moses could not utter a word at the Red Sea, though he did strive in his spirit (*Exod.* 14:15). In such cases they must be beholden to the help of others.

Sometimes a man is in body sick, as James saith, 'If any man be sick, let him send for the elders, and let them pray' (*James* 5:14). There may be such distemper of body and soul, that we are unfit to lay open our estate to our own content. It is oft so with the best of God's children; not that God doth not respect those broken sighs and desires, but they give not content to the soul. The poor palsy man in the gospel, not able to go himself, was carried on the shoulders of others, and let through the house to Christ (*Mark* 2:2, 3). Ofttimes we may be in such a palsy estate, that we cannot bring ourselves to Christ, but we must be content to be borne to him by others.

'I charge you, O daughters of Jerusalem, that ye tell my beloved I am sick of love.'

Whence the point that I desire you would observe is,

That at such times as we find not our spirits enlarged from any cause outward and inward, to comfort and joy, then is a time to desire the prayers and help of others.

It is good to have a stock going everywhere; and those thrive the best that have most prayers made for them; have a stock going in every country. This is the happiness of the saints. To enforce this instruction, to desire the prayers of others, we must discover that there is a wondrous force in the prayers of Christians one for another. It is more than a compliment. Would it were so!

The great Apostle Paul, see how he desires the Romans, that they would strive and contend with God after a holy violence, by their joint prayers for him (*Rom.* 15:30); so he desires the Thessalonians that they would pray for him, 'that he might be delivered from unreasonable men' (*2 Thess.* 3:2). It is usual with him to say,

'Pray, pray', and for us too; for such are gracious in the court of heaven. Despise none in this case. A true, downright, experienced Christian's prayers are of much esteem with God. Our blessed Saviour himself, when he was to go into the garden, though his poor disciples were sleepy, and very untoward, yet he would have their society and prayers (*Matt.* 26:38).[1]

'I charge you, O daughters of Jerusalem, if you find my beloved, that ye tell him I am sick of love.'

To speak a little of the matter of the charge, 'I am sick of love.' I love him, because I have found former comfort, strength, and sweetness from him, that I cannot be without him. To be lovesick, then, in the presence of the church, is to have strong affections to Christ; from which comes wondrous disquietness of spirit in his absence. Here is somewhat good, and somewhat ill. This is first her virtue, that she did fervently love. This was her infirmity, that she was so much distempered with her present want. These two breed this sickness of love. Whence we observe,

Where the thing loved is not present, answerable to the desires of the soul that loves, there follows disquiet and distemper of affections. That is here termed[2] sickness of love.

The reason hereof is, natural contentment is in union with the thing loved. The more excellent the thing is that is loved, the more contentment there is in communion with it; and where it is in any degree or measure hindered, there is disquiet. Answerable to the contentment in enjoying, is the grief, sorrow, and sickness in parting. The happiness of the church consisting in society with Christ, therefore it is her misery and sickness to be deprived of

[1] This is the popular view, but, like the popular understanding of Thomas, thrusting his fingers into the side and nail-prints of the risen Saviour, is probably a popular mistake. Our Lord sought the society of his disciples certainly; but nowhere do we read of his asking anyone to pray *for* him. It is an awful peculiarity of the divine man 'Emmanuel', that he never did that,—one of a multitude of subsidiary assertions of his divinity.—G.

[2] That is, termed.—G.

him, not to enjoy him whom her soul so dearly loveth. There are few in the world sick of this disease. I would there were more sick of the love of Christ. There are many that surfeit rather of fulness, who think we have too much of this manna, of this preaching, of this gospel. There is too much of this knowledge of the ordinances. These are not sick of love.

Use. Make a use, therefore, of trial, whether we be in the state of the church or no, *by valuing and prizing the presence of Christ in his ordinances, the Word and sacraments.*

There are many fond[1] sicknesses in the world. There is Amnon's sickness, that was sick of love for his sister Tamar (*2 Sam.* 13:2); his countenance discovered it. And Ahab, he is sick in desiring his neighbour's vineyard (*1 Kings* 21:1ff.). You have many strange sicknesses. Many sick with fires kindled from the flesh, from hell, but few sick of this sickness here spoken of.

1. If we find ourselves carried to Christ, to run in that stream as strong as the affections of those that are distempered with sickness of the love of other things, *it will discover to us whether we be truly love-sick or not.*

2. Take a man that is sick for any earthly thing, whether of Ahab's or Amnon's sickness, or of anything, take it as you will, *that which the soul is sick of in love, it thinks of daily.* It dreams of it in the night. What do our souls therefore think of? What do our meditations run after? When we are in our advised and best thoughts, what do we most think of? If of Christ, of the state of the church here, of grace and glory, all is well. What makes us, in the midst of all worldly discontentments, to think all dung and dross in comparison of Christ, but this sickness of love to Christ. If our love be in such a degree as it makes us sick of it, it makes us not to hear what we hear, not to see what we see, not to regard what is present. The soul is in a kind of ecstasy; it is carried so strongly, and taken up with things of heaven. It is deaded to other

[1] That is, foolish.—G.

things, when our eyes are no more led with vanity than if we had none, and the flesh is so mortified as if we were dead men, by reason of the strength of our affections that run another way, to better things which are above.

3. *Thus we see it is in love.* Talk with a man that is in any heat of affections, you talk with one that is not at home, you talk with one absent. The soul is more where it loves than where it dwells. Surely where love is in any strength it draws up the soul, so that a man ofttimes, in his calling and ordinary employments, doth not heed them, but passeth through the world as a man at random. He regards not the things of the world; for Christ is gotten into his heart, and draws all the affections to himself. Where the affection of love is strong, it cares not what it suffers for the party loved, nay, it glories in it. As it is said of the disciples, when they were whipped and scourged for preaching the gospel, it was a matter of glory to them (*Acts* 5:41). It is not labour, but favour. It is not labour and vexation, but favour that is taken, where love is to the party loved. Where the love of Christ is, which was here in the church, labour is no labour, suffering is no suffering, trouble is no trouble.

4. Again, *it is the property of the party that is sick of this disease, to take little contentment in other things.* Tell a covetous worldling that is in love with the world a discourse of learning, what cares he for learning? Tell him of a good bargain, of a matter of gain, and he will hearken to that. So it is with the soul that hath felt the love of Christ shed abroad in his heart. Tell him of the world, especially if he want[1] that which he desires, the peace and strength that he found from Christ in former times, he relisheth not your discourse.

Labour we, therefore, every day more and more to have larger and larger affections to Christ. The soul that loves Christ, the nearer to Christ the more joyful it is; when he thinks of those mutual

---

[1] That is, lack.—G.

embracings, when Christ and his soul shall meet together there. This happiness is there, where the soul enjoys the thing loved; but that is not here, but in heaven. Therefore, in the meantime, with joy he thankfully frequents the places where Christ is present in the Word and sacrament. And, that we may come to have this affection, let us see what our souls are without him; mere dungeons of darkness and confusion, nothing coming from us that is good. This will breed love to the ordinances; and then we shall relish Christ both in the Word and sacrament. For he is food for the hungry soul, and requires nothing of us but good appetites; and this will make us desire his love and presence.

SERMON 13

I charge you, O daughters of Jerusalem, if ye find my beloved,
that ye tell him I am sick of love. What is thy beloved more
than another beloved, O thou fairest among women? &c.
SONG OF SOLOMON 5:8, 9

THE soul, as it is of an immortal substance, so in the right
and true temper thereof, [it] aspireth towards immortality, unless when it is clouded and overpressed with that
'which presseth downwards, and the sin which hangeth so fast
on', as the apostle speaks (*Heb.* 12:1),[1] which is the reason of those
many and diverse tossings and turmoilings of the enlightened
soul, now up, now down, now running amain homewards, and
now again sluggish, idle, and lazy; until roused up by extraordinary means, it puts on again. As the fire mounteth upwards unto
its proper place, and as the needle still trembleth till it stand at
the north; so the soul, once inflamed with an heavenly fire, and
acquainted with her first original, cannot be at rest until it find
itself in that comfortable way which certainly leads homewards.
An instance whereof we have in the church here, who, having
lost her sweet communion with Christ, and so paid dearly for
her former neglect and slighting his kind invitations, as being
troubled, restless in mind, 'beaten and wounded by the watchmen', bereft of her veil, &c. Yet this heavenly fire of the blessed
Spirit, this 'water of life' (*John* 4:10), so restlessly springing in
her, makes her sickness of love and ardent desire after Christ to

[1] See note, p. 166.—G.

be such, that she cannot contain herself, but breaks forth in this passionate charge and request—

'I charge you, O daughters of Jerusalem, if ye find my beloved, that ye tell him I am sick of love.'

Thus we may see that the way to heaven is full of changes. The strength of corruption overclouds many times, and damps our joys. How many several tempers hath the church been in! Sometimes she is all compounded of joy, vehemently desiring kisses of her best beloved. She holds her beloved fast, and will not let him go; and sometimes, again, she is gone, hath lost her beloved, is in a sea of troubles, seeks and cannot find him, becomes sluggish, negligent, overtaken with self-love, after which when she hath smarted for her omissions, as here again, she is all a-fire after Christ, as we say, no ground will hold her, away she flies after him, and is restless until she find him. Where by the way we see, that *permanency and stability is for the life to come; here our portion is to expect changes, storms, and tempests.* Therefore they must not be strange to particular persons, since it is the portion of the whole church, which thus by sufferings and conformity to the head (2 *Cor.* 4:17, 18) must enter into glory, while God makes his power perfect in our weakness (2 *Cor.* 12:9), overcomes Satan by unlikely means, and so gets himself the glory, even out of our greatest infirmities, temptations, and abasements.

But God, though he make all things work for good unto his children (*Rom.* 8:28), even the devil, sin, and death, desertions, afflictions and all; yet we must be warned hereby not to tempt God, by neglecting the means appointed for our comfortable passage, but open to Christ when he knocks, embrace him joy-fully in his ordinances, and let our hearts fly open unto him. For though, through his mercy, our wounds be cured, yet who would be wounded to try such dangerous experiments, as here befell the church in her desertions, for her sluggish negligence, deadness, and self-love?

So that we see there is nothing gotten by favouring ourselves in carnal liberty, security, or by yielding to the flesh. The church stood upon terms with Christ when he would have come in to her; but what ensued hereupon? She fell into a grievous desertion, and not only so, but finds very hard usage abroad, all which she might have prevented by watchfulness, carefulness, and opening to Christ knocking. It is a spiritual error, to which we are all prone, to think that much is gained by favouring ourselves, but we shall find it otherwise. See here, again, that God will bear with nothing, though in his own, but he will sharply punish them even for omissions, and that not only with desertion, but sometimes they shall meet with oppositions in the world.

David cannot scape with a proud thought in numbering of the people, but he must smart for it, and his people also (*2 Sam.* 24:1). God is wondrous careful of his children to correct them, when he lets strangers alone (*Amos* 3:2). It is a sign of love, when he is at this cost with us. And it should tie us to be careful of our behaviour, not to presume upon God's indulgence; for the nearer we are to him, the more careful he is over us: 'He will be sanctified in all that come near him' (*Lev.* 10:3). We see the Corinthians, because they come unreverently to the Lord's table, though otherwise they were holy men, 'some of them are sick, some weak, others sleep, that they might not be condemned with the world' (*1 Cor.* 11:30-32).

Let none, therefore, think the profession of religion to imply an immunity, but rather a straighter[1] bond; for 'judgment begins at the house of God' (*1 Pet.* 4:17). Whatsoever he suffers abroad, he will not suffer disorders in his own house, as the prophet says, 'You only have I known of all the families of the earth, therefore you shall not go unpunished' (*Amos* 3:2). The church is near him, his spouse whom he loveth, and therefore he will correct her, not enduring any abatement, or decay of the first love in her. And for

[1] Qu. straiter?—Ed

this very cause he threateneth the church of Ephesus, 'to remove her candlestick' (*Rev.* 2:5).

To proceed. The poor church here is not discouraged, but discovers and empties herself to the daughters of Jerusalem. As it is the nature of culinary fire, not only to mount upwards, but also to bewray[1] itself by light and heat, so of this heavenly fire, when it is once kindled from above, not only to aspire in its motion, but to discover itself, in affecting others with its qualities. It could not contain itself here in the church, but that she must go to the daughters of Jerusalem. 'I charge you, O daughters of Jerusalem, if ye find my beloved, that ye tell him that I am sick of love.' Therefore they may doubt that they have not this heavenly fire kindled in them, that express it not seriously; for of all affections, it will not be concealed. David wonders at his own love: 'Oh, how I love thy law! Oh, how amiable are thy tabernacles!' (*Psa.* 119:97; 84:1).

Again, we see here, that *where the soul is sick of love, it stands not upon any terms, but it humbleth and abaseth itself.* We say that affection stands not with majesty. Therefore Christ's love to us moved him to abase himself in taking our nature, that he might be one with us. Love stood not upon terms of greatness. We see the church goes to those that were meaner proficients in religion than herself, to pour out her spirit to them, 'to the daughters of Jerusalem'. She abaseth herself to any service (*1 Thess.* 2:2). Love endureth all things (*1 Cor.* 13:7), anything to attain to the thing loved; as we see Hamor the son of Shechem,[2] he would endure painful circumcision for the love he bore to Dinah (*Gen.* 34:24). So in Acts 5:41, it is said they went away rejoicing, after they were whipped, because they loved Christ. The spirit of love made them rejoice, when they were most disgracefully used.

Sometimes where this affection of heavenly love is prevalent, so that a man is sick of it, the distempers thereof redounds to the

---

[1] Reveal or expose.—P.

[2] Shechem the son of Hamor.—Ed.

body, and reflects upon that, as we see in David: 'That his moisture became as the drought of summer' (*Psa.* 32:4); because there is a marriage and a sympathy between the soul and the body, wherein the excessive affections of the one redound and reflect upon the other.

'Tell him that I am sick of love.' Here is a sickness, but not unto death, but unto life; a sickness that never ends but in comfort and satisfaction. Blessed are those that hunger and thirst after Christ, they shall be satisfied (*Matt.* 5:6), as we shall see afterwards more at large.

Knowledge gives not the denomination, for *we may know ill and be good, and we may know good and be evil*; but it is the affection of the soul which cleaves to the things known. The truth of our love is that gives the denomination of a state to be good or ill. Love is the weight and wing of the soul, which carries it where it goes; which, if it carry us to earth, we are base and earthly; if to heaven, heavenly. We should have especial care how we fix this affection; for thereafter as it is, even so is our condition. 'Ask thy love of what city thou art, whether of Jerusalem or Babylon', as Augustine saith. Now the daughters of Jerusalem reply unto the church, wondering at her earnestness,

'What is thy beloved more than another beloved, O thou fairest among women? what is thy beloved more than another beloved, that thou dost so charge us?'

Instead of giving satisfaction to her, they reply with asking new questions, 'What is thy beloved more than another beloved, O thou fairest among women? what is thy beloved', &c. Wherein ye have a doubling of the question, to show the seriousness of it. Of this their answer there are two parts.

1. A loving and sweet compellation, 'O thou fairest among women.'

2. The question doubled, 'What is thy beloved more than another beloved?' And again, 'What is thy beloved', &c., 'that thou

THE LOVE OF CHRIST

dost so charge us?' As if they should say, 'Thou layest a serious charge upon us; therefore there is some great matter surely in thy beloved that thou makest such inquiry after him.' Thus the weaker Christians being stirred up by the example of the stronger, they make this question, and are thus inquisitive. But to speak of them in their order.

'O thou fairest among women.' Here is the compellation. The church is the fairest among women in the judgment of Christ. So he calls her, 'O thou fairest among women' (*Song of Sol.* 1:8); and here the fellow-members of the church term her so too; fair, and the fairest, incomparably fair.

Quest. But how cometh she to be thus fair?

Ans. 1. *It is in regard that she is clothed with Christ's robes.* There is a woman mentioned clothed with the sun (*Rev.* 12:1). We were all ennobled with the image of God at the first, but after we had sinned we were bereft of that image. Therefore now all our beauty must be clothing, which is not natural to man, but artificial; fetched from other things. Our beauty now is borrowed. It is not connatural with us. The beauty of the church now comes from the Head of the church, Christ. She shines in the beams of her husband, not only in justification, but in sanctification also.

Ans. 2. The church is lovely and fair again, *as from Christ's imputative righteousness, so from his righteousness inherent in her, the graces she hath from him.* For of him we receive grace for grace. There is never a grace but it is beautiful and fair; for what is grace but the beams of Christ, the Sun of righteousness? So that all must be fair that comes from the first fair, all beautiful that comes from the first beauty.

This beauty of grace, whereby it makes the church so fair, springs from these grounds.

First. In that it is from a divine principle and original. It is not basely bred, but from heaven. And therefore it raiseth the soul above nature, and makes the subjects wherein it is as far surpass all other men, as men do beasts.

Secondly. In regard of the continuance, *it is everlasting, and makes us continue for ever.* 'All flesh is grass, and as the flower of grass', saith the prophet (*Isa.* 40:6); and it is repeated in the New Testament in divers places. All worldly excellency is as the flower of grass. 'The grass withereth and the flower fadeth, but the word of the Lord (that is, the grace that is imprinted in the soul by the Spirit with the Word), that abideth for ever' (*1 Pet.* 1:24, 25), and makes us abide likewise.

Use 1. From this fairness of the church, let us take occasion *to contemplate of the excellency of Christ that puts this lustre of beauty upon the church.* Moses married a woman that was not beautiful, but could not alter the complexion and condition of his spouse. But Christ doth. He takes us wallowing in our blood, deformed and defiled. He is such a husband as can put into his church his own disposition, and transform her into his own proportion. He is such a head as can quicken his members; such a root as instils life into all his branches; such a foundation as makes us living stones. There is a virtue and power in this husband above all.

Obj. But she is black.

Ans. She is so, indeed, and she confesseth herself to be so. 'I am black, but comely' (*Song of Sol.* 1:5). 1, Black in regard of the afflictions and persecutions of others she meets with in this world.

2. Black, again, in regard of scandals; for the devil hates the church more than all societies in the world. Therefore, in the society of the church there are often more scandals than in other people; as the apostle tells the Corinthians there was incest amongst them, the like was not among the heathen (*1 Cor.* 5:1).

3. She is black through the envy of the world, that looks more at the church's faults than virtues.

4. The church is black and unlovely, nothing differing from others, in regard of God's outward dealing. 'All falls alike to all' (*Eccles.* 9:2). They are sick and deformed. They have all things outwardly whatsoever in common with others.

(5.) Lastly and principally, she is black, in respect of her infirmities and weaknesses; subject to weakness and passions, as other men. The beauty of the church is inward, and undiscerned to the carnal eye altogether. The scribes and Pharisees see no virtue in Christ himself. It is said, 'that he came among his own, and his own could not discern of him: the darkness could not comprehend that light' (*John* 1:5, 11). Now, as it was with Christ, so it is much more with the church. Let this, then, be the use of it.

Use 2. *Oppose this state of the church to the false judgment of the world.* They see all black, and nothing else that is good. Christ sees that which is black, too; but then his Spirit in them (together with the sight of their blackness) seeth their beauty, too. 'I am black, but comely', &c. Be not discouraged, therefore, at the censure of the world. Blind men cannot judge of colours. It is said of Christ, 'he had no form or beauty in him, when we shall see him' (*Isa.* 53:2). (1.) Not in outward glory, nor (2.) in the view of the world. If we be, therefore, thought to be black, we are no otherwise thought of than the church and Christ hath been before us.

Use 3. Again, let us make this use of it *against Satan in the time of temptation.* Doth Christ think us fair for the good we have? Doth he not altogether value us by our ill? and shall we believe Satan, who joins with the distempers of melancholy or weakness we are in (which he useth as a weapon against the soul), to make us think otherwise? 'Satan is not only a murderer, but a liar from the beginning' (*John* 8:44). We must not believe an enemy and a liar withal. But consider how Christ and the church judgeth, that have better discerning. And let us beware we be not Satans[1] to ourselves; for if there were no devil, yet in the time of temptation and desertion we are subject to discouragement, to give false witness against ourselves. We are apt to look on the dark side of the cloud. The cloud that went before the Israelites had a double aspect, one dark, the other light (*Exod.* 14:20). In temptation we look on the

---

[1] That is, accusers or adversaries.—G.

dark side of the soul, and are witty in pleading against ourselves. Oh, but consider what Christ judgeth of us, 'O! thou fairest among women;' and what those about us that are learned, who can read our evidences better than we ourselves, do judge of us. Let us trust the judgment of others in time of temptation more than our own.

Use 4. Learn again here, *what to judge of the spirits of such kind of men as are all in disgracing and defacing the poor church.* Their table talk is of the infirmities of Christians. They light upon them as flies do upon sore places, and will see nothing that is good in them. Oh! where is the Spirit of Christ, or of the church of Christ, in them that thus bescratch the face of the church? when yet oft-times their hearts tell them these poor despised ones will be better than themselves one day, for grace shall have the upper hand of all excellences.

The church is fair and fairest. Grace is a transcendent good. All the excellency of civility and morality is nothing to this. This denominates the church the fairest. She is not gilt, but pure gold; not painted, but hath a true natural complexion. All other excellencies are but gilt, painted excellencies. 'The whore of Babylon', she is wondrous fair! But wherein doth her beauty consist? In ornaments and ceremonies to abuse silly people that go no further than fancy. It is an excellency that comes not to the judgment, but the excellency of the church is otherwise. She is 'the fairest among women'. She hath a natural fairness. As gold is pure gold, so the church is of a pure composition, glorious within. It is for the false, whorish church to be glorious without only, but the true church is glorious within. But that which we should especially observe is, *that we should labour to answer this commendation; not only to be fair, but the fairest; to be transcendently, singularly good; to do somewhat more than others can; to have somewhat more in us than others have.*

For it is answerable to the state of a Christian. Is a Christian in an excellent rank above other men? Let him show it by a carriage more gracious, more fruitful and plentiful in good works. There is a kind of excellency affected in other things, much more should we desire to be excellent in that that is good, that we may not be fair only, but the fairest. This the apostle St Paul excellently presseth to Titus, his scholar (*Titus* 2:14),[1] and to all of us in other places, that we should be 'a peculiar people, zealous of good works', not only to do them, but to be zealous of them, and to go before others in them, standing as standard-bearers. Therefore those that think they may go too far in religion, that they may be too fruitful, are not worthy the name of the spouse of Christ; for she is fair, yea, the fairest among women, 'The righteous is more excellent than his neighbour' (*Prov.* 12:26). Therefore we should excel in good works, as the apostle exhorts us, 'to labour after things that are excellent' (*1 Cor.* 12:31, *2 Pet.* 1:8), as if he should say, Is there anything better than other, labour for that. You have some so far from this disposition that they cry down the excellencies of others, lest the fairness of others might discover their blackness. Thus we leave the compellation, and come to the question.

Quest. 'What is thy beloved more than another beloved?' And they double it, 'What is thy beloved more than another beloved, that thou so chargest us?'

Questions are of divers natures. We shall not stand upon them. This is not a question merely of ignorance, for they had some knowledge of Christ, though weak. Nor was it a curious nor a catching question, like those of the scribes and Pharisees unto Christ, to instance in that of Pilate, 'What is truth ?' (*John* 18:38), when Christ had told him the truth. 'What is truth?' saith he, in a scornful, profane manner, as indeed profane spirits cannot hear savoury words, but they turn them off with scorn, 'What is truth?' This here in the text is not such, but a question tending to further resolution and satisfaction, 'What is thy beloved more than another beloved?'

---

[1] 'Jesus Christ, who gave himself for us that he might redeem us from all iniquity, and purify unto himself a *peculiar* people.'—G.

First of all, observe that these of the church here were stirred up by the examples of other members of the church to be inquisitive after Christ, so to be satisfied. Hence observe that *there is a wondrous force in the examples of Christians to stir up one another.* We see here, when the church was sick of love, the other part of the members began to think, what is the reason the church is so earnest to seek after Christ? There is some excellency sure in him. For wise men do not use great motions in little matters. Great things are carried with great movings. We use not to stir up tragedies for trifles, to make mountains of mole-hills. The endeavours and carriages of great persons that be wise, judicious, and holy are answerable to the nature of things. And indeed the church judgeth aright in this. Then see the force of good example. Any man that hath his wits about him, when he sees others serious, earnest, and careful about a thing, whereof for the present he can see no reason, especially if they have parts equal or superior to himself, will reason thus presently:—

What is the matter that such a one is so earnest, so careful, watchful, laborious, inquisitive? It is not for want of wit; surely he hath parts enough, he understands himself well. And then he begins to think, sure I am too cold. Hereupon come competition and co-rivality,[1] surely I will be as good as he.

Use. Let us labour, therefore, to be exemplary to others, and to express the graces of God; for thus we shall do more than we are aware. There is a secret influence in good example. Though a man say nothing, saith one, there is a way to profit from a good man though he hold his peace. His course of life speaks loud enough. We owe this to all, even to them that are without, to do them so much good as to give them a good example, and we wrong them when we do not, and hinder their coming on by an evil or a dead example.

Let this be one motive to stir us up to it, *that answerable to the good we shall do in this kind shall be our comfort in life and death,*

[1] That is, mutual emulation.—G.

and our reward after death. For the more spreading our good is either in word, life, or conversation, the more our consciences shall be settled in the consideration of a good life well spent, our reward shall be answerable to our communication and diffusion of good; and whereas otherwise it will lie heavy on the conscience, not only in this life, but at the day of judgment and after; when we shall think not only of the personal ill that we stand guilty of, but exemplary ill also.

It should move those therefore of inferior sort to look to all good examples, as the church here to the love of the other part of the church. Wherefore are examples among us but that we should follow them? We shall not only be answerable for abuse of knowledge, but also of good examples we have had and neglected. Doth God kindle lights for us, and shall not we walk by their light? It is a sin not to consider the sun, the moon, the stars, the heavens, and works of nature and providence, much more not to consider the works of grace. But one place of Scripture shall close up all, which is, Romans 11:11, that the example of us Gentiles at length shall stir up and provoke the Jews to believe. To those stiff-necked Jews example shall be so forcible that it shall prevail with them to believe and to be converted. If example be of such force as to convert the Jews that are so far off, how much more is it or should it be to convert Christians! Wondrous is the force of good example! So we come to the question itself,

'What is thy beloved more than another beloved?' &c.

We see there is excellent use of holy conference. The church coming to the daughters of Jerusalem, speaking of Christ her beloved, that she is 'sick of love', &c., the daughters of Jerusalem are inquisitive to know Christ more and more. Here is the benefit of holy conference and good speeches. One thing draws on another, and that draws on another, till at length the soul be warmed and kindled with the consideration and meditation of heavenly things. That that is little in the beginning may bring forth great matters.

This question to the church and talking with her, 'I charge you, if you find my beloved, to tell him that I am sick of love', breeds questions in others, 'What is thy beloved?' &c. Whence, upon the description of her beloved, her heart is kindled, she findeth her beloved; so that talking of holy and heavenly things is good for others and ourselves also.

1. *It is good for others*, as it was good for the daughters of Jerusalem here; for thereupon they are stirred up to be inquisitive after Christ. And it was good for the church herself, for hereupon she took occasion to make a large commendation of Christ, wherein she found much comfort.

2. Good conference, then, is *good for ourselves*; for we see a little seed brings forth at length a great tree, a little fire kindleth much fuel, and great things many times rise out of small beginnings. It was a little occasion which Naaman the Assyrian[1] had to effect his conversion (2 *Kings* 5:2). There was a poor banished woman, a stranger, who was a Jewish maidservant. She told her lord's servants that there was a prophet in Jewry that could heal him, whereupon he came thither, and was converted and healed. And Paul showeth that the very report of his bonds did a great deal of good in Caesar's house (*Phil.* 1:13). Report and fame is a little matter, but little matters make way for the greater.

This may put us in mind *to spend our time fruitfully in good conference, when in discretion it is seasonable.* We know not, when we begin, where we may make an end. Our souls may be carried up to heaven before we are aware, for the Spirit will enlarge itself from one thing to another. 'To him that hath shall be given more and more still' (*Matt.* 13:12). God graciously seconds good beginnings. We see the poor disciples, when they were in a damp[2] for the loss of Christ, after he comes, meets them, and talks of holy things. In that very conference their hearts were warmed

---

[1] Syrian.—Ed.

[2] State of gloom and discouragement.—P.

and kindled (*Luke* 24:32). For, next to heaven itself, our meeting together here, it is a kind of paradise. The greatest pleasure in the world is to meet with those here whom we shall ever live with in heaven. Those who are good should not spend such opportunities fruitlessly.

And to this end, labour for the graces of the communion of saints; for there is such a state. We believe it as an article of our creed. How shall we approve ourselves to be such as have interest unto the communion of saints, unless we have spirits able to communicate good to others? pitiful and loving spirits, that we may speak a word in due season.

What a world of precious time is spent in idle conversing, as if the time were a burden, and no improvement to be made of the good parts of others. Sometimes, though we know that which we ask of others as well as they do, yet notwithstanding good speeches will draw us to know it better, by giving occasion to speak more of it, wherewith the Spirit works more effectually and imprints it deeper, so that it shall be a more rooted knowledge than before; for that doth good that is graciously known, and that is graciously known that the Spirit seals upon our souls. Perhaps the knowledge I have is not yet sealed sufficiently; it is not rooted by conference. Though I hear the same things again, yet I may hear them in a fresh manner, and so I may have it sealed deeper than before. Experience finds these things to be true.

Again, *we should labour here to have our hearts inquisitive.* The heathen man accounted it a grace in his scholar, and a sign that he would prove hopeful, because he was full of questions. Christians should be inquisitive of the ways of righteousness; inquisitive of the right path which leads to heaven; how to carry themselves in private, in their families; how in all estates; inquisitive of the excellency of Christ. 'What is thy beloved more than another beloved?' Questions end usually in resolutions; for the soul will not rest but in satisfaction. Rest is the happiness of the soul, as it were. When a question is moved, it will not be quiet till it have satisfaction. Therefore doubting at the first, breeds resolution at the last. It is good therefore to raise questions of the practice of all necessary points; and to improve the good parts and gifts of others that we converse with, to give satisfaction. What an excellent improvement is this of communion and company, when nothing troubles our spirit, but we may have satisfaction from others upon our proposing it. Perhaps God hath laid up in the parts of others, satisfaction to our souls; and hath so determined that we shall be perplexed and vexed with scruples, till we have recourse to some whom he hath appointed to be helpful to us in this kind. Many go mourning a great part of their days in a kind of sullenness this way, because that they do not open their estate to others. You see here the contrary practice of the church. She doubles the question: 'What is thy beloved more than another beloved, O thou fairest among women? what is thy beloved more than another beloved, that thou dost so charge us?'

SERMON 14

What is thy beloved more than another beloved, O thou fairest
among women? what is thy beloved more than another beloved,
that thou dost so charge us? My beloved is white and ruddy,
the chiefest among ten thousand.
SONG OF SOLOMON 5:9, 10

THE last time we met we left the church sick of love; which
strange affection in her, together with her passionate
charge to the daughters of Jerusalem, moved them to
make this question unto her, 'What is thy beloved more than another beloved', &c. To be in love is much; to conceal it is grievous;
to vent it with such fervency and passion breeds astonishment in
these younger Christians, who wonder what that is which can so
draw away the church's love, and run away with her affections.
They knew no such excellencies of the person the church so ad-
mired, and therefore they double the question unto her, 'What is
thy beloved?' &c. 'what is thy beloved?' &c. Whereby we see the
excellency of the soul which aspires still towards perfection; not
resting in any state inferior to the most excellent. Therefore also is
the church's sickness of love here, who desires a nearer union and
communion with Christ than she at this time had.

For there are degrees of spiritual languishing. *Till we be in*
heaven we are always under some degree of this sickness of love;
though the soul have more communion at one time than at another. Yea, the angels are under this wish to see Christ, together
with his church, in full perfection. So that until we be in heaven,

where shall be a perfect reunion of soul and body, and of all the members of the church together, there is a kind of sickness attending upon the church and a languishing.

The question asked is,

'What is thy beloved more than another's beloved, O thou fairest among women?'

What! now fair when her veil was taken away? now fair when the watchmen abased[1] her? now fair when she was disgraced? Yes; now fair, and now fair in the sight of the daughters of Jerusalem, and in the sight of Christ that calls her the fairest among women. So that under all disgraces, infirmities, and scandals; under all the shame that riseth in the soul upon sin; under all these clouds there is an excellency of the church. She is, 'the fairest among women', notwithstanding all these. 'O thou fairest among women.'

Quest. Whence comes this fairness, under such seeming foulness and disgrace?

Ans. It comes from without. It is borrowed beauty (*Ezek.* 16:1-6). By nature we lie in our blood. There must be a beauty put upon us. We are fair with the beauty that we have out of Christ's wardrobe. The church shines in the beams of Christ's righteousness; she is not born thus fair, but new-born fairer. The church of Christ is all glorious, but it is within, not seen of the world (*Psa.* 45:13). She hath a life, but it is a hidden life, 'our glory and our life is hidden in Christ' (*Col.* 3:3). It is hid sometimes from the church itself, who sees only her deformity and not her beauty, her death but not her life, because her 'life is hid'. Here is a mystery of religion, *The church is never more fair than when she judgeth herself to be most deformed; never more happy than when she judgeth herself to be miserable; never more strong than when she feels herself to be weak; never more righteous than when she feels herself to be most burdened with the guilt of her*

[1] Qu. abused?—G.

own sins, because the sense of one contrary forceth to another. The sense of ill forceth us to the fountain of good, to have supply thence. 'When I am weak, then am I strong', saith Paul (*2 Cor.* 12:10). Grace and strength is perfect in weakness.

Use. This should teach us what to judge of the church and people of God; even under their seeming disgraces, yet to judge of them as the excellentest people in the world, 'All my delight is in those that are excellent' (*Psa.* 16:3); to join ourselves to them. Especially this is here to be understood of the church, as it is the mystical body of Christ; not as a mixed body, as a visible church, 'but as it is the temple of the Holy Ghost' (*1 Cor.* 3:17).

The visible church hath terms of excellency put upon it sometimes, but it is in regard of the better part. As gold unrefined is called gold, because gold is the better part; and a heap of wheat unwinnowed is called wheat, though there be much chaff in it. The body of Christ itself hath always excellent terms given it, 'O thou fairest among women.'

Those that look upon the church with the spectacles of malice can see no such beauty in her, though to espy out faults (as the devil could in Job (*Job* 1:9ff.), to quarrel, to slander, they are quick-sighted enough. But we see here the church in the judgment of the 'daughters of Jerusalem', that she is the 'fairest among women'.

The papists have a painted beauty for their catholic church, but here is no such beauty. It becomes a whore to be painted to be as fair as her hands can make her, with feigned beauty. But the church of Christ hath a beauty from her husband, a real, spiritual beauty, not discerned of the world.

Use. This should be of use to God's children themselves, *to help them in the upbraidings of conscience* (as if they had no goodness in them), *because they have a great deal of ill.* Christians should have a double eye, one to set and fix upon that which is ill in them, to humble them; and another upon that which is supernaturally gracious in them, to encourage themselves. They should look upon themselves as Christ looks upon them, and judge of themselves as he judgeth of them, by the better part. He looks not so much what ill we have, for that shall be wrought out by little and little, and be abolished. It is condemned already, and it shall be executed by little and little, till it be wholly abolished. But he looks upon us in regard of the better part. So should we look upon ourselves, though otherwhiles upon our black feet (our infirmities) when we are tempted to pride and haughtiness. But always let the mean thoughts we conceive of ourselves make us to fly to Christ.

'What is thy beloved more than another beloved? '

Here is a question, and a question answered with a question. Questions, they breed knowledge; as the Greek proverb is, doubtings breed resolution. Whereupon the inquisitive soul usually proves the most learned, judicious, and wise soul. Therefore that great philosopher[1] counted it as a virtue amongst his scholars that they would be inquisitive. So the scholars of righteousness are inquisitive, 'They inquire the way to Canaan, and the way to Zion with their faces thitherwards' (*Jer.* 50:5).

It is a special part of Christians' wisdom to improve the excellency of others by questions; to have a bucket to draw out of the deep wells of others. As Solomon saith, 'The heart of a wise man is as deep waters, but a man of understanding can tell how to fetch those waters out.' There be many men of deep and excellent parts which are lost in the world, because men know not how to improve them. Therefore it is good, while we have men excellent in any kind, to make use of them. It is an honour to God as well as a commodity to ourselves. Doth God suffer lights to shine in the world that we should take no notice of them? It is a wrong to ourselves and a dishonour to God.

'What is thy beloved more than another beloved?' &c.

---

[1] That is, Socrates in Plato's *Dialogues*.—G.

A further point from hence is, that *if we would give encouragement to others to repair to us for any good, we should learn to be so excellent as to adorn religion.*

'O thou fairest among women, what is thy beloved?' &c. They inquire of her, because they have a good conceit of her. A world of good might be done if there were bred a good conceit of men in others. We say in sickness, A good conceit of the physician is half the cure. So in teaching, a good conceit of the teacher is half the learning. 'The daughters of Jerusalem' had a good conceit here in their questioning of the church. 'O thou fairest among women, what is thy beloved more than another beloved?'

Let us labour, therefore, to be such as may bring honour and credit to religion, and make it lovely; that what we do may make others think we do what we do to great purpose; which is ofttimes a special means and occasion of their conversion. Though properly the cause of conversion be the Spirit of God in the ordinances, yet the inducement, many times, and occasion, is the observation of the course and carriage of those that excel and are known to be eminent in parts and in graces. Emulation adds spurs to the soul. Do they take such courses that are wiser than I, and shall not I take the like course too? Paul saith, the emulation of the Gentiles shall be a means of the conversion of the Jews (*Rom.* 11:11). When they shall see them embrace Christ, they will be encouraged to do so also. What shall we think, therefore, of them that live so as that they bring an evil report, scandal, and reproach upon religion? Great and fearful is their wickedness, that by their ill conversation, like Hophni and Phinehas, discredit the ordinances of the Lord (*1 Sam.* 2:17).

Now the church thus answers the former question touching Christ, 'My beloved is white and ruddy, the chiefest of ten thousand.' She is not afraid to set out her beloved's beauty; for there is no envy in spiritual things. It is want of wisdom amongst men to commend a thing that is very lovely to others, and so to set an edge upon their affections when they cannot both share; and the more one hath, the less another hath of all things here below. But in spiritual things there is no envy at the sharing of others in that we love ourselves, because all may be loved alike. Christ hath grace and affection enough for all his. He hath not, as Esau speaks, but 'one blessing'. No, he can make all his happy. Therefore the church stands not upon terms. When the 'daughters of Jerusalem' inquire about her beloved, I tell you freely, says she, what my beloved is. First, in general, the answer is, 'My beloved is white and ruddy, the chiefest among ten thousand.' Then afterwards there is a specification of the particulars. She will not stand upon the gross, but admires[1] at every parcel in the thing beloved. Every thing is lovely, as we shall see in particulars afterwards.

'My beloved is white and ruddy, the chiefest among ten thousand.'

We will take that which is safe, because we will have sure footing, as near as we can, in this mystical portion of Scripture.

Quest. What is that white and ruddy? Why doth the church set forth the spiritual excellencies of Christ by that which is most outwardly excellent and most beautiful?

Ans. Because of all complexions, the mixed complexion of these two colours, white and ruddy, is the purest and the best. Therefore she sets out the beauty and the spiritual excellency of Christ by this 'white and ruddy'. Beauty ariseth of the mixture of these two. First, she sets out the beauty of Christ positively; and then, by way of comparison, 'the chiefest among ten thousand'.

But what is this white and ruddy? what is beauty?

1. To the making of beauty there is required a sound, healthy constitution, so as *the particulars have a due proportion.* There must be a harmony of the parts, one suiting with one another; for comeliness stands in oneness, when many things, as it were,

---

[1] That is, wonders.—G.

are one. Uncomeliness is in diversity, when diverse things are jumbled together that belong to many heads; as we say it is uncomely to have an old man's head on a young man's shoulders. But when all things are so suited that they make one, agreeing exactly, there is beauty and comeliness.

2. Besides soundness of constitution and comeliness of proportion, *there is a grace of colour* that maketh beauty, which ariseth out of the other. So that soundness and goodness of constitution, together with the exact proportion of the variety of parts, having with it this gracefulness of colour and complexion, makes up that which we call beauty. In a word, then, this carnation colour, white and ruddy, may be understood of that excellent and sweet mixture that makes such a gracefulness in Christ. In him there is wonderful purity and holiness, and yet a wonderful weakness. There is God the 'great God' and a piece of earth, of flesh in one person; a bloody, pierced, and a glorious shining body; humility and glory: justice, wonderful justice, and yet exceeding love and mercy: justice to his enemies, mercy to his children.

Obs. Christ is a most beautiful person, not as God only, but as man, the Mediator, God and man. The person of the Mediator is a beautiful person, as Psalm 45:2, there is a notable description of Christ and of his church, 'Thou art fairer than the children of men: grace is poured into thy lips', &c.

But the loveliness and beauty of Christ *is especially spiritual*, in regard of the graces of his Spirit. A deformed person, man or woman, of a homely complexion and constitution, yet, notwithstanding, when we discern them by their conversation to be very wise and of a lovely and sweet spirit, very able and withal wondrous willing to impart their abilities, being wondrous useful; what a world of love doth it breed, though we see in their outward man nothing lovely? The consideration of what sufficiency is in Christ, wisdom, power, goodness, and love, that made him come from heaven to earth, to take our nature upon him, to marry us, and join our nature to his (that he might join us to him in spiritual bonds): the consideration of his meekness and gentleness, how he never turned any back again that came to him, should make us highly prize him. Indeed some went back of themselves (as the young man in discontent (*Matt.* 19:2), Christ turned them not back; nay, he loved the appearance of goodness in the young man, and embraced him. He is of so sweet a nature that he never upbraided those that followed him with their former sins, as Peter with denial, and the like. He is of so gracious a nature that he took not notice of petty infirmities in his disciples, but tells them of the danger of those sins that might hurt them: being of so sweet a nature that 'he will not quench the smoking flax, nor break the bruised reed' (*Isa.* 42:3); his whole life being nothing but a doing of good, 'he did all things well' (as the gospel speaks), excellent well (*Mark* 7:37).

Now, the consideration of what a gracious Spirit is in Christ, must needs be a loadstone of love, and make him beautiful. Therefore Bernard saith well, 'When I think of Christ, I think at once of God, full of majesty and glory; and, at the same time, of man, full of meekness, gentleness, and sweetness.' So, let us consider of Christ as of the 'mighty God', powerful; and withal consider of him as a gentle and mild man, that came riding meekly on an ass, as the Scripture sets him out (*Matt.* 21:5). He was for comers, and gave entertainment to all: 'Come unto me, all ye that are weary and heavy laden', &c. (*Matt.* 11:28). For the most weak and miserable person of all had the sweetest entertainment of him, 'He came to seek and to save that which was lost' (*Luke* 19:10). Let us, I say, think of him both as of the great God, and withal as of meek man: the one to establish our souls, that he is able to do great matters; the other to draw us to him because he loves us. We are afraid to go to God, 'a consuming fire' (*Heb.* 12:29); but now let us think we go to bone of our bone and flesh of our flesh, to our brother, to one that out of his goodness abased himself of purpose that we might be one with him: who loved us more than his own life, and was contented to carry the curse for us, that we might be blessed of God for ever, and to suffer a most painful and shameful death, that so he might make us heirs of everlasting life.

Christ is spiritually lovely, 'the chiefest of ten thousand'. The church sets him out by comparison, 'a standard-bearer', a carrier of the 'banner of ten thousand'. For, as the goodliest men use to carry the ensign, the banner; so he, the goodliest of all other, is the standard-bearer.

Obs. Whence we gather, *that Christ, as he is beautiful and good, so he is incomparably, beyond all comparison good*; 'He is a standard bearer, one among ten thousand; anointed with the oil of gladness above his fellows' (*Psa.* 45:7).

First, *for that he is so near to God by the personal union.*

And in regard likewise, *that all others have all from him.* Of his fulness we receive grace for grace (*John* 1:16). Ours is but a derivative fulness. His glory and shining is as the shining of the body of the sun; ours as the light of the air, which is derived from the glory of the sun. Ours is but the fulness of the stream, and of the vessel, but the fulness of the fountain and of the spring is his. Thereupon he is called 'the head of the church' (*Col.* 1:18); the head is the tower of the body which hath all the five senses in it, and wisdom for the whole body. It seeth, heareth, understandeth, and doth all for the body; having influence into the other parts of it. So Christ is above all, and hath influence into all his church, not only eminence, but influence.

What is excellent in the heavens? The sun. So Christ is the 'Sun of righteousness' (*Mal.* 4:2). The stars. He is the 'bright morning star' (*Rev.* 22:16). The light. He is the 'light of the world' (*John* 9:5). Come to all creatures; you have not any excellent amongst them but Christ is styled from it. He is 'the lion of the tribe of Judah' (*Rev.* 5:5), the 'lily' (*Song of Sol.* 2:1), and the 'rose' (*Song of Sol.* 2:1), and 'the Lamb of God that taketh away the sins of the world' (*John* 1:29), 'the tree of Life', &c. (*Rev.* 22:2). There is not a thing necessary to nature, but you have a style from it given to Christ, to show that he is as necessary as bread and water, and the food of life (*John* 6:35; 4:14). When we see light, therefore, think of the 'true light' (*John* 9:5). When the sun, think of the 'Sun of righteousness' (*Mal.* 4:2). So remember 'the bread and water of life', in our common food. Therefore the sacraments were ordained, that as we go to the sea by the conduct of rivers, so we might go to the sea of all excellency and goodness by the conduct of these rivers of goodness, to be led by every excellency in the creature, to that of our mediator Christ, who is 'the chiefest among ten thousand'.

To come more particularly to speak of his excellencies, omitting his two natures in one person, God and man; that we may consider his offices, a king, priest and prophet. He being the chief in all these, so all good kings before him were types of him, as also the prophets and priests. He was all in one. Never any before him was king, priest, and prophet, as he was king, priest, and prophet in one. So in every respect he was incomparable above all.

1. *Such a king, as is king of kings*; and subdueth things unconquerable to all other kings, even the greatest enemies of all; such a king as conquered the world, death, hell, and sin, all things that are terrible. Death you know is called 'the king of fears',[1] because it terrifieth even kings themselves. Christ is such a king as takes away these terrible greatest ills of all; such a king as rules over the soul and conscience, the best part of man, where he settles and stablisheth peace; such a king as sets up his kingdom in our very souls and hearts, guides our thoughts, desires, actions, and affections, setting up a peaceable government there.

---

[1] Cf. *Job* 18:14.—G.

So he is an incomparable king even in regard of that office. 'He is the chiefest of ten thousand'; such a king as carries the government upon his own shoulders (*Isa.* 9:6). He devolves not the care to another, to make it as he list and so be a cypher himself, but he carries all upon his own shoulder. He needs not a pope for his vicar.

2. Again, as a priest, *such a high priest as offered himself a sacrifice by his eternal Spirit.* He as God offered up his manhood. Such a priest as hath satisfied the wrath of God, and reconciled God to man. All other priests were but types of this priest, who is such a priest as never dies, 'but lives for ever to make intercession for us in heaven', by virtue of that sacrifice which he offered in the days of his flesh. He was both priest and sacrifice. Such a 'priest as is touched with our infirmities;' so mild and gentle, full of pity and mercy. No priest to this priest. God only smelt a sweet smell from this sacrifice.

3. And *for his prophetical office, he is a prophet beyond all others.* Such a one as can instruct the soul. Other men can propound doctrines, but he can open the understanding, and hath the key of the heart, the 'key of David which can open the soul' (*Luke* 24:45). By his Holy Spirit he can make the very simple full of knowledge (*Prov.* 1:4). Such a prophet as hath his chair in the very heart of man; this great 'Bishop of our souls' (*1 Pet.* 2:25), 'the Angel of the covenant', that Λογος (*logos*), 'the messenger of the Father'. So he is 'the chief of ten thousand', consider him as king, as priest, or as prophet.

Use. The use of this is exceeding pregnant, comfortable, and large, that we have such a Saviour, such an eminent person, so near, so peculiar to us. Our beloved, my beloved. If he were a 'beloved, the chief of ten thousand', it were no great matter, but he is mine. He is thus excellent; excellent considered with propriety in it, and a peculiar propriety.[1] Peculiarity and propriety,

---

[1] That is, property = right.—G.

together with transcendent excellency, makes happy if there be any enjoying of it. Therefore repent not yourselves of your repentings, but think I have not cast away my love, but have set it upon such an object as deserves it, 'for my beloved is the chiefest of ten thousand'.

SERMON 15

My beloved is white and ruddy, the chiefest among ten thousand.
Song of Solomon 5:10

LOVE is such a boundless affection, that where it once breaks forth in praises upon a good foundation, it knows no measure; as we see here in the church, who being provoked and, as it were, exasperated by the 'daughters of Jerusalem' to explain the excellency of him she had with so much affection incessantly sought after, that she might justify her choice (ere she descend into particulars), she breaks forth into this general description of her beloved; whereby she cuts off from all hopes of equalling him, 'My beloved is white and ruddy' (exceeding fair), nay, 'the chief among ten thousand' (none like him). She would not have us think she had bestowed her love but on the most excellent of all, 'the chief of ten thousand'. Well were it for us that we could do so in our love, that we might be able to justify our choice; not to spend it on sinful, vain, and unprofitable things, which cause repentance and mourning in the conclusion, whereof the church here worthily cleareth herself; in that she had chosen 'the chief among ten thousand'.

And most justly did she place her affections upon so excellent an object, who was so full of 'all the treasures of wisdom and knowledge', the life of our life, in whom 'dwelt all the fulness of the Godhead bodily' (*Col.* 2:3; 1:19); in whom was a gracious mixture and compound of all heavenly graces; where greatness and goodness, justice and mercy, God and man, meet in one person.

Such an one *who breaks no 'bruised reed, nor quenches the smoking flax' (Matt.* 12:20), who refuses not sinners, but invites them unto him, offering to heal all and cure all who come unto him. He is a king indeed (*John* 18:37). But this also approves her choice; he rules all, commands all, judges all. What then can she want who hath such a friend, such a husband? whose government is so winning, mild, and merciful?

He is not such a monarch as loves to get authority by sternness, like Rehoboam (*1 Kings* 12:14), but by those amiable graces of gentleness and love. All the excellencies of holiness, purity, and righteousness, are sweetly tempered with love and meekness in him. You may see, for instance, how he takes his disciples' part against the Pharisees, and the poor woman's that came to wash his feet and kissed them, against the Pharisee that had invited him to dinner (*Luke* 7:44). The church is a company of despised people, that are scorned of Pharisaical proud spirits; who perhaps have morality and strength of parts to praise them with. Now Christ takes part with the broken spirits, against all proud spirits. Howsoever he be gone to heaven (where he is full of majesty), yet he hath not forgotten his meekness nor changed his nature, with change of honour. He is now more honoured than he was, for 'he hath a name above all names, in heaven or in earth' (*Acts* 4:12); yet he is pitiful still. 'Saul, Saul, why persecutest thou me?' (*Acts* 9:4). He makes the church's case his own still. Together with beams of glory, there are bowels of pity in him, the same that he had here upon earth; which makes him so lovely to the truly brokenhearted, believing soul, 'My beloved is white and ruddy.'

He is set out likewise by comparing him with all others whatsoever, 'He is the chief of ten thousand;' a certain number for an uncertain, that is, the chief among all. In all things Christ hath the pre-eminence. 'He is the first-born from the dead' (*Rom.* 8:29); 'he is the first-born of every creature' (*Col.* 1:15); he is the eldest brother; he is the chief among all. For all kings, priests, and prophets before were but types and shadows of him. He, the body, the truth, and the substance. And (as was showed before) he is all three in one, king, priest, and prophet; the great doctor[1] and prophet of his church, that spake by all the former prophets, and speaks by his ministers to the end of the world. 'The angel of the covenant', that Λογος (*logos*), the Word, that expresseth his Father's breast; that as he came from the bosom of his Father, so lays open his counsel to mankind. It was he that spake by Noah, and preached by his Spirit to the souls that are now in prison, as Peter speaks (*1 Pet.* 3:19). So, 'he is the chief among all'. But especially in regard of his righteousness; for which Paul 'accounted all dung and dross, to be found in Christ, not having his own righteousness, but the righteousness that is in Christ' (*Phil.* 3:8, 9); which is more than the righteousness of an angel, being the righteousness of God-man, and above all the righteousness of the law.

Quest. But what is this to us or to the church?

Ans. Yes; for his beauty and excellency is the church's, because he is the church's. 'My beloved is white and ruddy, and my beloved is the chief among ten thousand.' It is the peculiar interest that the church hath in Christ that doth relish her spirit; excellency with propriety in him; 'I am my beloved's, and my beloved is mine.' The more excellent the husband is, the more excellent is the wife. She only shines in his beams. Therefore it is the interest that we have in Christ that endears Christ to us. But to come to more particular application of it. Is Christ thus excellent, super-excellent, thus transcendently excellent, 'white and ruddy', 'the chief of ten thousand'? This serves,

1. *To draw those that are not yet in Christ unto him.*

2. *To comfort those that are in Christ.*

Use 1. First, those that are not yet in Christ, not contracted to him, to draw them; *what can prevail more than that which is in Christ?* Beauty and excellencies, greatness and goodness. And

---

[1] That is, teacher.—G.

indeed one main end of our calling, the ministry, is, to lay open and unfold the unsearchable riches of Christ; to dig up the mine, thereby to draw the affections of those that belong to God to Christ.

Use 2. But it is not enough to know that there are excellencies in Christ to draw us to him, but, *there must be a sight of our misery; what beggars we are, and how indebted.* Before we are in Christ we are not our own. The devil lays claim to us that we are his; death lays claim to us. We are under sin; we cannot satisfy one of a thousand; therefore this enforceth to make out to join with him that can discharge all our debts, answer all our suits, and non-suit Satan in the court of heaven. When once we are married to the Lord of heaven and earth, all is ours. We have a large charter, 'All things are yours, and you are Christ's, and Christ is God's' (*1 Cor* 3:22, 23).

Quest. Why are all things ours?

Ans. Because we are married to Christ, who is Lord of all. It is the end of our calling to sue for a marriage between Christ and every soul. We are the friends of the bride, to bring the church to him; and the friends of the church, to bring Christ to them. It is the end of our ministry to bring the soul and Christ together; and let no debts, no sins hinder. For especially he invites such as are sensible of their sins. 'Where sin abounds, grace abounds much more' (*Rom.* 5:20). 'Come unto me, all ye that are weary and heavy laden' (*Matt.* 11:28). And, 'he came to seek and to save that which was lost' (*Luke* 19:10). He requires no more, but that we be sensible of our debts and miseries, which sense he works likewise by his Holy Spirit.

Use 3. Again, for those that have entertained Christ, *let them see what an excellent gracious person they have entertained*, who is 'the chief of ten thousand'. The world thinks them a company of silly, mean people, that make choice of Christ, religion, the Word, and such things; but there is a justification of their choice. They choose him that is 'the chief of ten thousand'. 'Let him kiss me with the kisses of his mouth', saith the spouse, 'for thy love is better than wine, nay, than life itself' (*Song of Sol.* 1:2). A Christian must justify the choice that he hath made with Mary 'of the good part' (*Luke* 10:42); against all those that shall disparage his choice. Let the world account Christians what they will; that they are a company of deluded, besotted persons, fools and madmen; the Christian is the only wise man. Wisdom is seen in choice especially; and here is the choice of that which is excellent and most excellent of all, 'the chief of ten thousand'.

Use 4. So also, *we may see here the desperate and base folly of all whatsoever,* save true Christians. What do they make choice of to join to? that which is base, the condemned world, vain, transitory things; and refuse Christ. Are they in their right wits who refuse a husband that is noble for birth, rich for estate, mighty for power, abundant in kindness and love itself, every way excellent, and take a base, ignoble, beggarly person? This is the choice of the world. God complains, 'Israel would none of me', &c. (*Psa.* 81:11). What shall we judge therefore of those that will none of Christ when he woos and sues them; but prefer with Esau a 'mess of pottage', before their eternal birthright (*Heb.* 12:16); with Adam, an apple before paradise; and with Judas, thirty pieces of silver before Christ himself. This is the state of many men. To be married to Christ is to take him for an husband; to be ruled by him in all things. Now when we prefer base commodities and contentments before peace of conscience and the enjoying of his love—what is it, but for pelf[1] and commodity, thirty pieces of silver (perhaps for sixpence, a thing of nothing), to refuse Christ. Yet this is the condition of base worldlings that live by sense and not by faith. So then as it serves to comfort those that have made a true choice; so it serves to show the madness and folly of all others, which one day will feel their hearts full of horror and confusion, and their

---

[1] Riches, wealth—in a derogatory sense.—P.

faces of shame, when they shall think, What? hath Christ made such suit to my heart to win my love? hath he ordained a ministry for to bring me in? made such large promises? is he so excellent? and was this discovered to me, and yet would I none of him? what did I choose, and what did I leave? I left Christ with all his riches, and made choice of the 'pleasures and profits of sin, which are but for a season' (*Heb.* 11:25). When the conscience is once thoroughly awaked, this will torment it,—the punishment of loss, not of loss simply, as the loss of Christ and the loss of heaven, but the loss of Christ and of heaven so discovered and opened. Therefore there is no condition in the world so terrible as of those that live in the church, and hear those things of Christ crucified unfolded to them before their eyes. As Paul speaks of the ministry, it makes Christ's cross so open to them as if he had been crucified before their eyes (*Gal.* 3:1). Yet notwithstanding [they] yield to their base heart's desires and affections before these excellencies; which if they had a spirit of faith would draw their hearts to him.

Therefore let us consider how we hear those things. It concerns us nearly. On the one side we see what we get if we join with Christ; we have him and his. On the contrary, we lose him; and not only so, but we gain eternal misery, and perish eternally. O what baseness of mind possesseth us! Christ left all things in love to us, and we leave Christ for any paltry thing in the world; almost to please and content the humours of sinful men, to attain a few empty titles, to get a little wealth, enjoy a little pleasure. You see then the equity of that terrible commination[1] that you have, 'If any man love not the Lord Jesus Christ, let him be Anathema Maranatha' (*1 Cor.* 16:22). Let him be accursed for ever that loves not the Lord Jesus Christ. If any man sin there is a remedy to discharge his sin in Jesus Christ, if he will marry him and take him; but when Christ is offered and we will have none of him, we sin against the gospel; and then there is no remedy; there is nothing

---

[1] That is, denunciation, threatening.—G.

but 'Anathema and Maranatha.' Therefore the most dangerous sins of all, are those against the light of the gospel; when yet we choose rather to live as we list,[1] than to join ourselves to Christ. To this purpose (*Heb.* 1) St Paul makes an use of the first chapter, wherein he sets out the excellency of Christ, whom the angels adore. He is so beautiful, so lovely that God the Father is in love with him, and pronounceth, 'This is my beloved Son' (*Matt.* 3:17). In the beginning of the second chapter, 'Wherefore', saith he, 'how shall we escape if we neglect so great salvation; for if they escaped not that despised Moses' law, &c., how shall we escape if we neglect so great salvation?' (*Heb.* 2:1-3). He says not, if we oppose Christ, but if we neglect him, if we do not love so great salvation; as it is said, 'Christ will come in flaming fire to take vengeance of all those that do not know God, and obey not the gospel of Christ' (*2 Thess.* 1:8), though they do not persecute it.

Use 1. Therefore this *reproves all civil, moral persons that think they have riches enough.* Not only debauched persons, but self-sufficient persons, that think they have any righteousness of their own. Let them know that 'Christ shall come in flaming fire, to take vengeance of such.' This is the scope of the second psalm, which ye know sets out the excellency of Christ, 'I have set my king upon Zion' (*Psa.* 2:6). God the Father there anoints Christ king of the church. To what end? 'That we should kiss the Son', kiss him with the kiss of subjection, as subjects do their prince; with the kiss of love, as the spouse doth her husband; and with the kiss of faith. But what if we do not kiss him, and subject ourselves to him, love him, and believe in him? 'If his wrath be once kindled, happy are all those that trust in him.' He is a lamb, but such a one as can be angry. It is said, 'The kings and great persons of the world fly from the wrath of the Lamb' (*Rev.* 6:16). He that is so sweet, mild, and gentle, if we join with him, on the contrary, if we come not unto him, we shall find the wrath of the Lamb a terrible wrath, which

[1] As we please.—P.

the greatest potentates in the world shall desire to be hid from. 'If his wrath be once kindled, blessed are all those that trust in him', and woe be to them that do not receive him.

Use 2. For us that profess ourselves to be in Christ, and to be joined to him that is thus excellent, let us make this use, *to make him the rule of our choice in other things*. In the choice of friends, choose such as are friends to Christ. Take heed of society with idolaters, or with profane, wretched persons. If you will be joined to Christ, and profess yourselves to be so, then let us join to none but those that we can enjoy and Christ too. So in marriage, let the rule of choice be the love of Christ. And likewise, let the measure of our respect to all things be the respect to Christ. Let us measure our love to wife and children, to kindred, friends, and to all creatures whatsoever, as it may stand with love to Christ. Obey in the Lord, marry in the Lord, do all things in the Lord, so as may stand with the love and allowance of the Lord (*1 Cor.* 7:39, 40).

Use 3. Make also a use of direction, *how to come to value Christ thus*, as to keep an high esteem of him. For this follows infallibly and undeniably, if Christ be 'the chief of ten thousand', he must have the chief of our affections 'above ten thousand'. For, as he is in excellency, he must have place in our hearts answerable thereunto; for then our souls are as they should be, when they judge of, and affect things as they are in themselves.

1. First, let us enter into a serious consideration *of the need we have of Christ, of our misery without him, of our happiness if we be joined with him*. The soul being thus convinced, the affections must needs follow the sanctified judgment.

What will come of it if Christ be set in the highest place in our heart? If we crown him there, and make him 'King of kings and Lord of lords', in a hearty submitting of all the affections of the soul to him? While the soul continues in that frame it cannot be drawn to sin, discomfort, and despair. The honours, pleasures, and profits that are got by base engagements to the humours of men, what are these to Christ? When the soul is rightly possessed of Christ and of his excellency, it disdains that anything should come in competition with him.

2. Again, *it stands firm against all discouragements whatsoever*: for it sets Christ against all, who is the 'chief of ten thousand'. The soul in this case will set Christ against the anger and wrath of God, against Satan, and all our spiritual enemies. Christ is the angel of the covenant. Satan is a lion, a roaring lion; Christ the lion of the tribe of Judah. Satan a serpent, a dragon; but Christ, the true brazen serpent, the very looking upon whom will take away all the stings and fiery darts of Satan whatsoever. Wherefore it is said (*1 John* 5:4) that faith is that that 'overcometh the world'. How doth faith overcome the world? Because it overcomes all things in the world, as, on the right hand, pleasures and profits and honours, and on the left hand, threatenings, pains, losses, and disgraces, by setting Christ against all.

3. Again, if we would have a right judgment and esteem of Christ, *let us labour to wean our affections as much as may be from other things.* Fleshly hearts that have run so deeply into the world, and vanities of this present life, it is in a sort an extraordinary task for them to be drawn away and pulled from the world, as a child from a full breast, which they have sucked so long. Now, for sweet affections that are tender, it is an excellent advantage they have to consider betimes that there is that in religion and in the gospel which is worth their best and prime affections, the flower and marrow of them. Let them begin, with young Timothy (*2 Tim.* 3:15), Daniel, and Joseph, to love Christ from their childhood. It is a desperate folly, on the other hand, to put off the regard of good things till after, when we shall be less fit, when the understanding will be darkened, and the affections blunted, when we shall not have that edge, nature being decayed, and the world having taken such possession of the soul that we shall not value this excellency. Therefore let us begin betimes to make up the marriage between Christ and the soul. No time, indeed, is too late, but it were to

be wished that those that are young would be thus wise for their souls betimes.

4. Besides, if we would highly value Christ, *beg of God a spirit that we may judge aright of our corruptions, for in what measure we can discern the height, and breadth, and depth of our corrupt nature, in that measure shall we judge of the height, and breadth, and depth of the excellency of Christ.* The sweetest souls are the most humble souls. Those that love Christ most are those that have been stung most with the sense of their sins. Where sin most abounds in the sense and feeling of it, grace much more abounds in the sense and feeling of that (*Rom.* 5:20). Did ever soul love Christ more than that woman that had so many devils cast out of her? (*Luke* 8:2). And Paul, that had such great sins forgiven? Doth any man so love his creditor as he that hath much debt forgiven him? It is our Saviour Christ's own reason. Therefore these two go always with the true church. (1.) The true knowledge of the corruption of nature, and misery by reason of it; and (2.) The true sense and feeling of it, with true and hearty sorrow for it, &c. In popery they slight original sin, that mother, breeding sin. Actual sins be venial, and many sins no sins. And therefore they esteem so slightly of Christ that they join saints, the pope, works and satisfaction with him. Because they know not the depth of the malady, how black sin is, what a cursed estate we are in by nature, they have slight, shallow, and weak conceits of sin. Therefore they have answerable weak and shallow conceits of Christ and of his righteousness and excellency. Therefore the conviction of our sins goeth before the conviction of righteousness in Christ, as it is said, 'The Holy Ghost shall convince the world of sin and then of righteousness' (*John* 16:8). For except the soul be convinced of sin, and of ill in itself, it will never be truly convinced of good and of righteousness in Christ.

The Passover was always eaten with sour herbs, because it should add a relish to the feast. So Christ, the true Passover, we never relish truly without sour herbs, the consideration of sin, with the desert of it. Christ savours otherwise to a man humbled for his sins than he doth to another man not touched therewith; otherwise to a poor man than he doth to a rich; otherwise to a man that the world goes not well on his side than to a prosperous man. One savoury discourse of Christ relisheth more to an afflicted soul than seven discourses with such as are drunk with prosperity, not having a brain strong enough to conceive, nor an appetite to relish heavenly things.

Therefore why do we murmur at the cross, when all is to recover our spiritual taste and relish? Solomon had lost his taste and relish of Christ. He never made his song of songs when he was in his idolatrous way, nor was so in love with Christ and his excellencies when he doted so much upon his wives. No; but when he had recovered his spirit's taste and relish of heavenly things once, then made he the book of the preacher. When he had run through variety of things, and saw all to be nothing but vexation of spirit, and besides that vanity, then he passeth his verdict upon all things, that they were vanity. So it is with us, we can hardly prize Christ without some afflictions, some cross or other. Therefore here the church is fain to endure a spiritual desertion, to set an edge upon her affections, Now, when she is thus in her desertions, 'Christ is white and ruddy, the chief of ten thousand.'

We value more, and set a higher price on things in the want of them—such is our corruption—than in the enjoying of them. And if God remember us not with affliction, then let us afflict, humble, and judge ourselves; enter into our own souls, to view how we stand affected to Christ, to heaven, and to heavenly things. How do I relish and esteem them? If I have lost my esteem and valuing, where have I lost it? Consider in what sin, in what pleasure, in what company I lost it; and converse no more with such as dull our affections to heavenly things.

Use 4. And *let us make use likewise of our infirmities and sins to this purpose, to set an high price on the excellencies of Christ.* We carry about us always infirmities and corruptions. What use shall we make of them? Not to trust to our own righteousness, which is 'as a defiled cloth' (*Isa.* 64:6), but fly to Christ's righteousness, which is the righteousness of God-man, all being as dung and dross in regard of that. Often think with thyself, What am I? a poor sinful creature; but I have a righteousness in Christ that answers all. I am weak in myself, but Christ is strong, and I am strong in him. I am foolish in myself, but I am wise in him. What I want in myself I have in him. He is mine, and his righteousness is mine, which is the righteousness of God-man. Being clothed with this, I stand safe against conscience, hell, wrath, and whatsoever. Though I have daily experience of my sins, yet there is more righteousness in Christ, who is mine, and who is the chief of ten thousand, than there is sin in me. When thus we shall know Christ, then we shall know him to purpose.

SERMON 16

My beloved is white and ruddy, the chiefest among ten thousand.
His head is as fine gold; his locks are bushy and black as a raven;
his eyes are as the eyes of doves, by the rivers of waters,
washed with milk; and fitly set, &c.
SONG OF SOLOMON 5:10-13

OBJ. Hence likewise we may answer some doubts that may arise; as why the death of one man, Christ, should be of value for satisfaction for the sins of the whole world. How can this be?

Ans. O but what kind of man was he? 'The chief among ten thousand', especially considering that his excellency ariseth from the grace of his personal union of God and man. The first Adam tainted thousands, and would have tainted a world of men more if there had been more; but he was mere man that did this. And shall not Christ, God and man, the second Adam, advance the world, and ten thousand worlds if there had been more? He is chief among ten thousand.

'His head is as most fine gold; his locks are bushy and black as a raven', &c.

1. Positively, 'He is white and ruddy.' 2. Comparatively, 'He is the chiefest of ten thousand.'

The church doth not think it sufficient, in general, to set out Christ thus; but she descends into a particular description of him by all the parts of a body that are conspicuous. First, in general observe hence, that *it is the nature of love upon all occasions to reflect upon the thing loved.* As the church here, from things that are excellent in the world, borrows phrases and comparisons to set out the excellency of Christ, exalting him above any other thing. Whatsoever the soul of a Christian sees in heaven or earth, it takes occasion thence to think of Christ.

Again, in general, observe from hence, seeing the church fetcheth comparison from doves' eyes, from the body of a man and other things, that *there are some beams of excellency in every creature.* There is somewhat of God in every creature. This makes the meditation of the creature to be useful. There is none, even the meanest, but it hath a being, and thereby in a sort sets out the being of God. Why doth God style himself a shield, a rock, a buckler, a shadow, and the like? but to show that there is something of him in these. And therefore to teach us to rise from them to him, in whom all those excellencies that are scattered in them are united.

In innocency we knew God, and in him we had knowledge of the creature; but now we are fain[1] to help ourselves from the knowledge of the creature to rise to the knowledge of God.

'His head is as fine gold.' A little in general. See the boldness and largeness of the church's affections, who, though she had been ill entreated by the watchmen and others, yet is she not disheartened for all this. No; she goes on and sets out particular commendations of her beloved. Where love hath any strength, no water can quench it. You see the church here found but cold entertainment from the watchmen and others that should have been better.

Nay, she was in desertion, yet she was not discouraged. Nay, not from the desertion that Christ left her in; but she seeks after him whom her soul loved. Oh! this is the sign of a true, sanctified soul, touched from heaven, never to give over seeking of Christ; nor setting out his praises. No, though it thinks itself not beloved of Christ. Ask such ones, Do you love God, his children, and his

[1] Glad, eager.—P.

Word? Oh! you shall have them eloquent. No words are enough to set out their affections.

And this is one reason, which we may note by the way, why God plants in his children, at their first conversion, a sweet love, which we call, 'the first love', that when desertions come they may call to mind what they felt from Christ, and what they bore to him; and thereupon the church concludes, 'I will return to my first love, for then was I better than now' (*Hos.* 2:7). The church here, from what doth she commend her beloved, but from somewhat that was left in her soul, some inward taste of the love of Christ in her? She called to mind how it was with her before in the former part of this, and in the latter end of the former chapter; what an excellent estate she had been in. This helped her to recover herself.

Now you may say, Why is she so exact in reckoning up so many particulars of her beloved, his head, locks, eyes, lips, and such like?

Why? 1. It is from largeness of affection. A large heart hath always large expressions. When we are barren in expressions towards Christ, and of good things, whence comes this but from narrow, poor affections? The church had large affections; therefore she had suitable expressions.

And then, 2. She is thus particular, because Christ hath not one but many excellencies. Everything in him is excellent, inward and outward, as his head, &c. For indeed beauty consists not in sweetness of colour only, but in affinity and proportion of all parts. Now there is all sweet proportion in Christ. So it should be with Christians. They should not have one excellency, but many. Those that receive grace for grace from Christ (*John* 1:16), have not only head, eyes, hands, and feet good; but all lovely, 'grace for grace', answerable to the variety of graces in Jesus Christ, in whom all things jointly, and everything severally, are lovely.

Then, 3. She showeth her particular care and study, to be exact in this knowledge of Christ. To rip him up and anatomise him thus, from head to foot, it argueth she had studied Christ well, ere she could attain this excellency. So it should be the study and care of every Christian, to study the excellencies of Christ, not only in the gross, to say as much as you have in the Creed; he was born for us of the Virgin Mary, was crucified, dead, and buried, &c., which every child can say; but to be able to particularize the high perfections and excellencies of Christ, as the church here; to study his nature, offices, the state he was in, and how he carried himself in his humiliation and exaltation; what good we have by both states, redemption by his abasement; application of it by his advancement; what he did for us on earth; what he doth in heaven; what in justification, adoption, sanctification, and in the glory to come. Study everything, and warm the heart with the meditation of them.

This particular spreading and laying open the excellencies of Christ is a thing worthy of a Christian. We make slight work of religion. We can be particular and eloquent enough in other things, but in that wherein all eloquence is too little, how barren are we! how shamefaced to speak of Christ and his excellencies in base company, as if it were a dishonour! Let us therefore learn this from the church here, to be much in thoughts and meditations of the excellencies of Christ, and so our expressions will be answerable to our meditations. So the holy fathers that were godly (till another kind of divinity came into the world, of querks[1] and subtleties) there was none of them but was excellent this way. Paul [was] admirable, accounting 'all dung and dross in comparison of Christ'. In speaking of him, when he begins, he goes on from one thing to another, as if he were ravished, and knew not how nor where to end.

The soul hath sights of Christ that God shows to it, and which the soul presents to itself by the help of the Spirit. The sights that God in this kind shows, are to those in affliction especially; as

[1] That is, 'quirks' = tricks.—G.

Daniel and Isaiah saw Christ in his glory in a vision. So Ezekiel had a vision, and John (*Rev.* 1), where Christ was presented to him gloriously. So there is a glorious, description of Christ present to the church (*Rev.* 4:3-5).

And as there are sights let down from God into the soul, so there are sights that the soul frames of Christ, such as the church here conceives of him by faith. Thus Moses saw him before he was incarnate, and Abraham saw his day and rejoiced (*John* 8:56): so should we now have spiritual sights, ideas of Christ framed to our souls. This is to bestow our souls as we should do.[1] So much for general, now we come to some particulars. 'His head is as fine gold; his locks are bushy and black as a raven.'

'His head is as fine gold.' He begins to set out the excellency of the chief part, the head. The head of Christ is God (*1 Cor.* 11:3). He is above all, and God only is above him. All is yours, and you are Christ's, and Christ is God's (*1 Cor.* 3:22, 23). But that is not so much intended here, as to show Christ's headship over the church, as God and man. His head is as fine gold, that is, his government and headship is a most sweet and golden government.

Daniel 2. You have an image of the monarchies; the first whereof had a golden head, which was the Chaldean. The best monarchy is set out by the best metal—gold; so Christ, the head of the church, is a precious head, a head of gold.

A head hath an eminency above all others; an influence and motion above all other parts. It is the seat of the senses. So this

[1] For a very valuable, and, in many respects, remarkably acute and suggestive discussion of the question of framing 'ideas of Christ', a subject keenly debated in the last century in Scotland, consult the following little-known book, by Ralph Erskine—'*Faith no Fancy*; or a Treatise of Mental Images . . . showing that our imaginary idea of Christ as Man (when supposed to belong to saving faith, whether in its act or object), imports nothing but ignorance, atheism, idolatry, great falsehood, and gross delusion . . .' Edinburgh, 1745, 12mo. This little work may be pronounced the pioneer of the philosophy known as Scottish. Apart from its bearing on the passage of Sibbes, it will be found to contain much uncommon thought on 'ideas' equal, to say the least, to the subsequent writings of Reid.—G.

golden head is more eminent than all, governs the whole church and hath influence into all. In him we live, and move, and have our being (*Acts* 17:28).

Quest. Why is Christ as king thus resembled to an head of gold?

Ans. Because gold is the chief, the most precious, durable metal of all others. Christ is a king for ever, and hath an everlasting government. Gold is also the most pliable metal. You may beat it out to leaves more than any other metal whatsoever. Christ is all gold indeed. His love hath beat himself out as low as may be, all for our good. What abasement like to Christ's? That which is most precious is most communicating, as the sun, a glorious creature. What doth so much good as it? So Christ, as he is the most excellent of all, 'the chief of ten thousand', so is he also the most communicative. What good to the good that Christ did? He was beaten, out of love to mankind, to lowest abasement for us. Though this be not mainly aimed at here, yet, by the way, speaking of gold, we may present to ourselves such comfortable meditations.

Use 1. Well then, is Christ such an excellent head, a golden head, 'in whom are hid all the treasures of wisdom' (*Col.* 2:3), to govern his church? *What need we then go to that triple crown, having such a golden head?* The apostasy of the church hath found out another golden head. Is not Christ precious enough? Let us take heed of leaving the head Christ, as it is Colossians 2:19. It is a damnable thing to forsake him. Let the apostatical[1] church alone with her antichrist.

2. Again, if Christ be a golden head, let us his members *labour every one to be suitable*. Though there be difference between the head and the members in many respects, especially in those three formerly named, eminency, government, and influence, yet for nature they are one. Head and members make but one. So that as the head of the body is gold, so should every member

---

[1] That is, apostate.—Ed.

be. Therefore the seven churches are styled seven golden candlesticks. Everything in the tabernacle was gold, even to the snuffers, to show that in the church everything is excellent. The tabernacle was gold, most of it, though it was covered with badgers' skins. The church indeed hath a poor covering as of badgers' skins, not gilded as hypocrites; but it is precious within. Again, Christ, as he is gold, so he is fine gold, whole gold. He hath not only the crown on him, but his head is gold itself. Other kings, their crowns are of gold, but their heads are not so. But there is such a precious treasure of wisdom in him that his head is gold. So let the church and every Christian labour, not to be gilt, but gold; to be thoroughly good; to have the inside as good as the outside, the heart as good as the conversation. The church is glorious within (*Psa.* 45:13). Beloved, is Christ an excellent golden head, and shall we have a base body? Is he fit to be united to a golden head that is a common drunkard, a swearer, that is a beast in his life and conversation? Is this suitable?

3. Again, is our head so golden, and whatsoever excellency we have, is it from our head? Therefore as the church in the Revelation, '*let us cast all our crowns at his feet*' (*Rev.* 4:10). Have we crowns of gold? anything that is excellent within, any grace, any comfort? Let us lay it down at his feet, for all is from him. Natural men have golden images of their own. Israel would have golden calves. Nebuchadnezzar sets up a golden image, and all must worship it. So in the declining times of the church: they framed golden images, that is, a golden whorish religion, gilded, and painted, framed by their own brain, whereunto all must stoop. But the true gold is that we must respect and submit ourselves unto and admire. Others are but golden dreams and images, as Nebuchadnezzar's was. Christ's head is of fine gold.

All must be fine gold that comes from this head. His Word is gold, sometimes[1] purged in the fire. His ordinances gold, in the

---

[1] Qu. seven times?—Ed.

Scripture phrase (*Psa.* 19:10). The city, the new Jerusalem, which signifies the state of the church in this world, when it shall be refined to the utmost, all is of gold; the walls of precious stones; the gates of pearl; and the pavement of the streets of pure gold (*Rev.* 21:21) to show the excellency of reformation; which golden times are yet to come. In the meantime let us go on and wait for them.

'His locks are bushy, and black as a raven.' I think this is but complemental, to fill up the other. It is nothing but a commendation of his freshness, a foil to beauty. Therefore not particularly to be stood upon.

'His eyes are as doves' eyes by the rivers of waters', &c. His eyes are as doves' eyes, and such eyes as are by the rivers of waters; where they are cleansed and washed with milk that they may be the clearer, and fitly set; neither goggle eyes, nor sunk into the head, but fitly set, as a jewel in a ring; neither too much in, nor too much out, to set out the comeliness of this part, the eye, which is the glory of the face.

Quest. Why is Christ said to have the eyes of doves?

Ans. The dove hath many enemies, especially the white dove is a fair mark for the birds of prey. Therefore God hath given that creature a quick sight, that she might discern her enemies. Thus the Scripture helps us to conceive of the quickness of Christ's eye (*Rev.* 5:6). There are seven horns and seven eyes, which are the seven Spirits of God. Here Christ the lamb, hath seven eyes and seven horns. What be these? Christ hath not only horns of power, as the enemies have horns of violence.—He hath horn against horn; but seven eyes, that is, a quick sight to see all the danger the church is in, and seven eyes. Seven is a word of perfection, that is, he hath many eyes, an accurate sight. He hath not only an eye of providence over the whole world, but an eye of grace and favour, lively, and lovely in regard of his church. All things are naked and open before his eyes (*Heb.* 4:13). He can see through us, he knows our very hearts and reins, which he must do *ex officio*, because he must be our judge. He that is judge of all had need to have eyes that will pierce through all. It had need be a quick eye that must judge of the heart and affections. But what may we learn hence? That we have a Saviour that hath doves' eyes, that is, clear eyes, able to discern.

Use 1. Take it as a point first, *of all comfort to the church*, that when we have any imputation [that] lies upon us, that we are thus and thus, Christ hath quick eyes, he knows our hearts. 'Thou knowest', saith Peter, 'Lord, that I love thee' (*John* 21:15). In all false imputations, rest in the eyesight of Christ. He knows it is otherwise with us.

Use 2. Then again, *in all abasement, know that there is an eye that sees all*. He sees with his eye and pities with his heart. As he hath a quick eye, so he hath a tender heart. Though he seems to sleep and to wink, it is but that we may wake him with our prayers; which when we have done, we shall see that Christ hath seen all this while, and that the violence the enemies of God have offered to his church, the spouse, hath been in his sight, and that they shall know at length to their cost.

Likewise it is a point of terror to all hypocrites and others, that think to blindfold Christ again. Can they blindfold him in heaven that hath this sharp eye? No; he sees all their courses and projects, what they are and what they tend to; and as he sees them, so he will spread them all open ere long.

Use 3. And as it is a point of comfort and terror, so *it is a point of instruction to us all, that we have to deal with a judge that sees all, to worship Christ in spirit*. If we had knowledge that such an eye of God is fixed upon us in all places, in all our affections and actions, would we give liberty to base and filthy thoughts, to cruel designs, and to treacherous aims and intents? to hatch a hell, as it were, in our hearts, and to carry a fair show outwardly. It could not be. Men are not afraid of their thoughts, affections, desires, and inward delights of their soul, because there is no eye of justice upon them. But if they did consider that the all-seeing God did observe these inward evils, and would call them to account one day for them, then they would be as well afraid to think ill as to do ill.

'His cheeks are as beds of spices, and as sweet flowers.'

Cheeks are the grace of the face. They are used here to denote the presence of Christ, which is sweet as spices and flowers. Not only his presence is glorious in heaven, when we shall see that goodly person of Christ that became man for us, that transforming sight that shall make us like himself, but the spiritual presence of Christ in his ordinances which we are capable of here, this is as spices and flowers.

Obj. But you will say, cheeks, face, and presence present colours to the eye, and not smells, as spices and flowers, which are the peculiar object of another sense.

Ans. Oh, but Christ is the object of all the senses. Beloved, he is not only beauty to the eye, but sweetness to the smell, and to the taste. Therefore faith hath the name of all the senses, to see, hear, taste, and smell, and doth all, because it carries us to Christ, that is instead of all to us. But the point is,

That the manifestation of Christ to his church and children by his Spirit in any of his ordinances, is a sweet manifestation, and delectable as spices and flowers; 'Because of the savour of thy good ointments, thy name is as an ointment poured out, therefore the virgins love thee' (*Song of Sol.* 1:3). The very name of Christ, when he is known and laid open by the ministry, is a precious ointment, and the virgins, that is, all chaste souls, follow him by the smell of his ointments. All his ordinances convey a sweetness to the soul. His sacraments are sweet, his Word sweet, the communion of saints sweet. The presence of the sun, you know, is known in the spring time by the freshness of all things, which put forth the life and little liveliness they have in them, some in blossoming, and some in flowers. That which lay, as it were, dead in winter, it comes out when the sun draws near; so when Christ comes and shows his presence and face to the soul, he refresheth and delights it.

Hence we see they are enemies to Christ and to the souls of God's people that hinder the manifestation of Christ, whereby his face might be seen, and his lovely cheeks discerned. Those that hate and undermine the ordinances of God, they hinder the comforts of their own souls.

And they are enemies to Christ. For when hath Christ glory but when the virgins follow him in the scent of his sweet ointments? When the soul, in the sense of his sweetness, follows him, and cleaves to him with joy, love, and delight, this makes Christ Christ, and sets him up in the heart above all others. This is the proper work of the ordinances. Those, therefore that are enemies to the ordinances of Christ, are enemies to the souls of God's people, and to the glory and honour of Christ himself. Thus far we may go safely, upon comparison of this with the other Scriptures.

SERMON 17

*His lips are like lilies, dropping sweet-smelling myrrh; his hands
are as gold rings set with beryl; his belly is as bright
ivory overlaid with sapphire: his legs, &c.*
Song of Solomon 5:13-15

I N speaking of these particulars we are to be very wary, for we
have not that foundation as we have in other generals. For no
doubt but the Spirit of God here did more intend to set out
the large affection that the church had to Christ, than to insinuate
any great particularity in every one of these. Therefore let us only
cull out, and take those things that are of more easy explication.

'His lips are as lilies, dropping down sweet myrrh.'

That is, his doctrine is as sweet as the lilies, and sound as the
myrrh, keeping from putrefaction, it being the nature of myrrh,
as it is sound itself, so to make other things sound. In like manner, the speech of Christ makes the soul sound that embraceth
it. What was ever more sweet than the truth of Christ? When
he spake himself, they all hung upon his lips (*Luke* 4:20), as the
phrase is in the gospel,[1] as a man hangs upon the lips of another
whom he desires and delights to hear speak, and they marvelled
at the gracious words that came out of his lips. Grace was in his
lips (*Psa.* 45:2). All was sweet that came from him, for it came
from the excellency of his Spirit. His words were dyed in these
affections of his heart. In the learned language, the same word

---

[1] The Greek word used is from ἀτενής = intent, earnestly fixed, from τείνω (cf.
Luke 22:56. *Acts* 3:12; 10:4; 14:9).—G.

signifieth speech and reason,[1] to intimate that speech is but the current of reason from the heart, the seat of reason. Therefore Christ's speeches were sweet, because his heart was sweet, full of all love, grace, mercy, and goodness (*Matt.* 12:34, 35). His heart was a treasure. His lips must needs then be sweet. Beloved, therefore let us hence take a trial of ourselves, what our condition is, whether the words that come from Christ when he speaks in his ministry to us be sweet or not.

The word, to some kind of men, is like the northern air, which parcheth and cutteth. Ahab could not endure the breath of Elijah (*1 Kings* 21:20), nor Herodias the breath of John Baptist (*Mark* 6:16), nor the Pharisees the breath of Stephen and Paul (*Acts* 7:54; 22:22). So too many now-a-days cannot endure the breath of divine truth, when it cuts and pierceth. These words are arrows that stick. If they stick not savingly, they stick to killing. If we cannot endure Christ's breath, we are not his spouse, nor have any communion with him.

'His lips are like lilies, dropping sweet myrrh', &c.

This is one excellency of Christ and of his truth, that it preserves the soul in a pure estate. It is pure itself, and so it preserves the soul. Myrrh is a liquor that keeps from putrefaction. There is nothing that keeps the soul, but the Word that endures for ever. Whereas, on the other side, error is of a putrefying nature, corrupting and defiling the soul.

'His hands are as gold rings set with beryl', &c.

Hands are the instruments of actions. Christ's actions are precious. Whatsoever he doth to the church, nay, even when he doth use evil men to afflict and exercise the church, he hath a hand there, a golden, a precious hand, in the evil hand of wicked men. God doth all things by Christ. He is, as it were, God's hand, which all things pass through (*Heb.* 1:2, *John* 5:22). Joseph was the second man of Egypt, through whose hands all things came to the rest;

---

[1] Query—Is the allusion to λογος?—G.

so all things come through Christ's hands to us; and whatsoever is his handiwork is good. Even as it is said in the days of his flesh, 'he did all things well' (*Mark* 7:37), so still, in the church all his workmanship is exceeding well. Though we cannot see the excellency of it, it is all well both in the government of the church and his workmanship in our hearts, 'the new creature'.

'His belly is as bright ivory overlaid', &c.

His belly, that is, his inward parts. In the Hebrew, it is used for the inward affections. They are as bright ivory overlaid with sapphires, that is, they are pure. All the inside of Christ, all his affections that he bears, are wondrous good. His love, his desires, his joys, his hatred, all pure, like pure water in a crystal glass. It may be stirred sometimes, but still it is clear. There are no dregs at the bottom, because there was no taint of sin in him.

'His legs are as pillars of marble set on sockets of fine gold', &c.

That is, all his passages and ways are constant and firm, even as pillars of marble. His children are so likewise, as far as they are endued with his Spirit. Christ is yesterday, today, and the same for ever (*Heb.* 13:8). In regard of his enemies, he is set out in another manner of similitude, 'as having legs of brass to trample them all in pieces' (*Rev.* 1:15). But in respect of his constant truth and ways of goodness to his church, his legs are as pillars of marble.

'His countenance is as Lebanon, excellent as the cedars.'

Lebanon was a goodly forest lying on the north side of Judea, wherein were excellent plants of all kinds, especially cedars. Christ his countenance is as Lebanon; excellent as the cedars, that is, his presence is goodly, stately, and majestical. So it is and will be when he shows himself, indeed, for the vindicating of his church. Then the enemies thereof shall know that his presence is as Lebanon, and excellent as the cedars.

The children of God are like to cedars, too, for they are Christ mystical. Other men are as shrubs to them, men of no value; but

THE LOVE OF CHRIST

they are cedars, and grow as cedars in Lebanon, from perfection to perfection, bearing most fruit in their age. Wicked men sometimes are cedars, too, and are said to grow and flourish as the cedars in Lebanon. But look a while, and you shall see their place no more (*Psa.* 37:10). They have no good root, no good foundation. A Christian is a cedar set in Christ the chief cedar. He is a plant that grows in him. He hath an eternal root, and, therefore, he flourisheth eternally.

'His mouth is most sweet, he is altogether lovely.'

His mouth is most sweet. She doubles this commendation. She had said before, his lips are as lilies dropping sweet myrrh. Here she saith again of his mouth, it is most sweet, to show that this is the chief lovely thing in Christ. The repetition argueth the seriousness of the church's affection to Christ, and of the excellency of that part. The main lovely thing is that which comes from his heart by his words and his lips; as, indeed, the most excellent thing that we can think of is the expression of the heart of God in Christ, and of Christ's love to us. 'His mouth is most sweet.' And, indeed, the best discovery of a true affection to Christ, and of a true estate in grace, is from our affection to the Word of Christ. Wheresoever there is interest into Christ, there is a high respect to the Word. 'My sheep hear my voice' (*John* 10:4); and you know what Peter saith (*John* 6). Many of Christ's hearers and followers forsook him, upon some hard speeches, as they thought, that came from him. Saith Christ to Peter, 'Will ye also leave me?' Peter answered again, 'Whither, Lord, shall we go? Thou hast the words of eternal life' (*John* 6:68). The apostles, that had the Spirit of God, perceived an incredible graciousness to sit on his lips, and therefore they hung upon his lips. 'Whither shall we go? Thou hast the words of eternal life.' If we leave his speech, we leave our comfort, we leave our life.

As a comment hereupon, see Psalm 19, where we have a high commendation of God's excellency; first, from the book of nature, the works of God: 'the heavens declare the glory of God;' then from the Word of God; and herein the psalmist is wondrous large. 'The law of the Lord is perfect, converting the soul; the testimonies of the Lord are sure, making wise the simple; the statutes of the Lord are right, and rejoice the heart; the commandments of the Lord are sure, and enlighten the eyes; more to be desired than gold, yea, than fine gold; sweeter also than the honey or the honeycomb.'

But mark the order. When is the Word of God precious as gold, sweeter than the honey or the honeycomb, but when the former commendation takes place? Where the Word is perfect, converting the soul, and where it is sure, making wise the simple, and where the fear of the Lord is clean, &c., there it is more to be desired than fine gold, and sweeter than the honeycomb. So the church here finding, first of all, the word to be a converting word, and giving understanding to the simple, she cannot but speak of the sweetness of the word of Christ. His lips are as lilies dropping sweet-smelling myrrh. His mouth is most sweet. Thus a man may know his estate in grace by his relish of the Word.

There is a divine and a heavenly relish in the word of God; as, for instance, take the doctrine of his providence, 'that all things shall work together for the best to them that love God' (*Rom.* 8:28). What a sweet word is this! A whole kingdom is not worth this promise, that whatsoever befalls a Christian in this world, there is an overruling providence to sway all to good, to help forward his eternal good.

That Christ will be present with us in all conditions, what a sweet word and promise is this! (*Matt.* 28:20); that 'he will give his Holy Spirit, if we beg it' (*Luke* 11:13); that 'he will not fail us nor forsake us' (*Heb.* 13:5); that 'if we confess our sins, and lay them open, he is merciful to forgive them' (*1 John* 1:9); that 'if our sins were as red as scarlet, they shall all be white as wool' (*Isa.* 1:18). What kind of incredible sweetness is in these to a heart that is prepared for these comforts! The doctrine of reconciliation, of adoption, of glory to come, of the offices of Christ and such like, how sweet are they! They relish wondrously to a sanctified soul.

Let us therefore discern of our estate in grace by this, how do we relish divine truths? Are they connatural and suitable to us? Do we love them more than our appointed food? Are they dearer unto us than thousands of gold and silver? (*Psa.* 119:72, 127). Do we like them above all other truths whatsoever? Every truth in its rank is lovely, and is a beam of God. For truth is of God wheresoever we find it. But what are other truths to this heavenly, soul-saving truth? this gospel-truth that is from Christ? 'His mouth is most sweet.'

In our nature there is a contrary disposition and antipathy to divine truth. We love the law better than the gospel, and any truth better than the law. We love a story, any trifling, baubling thing concerning our ordinary callings, better than divine truth. In divine truth, as things are more spiritual, so the more remote they are naturally from our love and liking. Evangelical truths will not down with a natural heart; such an one had rather hear a quaint point of some vice or virtue finely stood upon than anything in Christ, because he was never truly convinced of his corrupt and miserable estate by nature. But when the grace of God hath altered him, and his eyes are open to see his misery, then of all truths the truth of Christ favours[1] best. Those truths that come out of the mouth of Christ, and out of the ministry concerning Christ, they are the most sweet of all. Oh! how sweet are those words in the gospel to the poor man, 'Thy sins are forgiven thee' (*Matt.* 9:2). Do you think they went not to his heart? So to the woman (*Luke* 7:47). Her many sins are forgiven her, for she loved much. Oh! they were words that went to her soul! And to the thief on the cross, 'This day thou shalt be with me in paradise' (*Luke* 23:43). How do you think those words affected him? So it is with us if ever we have been abased in the sense of our sins.

[1] Qu. savours?—Ed.

Oh! how sweet is a promise of mercy then! He that brings it is as one of ten thousand, that comes to declare to man his righteousness (*Job* 33:23); to lay open the mercy that belongs to a distressed soul. Oh! the very feet of those that bring these glad tidings are beautiful! (*Rom.* 10:15). When our blessed Saviour, after his resurrection, spake to Mary, and called her by her name, after that she had sought him and could not find him, 'O Rabboni', saith she. The words of Christ they melted her presently. Let Christ once call us by our names, for he knows us by name, as he knew Moses (*Exod.* 34:27, *Isa.* 43:1); let him by his Spirit speak to us by name, and own us, then we call him Rabboni. We own him again, for what is our love but the reflection of his back again? Therefore saith the psalmist, 'Let me hear the voice of joy and gladness, that the bones that thou hast broken may rejoice' (*Psa.* 51:8). 'Let me hear;' that is, I long for thy word to hear it; not the bare ministerial word, but the word of the Spirit. But the church resteth not here, but saith further,

'He is altogether lovely.' Altogether desirable; as if she should say, What should I stand upon particulars? he is altogether, from top to toe, amiable, lovely, and delectable.

'He is altogether lovely.' Lovely to God, to us, to the soul; lovely to him that can best judge of loveliness. The judgment of God I hope will go current with us; and what doth God the Father judge of Christ? 'This is my beloved Son' (*Matt.* 3:17). He is the Son of God's love (*Col.* 1:13), as God cannot but love his own image. He is lovely also as man, for he was pure and holy; lovely as mediator by office, for he was anointed by God to convey the Father's love to us. He must needs be lovely in whom all others are loved. This is my beloved Son, in whom I am well pleased; out of him I am well pleased with nobody. And indeed he was filled with all graces that might make him lovely. All the treasures of wisdom are in him, and of his fulness we all receive grace for grace. He is made a storehouse of all that is good for us.

He is lovely to God in whatsoever he did. He carried himself lovely, and pleased his Father in all his doings and sufferings. God loved him especially, 'because he was obedient, even unto the death of the cross. Therefore God gave him a name above all names; that at the name of Jesus every knee should bow, both in heaven and in earth' (*Phil.* 2:8-10). As for the angels, they look upon him with admiration. They attended him, and accounted it an honour to wait upon him. He is lovely to all above us, and shall he not be lovely to us?

Obj. But you will say, Was he lovely when he was nailed on the cross, hung between two thieves, when he wore a crown of thorns, was whipped, laid grovelling on the ground, when he sweat water and blood? What loveliness was in him when he was laid in his grave?

Ans. Oh! yes; then he was most lovely of all to us, by how much the more he was abased for us. This makes him more lovely that out of love he would abase himself so low. When greatness and goodness meet together, how goodly is it! That Christ, so great a majesty, should have such bowels of compassion! Majesty alone is not lovely, but awful and fearful; but joined with such condescending grace, is wondrous amiable. How lovely a sight is it to see so great a person to be so meek and gentle! It was so beyond comparison lovely in the eyes of the disciples, that they stood and wondered to see him, who was the eternal Word of the Father, condescend to talk with a poor Samaritan woman (*John* 4:6ff.). And what loveliness of carriage was in him to Peter, undeserving, after he had denied and forsworn him, yet to restore him to his former place that he had in his heart, loving him as much as ever he did before! In a word, what sweetness, gentleness, bowels of meekness, pity, and compassion did he discover to those that were in misery! We cannot insist upon particulars.

There is a remarkable passage in the story of Alphonsus the king, not very well liked of some. When he saw a poor man pulling of his beast out of a ditch, he put to his hand to help him; after which, as it is recorded, his subjects ever loved him the better. It was a wonderful condescending. And is it not as wonderful that the King of heaven and earth should stoop so low as to help us poor worms out of the ditch of hell and damnation? and that, when he hath set us in a state of deliverance, he should not leave us there, but advance us to such a state and condition as is above our admiration, which neither heart can conceive nor tongue express? Is not this wonderful condescending?

Use 1. That we may further improve this point, Is Christ altogether lovely; so lovely to us, and so beloved of God the Father? *Let us then rest upon his obedience and righteousness*; build upon it, that God cannot refuse that righteousness whose whole subject is altogether lovely. Let us come clothed in the garments of our Elder Brother, and then doubt not of acceptance; for it is in Christ that he loves us. In this well-beloved Son it is that God is well pleased with us. If we put on Christ's righteousness, we put on God's righteousness; and then how can God hate us? No more than he hates his own Son. Nay, he loves us, and that with the same love wherewith he loves him; for he loves whole Christ mystical, Head and members (*John* 17:23). Let this strengthen our faith, that if Christ be so altogether lovely in himself and to the Father, then we may comfortably come before the Father, clothed with the garments of him our Elder Brother, and so rest ourselves on the acceptation of his mediation, that is so beloved a mediator.

Use 2. Again, if Christ be so lovely, 'altogether lovely', then *let us labour to be in him*, that so we may be lovely to God; because he is the first amiable thing in the world, in whom we are all lovely. All our loveliness is in beloved Christ.

Use 3. Again, if Christ be so lovely, *here only we have whereupon to spend the marrow of our best affections*. Is it not pity we should lose so much of our affections as we do upon other things? Christ is altogether lovely; why should we dote upon other things so much, and set up idols in our hearts above Christ? Is he

293

altogether lovely, and shall not he have altogether our lovely affections, especially when we are commanded, under pain of a curse, to love the Lord Jesus? *Anathema Maranatha* to those that love not Christ (*1 Cor.* 16:22). Let us therefore labour to place all our sweet affections that are to be exercised upon good, as love, joy, and delight, upon this object, this lovely deserving object, Christ, who is 'altogether lovely'. When we suffer a pure stream, as it were, to run through a dirty channel, our affections to run after the things of the world, which are worse than ourselves, we lose our affections and ourselves.

Let, therefore, the whole stream of our affections be carried unto Christ. Love him, and whatsoever is his; for he being altogether lovely, all that comes from him is lovely. His promises, his directions, his counsels, his children, his sacraments, are all lovely. Whatsoever hath the stamp of Christ upon it, let us love it. We cannot bestow our hearts better, to lose ourselves in the love of Christ, and to forget ourselves and the love of all. Yea, to hate all in comparison of him, and to account all 'dung and dross' compared with Christ, is the only way to find ourselves. And indeed we have a better condition in him, than in the world or in ourselves. Severed from him, our condition is vain, and will come to nothing; but that we have in him is admirable and everlasting. We cannot conceive the happiness which we poor wretches are advanced to in Christ; and what excellent things abide for us, which come from the love of God to us in Christ, who is so altogether lovely. Therefore let us labour to kindle in our hearts an affection towards Christ, all that we can, considering that he is thus lovely.

Use 4. And let us make an use of trial, *whether he be thus lovely to us, or no*. We may see hence whether we love Christ or no. We may judge of our love by our esteem.

1. How do we value Christ? what price doth the church set on him? 'He is the chief of ten thousand.' What place, then, should he

have in our hearts? If he be the chief of ten thousand, let us rather offend ten thousand than offend him. Let us say, with David, 'Whom have I in heaven but thee?' &c. (*Psa.* 73:25). And when the soul can say to Christ, or any that is Christ's (for I speak of him in the latitude of his truths, promises, sacraments, and communion with his children), 'What have I in heaven but thee?' &c., then it is in a happy condition. If these things have the same place in our esteem, as they have in respect of their own worth, then we may say truly, without hypocrisy, 'He is altogether lovely to us', that we truly love him.

2. In the next place, *are we ready to suffer for Christ?* We see the church here endures anything for Christ. She was misused of the watchmen. They scorned her, and her 'veil is taken away', yet notwithstanding, she loves Christ still. Do we stand ready disposed to suffer for Christ? of the world to be disgraced and censured? and yet are we resolved not to give over? Nay, do we love Christ the more, and stick to his truth the faster? Certainly where the love of Christ is, there is a spirit of fortitude, as we may see in the church here, who is not discouraged from Christ by any means. He is still the chief of ten thousand. When she was wronged for seeking after him, yet he was altogether lovely. Whereas, on the other hand, you have some that, for frowns of greatness, fear of loss, or for hope of rising, will warp their conscience, and do anything. Where now is love to Christ and to religion? He that loves Christ, loves him the more for his cross, as the Holy Ghost hath recorded of some, that they 'rejoiced that they were thought worthy to suffer for Christ' (*Acts* 5:41). So the more we suffer for him, the more dear he will be to us. For indeed he doth present himself in love and comfort most, to those that suffer for his sake; therefore their love is increased.

3. Again, where love is, *there it enlargeth the heart*, which being enlarged, enlargeth the tongue also. The church hath never enough of commending Christ, and of setting out his praise. The

tongue is loosed, because the heart is loosed. Love will alter a man's disposition. As we see in experience, a man base of nature, love will make him liberal; he that is tongue-tied, it will make him eloquent. Let a man love Christ, and though before he could not speak a word in the commendation of Christ, and for a good cause, yet, I say, if the love of Christ be in him, you shall have him speak and labour earnestly in the praises of God. This hot affection, this heavenly fire, will so mould and alter him, that he shall be clean[1] another man. As we see in the church here, after that there was kindled a spirit of love in her, she cannot have done with Christ. When she had spoke what she could, she adds, 'He is altogether lovely.' Those that cannot speak of Christ, or for Christ, with large hearts in defence of good causes, but are tongue-tied and cold in their affections, where is their love? Put any worldly man to a worldly theme that he is exercised in, and speaks of daily, he hath wit and words at will; but put him to a theme of piety, you lose him: he is out of his theme, and out of his element. But 'tis not so with those that have ever felt the love of God in Christ. They have large affections. How full is Saint Paul! He cannot speak of Christ, but he is in the height, breadth, length, and depth of the love of God in Christ, and the knowledge of God above all knowledge. Thus we may discern the truth of our love by the expressions of it here as in the church.

4. Again, *the church here is never content till she find Christ*; whatsoever she had, nothing contents her. She wanted her beloved. As we see here, she goes up and down inquisitive after him till she find him. So it is with a Christian. If he have lost, by his own fault, his former communion with Christ, he will not rest nor be satisfied; but searcheth here and there in the use of this and that means. He runs through all God's ordinances and means till he find Christ. Nothing in the world will content him, neither honour, riches, place, or friends, till he find that which he once

---

[1] Clear, clear-cut, sharply defined.—P.

enjoyed, but hath now for a season lost, the comfort and assurance of God's love in Christ.

Now, if we can sit down with other things, and can want Christ and the assurance of salvation, that sweet report of the Spirit that we are his, and yet be contented well enough, here is an ill sign that a man is in an ill condition. The church was not so disposed here. She was never quiet, nor gives over her inquisition and speaking of Christ (that by speaking of the object she might warm her affections), until at the last she meets with Christ. These and the like signs there are of the truth of the love of Christ. But where there is a flaming love of Christ there is this degree further, a desire of the appearance of Christ, a desire of his presence. For if Christ be so lovely in his ordinances, if we find such sweetness in the Word and sacraments, in the communion of saints, in the motions of the Spirit, what is the sweetness, think you, which the souls in heaven enjoy, where they see Christ face to face, see him as he is? Hereupon the spouse saith, 'Let him kiss me with the kisses of his mouth.' Oh, that I might live in his presence. This is the desire of a Christian soul when the flame of love is kindled in any strength, 'Oh, that I might see him.' And therefore it longs even for death; for as far as a man is spiritual, he desires to be dissolved and to be with Christ; as Simeon, when he saw him, though in his abasement, 'Now I have enough; let thy servant depart in peace, for mine eyes have seen thy salvation' (*Luke* 2:29, 30). The presence of Christ, though it were but in the womb, when Mary, the mother of Christ, came to Elizabeth, it caused the babe that was in her womb to spring. Such comfort there is in the presence of Christ, though he be but in the womb, as it made John to spring. What, then, shall be his presence in heaven? How would it make the heart spring there, think you? For that which is most lovely in Christ is to come. Therefore the saints that have any degree of grace in the New Testament, they are set out by this description. They were such as loved the appearing of our Lord

Jesus Christ. How can it be otherwise? If they love Christ, they love the appearing of Christ, wherein we shall be made lovely, as he is lovely.

Here we are not 'altogether lovely;' for we have many dregs of sin, many infirmities and stains. Shall we not, then, desire that time wherein, as he is 'altogether lovely', so shall we be made a fit spouse for so glorious a husband?

To conclude this point, let us try our affections by the church's affections in this place, whether Christ be so lovely to us or not. It is said, 'There is no beauty in him when we shall see him, and he was despised of men' (*Isa.* 53:2, 3). He was so, in regard of his cross and sufferings, to the eye of the world and of carnal men. Herod scorned him; when Pilate sent him to him, made nobody of him, as the word in the original is.[1] They looked upon the outside of Christ in the flesh when he was abased. 'There was no form nor beauty in him', saith the Holy Ghost, that is, to the sight of carnal men; but those that had the sight of their sins with spiritual eyes, they could otherwise judge of Christ. The poor centurion saw an excellency in him when he said, 'He was not worthy that he should come under his roof' (*Matt.* 8:8). The poor thief saw the excellency of Christ upon the cross in those torments. 'Lord, remember me when thou comest into thy kingdom' (*Luke* 23:42).

So those souls that were enlightened, that had the sight of their misery and the sight of God's love in Christ, had a high esteem of Christ in his greatest abasement. Therefore, if we have a mean esteem of the children of God as contemptible persons, and of the ordinances of God as mean things, and of the government of Christ (such as he hath left in his Word) as base, it is an argument of a sinful, unworthy disposition. In such a soul Christ hath never been effectually by his Spirit; for everything in him is lovely,

---

[1] Sibbes' reference is to Luke 23:11, rendered in the Authorised Version, 'set him at nought', but literally runs, 'having set him at nought', i.e., etymologically, treated him as if he were nobody, or of no consideration. The verb is ἐξουθενέω—G.

even the bitterest thing of all. There is a majesty and excellency in all things of Christ. The censures of the church are excellent when they proceed and issue forth with judgment, as they should do, 'to deliver such a man over to Satan, that he may be saved in the day of the Lord' (*1 Cor.* 5:5).

Now, if the ordinances of Christ, the Word and sacraments, and the shutting sinners out of the church, if these things be vilified as powerless things, it shows a degenerate, wicked heart, not acquainted with the ways of God. If we have a mean esteem of men that suffer for Christ and stand out for him, if we account them so and so, shall we think ourselves Christians in the meantime? When Christ is altogether lovely, shall they be unlovely that carry the image of Christ? Can we love him that begets, and hate them that are begotten of him? Can we love Christ, and hate Christians? It cannot be.

Now, that we may get this affection and esteem of Christ that is so lovely,

1. *Let us labour to make our sins bitter and loathsome, that Christ may be sweet.*

Quest. What is the reason we set no higher a price of Christ?

Ans. Because we judge not of ourselves as we are indeed, and want spiritual eye-salve to see into ourselves rightly.

2. *And let us attend upon the means of salvation, to hear the unsearchable riches of Christ.* What makes any man lovely to us, but when we hear of their riches, beauty, and good intent to us? In the Word we are made acquainted with the good intent of Christ towards us, the riches of mercy in forgiving our sins, and riches of glory prepared for us. The more we hear of him, of his riches and love to us, the more it will inflame our love to Christ. Those that live where the ordinances of Christ are held forth with life and power, they have more heavenly and enlarged affections than others have, as the experience of Christians will testify.

3. Again, if we would esteem highly of Christ that he may be lovely to us, *let us join with company that highly esteem of Christ, and such as are better than ourselves.* What deads the affections so much as carnal, worldly company, who have nothing in them but civility? By converse with them who have discourse of nothing but the world, if a man have heavenly affections, he shall quickly dull them, and be in danger to lose them. They may be conversed with in civil things, but when we would set to be heavenly and holy minded, let us converse with those that are of an heavenly bent. As we see here, 'the daughters of Jerusalem' are won to love Christ. By what? By conversing with the church. Upon the discourse that the church makes of his excellencies, in particular, they begin to ask, Where is Christ, as in the next chapter; and so are all brought to the love of Christ.

SERMON 18

*His mouth is most sweet; yea, he is altogether lovely. This is my
beloved, and this is my friend, O daughters of Jerusalem.*
SONG OF SOLOMON 5:16
*Whither is thy beloved gone, O thou fairest among women?
whither is thy beloved turned aside? that we may seek
him with thee. My beloved is gone down, &c.*
SONG OF SOLOMON 6:1, 2

B Y this time the church hath well quit herself in that safe
subject, commending her beloved; first in general, and
then in particular. She affirms in effect, there was none like
him in general; which she after makes good, in all the particulars
of her description. Now she sums up all with a kind of superabun-
dant expression. What shall I say more of him? if that which is said
be not enough, then know farther, he is altogether lovely. There
were no end to go through all his perfections; but look on him
wholly, 'he is altogether lovely', and therefore deserves my love.
So that there is no cause why you should wonder at the strength
of my affections, and care to find out this my beloved and this my
friend, O ye daughters of Jerusalem. Thus we see how the pitch of
an enlightened soul is bent. It aspires to things suitable to itself; to
God-wards; to union and communion with Christ; to supernatural objects. Nothing here below is worthy the name of its beloved.
It fastens not on earthly, base things. But this is my beloved, and
this is my friend, this so excellent a person, this Jedidiah,[1] this

[1] That is, beloved of Jehovah.—G.

beloved Son, this judge of all, Lord of all, this chief of ten thousand. Here the church pitches her affections, which she conceals, not as ashamed thereof, but in a kind of triumphing, boasting of her choice. She concludes all with a kind of resolute assurance, that the object of this her choice is far beyond all comparison.

'This is my beloved, and this is my friend, O daughters of Jerusalem.' Which is the closing up of her commendations of Christ. 'This is my beloved, and this my friend', &c. Which shall only be touched, because we had occasion to speak thereof before. She calls Christ her beloved. Howsoever he had withdrawn himself in regard of the comfort and communion she had with him before, yet he is her beloved still.

That which is specially to be stood upon is, that the church here doth set out not only in parcels, but in general, her beloved Christ. This is my beloved. She doth, as it were, boast in her beloved. Whence observe:

A Christian soul seems to glory as it were in Christ.

'This is my beloved, and this is my friend, O ye daughters of Jerusalem.' But to unfold more fully this point, there be three or four ends why the church thus stands upon the expression of the excellencies of Christ, in particular and in general.

1. The one, *to show that it is most just that she should love and respect him in whom there is all this to deserve love.* Both in himself, in regard of his own excellencies, so, and in relation to us, in regard of his merits and deserts.

2. Secondly, *to justify her large affections before the world and all opposites.*[1] For the world thinks, what mean these who are called Christians to haunt the exercises of religion, to spend so much time in good things? They wonder at it for want of better information. Now the church here, to justify her large expressions, says, 'This is my beloved, this is my friend, O ye daughters of Jerusalem.'

---

[1] That is, opponents.—Ed.

3. *And not only to justify, but likewise to glory therein*, as you have it (*Psa.* 44:8). The church there boasts of God, 'I will make my boast of thee all the day long.' So that Christians may not only justify their course of life against enemies, but in some sort boast of Christ, as Paul oft doth. And he shows the reason of it, that God hath made Christ to us all in all, wisdom, righteousness, sanctification, and redemption (*1 Cor.* 1:30), that whosoever glorieth might glory in the Lord (verse 31). For it is not a matter of glorying in the church when she hath such a head and such a husband. 'This is my beloved.' The wife shines in the beams of her husband. Therefore this yields matter not only of justification but of glory.

4. And next, in the fourth place, the church is thus large and shuts up all with a repetition, 'This is my beloved', *to enlarge her own affections and to feed our[1] own love.* For love feeds upon this fuel, as it were; upon expressions and meditations of the person or thing loved. Love is, as it were, wages of itself. The pains it takes is gain to itself. To the church here, it is an argument pleasing. She dilates upon a copious theme. I may truly say there is no greater comfort to a Christian, nor a readier way to enlarge the affections after Christ, than to speak oft of the excellencies of Christ; to have his tongue as the pen of a ready writer furnished this way, 'This is my beloved', &c.

5. In the fifth place, another end of this may be, *to aggravate her own shame*, as indeed God's children are much in this argument; that upon their second thoughts of Christ's worthiness, and therewithal reflecting upon their own unworthiness and unkindness, they may relish Christ the better. Therefore the church here, that it might appear to herself, for her humiliation, how unkind she had been to shut the door against Christ when he knocked (whereupon he deservedly did withdraw himself, and made her seek him so long sorrowing), I tell you, says she, what a kind of

[1] Qu. her?—Ed.

beloved he is, thus and thus excellent. How did the consideration of God's kindness and love melt David's heart after that horrible sin in the matter of Uriah (2 *Sam.* 12:13); and the sweet looks of Christ upon Peter (*Luke* 22:61), that had been so unkind, melted him. So here the church, when she considered how unkind she had been to Christ her beloved, so incomparably excellent above other beloveds, to let him stand at the door, till his locks were wet with the dew of the night, the consideration hereof made her ashamed of herself. What! so excellent, so deserving a person as my beloved is to me, to be used of me so! what indignity is this! Thus to raise up the aggravation of her unkindness, no question but the church takes this course. For God's children are not as untoward worldlings and hypocrites, afraid to search and to understand themselves. The child of God loves to be well read in his own heart and unworthy ways. Therefore he lays all the blame he can upon himself every way. He knows he loseth nothing by this; for there is more mercy in Christ than there is sin in him. And the more sin abounds in his own feeling, the more grace shall abound. He knows the mystery of God's carriage in this kind. Therefore for this end, amongst the rest, she says, 'This is my beloved, and this is my friend', whom I have so unkindly used.

6. And the last reason why the church is thus large was, *to draw and wind up the affections of those well-meaning Christians that were comers on, who were inquisitive of the way to Zion*. O ye daughters of Jerusalem, that you may know that there is some cause to seek after Christ more than you have done before, I tell you what an excellent person my beloved is; to whet their affections more and more. And we see the success of this excellent discourse in the beginning of the next chapter. 'Whither is thy beloved gone?' &c.

These and the like reasons there are of the large expressions of the church, of the excellencies of Christ. 'This is my beloved, and this is my friend, O ye daughters of Jerusalem.' But we will single out of these reasons for use, that which I think fittest for us to make use of.

Let us then oft think of the excellencies of Christ for this end, *to justify our endeavours and pains we take in the exercises of religion, and to justify God's people from the false imputations of the world, that they lay upon them*; as if they were negligent in other matters, and were too much busied in spiritual things. You see how large the church is in setting out the excellencies of her beloved, and then she shuts up all (being able to say no more) justifying our cause, 'This is my beloved, and this is my friend.' Do you wonder that I seek so much after him then? or wonder you at Christians, when they take such pains to keep their communion with Christ in a holy walking with, and depending upon God? These are no wonders, if you consider how excellent Christ is, what he hath done for us, and what he keeps for us in another world? that he will preserve us to his heavenly kingdom, till he put us into possession of that glorious condition that he hath purchased? Let the hearts of men dwell upon the consideration of these things, and then you shall see that God's children are rather to be blamed that they are no more careful, watchful, and industrious, than to be taxed that they are so much. Our Saviour Christ said, 'Wisdom is justified of all her children' (*Matt.* 11:19). If you will make good that you are children of wisdom, you must be able to justify the wisdom of God every way, to justify your reading, hearing, your communion of saints; to justify all the exercises of religion from an experimental taste and sweetness of them, as the church doth here, 'This is my beloved.' What says Joshua? 'This choice I have made; do you what you will, it matters me not, but I and my house will serve the Lord' (*Josh.* 24:15). So Paul makes a voluntary profession of his affection (*Rom.* 1:16), 'I am not ashamed of the gospel of Jesus Christ.' Let the gospel be entertained in the world as it will, and let others think of me as they will, that I am forward in the preaching of it; I am not ashamed of it. And good reason he had not to be ashamed; for it is the power of God to salvation, to all that believe; yea the saving power to us. And have not I cause to stand in the defence of it? And so he saith, 'I know whom I have believed', &c. (2 *Tim.* 1:12). I am not ashamed to suffer bonds for his sake. Though the world thought him a mean person, 'I will not be scorned out of my faith and religion by shallow, empty persons, that know not what Christ and religion meaneth.' No; 'I know whom I have believed; he is able to keep that that I have committed to him against that day.' Let us therefore be able to justify from a judicious apprehension, sweet divine truths. You see what justifications there are of the church of God, 'Wherefore should the heathen say, Where is now their God?' (*Mic.* 7:10, *Psa.* 42:10). Oh, it went to David's heart, when they said, 'Where is now their God?' 'What was become of his God?' when he was left in trouble, as the church here. And what doth he answer? Doth he let it go with a question? No, says he; our God is in heaven (*Psa.* 113:4), and hath done whatsoever he pleased.

And this justification of religion, you may know by this sign. It is with the desertion of all discourses opposite to religion whatsoever. He that justifies the truth, he esteems meanly of other courses and discourses. Therefore in the next verse the church vilifies the idols. Our God is in heaven, and doth whatsoever he pleaseth; the idols are silver and gold, the work of men's hands: they have eyes and see not, ears and hear not (*Psa.* 115:6). And the more we justify Christ, the more we will be against antichrist and his religion. We may know the owning of the one truth by the vilifying the other. Let us labour therefore to grow to such a convincing knowledge of Christ; the good things in him; and the ways of God, as we may be able to stand out against all opposition of the gates of hell whatsoever.

And to this end proceed in the study of Christ, and to a deeper search of him, and of the excellencies and good things in him, that we may say as Micah 7:18, 'Who is a God like to thee, that pardons sins and iniquities?' and as David, 'Who is a God like our God, that humbleth himself to behold the things done here below?' (*Psa.* 113:5, 6).

And desire also to this purpose, the spirit of revelation, that which Paul prays for (*Eph.* 3:18, 19), 'that we may know that knowledge that is above all knowledge, the height, depth, and breadth of God's love in Christ'. So sweet is God in the greatest abasements of his children, that he leaves such a taste in the soul of a Christian, that from thence he may be able to say, 'This is my beloved', when his beloved seems not to care for him. When the church seemed to be disrespected and neglected of Christ, yet she says, 'This is my beloved, and this is my friend, O ye daughters of Jerusalem.'

Shall rich men boast of their riches? Shall men that are in favour, boast of the favour of great persons? Shall a man that hath large possessions boast and think himself as good and as great as his estate is? Shall a base-minded worldling be able to boast? 'Why boastest thou thyself, O mighty man?' (*Psa.* 52:1). Nay, you shall have malignant-spirited men boast of their malignant destructive power. I can do this and that mischief. Shall a man boast of mischief, that he is able to do mischief? and hath not a Christian more cause to boast in God and in salvation? Lord, shine on me, says David (*Psa.* 4:6), let me enjoy the light of thy countenance; and that shall bring me more joy than they have, when their corn and wine increaseth. Know this, as he goes on in the same psalm, that God accepts the righteous man.

Therefore let us think we have much more cause to boast of God and of Christ in a spiritual manner, than the worldling hath of the world. Is not God and Christ our portion? and having Christ, have we not all things with Christ? Put case all things be took from us. If a man have Christ, he is rich though he have nothing else. If he have all without him, his plenty is (as a father saith, and as it is in truth) beggary. But whosoever hath Christ may thus rejoice with David, 'The lot is fallen to me in pleasant places; yea, I have a goodly heritage' (*Psa.* 16:6). Would we have more than God in Christ, a ring with a diamond very precious in it? Now the daughters of Jerusalem, hearing this large expression of affection, ask,

'Whither is thy beloved gone, O thou fairest among women? whither is thy beloved turned aside? that we may seek him with thee' (chap. 6:1).

Here is another question. The first which the daughters of Jerusalem ask is, 'What is thy beloved?' whereupon the church took occasion to express what her beloved was: upon her expression closing up all with this general, 'This is my beloved, and this is my friend.'

Then the second question is, 'Whither is thy beloved gone?' One question begets another; and indeed if this question be well satisfied, what is Christ above others? this will follow again. Where is he? How shall I get him? How shall I seek him? What is the reason this second question is seldom made? Whither is he gone? how shall I get Christ? Because the former question, namely, 'What is Christ?' is so seldom made. For if we did once know what Christ is, we would be sure with the daughters of Jerusalem to ask whither is he gone, that we may seek him with thee.

We see here is a growth in the desires of the daughters of Jerusalem, whence we learn,

That grace, though it be in never so little proportion at the first, it is growing still.

From the first question, 'What is thy beloved?' here is a second, upon better information, 'Whither is thy beloved gone, that we may seek him with thee?' Nothing is less than grace at the first, nothing in the world so little in proportion. The kingdom of heaven is compared to a grain of mustard seed (*Matt.* 13:31ff.). That is, the work of grace in the heart, as well as in the preaching of the gospel, in the beginning is little. It is true of the work of grace, as well as of the word of grace, that it is like a grain of mustard seed at first. 'What is thy beloved?' inquires the church at first; but when she hears of the excellency of Christ, then, 'Whither is thy beloved gone?' Grace begets grace. There is a connection and knitting together in religion. Good things beget good things. It is a strange thing in religion how great a matter ariseth of a little beginning. The woman of Samaria had but a small beginning of grace, and yet she presently drew many of her neighbours to believe in Christ. So Andrew (*John* 1:41). As soon as he was converted, he finds his brother Simon, and tells him that he had found the Messiah, and so brings him to Christ. And Philip, as soon as he had got a spark of faith himself, he draws also Nathanael to come to Christ. Paul speaks of his bonds, how the noise of them was in Caesar's court (*Phil.* 1:13), and many believed the very report, which, howsoever it is not a working cause, yet it may be a preparing, inducing, leading cause to such things, from one thing to another, till there follow this change and full conversion. You see here the daughters of Jerusalem growing. Therefore, let us labour to be under good means. Some of the Romists and others, which are ill affected and grounded in that point, they think that the efficacy of grace is, as we call it, from the congruity, fitness, and proportion of the means to the heart and will of man. And thereupon God converts one and not another, because there is a congruous and fit offering of means to him when he is fitly disposed, and another is not fitly disposed. Therefore, there follows not upon it effectual calling. So that the virtue of the means offered depends upon suitableness and fitness in the party to whom the means are offered, and not upon the power and blessing of God. Verily, this is plausible, and goes down very roundly with many weak persons; but this is a false and a gross error, for unless God by his Holy Spirit do work by the means, no planting and watering will bring any increase, and change the heart and mind. Though there were greater means in Christ's time when he wrought these miracles, than any time before, yet all those could not convert that froward generation; and it was Moses's complaint in the wilderness, where they had abundance of means, 'God hath not given you a heart to perceive, and eyes to see, and ears to hear until this day' (*Deut.* 29:4). When a man is planted under good means and frequents them, then ordinarily it pleaseth God, by the inward workings of his own powerful Spirit, to work greater matters; and those that keep out of God's reach, that will not come into places where they may hear good things, there is no hope of them. Though there be many ill fish in the net, yet there is no hope to catch them that are without the net. So those that are kept out of all opportunities and occasions whereby God's Spirit may work upon them, there is no hope of them.

Let us learn this heavenly wisdom, to advantage ourselves this way, by improving all good opportunities whatsoever whereby we may learn; for God works by outward means. Good company and good discourse, these breed excellent thoughts. As, therefore, we love our souls, take all advantages wherein the Spirit of God works. We shall find incredible fruit thereof, more than we would believe. But to come to the question.

1. See here, first of all, in this question *the blessed success of the church's inquiry after Christ* in the daughters of Jerusalem after they heard the large explications of the excellencies of Christ, especially by the church, whom they had a good conceit of, for they call her 'the fairest among women'.

And seeing, likewise, the confidence of the church, she stands to it, 'This is my beloved;' yea, also, eagerness in the church to seek after him, they would seek him with her. So that where these meet, a large unfolding of the truth of God, and that by persons that are known to be good, well accepted, and conceited of, and where there is a large demonstration of real affection, and the things are spoken of with confidence, as knowing what they say; the Word, I say, so managed, it is never without wondrous success.

(1.) For in the course of reason, what can I have to say, considering the party who speaks is an excellent person? He is wiser and holier than I; he takes to heart these things; and shall not I affect that which those that have better parts and graces do?

(2.) Then, withal, I see not only excellent persons do it, but I see how earnest they are. Surely there is some matter in it; for persons so holy, so wise, and gracious to be so earnest, surely either they are to blame, or I am too dull and too dead; but I have most cause to suspect myself.

(3.) And to see them carried with a spirit of confidence, as if they were well enough advised when they deliver this, 'This is my beloved', in particular, and then to shut up all in general, 'This is my beloved, and this is my friend;' I say, when there is grace and life in the heart, and earnestness with confidence, this, together with the explication of the heavenly excellencies of Christ and of religion, it hath admirable success. As here in the church, 'the fairest among women', the 'daughters of Jerusalem', seeing the church was so earnest, confident, and so large in the explication of the excellencies of Christ, see how it works. It draws out this question with resolution. They join with the church in seeking Christ, 'Whither is thy beloved gone, O thou fairest among women? whither is thy beloved turned aside? that we may seek him with thee.' Where by the way observe, as the church before doubles it, 'This is my beloved, and this is my friend', so they answer with a double question, 'Whither is thy beloved gone? whither is he turned aside? O thou fairest among women', &c. From this appellation note,

2. If we would be happy instruments to convert others, being converted ourselves, *labour to be such as the world may think to be good and gracious.* 'O thou fairest among women', fair in the robes of Christ took[1] out of his wardrobe. All the beauty and ornaments that the church hath she hath from Christ. Let us labour to be such as the world may conceit are good persons. We say of physicians, when the patient hath a good conceit of them, the cure is

---

[1] That is, taken.—G

half wrought. So the doctrine is half persuaded when there is a good conceit of the speaker.

3. Again, *labour to be earnest.* If we would kindle others, we must be warmed ourselves; if we would make others weep, we must weep ourselves. Naturalists could observe this. The church spake this with large expressions, indeed, more than can be expressed. Let us labour to be deeply affected with what we speak, and speak with confidence as if we knew what we spoke, as the apostle John doth, in the beginning of his epistle, to bring others to be better persuaded of his doctrine. He affirmeth 'that which was from the beginning, which we have heard, which we have seen with these our eyes, which we have looked upon, and these hands of ours have handled of the word of life' he delivered to them (*1 John* 1:1).

For when we are confident from spiritual experience, it is wonderful how we shall be instruments of God to gain upon others. So Peter. 'We followed not', says he, 'deceivable fables, when we opened unto you the power and coming of our Lord Jesus Christ, but with our eyes we saw his majesty' (*2 Pet.* 1:16).

Do not think it belongs only to the ministry. There is an art of conversion that belongs to every one that is a grown Christian, to win others.

'Whither is thy beloved gone, O thou fairest among women?'

The next observation out of the words, because it is the especial, which works upon the daughters of Jerusalem, is from the large explication of Christ.

That which most of all stirs up holy affections to search after Christ is the large explications of his excellencies.

Then be in love with the ministry of the gospel and the communion of saints, who have their tongues and their hearts taught of God to speak excellently. Their tongues are as refined silver; their hearts are enriched to increase the communion of saints (*Prov.* 10:20). Mark this one excellency of that excellent ordinance of God in Christ, whereof Paul saith (*Eph.* 3:7, 8), 'To me is committed this excellent office, to lay open the unsearchable riches of Christ;' such riches as may draw you to wonder, such 'as eye hath never seen, nor ear heard, nor hath entered into the heart of man to conceive' (*1 Cor.* 2:9); and so to draw the affections of people after them.

And because it is the special office of the ministry to lay him open, to hold up the tapestry, to unfold the hidden mysteries of Christ, labour we, therefore, to be always speaking somewhat about Christ, or tending that way. When we speak of the law, let it drive us to Christ; when of moral duties, to teach us to walk worthy of Christ. Christ, or somewhat tending to Christ, should be our theme and mark to aim at.

Therefore what shall we judge of those that are hinderers of this glorious ordinance of Christ in the gospel? They are enemies of conversion and of the calling of God's people; enemies of their comfort. And what shall we think of those wretched and miserable creatures that, like Cain, are vagabonds? who wander, and will not submit themselves to any ordinance meekly, but keep themselves out of this blessed opportunity of hearing the excellencies of Christ, which might draw their hearts to him? We are made for ever, if Christ and we be one. If we have all the world without him, it is nothing; if we have nothing in the world but Christ, we are happy. Oh! happy then when this match is made between Christ and the soul! The friends of the bride and of Christ, they, laying open the unsearchable riches of Christ to the spouse, draw the affections, work faith, and so bring the bride and the bridegroom together.

Thus far of the question. Now we have the church's answer to the daughters of Jerusalem.

'My beloved is gone into his garden, to the beds of spices, to feed in the gardens, and to gather lilies.'

The question was not for a bare satisfaction, but from a desire the church had to seek Christ. 'Whither is thy beloved gone, that we may seek him?' It was not a curious question, but a question of inquisition tending to practice. Many are inquisitive; but when they know another man's meaning, it is all they desire. Now I know your meaning, will they say, but I mean not to follow your counsel. The daughters of Jerusalem had a more sincere intention, 'O thou fairest among women, whither is thy beloved turned aside? *that we may seek him with thee.*' Whereunto the church answered,

'My beloved is gone into his garden, to the beds of spices, to feed in the gardens.' Where we see,

The church is not squeamish, but directly answers to the question. For there is no envy in spiritual things, because they may be divided *in solidum*.[1] One may have as much as another, and all alike. Envy is not in those things that are not divisible; in other things, the more one hath, another hath the less. But there is no envy in grace and glory, because all may share alike. Therefore here is no envy in the answer, as if she denied the daughters of Jerusalem the enjoying of her beloved. No. If you will know, says she, I will tell you directly whither my beloved is gone.

'My beloved is gone into his garden, to the bed of spices', &c.

God hath two gardens. The church catholic is his garden, and every particular church are gardens and beds of spices, in regard that many Christians are sown there that Christ's soul delights in, as in sweet spices. This was spoken of before at large in chapter 5:1, why the church is called a garden, being a severed place from the waste.[2] The church is severed from the wilderness of the world in God's care and love; likewise he tends and weeds his church and garden. As for the waste of the world, he is content the wilderness should have barren plants, but he will not endure such in his garden. Therefore those that give themselves liberty to be naught in the church of God, he will have a time to root them out. Trees that are not for fruit shall be for the fire; and above all other trees their doom shall be the heaviest that grow in God's garden without fruit. That fig-tree shall be cursed (*Luke* 13:6-9).

[1] 'For the whole', meaning that each has a full part (or liability, in the case of a contract), as is explained by Sibbes.—P.

[2] See pp. 10-12.—P.

Men are pleased with answering the bill of accusation against them thus: Are we not baptized? and do we not come to church? &c. What do you make of us? Yet they are abominable swearers, and filthy in their lives. To such I say, the more God hath lifted you up and honoured you in the use of the means, the more just shall your damnation be, that you bring forth nothing but briers and brambles (*Heb.* 6:4ff.), the grapes of Sodom and the vine of Gomorrah (*Deut.* 32:32). Heavy will the doom be of many that live in the church's bosom, to whom it had been better to have been born in America,[1] in Turkey, or in the most barbarous parts in the world. They have a heavy account to make that have been such ill proficients under abundance of means. Therefore it ought to be taken to heart.

'My beloved is gone into his garden, to the beds of spices, to feed in the gardens, and to gather lilies.'

That is, having first planted them lilies here, to gather them, and to transport them out of the garden here to the garden in heaven, where there shall be nothing but lilies. For the church of God hath two gardens or paradises since the first paradise (whereof that was a resemblance), the paradise of the church and the paradise of heaven. As Christ saith to the good thief, 'This day thou shalt be with me in paradise' (*Luke* 23:43); so those that are good plants in the paradise of the church, they shall be glorious plants also in the paradise of heaven. We must not always be here; we shall change our soil, and be taken into heaven. 'He is gone into his garden to gather lilies.'

1. Christians are compared to lilies for their *purity and whiteness*, unspotted in justification; and for their endeavours in sanctity

---

[1] The juxtaposition of America and Turkey is in curious contrast with the present position of America among the *Christian* nations of the world. Yet with all this idea of the 'barbarousness' of America (which was common to Sibbes with his contemporaries), the Puritans shrank not from exiling themselves thither when the question of their religious liberties came up. Hooker, Davenport, Cotton, Stone, and numerous others of Sibbes' friends thus expatriated themselves.—G.

and holiness, wherein also at length they shall be wholly unspotted. It is the end they are chosen to, 'to be holy without blame
before him in love' (*Eph.* 1:4). God and Christ look upon them
without blame, not as they are here defiled and spotted, but as
they intend, by little and little, to purge and purify themselves
by the Spirit that is in them, that they may be altogether without
blame. They are lilies, being clothed with the white garment of
Christ's righteousness, not having a natural whiteness and purity.[1]
The whiteness and purity of God's children is borrowed. All their
beauty and garments are taken out of another's wardrobe. The
church is all glorious within; but she borrows her glory, as the
moon borrows all her light from the sun. The church's excellency
is borrowed. It is her own, but by gift; but being once her own, it
is her own for ever.

The church before was likened to a garden culled out, an
Eden, a paradise. Now there, you know, were four streams, sweet
and goodly rivers, which watered paradise; the heads of which
rivers were without it. So the church of God, her graces are her
own; that is, the Spirit of God comes through her nature, purgeth
and purifieth it; but the spring of those graces, as in paradise, is
out of herself.

2. And then the lily is *a tall, goodly plant.* Therefore the church
is compared to them. Other men are compared to thorns, not
only for a noxious, hurtful quality in them, but for their baseness
likewise. What are thorns good for, but to cumber the ground,
to eat out the heart of it, to hide snakes, and for the fire? Wicked
men are not lilies, but thorns. They are base, mean persons. An-
tiochus (*Dan.* 11:21), is said to be a vile person, though he were a
king, because he was a naughty[2] man. Wicked men, though they

---

[1] It is pity to destroy the 'fine fancies' of Sibbes on the supposed 'whiteness' of
the lily; but he was thinking of the home, not of the eastern 'lily', which is purple
coloured, not 'white'. The 'purple' gives greater vividness to the Lord's allusion to
the imperial robes of Solomon (*Matt.* 6:28-29).—G.

[2] That is, 'wicked'—G.

be never so great, being void of the grace of God, are vile persons. Though we must respect them in regard of their places, yet as they are in their qualification, they are vile and base thorns. But the church is not so, but as a lily among thorns, that is, among vile and abominable persons.

Use 1. The use is *to comfort God's children*. They have an excellency and glory in them, which, howsoever it is not from them, yet it is theirs by gift, and eternally theirs. Therefore let them comfort themselves against all the censures of sinful persons that labour to trample them under foot, and think basely and meanly of them, as of the offscouring of the world. Let the unworthy world think of them as they will, they are lilies in God's esteem, and are so indeed; glorious persons that have the Spirit of glory resting upon them (*1 Pet.* 4:14), and whom the world is not worthy of (*Heb.* 11:38), though their glory be within. Therefore let us glory in it, that God vouchsafeth saving grace to us above any other privilege.

Use 2. Again, it comforts us in all our wants whatsoever, that *God will take care for us*. Christ useth this argument. God saith, he clotheth the lilies of the field with an excellent beauty; he cares even for the meanest plants, and will he not take care for you, O ye of little faith? (*Matt.* 6:29, 30). Doth he care for lilies, that are today, and to-morrow are cast into the oven? and shall he not care for the lilies of paradise, the living lilies, those holy reasonable lilies? Undoubtedly he will. Our Saviour Christ's reason is undeniable. He that puts such a beauty upon the poor plants, that flourish today in the morning, and wither before night; he that puts such a beauty upon the grass of the field; will he not put more excellency upon his children? will he not provide for them, feed them? Undoubtedly he will. Thus we have showed why God's children in the church of God are compared to lilies.

'To gather lilies.' Christ is said to gather these lilies, that is, he will gather them together. Christ will not have his lilies alone, scattered. Though he leaves them oft alone for a while, yet he will gather them to congregations and churches. The name of a church in the original is *ecclesia*. It is nothing but a company gathered out of the world. Do we think that we are lilies by nature? No; we are thorns and briers. God makes us lilies, and then gathers us to other lilies, that one may strengthen another. The Spirit of God in his children is not a spirit of separation of Christians from Christians, but a spirit of separation from the waste, wild wilderness of the world, as we say of fire—It congregates all homogeneal things, as gold, which it gathers, but disgregates heterogeneal things, consumeth dross. So the Spirit of God severs thorns, and gathers lilies; gathers Christians together in the church, and will gather them for ever in heaven.

Thus we see the answer of the church to the daughters of Jerusalem, what it was, with the occasion thereof; the question of the daughters of Jerusalem, 'Whither is thy beloved gone?' So that the church was beholden to the daughters of Jerusalem for ministering such a question, to give her occasion to know better what her beloved was. Indeed, we many times gain by weaker Christians. Good questions, though from weak ones, minister suitable answers. It is a Greek proverb, that 'doubting begets plenty and abundance', for doubting at the first begets resolution at last. O! that we could take occasion hence to think of this. What excellent virtue is in the communion of saints, when they meet about heavenly exercises! What a blessing follows when, though at the entry their affections may be flat and dull, yet they part not so! Christ heats and inflames their hearts to do much good to one another. O! those that shall for ever live together in heaven, should they not delight to live more together on earth?

SERMON 19

I am my beloved's, and my beloved is mine:
he feedeth among the lilies.
SONG OF SOLOMON 6:3

THESE words are a kind of triumphant acclamation upon all the former passages; as it were, the foot of the song. For when the church had spoken formerly of her ill-dealing with Christ, and how he thereupon absented himself from her, with many other passages, she shuts up all at last with this, 'I am my beloved's, and my beloved is mine.'

Now she begins to feel some comfort from Christ, who had estranged himself from her. O! saith she, notwithstanding all my sufferings, desertions, crosses, and the like, 'I am my beloved's, and my beloved is mine', words expressing the wondrous comfort, joy, and contentment the church now had in Christ; having her heart inflamed with love unto him, upon his manifesting of himself to her soul. 'I am my beloved's, and my beloved is mine: he feedeth among the lilies.'

There is a mutual intercourse and vicissitude of claiming interest betwixt Christ and his church. I am Christ's, and Christ is mine. 'I am my beloved's, and my beloved is mine.'

From the dependence and order of the words coming in after a desertion for a while, observe,

That Christ will not be long from his church.

The spiritual desertions (forsakings, as we use to call them), howsoever they be very irksome to the church (that loves communion with Christ), and to a loving soul to be deprived of the sense of her beloved, yet notwithstanding they are but short. Christ will not be long from his church. His love and her desire will not let him. They offer violence. Why art thou absent? say they. Why art thou so far off, and hidest thyself? Joseph may conceal himself for a space, but he will have much ado so to hold long, to be straitened to his brethren. Passion will break out. So Christ may seem hard to be entreated, and to cross his own sweet disposition, as to the woman of Canaan, but he will not long keep at this distance. He is soon overcome. 'O! woman, great is thy faith; have what thou wilt' (*Matt.* 15:28). When she strove with him a little (as faith is a striving grace), see how she did win upon him! So the angel and Jacob may strive for a while, but Jacob at the length proves Israel; he prevails with God (*Gen.* 32:24ff.). So it is with the Christian soul and Christ. Howsoever there be desertion, for causes before mentioned, because the church was negligent, as we hear, and partly for the time to come, that Christ, by his estrangement, might sweeten his coming again howsoever there may be strangeness for a time, yet Christ will return again to his spouse.

Use 1. The use should be not only *for comfort to stay us in such times, but to teach us likewise to wait, and never give over.* If the church had given over here, she had not had such gracious manifestations of Christ to her. Learn hence, therefore, this use, to wait God's leisure. God will wait to do good to them that wait on him (*Isa.* 30:18). If we wait his leisure, he will wait an opportunity of doing good to us. When God seems not to answer our prayers, let us yet wait. We shall not lose by our tarrying. He will wait to do us good.

Use 2. In the next place, observe, after this temporary desertion, *Christ visits his church with more abundant comfort than ever before.*

Now, the church cannot hold, 'My beloved is mine, and I am his;' and Christ cannot hold, but falls into a large commendation of his spouse back again. As she was large in his commendations, so he is large in hers, and more large. He will have the last word. Therefore, learn by this experience, 'that all things work together for the best to them that love God' (*Rom.* 8:28). All things. What? evil? Ay, evil. Why, even sin turns to their humiliation; yea, and desertion (those spiritual ills), turns to their good; for Christ seems to forsake for a while, that he may come after with more abundance of comfort. When once he hath enlarged the soul before with a spacious desire of his coming, to say, O! that he would come; when the soul is thus stretched with desire in the sense of want, then he fills it again till it burst forth, 'My beloved is mine, and I am his.' It was a good experiment of Bernard, an holy man in ill times, speaking of Christ's dealing with his church. He comes and he goeth away for thy good. He comes for thy good to comfort thee; after which, if thou be not careful to maintain communion with him, then he goeth away for thy good, to correct thy error, and to enlarge thy desire of him again, to teach thee to lay sure and faster hold upon him when thou hast him, not to let him go again.

If you would see a parallel place to this, look in Song of Solomon 3, where there is the like case of the spouse and Christ, 'By night on my bed I sought him.' The church sought Christ not only by day, but by night, 'I sought him whom my soul loved.' Though she wanted him, yet her soul loved him constantly. Though a Christian's soul have not present communion with Christ, yet he may truly say, My soul loves him, because he seeks him diligently and constantly in the use of all the means. So we see the church, before my text, calls him my beloved still, though she wanted communion with him. Well, she goes on, 'I sought him, but I found him not.' Would the church give over there? No; then she riseth and goeth about the city, and about the streets, and 'seeks him whom her soul loved', seeks him, and will not give over. So I sought him, but I wanted the issue of my seeking, I found him not. What comes upon that? 'The watchmen go about the city, and find her.' Of whom, when by her own seeking she could not find Christ, she inquires, 'Saw you him whom my soul loveth?' She inquires of the watchmen, the guides of God's people, who could not satisfy her fully. She could not find her beloved, yet what doth she, she shows (verse 4). It was but a little that she stayed, after she had used all means, private and public—in her bed, out of her bed—by the watchmen and others, yet, saith she, it was but a little that I was past from them. She had not an answer presently, though the watchmen gave her some good counsel. It was not presently, yet not long after. Christ will exercise us a while with waiting: 'It was but a little that I passed from them, but I found him whom my soul loved.' After all our seeking, there must be waiting, and then we shall find him whom our soul loveth. Perhaps we have used all means, private and public, and yet find not that comfort we look for. Oh, but wait a while! God hath a long time waited for thee. Be thou content to wait a while for him. We shall not lose by it, for it follows in the next verse; after she had found him whom her soul loved, 'I held him, I would not let him go.' So this is the issue of desertions. They stir up diligence and searching, in the use of means, private and public; and exercise patience to wait God's leisure, who will not suffer a gracious soul to fail of its expectation. At length he will fulfil the desires of them that fear him (*Psa.* 145:19); and this comes of their patience. Grace grows greater and stronger. 'I held him, and would not let him go, until I had brought him unto my mother's house.' Thus you see how the Spirit expresseth the same truth in another state of the church. Compare place with place. To go on.

'I am my beloved's, and my beloved is mine.' The words themselves are a passionate expression of long-looked-for consolation. Affections have eloquence of their own beyond words. Fear hath a proper expression. Love vents itself in broken words and sighs, delighting in a peculiar eloquence suitable to the height and pitch of the affection, that no words can reach unto. So that here is more in the words breathed from such an inflamed heart, than in ordinary construction can be picked out, 'I am my beloved's,' &c., coming from a full and large heart, expressing the union and communion between Christ and the church, especially after a desertion. 'I am my beloved's, and my beloved is mine.'

First, I say, the union, *viz.*, the union of persons, which is before all comfort and communion of graces, 'I am my beloved's, and my beloved is mine.' Christ's person is ours, and our persons are his. For, as it is in marriage, if the person of the husband be not the wife's, his goods are not hers, nor his titles of honour; for these come all to her, because his person is hers: he having passed over the right of his own body and of his person to his wife, as she hath passed over all the right of herself to her husband. So it is in this mystical marriage. That that entitles us to communion of graces is union of persons between Christ and his church. 'I am my beloved's, and my beloved himself is mine.' And indeed nothing else will content a Christian's heart. He would not care so much for heaven itself, if he had not Christ there. The sacrament, Word, and comforts, why doth he esteem them? As they come from Christ, and as they lead to Christ. It is but an adulterous and base affection to love anything severed from Christ.

Now, from this union of persons comes a communion of all other things whatsoever. 'I am my beloved's, and my beloved is mine.' If Christ himself be mine, then all is mine.[1] What he hath done, what he hath suffered, is mine; the benefit of all is mine. What he hath is mine. His prerogatives and privileges to be the Son of God, and heir of heaven, and the like, all is mine. Why? Himself is mine. Union is the foundation of communion. So it is here with the church, 'I am my beloved's.' My person is his, my life is his, to glorify him, and to lay it down when he will. My

---

[1] The well-known hymn, 'If God be mine' (anonymous), is little more than a paraphrase of these sweet words of Sibbes.—G.

goods are his, my reputation his. I am content to sacrifice all for him. I am his, all mine is his. So you see there is union and communion mutually, between Christ and his church. The original and spring hereof is Christ's uniting and communicating himself to his church first. The spring begins to[1] the stream. What hath the stream or cistern in it, but what is had from the spring? First we love him, because he loved us first (*1 John* 4:19). It was a true speech of Augustine, whatsoever is good in the world or lovely, it is either God or from God; it is either Christ or from Christ. He begins it. It is said in nature, love descends. The father and the mother love the child before the child can love them. Love, indeed, is of a fiery nature. Only here is the dissimilitude, fire ascends, love descends. It is stronger, descending from the greater to the less, than ascending up from the meaner to the greater, and that for this amongst other reasons,

Because the greater person looks upon the lesser as a piece of himself—sees himself in it. The father and mother see themselves in their child. So God loves us more than we can love him, because he sees his image in us. Neither is there only a priority of order. He loves us first, and then we love him. But also of causality. He is the cause of our love, not by way of motive only. He loves us, and therefore from an ingenuous spirit we must love him again. But he gives us his Spirit, circumciseth our hearts to love him (*Deut.* 30:6); for all the motives or moral persuasions in the world, without the Spirit, cannot make us love (*1 Thess.* 4:9). We are taught of God to love one another, our brethren whom we see daily, saith Paul, much more need we to be taught to love him whom we never saw, so that his love kindles ours by way of reflection.

In the new covenant God works both parts, his own and our parts too. Our love to him, our fear of him, our faith in him, he works all, even as he shows his own love to us.

If God love us thus, what must we do? Meditate upon his love. Let our hearts be warmed with the consideration of it. Let

---

[1] That is, originates, or gives its beginning to.—Ed.

us bring them to that fire of his love, and then they will wax hot within us, and beg the Spirit, 'Lord, thou hast promised to give thy Spirit to them that ask it' (*Luke* 11:10), and to circumcise our hearts to love thee, and to love one another, 'give thy Holy Spirit, as thou hast promised'.

In a word, these words, 'I am my beloved's, and my beloved is mine', to join them both together.

1. They imply a *mutual propriety*;[1] Christ hath a propriety in me, and I in Christ. Peculiar[2] propriety. Christ is mine, so as I have none in the world. So mine, 'whom have I in heaven but Christ?' and what is there in earth in comparison of him? He is mine, and mine in a peculiar manner, and I am his in a peculiar manner. There is propriety with peculiarity.

2. Then, again, these words, 'I am his', implies *mutual love*. All is mutual in them, mutual propriety, mutual peculiarity, and mutual love. I love Christ so as I love nothing else. There is nothing above him in my heart, as Christ loves me more than anything else, saith the church, and every Christian. He loves all, and gives outward benefits to all, but to me he hath given himself, so love I him. As the husband loves all in the family, his cattle and his servants, but he gives himself to his spouse. So Christ is mine, himself is mine, and myself am Christ's. He hath my soul, my affections, my body, and all. He hath a propriety in me, and a peculiarity in me. He hath my affection and love to the uttermost, as I have his, for there is an intercourse in these words.

3. Then, again, they imply *mutual familiarity*. Christ is familiar to my soul, and I to Christ. He discovers himself to me in the secret of his love, and I discover myself to him in prayer and meditation, opening my soul to him upon all occasions. God's children have a spirit of prayer, which is a spirit of fellowship, and talks, as it were, to God in Christ. It is the language of a new-born Christian. He cries to his Father. There is a kind of familiarity

[1] That is, property.—G.

[2] One's own property.—P.

between him and his God in Christ, who gives the entrance and access to God. So that where there is not a kind of familiarity in prayer and opening of the soul to Christ upon all occasions, there is not this holy communion. Those that are not given to prayer, they cannot in truth speak these words, as the church doth here, 'I am my beloved's, and my beloved is mine', for they imply sweet familiarity.

4. Then, again, they imply *mutual likeness* one to another. He is mine, and I am his. The one is a glass to the other. Christ sees himself in me, I see myself in him. For this is the issue of spiritual love, especially, that it breeds likeness and resemblance of the party loved in the soul that loveth; for love frameth the soul to the likeness of the party loved. I am his, I resemble him. I am his, I have given myself to him. I carry his picture and resemblance in my soul, for they are words of mutual conformity. Christ, out of love, became like me in all things, wherein I am not like the devil, that is, sin excepted. If he became like me, taking my nature that I might be near him in the fellowship of grace, 'My beloved is mine', I will be as like him as possibly I can, I am his. Every Christian carries a character of Christ's disposition as far as weakness will suffer. You may know Christ in every Christian; for as the king's coin carries the stamp of the king (Caesar's coin bears Caesar's superscription), so every Christian soul is God's coin, and he sets his own stamp upon it. If we be Christ's, there is a mutual conformity betwixt him and us.

Now, where you see a malicious, unclean, worldly spirit, know that is a stamp of the devil, none of Christ's. He that hath not the Spirit of God is none of his. Now, where the Spirit of Christ is, it stamps Christ's likeness upon the soul. Therefore we are exhorted (*Phil.* 2:5), to be likeminded to Christ.

5. Again, these words, 'I am my beloved's, and my beloved is mine', imply a *mutual care* that Christ and the soul have of the good of one another, of each other's honour and reputation. As Christ hath a care of our good, so a Christian soul, if it can say with

truth and sincerity I am Christ's, it must needs have care of Christ's good, of his children, religion, and truth. What! will such a soul say, Shall Christ care for my body, soul, and salvation, and stoop to come from heaven to save me, and shall I have no care for him and his glory? He hath left his truth and his church behind him, and shall not I defend his truth, and stand for the poor church to the utmost of my power against all contrary power? Shall not I stand for religion? Shall it be all one to me what opinions are held? Shall I pretend he cares for me, and shall I not care for that I should care for? Is it not an honour to me that he hath trusted me to care for anything? that he will be honoured by my care? Beloved, it is an honour for us that we may speak a good word for religion, for Christ's cause, for his church, against maligners and opposers; and we shall know one day that Christ will be a rewarder of every good word. Where this is said in sincerity, that Christ is mine, and I am Christ's, there will be this mutual care.

6. Likewise there is implied a *mutual complacency* in these words. By a complacency I mean a resting, contenting love. Christ hath a complacency and resting in the church; and the church hath a sweet resting contentment in Christ. Christ in us and we in him. A true Christian soul that hath yielded up its consent to Christ, when it is beaten in the world, vexed and turmoiled, it can rely on this, 'I have yet a loving husband;' yet I have Christ.

Let this put us upon a search into ourselves, what we retire to, when we meet with afflictions. Those that have brutish and beastly souls retire to carnal contentments, to good fellowship; forget, besot, and fly away from themselves; their own consciences and thought of their own trouble. Whereas a soul that hath any acquaintance with God in Christ, or any interest into Christ, so that it may say, that Christ is mine, and I am Christ's, there will be contentment and rest in such a soul, whatsoever it meets with in the world.

7. The last thing implied is *courage*, a branch of the former. Say all against it what they can, saith the resolved soul, I will be

Christ's. Here is courage with resolution. Agreeable hereto is that, 'One shall say I am the Lord's, and another shall call himself by the name of Jacob; another shall subscribe and surname himself by the name of Israel' (*Isa.* 44:5). Where there is not this resolution in good causes, there is not the Spirit of Christ; there is no interest into Christ. It is but a delusion and self-flattery to say I am Christ's, when there is not resolution to stand to Christ. These words are the expression of a resolved heart, I am, and I will be Christ's; I am not ashamed of my bargain; of the consent I have given him; I am and I will be his. You have the like in Micah 4:5, 'All people will walk every one in the name of his god, they will resolve on that, and we will walk in the name of the Lord our God for ever and for ever.' So that where these words are spoken in truth, that 'I am Christ's', there is necessarily implied, I will own him and his cause for ever and ever.

He hath married me for ever and ever; therefore, if I hope to have interest in him for comfort for ever and ever, I must be sure to yield myself to him for ever and ever; and stand for his cause, in all oppositions, against all enemies whatsoever. These and such like places in Scripture run parallel with this in the text, 'I am my beloved's, and my beloved is mine', not only holding in the person, but in the cause of Christ. Every man hopes his god will stand for him against the devil, who accuseth us daily. If we will have Christ to stand for us, and to be an advocate to plead our cause as he doth in heaven, we must resolve to stand for him against all enemies, heretics, schismatics, persecutors whatsoever; that we will walk in the name of our God for ever and ever.

Quest. But when the case is not thus with us, and that neither we can feel comfort from Christ, nor have this assurance of his love to us, what should we judge of such?

Solution. We should not wonder to see poor souls distempered when they are in spiritual desertions, considering how the spouse cannot endure the absence of Christ. It is out of love therefore in the deepest plunge she hath this in her mouth, 'my beloved'. Therefore let us not judge amiss of ourselves or others, when we are impatient in this kind.

But for a more full answer, in want of feeling of the love of Christ in regard of that measure we would (for there is never altogether a want of feeling, there is so much as keeps from despair always, yet), if we carry a constant love towards him, mourn to him and seek after him as the church here; if the desire of our souls be after him, that we make after him in the use of means, and are willing to speak of him as the church here, feel or feel not, we are his, and he will at length discover himself to us.

Let such drooping spirits consider, that as he will not be long from us, nor wholly, so it shall not be for our disadvantage that he retires at all. His absence at length will end in a sweet discovery of himself more abundantly than before. He absents himself for our good, to make us more humble and watchful for the time to come; more pitiful to others; more to prize our former condition; to justify the ways of God more strictly; to walk with him; to regain that sweet communion which by our negligence and security we lost. When we are thus prepared by his absence, there ensues a more satisfying discovery of himself than ever before.

But when is the time that he comes? Compare this with the former chapter. He comes after long waiting for him. The church waited for him, and waited in the use of all means. She runs to the watchmen, and then inquires after him of the daughters of Jerusalem. After this she finds him. After we have waited and expected Christ in the use of means, Christ at length will discover himself to us; and yet more immediately, it was after the church had so deservedly exalted him in such lofty praises, 'This is my beloved, the chief of ten thousand; he is altogether lovely.' When we set our hearts to the high exaltation of Christ above all things in the world, proclaiming him 'the chief of ten thousand', this at the last breeds a gracious discovery, 'I am my beloved's, and my beloved is mine', for Christ when he sees us faithful, and so loving that we will not endure his absence, and so constantly loving, that we love him notwithstanding some discouragements, it melts him at the last, as Joseph was melted by his brethren.

'I am my beloved's, and my beloved is mine.'

In the words, you see a mutual interest and owning between Christ and the church. Howsoever in the order of words, the church saith, 'I am my beloved's' first, yet in order of nature Christ is ours first, though not in order of discovery. There is one order of knowing, and another order of causing. Many things are known by the effect, but they issue from a cause. I know he is mine, because I am his. I have given myself to him. I know it is day, because the sun is up. There is a proof from the effect. So I know a man is alive, because he walks. There is a proof of the cause by the effect. 'I am his;' I have grace to give myself up to him. Therefore I know he loves me. He is mine. Thus I say in order of discovery; but in order of nature, he is first mine, and then I am his. 'My beloved is mine, and I am my beloved's.'

The union and communion betwixt us and Christ hath been already spoken of.

Now to speak of the branches, 'I am my beloved's, and my beloved is mine.' That Christ is first ours; and then we are his, because he is ours; and the wondrous comfort that issues hence—that Christ himself is ours.

How comes Christ to be ours?

1. Christ is ours by his Father's gift. God hath given him for us.

2. Christ is ours by his own gift. He hath given himself for us.

3. And Christ is ours by his Spirit that witnesseth so much to our spirits. For the Spirit is given for this purpose, to show us all things that are given us of God, whereof Christ is the chief. Therefore the Spirit of Christ tells us that Christ is ours; and Christ being ours, all that he hath is ours.

If he be ours, if we have the field, we have all the treasures in the field. If we have him, we have all his. He was born for us; his birth was for us; he became man for us; he was given to death for us. And so likewise, he is ours in his other estate of exaltation. His rising is for our good. He will cause us to rise also, and ascend with him, and sit in heavenly places, judging the world and the angels. We recover in this second, what we lost in the first, Adam.

Use 1. This is a point of wondrous comfort *to show the riches of a Christian*, his high estate, that Christ is his.

And Christ being ours, God the Father and the Holy Spirit and all things else in the world, the rich promises, are ours; for in Christ they are all made, and for him they shall be performed. For, indeed, he is the chief promise of all himself, and all are 'yea and amen in him' (2 *Cor.* 1:20). Can we want righteousness, while we have Christ's righteousness? Is not his garment large enough for himself and us, too? Is not his obedience enough for us? Shall we need to patch it up with our own righteousness? He is ours, therefore his obedience is ours.

Use 2. And this should be a ground likewise of *contentation*[1] *in our condition and state whatsoever,*—Christ himself is ours. In the dividing of all things, some men have wealth, honours, friends, and greatness, but not Christ, nor the love of God in Christ, and therefore they have nothing in mercy. But a Christian, he hath Christ himself. Christ is his by faith and by the Spirit's witness. Therefore, what if he want those appendencies,[2] the lesser things? He hath the main; what if he want a riveret, a stream? He hath the spring, the ocean; him, in whom all things are, and shall he not be content? Put case a man be very covetous, yet God might satisfy him. What! should anxious thoughts disquiet us, when we have such bills, such obligations from him who is faithfulness itself?

---

[1] That is, contentment.—G.

[2] That is, additions.—G.

When a Christian cannot say, honour, favour, or great persons are his, yet he can say, he hath that that is worth all, more than all; Christ is his.

Obj. Oh! may some say, this is but a speculation,—Christ is yours. A man may want and be in misery for all that.

Ans. No; it is a reality. Christ is ours, and all things else are ours. He that can command all things is mine. Why then, do I want other things? Because he sees they are not for my good. If they were, he would not withhold them from me. If there were none to be had without a miracle, no comfort, no friends, he could and would make new out of nothing, nay, out of contraries, were it not better for me to be without them.

Use 3. That you may the more fully feed on this comfort, *study the excellencies of Christ* in the Scripture, the riches and honour that he hath, the favour he is in with his Father, with the intercession that he makes in heaven (*John* 17). Study his mercy, goodness, offices, power, &c., and then come home to yourselves, 'All this is mine, for he is mine; the love of God is mine.' God loves him, and therefore he loves me, because we are both one. He loves me with the same love that he loves his Son. Thus we should make use of this, that Christ is ours. I come to the second.

'I am my beloved's.'

This is a speech of reflection, second in nature, though first in place and in discovery to us. Sometimes we can know our own love, when we feel not so much the love of Christ, but Christ's love must be there first (1 *John* 4:19). 'I am my beloved's.'

How are we Christ's beloved?

1. We are his, first of all, *by his Father's gift*; for God in his eternal purpose gave him for us, and gives us to him, as it is in the excellent prayer, 'Father, thine they were, and thou gavest them me' (*John* 17:6). I had not them of myself first, but thine they were before all worlds were. Thou gavest them me to redeem them, and my commission doth not extend beyond thy gift. I die for all those

that thou gavest me. I sanctify myself for them, that they may be sanctified. So we are Christ's in his Father's gift. But that is not all, though it be the chief, fundamental, principal ground of all.

For, 2. We are his likewise by *redemption*, Christ took our nature, that he might die for us, to purchase us. We cost him dear. We are a bloody spouse to Christ. As that froward woman wrongfully said to Moses, 'Thou art a bloody husband unto me' (*Exod.* 4:25), so Christ may without wrong say to the church, 'Thou art a spouse of blood to me.' We were, indeed, to be his spouse, but first he must win us by conquest in regard of Satan, and then satisfy justice. We were in such debt by sin, lying under God's wrath, so as, till all debts were paid, we could not in the way of justice be given as a spouse to Christ.

3. Nor is this all; but we are Christ's *by marriage* also. For when he purchased us, and paid so dear for us, when he died and satisfied divine justice, he did it with a purpose to marry us to himself. We have nothing to bring him but debt and misery; yet he took upon him our nature to discharge all, that he might marry us, and take us to himself. So we are his by marriage.

4. Then again, we are his *by consent*. We have passed ourselves over unto him. He hath given himself to us, and we have given ourselves to him back again. To come to some use of it, if we be Christ's, as Christ is ours.

Use 1. First, it is a point of *wondrous comfort*. God will not suffer his own to want. He is worse than an infidel that will suffer his family to perish. When we are once of Christ's family, and not only of his family, but of his body, his spouse, can we think he will suffer us to want that which is needful?

Use 2. Then again, as it comforts us against want, so, it likewise *fenceth us against all the accusations of Satan*. I am Christ's; I am Christ's. If he have anything to say, lo! we may bid him go to Christ. If the creditor comes to the wife, she is not liable to pay her own debts, but saith, Go to my husband. So in all temptations, learn hence to send Satan whither he should be sent. When we cannot answer him, send him to Christ.

Use 3. And for the time to come, what a ground of comfort is this, that we are Christ's, as well as he is ours. What a plea doth this put into our mouths for all things that are beneficial to us. 'Lord, I am thine; save me', saith the psalmist. Why? 'Save me; because I am thine, I am thine; Lord, teach me and direct me' (*Psa.* 27:11). The husband is to direct the spouse. The head should direct all the senses. All the treasures of wisdom are in Christ, as all the senses are in the head for the good of the body. All fulness dwells in him. Therefore, plead with him, I want wisdom; teach me and instruct me how to behave myself in troubles, in dangers, in fears. If it be an argument strong enough amongst men, weak men, I am thine, I am thy child, I am thy spouse, &c., shall we attribute more pity and mercy to ourselves than to the God of mercy and comfort, who planted these affections in the creature? Shall he make men tender and careful over others, and shall not he himself be careful of his own flock? Do we think that he will neglect his jewels, his spouse, his diadem, and crown? (*Isa.* 62:3). He will not.

But you will urge experience. We see how the church is used, even as a forlorn widow, as if she had no husband in the world, as an orphan that had no father. Therefore, how doth this stand good?

Ans. 1. The answer is, all that the church or any particular Christian suffers in this world, it is but that there may be *a conformity between the spouse and the husband*. The Head wore a crown of thorns, and went to heaven and happiness through a great deal of misery and abasement in the world, the lowest that ever was. And it is not meet that the church should go to heaven another way.

Ans. 2. Then again, all this is but *to fashion the spouse to be like to Christ*; but to bring the church and Christ nearer together. That is all the hurt they do, to drive the church nearer to Christ than before. Christ is as near to his church as ever in the greatest afflictions, by his Spirit. Christ cries out on the cross, 'My God, my God, why hast thou forsaken me?' It is a strange voice, that God should be his God, and yet, notwithstanding, seem to forsake him. But God was never more his God than at that present. Indeed, he was not his God in regard of some feelings that he had enjoyed in former times. He seemed to be forsaken in regard of some sense, as Christ seems to forsake the church in regard of some sense and feeling, but yet [is] his God still. So the church may say, I am thine still. Though she seem to be forsaken in regard of some feelings, yet she is not deserted in regard of God's care for support of the inward man and fashioning to Christ. The church hath never sweeter communion with Christ than under the greatest crosses; and, therefore, they many times have proved the ground of the greatest comforts. For Christ leads the church into the wilderness, and then speaks to her heart (*Hos.* 2:14). Christ speaks to the heart of his spouse in the wilderness, that is, in a place of no comfort. There are no orchards or pleasures, but all discomforts there. A man must have it from heaven, if he have any good in the wilderness. In that wilderness, that is, in a desolate, disconsolate estate, Christ speaks to the heart of his children. There is in the wilderness oftentimes a sweet intercourse of love, incomparably beyond the time of prosperity.

Ans. 3. Again, to stay your hearts, *know this will not be long*; as we see here, the church seemed to be forsaken and neglected, fell into the hands of cruel watchmen, and was fain to go through this and that means, but it was not long ere she met with him whom she sought after. It may be midnight at this time, but the night continues not long; it will be morning ere long. Therefore the church may well say, 'Rejoice not against me, O mine enemy; for though I be fallen, I shall rise again; though I sit in darkness, the Lord will be a light unto me' (*Mic.* 7:8). It shall not be always ill with the church. Those that survive us shall see other manner of days than we see yet, whatsoever we shall ourselves.

Use 4. Hence we have also an use of trial. Whosoever are Christ's, they have hearts to give themselves to him. As he gives himself, not his goods or his honours, but himself for his church, so the church gives herself to Christ. My delight is in him; he hath myself, my heart, my love and affection, my joy and delight, and all with myself. If I have any honour, he shall have it. I will use it for his glory. My riches I will give them to him and his church and ministry and children, as occasion shall serve. I am his, therefore all that I have is his, if he ask it at my hands. It is said of the Macedonians, they gave themselves to Christ, and then their riches and goods (2 *Cor.* 8:5). It is an easy matter to give our riches to Christ when we have given ourselves first. A Christian, as soon as ever he becomes a Christian, and ever after, to death, and in death too, he gives up himself to Christ. They that stand with Christ, and will give this or that particular, will part only with idle things that they may spare, are they Christ's? No. A Christian gives himself and all his to Christ. So we see here what we should do if Christ be ours. Let us give up ourselves to him (*Rom.* 12:1). The issue of all that learned profound discourse in the former part of the epistle, that Christ justifieth us by his righteousness and merit, and sanctifies us by his Spirit, and hath predestinated and elected us, and refused others, is this, 'I beseech you, give up your bodies and souls, and all as a living sacrifice, holy and acceptable unto God.'

In brief, these words imply renunciation and resignation. 'I am his', that is, I have given up myself to him, therefore I renounce all others that stand not with his love and liking. I am not only his by way of service, which I owe him above all that call for it, but I am his by way of resignation. If he will have me die, I will die. If he will have me live here, I will. I have not myself to dispose of any longer. I have altogether alienated myself from myself. I am his to serve him, his to be disposed of by him. I have renounced all other.

Therefore here we have another answer to Satan, if he come to us and solicit us to sin. Let the Christian's heart make this answer,

I am not mine own. What hath Satan and his instruments to do with me? Is my body his to defile? Is my tongue his to swear at his pleasure? Shall I make the temple of God the member of an harlot? As the apostle reasons, 'Shall I defile my vessel with sin?' (*1 Cor.* 6:15). What saith converted Ephraim? 'What have I any more to do with idols? for I have seen and observed him?' (*Hos.* 14:8). We ought to have such resolutions ready in our hearts. Indeed, when a Christian is resolute, the world counts such to be lost. He is gone. We have lost him, say your dissolute, profane persons. It is true they have lost him indeed, for he is not his own, much less theirs, any longer. But he is found to God and himself and the church. Thus we see what springs from this, that Christ is ours, and that we are Christ's back again. Let us carry this with us even to death; and if times should come that God should honour us by serving himself of us in our lives, if Christ will have us spend our blood, consider this, I am not mine own in life nor death, and it is my happiness that I am not my own. For if I were mine own, what should I do with myself? I should lose myself, as Adam did. It is therefore my happiness that I am not mine own, that I am not the world's, that I am not the devil's, that none else hath to do with me, to claim any interest in me, but I am Christ's. If I do anything for others, it is for Christ's sake. Remember this for the time to come. If there be anything that we will not part with for Christ's sake, it will be our bane. We shall lose Christ and it too. If we will not say with a perfect spirit, I am his, my life, my credit, my person is his, anything his; look what we will not give for him, at length we shall lose and part with it and him too.

SERMON 20

I am my beloved's, and my beloved is mine:
he feedeth among the lilies.
Song of Solomon 6:3

THE church, you see here, though she stood out a while against all Christ's invitation and knocking, yet at length she is brought to yield herself up wholly unto Christ, and to renounce herself, which course God takes with most, yea, in a manner with all his people, ere they go out of this world, to lay all high things low, beat down every high thought and imagination which exalteth itself against him (*2 Cor.* 10:5), that they may give themselves and all they have to Christ (*Luke* 14:26), if he call for it. For he that doth not so is not worthy of Christ. If we do not this, at least in preparation of mind, let us not own the name of Christians, lest we own that which shall further increase and aggravate our condemnation, professing religion one way, and yet alienating our minds to our lusts and pleasures of the world another way. To have peculiar love-fits of our own, distinct from Christ, how stands this with 'I am my beloved's, and my beloved is mine'? How stands it with the self-resignation that was spoken of before?

Now this follows upon apprehension of Christ being ours. 'I am my beloved's, because my beloved is mine first.' There are four reasons why Christ must be given to us before we can give ourselves to him by this self-resignation.

1. *Because he is the chief spring of all good affections*, which he

must place in us; loving us, ere we can love him (*1 John* 4:10, 19).

2. *Because love descends.* Though it be of a fiery nature, yet in this it is contrary, for love descends, whereas fire ascends. The superior, first loves the inferior. Christ must descend in his love to us, ere we can ascend to him in our affections.

3. *Because our nature is such that we cannot love but where we know ourselves to be loved first.* Therefore God is indulgent to us herein; and that we may love him, he manifests his love first to us.

4. *Because naturally ourselves, being conscious of guilt, are full of fears from thence.* So that if the soul be not persuaded first of Christ's love, it runs away from him, as Adam did from God, and as Peter from Christ, 'Depart from me, for I am but a sinful man' (*Luke* 5:8). So the soul of every man would say, if first it were not persuaded of God's love in Christ, 'Who amongst us shall dwell with the everlasting burnings?' (*Isa.* 33:14). Therefore to prevent that disposition of soul which would rise out of the sense of guilt and unworthiness, God first speaks to us in Christ; at length saying unto our souls, 'I am thy salvation', whereupon the soul first finding his love, loves him back again, of whom it finds itself so much beloved; so that our love is but a reflection of his, 'I am my beloved's, because my beloved is mine.'

It is with the Spirit of God as with the spirits in the soul and body of a man, there is a marriage betwixt the body and soul. The spirits join both together, being of a middle nature; for they have somewhat spiritual near the soul, and somewhat bodily near the body. Therefore they come between the body and the soul, and are the instruments thereof, whereby it works. So it is with the Spirit of God. The same Spirit that tells the soul that Christ is ours, the same Spirit makes up the match on our part, and gives us up to Christ again.

Let this then be the trial that we are Christ's, by the spiritual echo that our souls make to that report which Christ makes to our souls, whether in promises or in instructions.

Use 1. See hence likewise the nature of faith, for these are the words of faith as well as of love. Faith hath two branches, it doth give as well as take. Faith receives Christ, and says, Christ is mine; and the same faith saith, I am Christ's again. Indeed, our souls are empty; so that the main work of faith is to be an empty hand, a beggar's hand to receive (as Luther calls it). But when it hath received it gives back again, both ourselves and all that we can do. The churches of Macedonia 'gave themselves', and then 'they gave their goods' (*2 Cor.* 8:5). Where faith is, there will be a giving of ourselves and our goods; and, by a proportion, our strength, wits, and all back again. This discovers a great deal of empty false faith in the world; for undoubtedly if it were true faith there would be a yielding back again.

Use 2. And again, these words discover the mutual coherence of justification and sanctification, and the dependence one upon another. 'I am my beloved's, and my beloved is mine.' Christ is mine; his righteousness is mine for my justification; I am clothed with Christ as it is, 'The spouse there is clothed with the sun' (*Rev.* 12:1), with the beams of Christ. But is that all? No. 'I am my beloved's;' I am Christ's. There is a return of faith in sanctification. The same Spirit that witnesseth Christ is ours, it sanctifies and alters our disposition, that we can say, I am Christ's. It serves to instruct us therefore in the necessary connection of these two, justification and sanctification, against the idle slander of papists, that sinfully traduce that doctrine, as if we were Solifideans,[1] as

---

[1] This sect derived its name from *solus*, alone, and *fides*, faith. The following quotations will illustrate Sibbes:—

'Such is first the persuasion of the *solifidians*, that all religion consists in believing aright, that the being of orthodox (as that is opposed to erroneous) opinions is all that is on our part required to render our condition safe, and our persons acceptable in the sight of God.'—Hammond, *Works*, i., p. 480.

'That we may be able to answer the Papists, who charge us with *solifidianism*, as if we were of this opinion, that if a man do but trust in Christ, that is, be but confidently persuaded that he will save him, and pardon him, this is sufficient, and, consequently, he that is thus persuaded need not take any farther care of his salvation, but may live as he list.'—Tillotson, iii., ser. 174. —G.

if we severed justification from sanctification. No. We hold here that whensoever Christ is ours, there is a spirit of sanctification in us, to yield all to Christ, though this resignation be not presently perfect.

Use 3. This likewise helps us, by way of direction, to understand the covenant of grace, and the seals of the covenant, what they enforce and comprise; not only what God will do to us, but the duty we are to do to him again, though we do it in his strength. A covenant holds not on one side, but on both. Christ is mine, and I am Christ's again. 'I will be their God', but they must have grace 'to be my people' (*Lev.* 26:12); and then the covenant is made up. The covenant of grace is so called, because God is so gracious as to enable us to perform our own part.

And so in the seals of the covenant in baptism. God doth not only bind himself to do thus and thus to us, but binds us also to do back again to him. So in the communion, we promise to lead a new life, renewing our covenant; and therefore we must not think that all is well (when we have received our Maker), though we continue in a scandalous, fruitless course of life. No. There is a promise in the sacrament (the seal of the covenant of grace), to yield up ourselves to God, to return to Christ again with our duty. Then we come as we should do when we come thus disposed. This for direction, 'My beloved is mine, and I am my beloved's.'

Use 4. To proceed to make an use of comfort *to poor, doubting Christians.* 'I am my beloved's', is the voice of the whole church, that all ranks of Christians, if they be true, may without presumption take up. I have not so much faith, so much love, so much grace, so much patience as another, saith a poor Christian; therefore I am none of Christ's. But we must know that Christ hath in his church of all ranks, and they are all his spouse, one as well as another, there is no exception. There is a little spirit of emulation, and a spice of envy, in Christians that are weaker. If they have not all that great measure of grace which they see in others, they fear they have none at all; as if there were no babes in Christ's school as well as men and grown persons.

Then again, we see here the nature of faith in the whole church. It is the same that is in every particular, and the same in every particular as it is in the whole church. The whole church saith, 'I am my beloved's, and my beloved is mine.' I appropriate him. There is a spirit of appropriation in the whole, and there is so in each particular. Every Christian may say with Paul, 'I live by faith in the Son of God, that hath loved me, and gave himself for me' (*Gal.* 2:20); and with Thomas, 'My God, and my Lord' (*John* 20:28).

The ground hereof is, because they are all one in Christ, and there is one and the same Spirit in the whole church and every particular Christian, as in pipes, though of different sounds, yet there is the same breath in them. So Christians may have different sounds, from the greater or lesser strength of grace that is in the one and in the other, but all comes from the same breath, the same Spirit. The Spirit in the bride saith 'Come' (*Rev.* 22:17), the whole church saith it, and every particular Christian must say it; because, as the body is acted by one spirit, and makes but one natural body, though consisting of many parts weaker and stronger, so should there be a harmony in this mystical body acted by that one Spirit of Christ, who so regards all, as if there were but one, and regards every one so, as he doth not forget the whole. Christ so attends to all, that he is not detained from any particular, and he so attends every particular, that he is not restrained from all. There is the same love to all as to one, and to everyone, as if there were no other. He so loves each one, that every Christian may say as well as the whole church, Christ is mine, and I am Christ's.

In those things that we call homogeneal, there is the same nature in each quantity as in the whole, as there is the same nature in one drop of water as in the whole ocean, all is water; and the same respect of a spark, and of all the element of fire. So Christ bears the same respect to the church as to every particular, and to every particular as to the church.

Use 5. To come to make an use of direction, *how to come to be able to say this*, 'I am my beloved's, and my beloved is mine.' For answer hereto, take notice in the first place, from the dependence. Christ must be first ours, before we can give ourselves to him.

(1.) Therefore, we must dwell on the consideration of Christ's love. This must direct and lead our method in this thing. Would we have our hearts to love Christ, to trust in him, and to embrace him, why then think what he is to us. Begin there; nay, and what we are: weak, and in our apprehension, lost. Then go to consider his love, his constant love to his church and children. 'Whom he loves, he loves to the end' (*John* 13:1). We must warm our souls with the consideration of the love of God in him to us, and this will stir up our faith to him back again. For we are more safe in that he is ours (*Gal.* 4:9, *Phil.* 3:12), than that we give ourselves to him. We are more safe in his comprehending of us, than in our clasping and holding of him. As we say of the mother and the child, both hold, but the safety of the child is that the mother holds him. If Christ once give himself to us, he will make good his own part always. Our safety is more on his side than on ours. If ever we have felt the love of Christ, we may comfort ourselves with the constancy and perpetuity thereof. Though, perhaps, we find not our affections warmed to him at all times, nor alike, yet the strength of a Christian's comfort lies in this, that first, 'Christ is mine', and then, in the second place, that 'I am his.' Now, I say, that we may be able to maintain this blessed tradition of giving ourselves to Christ,

(2.) Let us dwell on the consideration of his love to us, and of the necessity that we have of him; how miserable we are without him, poor, beggarly, in bondage to the devil. Therefore we must have him to recover us out of debt, and to enrich us. For Christ's love carries him forth, not only to pay all our debts for us, but to enrich us; and it is a protecting, preserving love, till he brings us to heaven, his own place, where we shall ever be with him. The consideration of these things will warm our hearts, and for this purpose serves the ministry.

(3.) We should therefore, in the next place, attend upon the Word, for this very end. Wherefore serves the ministry? Among many others, this is one main end—'to lay open the unsearchable riches of Christ'. Therein you have something of Christ unfolded, of his natures, offices, and benefits we have by him,—redemption, and freedom, and a right to all things in him, the excellencies of another world. Therefore attend upon the means of salvation, that we may know what riches we have in him. This will keep our affections close to Christ, so as to say, 'I am his.'

(4.) And labour we also every day more and more to bring all our love to him. We see in burning-glasses, where the beams of the sun meet in one, how forcible they are, because there is an union of the beams in a little point. Let it be our labour that all the beams of our love may meet in Christ, that he may be as the church saith, our beloved. 'My beloved is mine, and I am my beloved's', saith she, as if the church had no love out of Christ. And is it love lost? No; but as Christ is the church's beloved, so the church is Christ's love again, as we see in this book oft, 'My love, my dove.' As all streams meet in the great ocean, so let all our loves meet in Christ. We may love other things, and we should do so, but no otherwise than as they convey love to us from Christ, and may be means of drawing up our affections unto Christ. We may love our friends, and we ought to do so, and other blessings of God; but how? No otherwise than as tokens of his love to us. We love a thing that our friends send to us. O, but it is as it doth convey his affection to us. So must we love all things, as they come from God's love to us in Christ.

And, indeed, whatsoever we have is a love-token, even our very afflictions themselves. 'Whom I love, I rebuke and chastise' (*Heb.* 12:6).

(5.) Again, that we may inflame our hearts with the love of Christ, as we are exhorted by Jude, verse 21, let us consider the vanity of all things that entice us from Christ, and labour every day more and more to draw our affections from them, as we are exhorted—'Hearken, O daughter, and consider, and incline thine ear; forget also thine own people, and thy father's house: so shall the king greatly desire thy beauty' (*Psa.* 45:10, 11). So, if we will have Christ to delight in us, that we may say we are his, let us labour to sequester our affections more and more from all earthly things, that we may not have such hearts, as St James speaketh of, adulterous hearts. 'O ye adulterers and adulteresses! know ye not that the love of the world is enmity with God?' (*James* 4:4).

Indeed there is reason for this exhortation; for all earthly things, they are all vain and empty things. There is an emptiness in whatsoever is in the world, save Christ. Therefore we should not set our affections too much upon them. A man cannot be wise in loving anything but Christ, and what he loves for Christ. Therefore let us follow that counsel, to draw ourselves from our former company, acquaintance, pleasures, delights, and vanities. We cannot bestow our love and our affections better than upon Christ. It is a happiness that we have such affections, as joy, delight, and love, planted in us by God; and what a happiness is it, that we should have such an excellent object to fill those affections, yea, to transcend and more than satisfy them! Therefore the apostle wisheth that they might know all the dimensions of God's love in Christ. There is a 'height, breadth, length, and depth of the love of God' (*Eph.* 3:18, 19).

And let us think of the dimensions, the height, breadth, and depth of our misery out of Christ. The more excellent our natures are, the more miserable they are if not changed; for look what degree of excellency we have, if it be not advanced in Christ, we have so much misery being out of him. Therefore let us labour to see this, as to value our being in him, so to be able, upon good grounds, to say, 'I am my beloved's, and my beloved is mine.'

(6.) Again, let us labour to walk in the light of a sanctified knowledge to be attained by the gospel, for as it is, 'the end of all our preaching is to assure Christ to the soul' (*1 John* 5:13), that we may be able to say without deceiving our own souls, 'I am my beloved's, and my beloved is mine.' All preaching, I say, is for this end. The terror of the law and the discovery of corruption is to drive us out of ourselves to him; and then to provoke us to grow up into him more and more. Therefore saith John, 'All our preaching is that we may have fellowship with the Father and the Son, and they with us' (*1 John* 1:3). And what doth he make an evidence of that fellowship? 'walking in the light, as he is light', or else we are liars. He is bold in plain terms to give us the lie, to say we are Christ's, and have communion with the Father and the Son, when yet we walk in darkness. In sins against conscience, in wilful ignorance, the darkness of an evil life, we have no communion with Christ. Therefore if we will have communion with him, let us walk in the light, and labour to be lightsome in our understandings, to have a great deal of knowledge, and then to walk answerable to that light and revelation that we have. Those that live in sins against conscience, and are friends to the darkness of ignorance, of an evil life, Oh they never think of the fellowship with Christ and with God! These things are mere riddles to them; they have no hope of them, or if any, their hope is in vain. They bar themselves of ever having comfortable communion with Christ here; much less shall they enjoy him hereafter in heaven.

Therefore labour every day more and more to grow rich in knowledge, to get light, and to walk in that light; to which end pray with the holy apostle, 'That you may have the Spirit of revelation' (*Eph.* 1:17), that excellent Spirit of God, to reveal the things of God, that we may have the light discovered to us.

What a world of comfort hath a Christian that hath light in him and walks in that light, above another man. Whether he live or die, the light brings him into fellowship with the Father of lights. He that hath this light knows his condition and his way, and whither he goeth. When he dieth he knows in what condition he dieth, and upon what grounds. The very light of nature is comfortable, much more that of grace. Therefore labour to grow daily more and more in the knowledge and obedience of the light.

All professors of the gospel are either such as are not Christ's, or such as are his. For such as are not yet, that you may be provoked to draw to fellowship with Christ, do but consider you are as branches cut off, that will wither and die, and be cast into the fire, unless you be grafted into the living stock, Christ. You are as naked persons in a storm, not clothed with anything to stand against the storm of God's wrath. Let this force you to get into Christ.

Use 6. And next for encouragement consider, *Christ offereth himself to all in the gospel*; and that is the end of the ministry, to bring Christ and our souls together, to make a spiritual marriage, to lay open his riches and to draw you to him. If you confess your sins, he will forgive them, and you shall have mercy (*1 John* 1:9). 'He relieves those that are wearied and heavy laden' (*Matt.* 11:28), and bids those come to him that are thirsty (*Isa.* 55:1). Christ came to seek and to save that which was lost. Christ offers himself in mercy to the worst soul.

Therefore if there be any that have lived in evil courses, in former times, consider that upon repentance all shall be forgotten, and as a mist scattered away and cast into the bottom of the sea. Christ offers himself to you. These are the times, this is the hour of grace. Now the water is stirring for you to enter; do but entertain Christ, and desire that he may be yours to rule you and guide you, and all will be well for the time to come.

Obj. Do not object, *I am a loathsome creature, full of rebellions.*

Ans. Christ doth not match with you, because you are good, but to make you good. Christ takes you not with any dowry. All that he requires is to confess your beggary and to come with emptiness. He takes us not because we are clean, but because he will purge us. He takes us in our blood when he first takes us (*Ezek.* 16:9). Let none despair either for want of worth or of strength

(*Eph.* 5:27). Christ seeth that for strength we are dead, and for worth we are enemies; but he gives us both spiritual strength and worth, takes us near to himself and enricheth us. Let none therefore be discouraged. It is our office, thus to lay open and offer the riches of Christ. If you will not come in, but love your sinful courses more than Christ, then you perish in your blood, and we free our hands, and may free our souls from the guilt thereof. Therefore as you love your own souls, come in at length and stand out no longer.

And for those that have in some measure given themselves up to Christ, and can say, 'He is mine and I am his', let them go on with comfort, and never be discouraged for the infirmities that hang about them. For one part of Christ's office is to purge his church by his Spirit more and more; not to cast her away for her infirmities, 'but to wash and cleanse it more and more till it be a glorious spouse like himself' (*Eph.* 5:27). For if the husband will, by the bond of nature, bear with the infirmities of the wife, as the weaker vessel, doth not Christ bind himself by that which he accounts us bound? Is there more love and mercy, and pity in us to those that we take near us, than there is in Christ to us? What a most blasphemous thought were this to conceive so! Only let us take heed of being in league with sin; for we cannot give our souls to Christ, and to sinful courses too. Christ will allow of no bigamy or double marriage. Where he hath anything to do, we must have single hearts, resolving, though I fall, yet I purpose to please Christ, and to go on in a good conversation; and if our hearts tell us so, daily infirmities ought not to discourage us. We have helps enough for these. First, Christ bids us ask forgiveness; and then we have the mercy of Christ to bear with weaker vessels. Then his advocation.[1] He is now in heaven to plead for us. If we were perfect, we needed not that office (*1 John* 2:1). Let none be discouraged therefore; but let us labour more and more that we

---

[1] That is, advocacy.—Ed.

may be able to comprehend in some measure the love of Christ, so will all duties come off sweetly and easily; and then we shall be enabled to suffer all things, not only willingly, but cheerfully, and rejoice in them. Love is of the nature of fire, which as it severeth and consumeth all that is opposite, all dross and dregs, and dissolves coldness, so it quickens and makes active and lively. It hath a kind of constraining force, a sweet violence. As the apostle saith, 'the love of Christ constraineth' (2 Cor. 5:14).

Let a man that loves the Lord Jesus Christ in sincerity, be called to part with his life, he will yield it as a sacrifice with comfort. Come what will, all is welcome, when we are inflamed with the love of Christ; and the more we suffer, the more we find his love. For he reserves the manifestation of his love most for times of suffering; and the more we find the manifestation of his love, the more we love him back again, and rejoice in suffering for him that we love so. Whether they be duties of obedience, active or passive, doing or suffering, all comes off with abundance of cheerfulness and ease, where the love of Christ is, that the soul can say, 'I am my beloved's, and my beloved is mine.' Nothing in the world is able to make such a soul miserable. It follows—

'He feedeth among the lilies.' The church here shows where Christ feeds.

Quest. But the question is, Whether it be the feeding of the church and people that is meant, or whether he feeds himself?

Ans. For answer, he both feeds his church among the lilies, and delights himself to be there. The one follows the other. Especially it is meant of the church. Those that are his, he feeds them among the lilies. How?

Lilies are such kind of flowers as require a great deal of nourishment, and grow best in valleys and fat ground. Therefore when she saith, 'He feeds among the lilies', the meaning is, he feeds his church and people in fat pastures, as sheep in such grounds as are sweet and fruitful. Such are his holy Word and the communion of saints. These are especially the pastures wherein he feeds his church. The holy truths of God are the food of the soul, whereby it is cherished and nourished up to life everlasting. This whole book is a kind of pastoral (to understand the word a little better), a 'song of a beloved' concerning a beloved. Therefore Christ in many places of this book, he takes upon him the term and carriage, as it were, of a loving shepherd, who labours to find out for his sheep the fattest, fruitfulest, best, and sweetest pastures, that they may grow up as calves of the stall, as it is [in] Malachi 4:2, that they may grow and be well liking.

You have, to give light to this place, a phrase somewhat like this, where he follows the point more at large (*Song of Sol.* 1:7). The church there prays to Christ, 'Tell me, O thou whom my soul loveth, where thou feedest, where thou makest thy flocks to rest at noon.' Those that are coming up in the church desire to know with whom they may join, and what truths they may embrace. 'Tell me where thou feedest, and where thou makest thy flock to rest at noon:' that is, in the greatest heat and storm of persecution, as at noon-day the sun is hottest. 'For why should I be as one that turns aside by the flocks of thy companions?' that is, by those that are not true friends, that are false shepherds; why should I be drawn away by them? I desire to feed where thou feedest among thy sheep. Why should I be as one that turns aside by the flocks of those that are emulators to thee? as antichrist is to Christ. Thus the church puts forth to Christ, whereunto Christ replies (verse 8), 'If thou know not, O thou fairest among women, go thy way forth by the footsteps of the flocks, and feed thy kids beside the shepherds' tents:' that is, if thou know not, go thy way forth, get thee out of thyself, out of the world, out of thy former course, put thyself forward, stay not complaining, go on, put thyself to endeavour, go thy way forth. Whither? 'In the footsteps of the flocks.' See the steps of Christians in the best times of the church in former times. Tread in the steps of those that lived in the best ages of the church. 'Feed thy kids', thy Christians, 'beside the shepherds' tents', the best shepherds. Mark where the apostles and prophets fed their sheep; there feed thou. And mark the footsteps of the flock that have lived in the best times; for of all times since the apostles and prophets, we must follow those virgin best times. All churches are so far true churches, as they have consanguinity with the primitive apostolical and prophetical churches.

Therefore, 'we are now to go out by the footsteps of the flock'. Mark the footsteps of former Christians, Abraham, Moses, and David; and in Christ's time, of John, Peter, and the rest. Blessed saints! walk as they walked, go their way, and 'feed yourselves by the shepherds' tents'. Mark the shepherds where they have their tents! So these words have reference to the prophetical, especially to the evangelical times, whereunto we must conform ourselves; for the latter times are apostate times. After a certain season the church kept not her purity; which the Scriptures foretold directly, that we should not take scandal at it. The church did fall to a kind of admiration of antichrist, and embraced doctrines of devils (*1 Tim.* 4:1). Therefore now we must not follow these companies that lead into by-paths, contrary to the apostolical ways, but see wherein our church agrees with the apostolical churches and truth, and embrace no truth for the food of our souls, but that we find in the gospel. For antichrist feeds his flocks with wind, and with poison, and with empty things. For what hath been the food in popery? Sweet and goodly titles; as if they, poor souls, had the best pastors in the world, whenas they administer to them nothing but that which will be the bane of their souls, full of poison and fraud. This is spoken to unfold that place which gives light to this, spoken of the pastoral care of Christ, 'he feeds his flock among the lilies', plentifully and sweetly. From hence may be briefly observed, first,

That Christ feeds as well as breeds. And we have need of feeding as well as breeding. Where dost thou feed? that is, build up thy children, and go on with the work begun in them. We have need to be fed after we are bred; and Christ (answerable to our exigence and necessity) he feeds as well as breeds; and that Word which is the seed to beget us, is that which feeds too (*1 Pet.* 1:23). What is the seed of the new birth? The Word of God, the holy promises, they are the seed, the Spirit mingling with them, whereby a Christian is born, and being born, is cherished and bred. Therefore, 'as new-born babes', saith the apostle, 'desire the sincere milk of the word, that you may grow thereby' (*1 Pet.* 2:2). So that the same thing is both the seed of a Christian, and that which breeds him; the blessed truth and promises of God.

Quest. If you ask, why we must grow up and be fed still?

Ans. 1. Do but ask your own souls, whether there be not a perpetual renewing of corruption, which still breaks out into new guilt every day. Therefore we have need to feed every day anew upon the promises, upon old promises with new affections. Somewhat breaks out ever and anon which abaseth the soul of a Christian, that makes him go with a sharp appetite to the blessed truths that feed his soul.

Ans. 2. And then again, we need a great deal of strength, which is maintained by feeding. Besides the guilt of the soul, there needs strength for duty, which must be fetched from the blessed Word of God; and the comforts thence, whereby we are able to withstand and resist, to stand and do all that we do.

Ans. 3. And then we are set upon by variety of temptations within and without, which require variety of wisdom and strength, all which must be gotten by feeding; and therefore you see a Christian for his subsistence and being, hath need of a feeding, cherishing, and maintaining still, by the sweet and blessed directions and promises out of the Word of God.

Therefore you may see what kind of atheistical creatures those are, and how much they are to be regarded, that turn off all with a

THE LOVE OF CHRIST

compendium in religion, Tush, if we know that we must love God above all, and our neighbours as ourselves, and that Christ died for all, we know enough, more than we can practise. They think these *compendiums* will serve the turn, as if there were not a necessity of growing still further and further in distinct knowledge. Alas! the soul needs to be fed continually. It will stagger else, and be insufficient to stand against temptation, or to perform duties.

A second general point out of the text is this, *that as Christ feedeth still his flock and people, so he feeds them fully, plentifully, and sweetly among the lilies.* There are saving truths enough. There is an all-sufficiency in the book of God. What need we go out to man's inventions, seeing there is a fulness and all-sufficiency of truth there? Whatsoever is not in that is wind, or poison. In the Word is a full kind of feeding. In former times when they had not the Scriptures, and the comforts of them to feed on, what did the poor souls then? and what do those remaining in popery feed on? Upon stones as it were. There was a dream of an holy man in those times, divers hundred years agone, that he saw one having a deal of manchet[1] to feed on, and yet all the while the poor wretch he fed on stones. What folly and misery is this, when there are delicate things to feed on, to gnaw upon stones! And what is all the school learning almost (except one or two that had better spirits than the rest) but a gnawing upon stones, barren distinctions, empty things, that had no substance in them? They had the Scriptures, though they were locked up in Latin, an unknown tongue. They had the sweet pastures of Christ to feed in; and yet all this while they fed, as it were, on stones.

This should show us, likewise, our own blessedness that live in these times, wherein the streams of the gospel run abundantly, sweetly, and pleasantly. There is a fulness among us, even in the spirits of the worst sort. There is a fulness almost to loathing of that heavenly manna: but those souls, who ever were acquainted

---

[1] That is, white bread. See Holinshed, *Description of England,* B. ii. c. 6.—G.

with the necessity of it, rather find a want than a fulness; and still desire to grow up to a further desire, that as they have plentiful means, so they may have plentiful affections after, and strength by those means. Let us know our own happiness in these times. Is it not a comfort to know where to feed and to have pastures to go to, without suspicion of poison? that we may feed ourselves with comforts fully without fear of bane, or noisome mingling of *coloquintida*[1] in the pot, which would disrelish all the rest? to know that there are truths that we may feed on safely? This the church in the former place (*Song of Sol.* 1:6, 7) accounted a great privilege, 'Oh, show me where thou feedest at noon.' In the greatest heat of persecution, that I may feed among them. So then it is a great privilege to know where to feed, and so to be esteemed, that thereby we may be stirred up to be thankful for our own good, and to improve these privileges to our souls' comfort.

But the second branch that must be touched a little is, *that there is fulness nowhere but in God's house; and that there, and there only, is that which satisfieth the soul with fatness and sweetness.*

Nay, not only the promises, but the very rebukes, of Scripture, are sweet. The rebukes of a friend, they feed the soul. For we have many corruptions which hinder our communion with God, so that a Christian delights to have his corruptions rebuked; for he knows, if he leave them, he shall grow into further communion with Christ, wherein stands his happiness in this world, and the fulness of his happiness in the world to come.

If this be so, let us know then that when we come to religion we lose not the sweetness of our lives, but only translate them to a far more excellent and better condition. Perhaps we fed before upon vain authors, upon (as it were) gravel, vain company; but now we have our delight (and perhaps find more pleasure) in better things. Instead of that which fed our idle fancy (vain treatises

[1] The colocynth, or bitter apple, a vine bearing fruits with a strong laxative effect.— P.

and the like), now we have holy truths to delight our souls. Believe it, a Christian never knows what comfort is to purpose till he be downright and sincere in religion. Therefore Augustine saith of himself, 'Lord, I have wanted thy sweetness over long. I see all my former life (that I thought had such sweetness in it) was nothing at all but husks, empty things. Now I know where sweetness is, it is in the word and truth.'[1] Therefore let us not misconceive of religion as of a mopish and dull thing, wherein we must lose all comfort. If we give ourselves over to the study thereof, must we so? Must we lose our comfort? Nay, we have no comfort till we be religious indeed. Christ feeds not his among thorns and briers and stinking weeds, but among lilies. Dost thou think he feeds thee among unsavoury, harsh, fretting, galling things? No; 'he feeds among lilies'. Therefore when thou comest to religion, think that thou comest to comfort, to refresh thy soul. Let us make use of this for our soul's comfort, to make us in love more with the ways of Christ.

Now, to seal this further, see what the Scripture saith in some parallel places. 'The Lord is my shepherd;' and what is the use that David presently makes hereof? Why, 'I shall want nothing' (*Psa.* 23:1). He will feed me plentifully and abundantly. The whole psalm is nothing but a commenting upon that word, 'the Lord is my shepherd'. How doth he perform the duty of a shepherd? 'He makes me to lie down in green pastures, and leads me by the still waters.' It is not only meant of the body, but of the soul chiefly, 'he restoreth my soul;' that is, when my soul languisheth and is ready to faint, he restores it, and gives me as it were a new soul; he refresheth it. We see say,[2] re-creation is the creating of a thing anew. So he restores my soul; he gives me my soul anew, with fresh comforts. Thus the blessed Shepherd doth, and how? Because 'he feeds among the lilies', the promises of the gospel. Then he doth not only do good to the body and soul, but he guides all

---

[1] *Confessions*, b. x. p. [xxviii.] 38.—G.

[2] That is, 'we see that people, etymologists, say.'—Ed.

our ways, all our goings out, 'he leads us in the paths of righteousness'. And why? Because I deserve so much at his hands? No; 'for his own name's sake', because he hath a love to me; because he hath purchased me with his blood, and given his life for his sheep; hath bought me so dear, though there be no worth in me. He goes on, 'Though I walk through all temptations and troubles', which are as 'the valley of the shadow of death', that is, where there is nothing but disconsolation and misery; 'yet I will fear none ill; thou, with thy rod and staff, dost comfort me'. If I, as a wandering sheep, venture to go out of the way, thou, out of thy care, being a sweet and loving shepherd, wilt pull me in with thy hook and staff again. He hath not care only to feed us, but to govern us also. What a sweet Shepherd and Saviour have we in covenant, that deals thus with us! And so he proceeds, 'Thou wilt prepare my table in the presence of mine enemies.' And for the time to come he promiseth himself as much, that God, as he hath been a Shepherd for the present, to provide all things necessary for body and soul and guidance, so surely the goodness of the Lord shall follow me all the days of my life; for he is a perpetual Shepherd. He will not leave us till he hath brought us to heaven. Thus we see in this place the sweet care of Christ.

The like place you have—'He shall feed his flock like a shepherd; he shall gather the lambs with his arms, and carry them in his bosom, and shall gently lead those that are with young' (*Isa.* 40:11). So he leads them into the pastures, and feeds them plentifully and sweetly, not only with sweet things, but with a tender care, which is sweeter. As a shepherd, he takes into his bosom the poor lambs that cannot walk themselves, and the sheep that are heavy with young. He cares for them; 'he gently leads them' that are poor, weak Christians, that struggle and conflict with many temptations and corruptions. Christ hath a tender care of them. He carries them, as it were, in his bosom and in his arms, and leads them gently; for indeed all Christ's sheep are weak. Everyone hath somewhat to complain of. Therefore he hath a tender

357

care; he feeds them tenderly and sweetly, or else they might perish.

Another place notable for this purpose (*Ezek.* 34:14ff.) wherein you have the same metaphor from a loving shepherd; and it is but a comment upon the text. Therefore, being parallel places, they may help our memories: 'I will feed them in good pastures upon the high mountains of Israel; there shall their fold be; there shall they lie in a good fold, and in a fat pasture. I will feed my flock, and cause them to lie down, saith the Lord God. I will seek that which is lost, and bring back that which was driven away; I will bind up that which was broken, and strengthen that which is sick, and destroy the fat and the strong, and feed them with judgment.' Those that are Christ's true sheep have somewhat to complain of. Either they are sick, or broken, or driven away. Somewhat is amiss or other. But Christ's care preventeth all the necessities of his sheep. He hath a fit salve for all their sores.[1] And, to apply this to the business in hand,[2] doth not Christ feed us 'among the lilies'? Doth he not now feed us with his own body and blood in the sacrament? Would you have better food? 'My body is meat indeed, and my blood is drink indeed',—that is, it is the only meat, with an emphasis; the only meat and drink that our souls could feed upon. God gave his Son to death, to shed his blood for my sins. What would become of the hunger-bitten, thirsty soul, that is stung with Satan and his temptations, were it not for the blood of Christ to quench our thirst, and the body of Christ given by the Father to death for sin? Were it not that the soul could think upon this, where were the comfort of the soul? All this is represented to us here in the sacrament. We feed on the body and blood of Christ spiritually, and are refreshed thereby, as verily as our bodies are refreshed with the bread and wine. For God doth not feed us with

[1] This is the title of one of Thomas Powell's excellent practical treatises, *viz.:— Salve for Soul-Sores.*—G.

[2] That is, celebration of the sacrament.—G.

empty symbols and representations, but with things themselves, that the soul which comes prepared by faith is partaker of Christ crucified, and is knit to him, though now in heaven. There is as sure an union and communion between Christ and the Christian soul, as there is between the food and the body, when it is once digested.

Therefore let us come to this blessed, to this sweet food of our souls with hungry appetites and thankful hearts, that God hath given us the best comforts of his Word, and fed us with the sweet comforts of the sacraments, as a seal of the Word. We should even spend our lives much in thankfulness for this, that he will feed us so sweetly, that thinks nothing is good enough for our food, but his own self, with his own gracious Word and truth. Thus we should be very thankful unto God, and now at this time labour to get hungry appetites fit for this blessed food to receive it.

How shall we do that?

1. Think seriously of the former part of thy life, and this week past. For Christ, the food of the soul, relisheth well with the sour herbs of repentance. Let us stir up in our hearts repentance for our sins, and sorrow in the consideration of our own corrupt nature and life; and when we have felt our corruptions and have the sense of our want, then Christ will be sweet to us. The paschal lamb was to be eaten with sour herbs; so Christ our passover must be eaten with repentance.

2. Then withal there must be purging. There are many things which clog the stomach. Come not with worldly, wicked, malicious affections, which puff up the soul (*James* 1:21); 'but lay aside', as the apostle wisheth, 'all guile, malice, and superfluity' (*1 Pet.* 2:1). Empty the soul of all sin and prepossessing[1] thoughts or affections.

3. And then consider the necessity of spiritual strength, that we have need to grow up more and more in Christianity, to be

---

[1] That is, pre-occupying.—G.

feeding still. We have need of strong faith and strong assurance that Christ is ours, and that we are his. Let us often frequent this ordinance, and come prepared as we should, and we shall find Christ making good his own ordinance, in his own best time; so as we shall be able to say, in truth of heart, experimentally and feelingly with the church, 'My beloved is mine, and I am his. He feedeth among the lilies.'

ALSO BY RICHARD SIBBES
AVAILABLE FROM
THE BANNER OF TRUTH

THREE TITLES IN THE
PURITAN PAPERBACKS SERIES

THE BRUISED REED

In this short exposition of Isaiah 42:1-3 Sibbes unfolds the tender ministry of Jesus Christ, who is a 'physician good at all diseases, especially at the binding up of the broken heart' (p. 8). There is comfort here for the weak and hurting Christian, help for the Christian struggling with assurance, and caution to ministers not to seek to be more pure than Christ.—Conrad Pomeroy in *Evangelical Times*

144pp. Paperback ISBN 978 0 85151 740 7

GLORIOUS FREEDOM

Sibbes examines the fuller self-revelation of God in the coming of Christ and its greater effect in those who behold that glory by the Spirit. The vitality of the new covenant brings about spiritual liberty and likeness to Christ.

208pp. Paperback ISBN 978 0 85151 791 9

JOSIAH'S REFORMATION

Contains four sermons by Sibbes on 2 Chronicles 34:26–28, where the Lord is said to have heard Josiah because his heart was tender, because he was humble, and because he mourned for his sin.

192pp. Paperback ISBN 978 1 84871 116 7

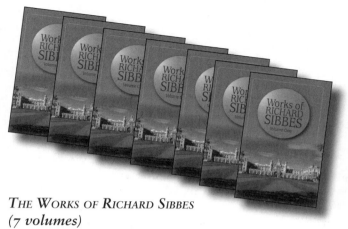

The Works of Richard Sibbes
(7 volumes)

Strong thoughts, simple sentences, deep knowledge of the Bible and the human heart, and a sure pastoral touch are here revealed in Sibbes' sustained concentration on the glory and grace of God in Christ.

More than anything else, Sibbes was a great preacher. He never lost sight of the fact that the best Christian counselling is done through the patient and lively exposition of the Word of God. Sibbes excelled as a comforter of the troubled and doubting, but he also possessed the rare gift of illuminating every passage of Scripture he handled by drawing out its significance for his hearers and readers.

The republication of the Nichol edition of his complete works is a notable event for all who have an appetite for helpful and faithful biblical preaching. Volume 1 contains a memoir of Sibbes by A. B. Grosart.

Approx 550pp. per volume. Clothbound
Set ISBN 978 0 85151 398 0